WINDOWS *across* MISSOURI

a culinary view

Enhance your culinary experience with the classic and contemporary cuisine represented in Windows Across Missouri.

A Missouri State Medical Association Alliance publication.

Founded over 75 years ago, the MSMA Alliance is dedicated to making a difference in Missouri communities through health awareness and education of health issues.

WINDOWS *across* MISSOURI

a culinary view

First Edition
ISBN Number 0-9717349-0-9

For your convenience, copies of *Windows Across Missouri* may be obtained using the order form found in the back of the cookbook or by sending $21.50 plus $3.50 shipping and handling to the following address:

Missouri State Medical Association Alliance
113 Madison Street ◆ P.O. Box 1028
Jefferson City, Missouri 65101
Tel: 573-636-5151 ◆ Fax: 573-636-8552
Internet: www.msma.org

Cover Art

On the front:

A Window to Missouri's past: the Missouri Children's Fountain and Plaza on the front lawn of the Governor's Mansion is a popular gathering spot for visitors who tour the 130-year-old landmark. Created by sculptor Jamie G. Anderson of Rolla, Missouri, the fountain was dedicated in September 1996. A photograph of the three children of Governor and Mrs. Herbert Hadley (1909-1913) playing on a previous fountain installed at the turn of the century on the same site as the newer fountain inspired the addition of figures of children to the design. The three dancing children represent the importance of preserving the health, the opportunities, and the environment for children in the future. The Missouri Children's Fountain and Plaza was made possible by Missouri Mansion Preservation, Inc., through private funds.

On the back and inside liner:

Previously called the Governor's Garden, the area was rededicated as the Carnahan Memorial Garden in October 2001 in memory of Governor Mel Carnahan who died in a plane crash on October 16, 2000. The garden began as a Depression-era project which ran out of funds. However, the love and care of Missouri First Lady Juanita Donnelly was instrumental in completing the Governor's Garden in 1948. Through her persistent efforts, the area was transformed by the addition of a sunken garden, shelter house, pergola, goldfish pool, terraces and walkways.

Photographs by William Helvey

1-800-548-2537

The Missouri State Medical Association Alliance

Celebrating its 75th Anniversary in the year 2000, the Missouri State Medical Association Alliance has a history and a future rich in the giving of its time, talents, and resources to improving the lives of countless Missouri citizens. During a time when proactive women's organizations were not in vogue, Auxiliary founders' beliefs in family values and the need for health education in their communities were turned into action. In 1924, in a letter of invitation to membership in a state Auxiliary, Mrs. George H. Hoxie, of Jackson County, Missouri, who became the first president of the state Auxiliary, wrote, *"Our immediate aim is to educate ourselves in matters of public health and to be prepared to secure the backing of women's organizations and other groups for legislative enactments which the Missouri State Medical Association desires to be passed."* Members traveled to that first meeting from 60 Missouri counties, and the Missouri State Medical Association Auxiliary was founded. County medical society Auxiliaries then formed across the state. In the early 1990s, many followed the trend and changed the name "Auxiliary" to "Alliance."

As you read the accomplishments throughout *Windows Across Missouri* of each county medical Alliance, you will see the intensity of this organization's commitment and the relevance of programs as they focus on family and community needs. The constants that remain strong through the MSMA Alliance's history are:

- advocacy for the profession of medicine and the patients served;
- education of the community on child health, safety, and protection issues;
- promotion of responsible legislation through awareness, education, and involvement.

On behalf of the MSMA Alliance, we thank you for your purchase of this cookbook. All proceeds from *Windows Across Missouri - A Culinary View* will support and fund the education of youth, adults, and families through a variety of health awareness and education projects and programs in Missouri communities. As you read, we encourage you to become acquainted with the 10 regions in Missouri and each MSMA county Alliance within them as described on the reverse of the division pages. History and descriptions include:

- Boone County Medical Society Alliance
- Buchanan County Medical Society Alliance
- Cape Girardeau County Area Medical Society Alliance
- Clay-Platte County Medical Society Alliance
- Cole County Medical Alliance
- Greene County Medical Society Alliance
- Jasper-Newton Metropolitan Medical Alliance
- Medical Alliance of the Metropolitan Medical Society of Greater Kansas City
- Members-At-Large
- Quad County Medical Society Alliance (Butler-Wayne-Ripley-Carter Counties)
- Tri-County Medical Alliance (Franklin-Gasconade-Warren Counties)
- St. Louis Metropolitan Medical Society Alliance

And introducing a Culinary View...

First Impressions 7

Appetizers & Beverages — *The Missouri Governor's Mansion*

Visions of Plenty 43

Breads & Breakfasts — *Mark Twain*
Members-At-Large

A Garden Panorama 73

Salads — *Heart of Missouri*
The Medical Alliances of Boone & Cole Counties

A Stirring Sight 101

Soups — *Pony Express*
The Medical Alliance of Buchanan County

Vistas of Bountiful Harvests 121

Pastas & Grains — *Trails West*
The Medical Alliances of Clay-Platte Counties & Greater Kansas City

A Sight to Behold 143

Fruits & Vegetables — *Water Wilderness, The Medical Alliance of Quad County*

Sporting Views 171

Fish, Seafood & Game — *Ozark Mountain, The Medical Alliances of Greene & Jasper-Newton Counties*

Reflections of the Fold 201

Beef, Veal, Lamb & Pork — *Wine Country, The Medical Alliance of Tri-County*

A Bird's - Eye View 227

Poultry — *River Heritage, The Medical Alliance of Cape Girardeau County*

A Kaleidoscope of Confections 253

Sweets & Desserts — *Gateway, The Medical Alliance of Metropolitan St. Louis*

Acknowledgments & Sources 312

Index 316

WINDOWS *across* MISSOURI

a culinary view

Favorite Recipes - Notes

First Impressions

Appetizers & Beverages

Photo: The Missouri Governor's Mansion, Jefferson City

A Missouri Window

The Missouri Governor's Mansion

Perched on a bluff within a short walking distance of the State Capitol stands the Governor's Mansion that has served as the home for 30 of Missouri's first families. It majestically overlooks the Missouri River and the well-travelled route of Lewis and Clark. Two previous structures that once served as the Governor's residence stood on this corner at Madison and Capitol Streets in Jefferson City, Missouri.

Completed in December 1871, the Mansion is an outstanding example of Renaissance Revival architecture with Italianate and French influences. The Mansion, designed by architect George Ingham Barnett, is one of the oldest governor's homes in the United States and one of the most beautifully restored.

The three-story red brick building richly trimmed in stone has an imposing portico with four stately pink granite columns. The columns were the gift of Governor and Mrs. B. Gratz Brown and began a tradition of first families leaving a gift to the Mansion.

The Mansion's first floor is restored beautifully and many experts consider it to be the most authentic and carefully researched example of the Renaissance Revival period in the United States. Designed for entertaining and official state functions, the main floor is rich in Victorian color. Fine stenciling, gold leaf, and handsome furniture reflect the period of the house. Works of art, including those of Missouri painters Thomas Hart Benton and George Caleb Bingham, as well as portraits of first ladies, are featured throughout the Mansion.

A Victorian atmosphere greets visitors as they enter the Great Hall containing one of nine fireplaces. From the hall, huge doorways open into the library, the double parlor and the dining room. The Grand Stairway winds gracefully upward from the inlaid parquet floor to the second floor private quarters of the First Family; a ballroom and additional bedrooms are on the third floor.

A visit to the 132-year-old Mansion is truly a "handclasp with history," as former First Lady Mrs. John Dalton once said.

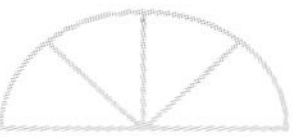

Camembert Sauté

Level: Easy
Serves 4
Preparation Time: 20 minutes

1	(4¼-ounce) round Camembert cheese, with rind
1	egg, beaten
½	cup Italian-seasoned bread crumbs
3	tablespoons butter, divided
⅓	cup chopped green onion tops
	Crackers, French bread or Melba toast rounds

- Dip cheese in egg then in bread crumbs to coat entire round.
- Melt 1½ tablespoons butter over medium high heat until it begins to brown.
- Slide coated cheese round into butter and warm on both sides until crumbs become golden.
- Remove cheese from pan. Plate and keep warm. Discard used butter.
- Add remaining 1½ tablespoons butter to a clean skillet. When foamy, sauté onion tops. Pour over top of cheese round.
- Serve immediately with assorted crackers, French bread or Melba toast rounds.

Chunky Gorgonzola Dip

Level: Easy
Yield: 2 cups
Preparation Time: 10 minutes

1	cup mascarpone cheese
⅓	cup sour cream
⅓	cup chopped fresh chives
½	teaspoon salt
¼	teaspoon ground white pepper
1	cup (4-ounces) crumbled Gorgonzola cheese
	Chopped fresh chives, for garnish
	Pear and apple slices
	Crackers or toasted crostini

- Combine mascarpone cheese and sour cream. Mix until smooth.
- Add chives, salt and white pepper. Mix.
- Fold in Gorgonzola, leaving crumbles of cheese in dip.
- Garnish with chopped chives.
- Serve with sliced pears, apples, crackers or on toasted crostini.
- Cook's Tip: Dip pear and apple slices in lemon water to prevent browning.

A Chef's View

Brie and Camembert are creamy French cheeses with a soft rind made from cows' milk. They are wonderful when melted. Camembert has more tang than Brie. Feta is a crumbly Greek cheese made from goats' milk. It adds a salty touch to salads. Gorgonzola is a semisoft Italian bleu cheese made from cows' milk and is delicious melted on bread or sprinkled on a salad. Monterey Jack is a mild semisoft American cheese made from cows' milk, and is a must for nachos. Roquefort is a French bleu cheese made from sheep's milk and can be a tasty addition to salads.

A Missouri Window

Missouri is known as the 'Show Me State.' This nickname is usually traced to a speech given by Congressman Willard Duncan Vandiver of Missouri in 1899. Speaking in Philadelphia, Vandiver said: "... frothy eloquence neither convinces nor satisfies me. I am from Missouri. You have got to show me."

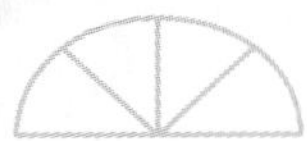

A Chef's View

Beluga is a highly-valued caviar. Coming from the beluga sturgeon in the Caspian Sea, it has the largest eggs. The beluga sturgeon can be 30 feet long and weigh 3,000 pounds, producing 350 pounds of caviar. Osetra and sevruga are among the 23 species of sturgeons. They are smaller than the beluga, so the eggs are smaller, but are still considered quite desirable. Alaskan salmon produce a superb red caviar with large beads. Whitefish from the Great Lakes produce a golden caviar that is actually more popular for its appearance than for its taste.

A Chef's View

Low-fat cream cheese may be substituted for regular cream cheese in hot dishes without changing the texture. Fat-free cream cheese may be substituted in cold recipes, but tends to separate in hot recipes.

Caviar Cream Cheese Spread

Level: Easy
Serves 24
Preparation Time: 30 minutes

5 (4-ounce) packages cream cheese, softened
1 cup mayonnaise
1 small onion, grated
1 tablespoon Worcestershire sauce
1 tablespoon lemon juice, freshly squeezed
Dash hot pepper sauce
1 (3½-ounce) jar black caviar
4 hard-boiled eggs, finely chopped
1 cup fresh parsley, chopped
Assorted crackers

- Beat softened cream cheese with mixer until smooth.
- Add mayonnaise, onion, Worcestershire sauce, lemon juice and hot pepper sauce; beat well.
- Spoon cream cheese mixture into a shallow serving dish. Top with caviar, eggs and parsley.
- Serve with assorted crackers.

Grecian Cheese Round

Level: Easy
Yield: 1 cheese ball
Preparation Time: 3 hours

4 ounces dry-packed feta cheese
1 (8-ounce) package cream cheese, softened
⅓ cup chopped ripe olives, divided
2 tablespoons thinly sliced green onion, white and green parts, divided
1 tablespoon chopped fresh basil, divided
Toasted pita bread wedges, crackers or crostini

- Cut feta and cream cheese into chunks and process in a food processor until smooth.
- Reserve 1 tablespoon olives and 1 tablespoon green onion.
- Mix remaining olives, green onion and 1 teaspoon basil into creamed cheeses.
- Shape mixture into a ball. Cover with plastic wrap and chill.
- Sprinkle with remaining basil, reserved olives and green onion before serving.
- Serve with toasted pita bread wedges, mild crackers or crostini.

Herbed Boursin

Level: Easy
Yield: 1 cup
Preparation Time: 15 minutes

- 1 garlic clove, minced
- 1 (8-ounce) package cream cheese, softened
- ¼ teaspoon dried oregano leaves
- ¼ teaspoon dried basil leaves
- ¼ pound (1 stick) butter, softened
- ¼ teaspoon dried thyme leaves
- 2 parsley sprigs, for garnish
- Assorted crackers or fresh vegetables

- ◆ Combine garlic, cream cheese, oregano, basil, butter and thyme in the bowl of a food processor. Process until creamy.
- ◆ Refrigerate in a covered container.
- ◆ Garnish with parsley sprigs before serving.
- ◆ Serve at room temperature with assorted crackers and fresh vegetables.

Herbed Goat Cheese

Level: Easy
Yield: 1½ cups
Preparation Time: 4 hours

- 8 ounces goat cheese, softened
- 3 tablespoons extra-virgin olive oil
- 4 tablespoons unflavored yogurt
- 3 tablespoons chopped fresh chives
- 2 tablespoons chopped fresh Italian parsley
- 1 teaspoon chopped fresh cilantro
- 1 teaspoon chopped fresh mint
- 1 teaspoon dried thyme leaves
- ½ teaspoon chopped fresh rosemary
- Salt and black pepper, to taste
- Assorted vegetables and toasted baguette slices

- ◆ Cream cheese, oil and yogurt in a food processor until smooth.
- ◆ Add chives, parsley, cilantro, mint, thyme and rosemary. Pulse until well-blended.
- ◆ Season dip to taste with salt and black pepper.
- ◆ Cover and refrigerate for 4 hours.
- ◆ Serve dip with raw vegetables and toasted baguette slices.

A Chef's View

Boursin (Boor SAHN) cheese is a smooth, white cheese with a buttery texture that is often flavored with herbs, garlic or cracked pepper. It can be used more than simply a spread or dip. It makes a delicious topping for broiled tomatoes, or mix with a little milk and toss with hot pasta. Spread some under the skin of chicken before baking or add to a potato mixture to give a new twist. For a quick and easy hors d'oeuvre, spread a small amount onto crinkle cut cucumber slices.

A Chef's View

When shopping for cheese, put your senses to work. Look, touch, smell, and, if possible, taste the cheese before you buy. The key to proper cheese storage is airtight packaging. Wrap unused cheese tightly in foil or plastic wrap, then seal in a plastic bag. Store on the bottom shelf of the refrigerator or in a vegetable bin. Cheese can be frozen, but its texture suffers. Semisoft and hard cheeses become crumbly, and soft cheeses tend to separate.

A Chef's View

Ever wonder what makes bleu cheese blue? It has been injected with or exposed to a mold that gives it the characteristic blue veining and then aged for 3 to 6 months. You may find it labeled as Roquefort, Stilton or Gorgonzola, but they are all bleu cheeses. Some of the cheeses are mild in flavor while others are quite potent.

Party Cheese Pâté

Level: Easy
Yield: 4½ cups
Preparation Time: 4 hours

3 (8-ounce) packages cream cheese, softened and divided
2 tablespoons milk
1 cup chopped pecans, toasted
1 (4.5-ounce) package Camembert cheese, softened
1 (4-ounce) package bleu cheese
1 cup (4-ounces) shredded Swiss cheese
Red and green grapes, cut in half, for garnish
Chive stems, for garnish
Assorted apples, gingersnaps or crackers

- Line a lightly greased 8-inch round baking pan or 9-inch springform pan with plastic wrap. Set aside.
- Cream 1 package cream cheese and milk, in a medium bowl with an electric mixer, until smooth.
- Spread cream cheese mixture into prepared pan. Sprinkle evenly with chopped toasted pecans. Cover and chill.
- Combine remaining 2 packages of cream cheese, Camembert cheese, bleu cheese and Swiss cheese in a large mixing bowl. Beat until blended.
- Spoon mixture over pecan layer, spreading to edge of pan.
- Cover and chill at least 4 hours for flavors to blend. Can be stored up to one week in the refrigerator.
- Invert pâté carefully onto a serving plate, removing plastic wrap with care.
- Use grape halves and chive stems to decorate top along one edge to resemble a bunch of grapes.
- Serve with apple wedges, gingersnaps or assorted crackers.

Pineapple Cheese Ball

Level: Easy
Yield: 1 cheese ball
Preparation Time: 15 minutes

- 2 (3-ounce) packages cream cheese, softened
- 1 (8-ounce) can crushed pineapple, drained
- 2 cups chopped pecans
- ¼ cup chopped green bell pepper
- 2 tablespoons finely chopped onion
- 1 cup chopped pecans, toasted
- Chopped fresh parsley, optional
- Assorted crackers

- Combine cream cheese, pineapple, 2 cups chopped pecans, green pepper and onion in a food processor. Process until a ball almost forms.
- Shape into a ball or log and refrigerate for 2-4 hours.
- Before serving, roll in toasted pecans or parsley. Keep cold until serving.
- Serve with crackers.

Strawberry Cheddar Cheese Carousel

Level: Easy
Serves 15
Preparation Time: 3 hours

- 1 cup chopped pecans, toasted and divided
- 4 cups finely shredded sharp Cheddar cheese
- 2 cups finely shredded mild Cheddar cheese
- 4 green onions, chopped, white and green parts
- 1 cup mayonnaise
- ½ teaspoon cayenne pepper, or to taste
- Chopped fresh parsley, for garnish
- 1 (16-ounce) jar strawberry preserves
- Butter crackers

- Coat a 7-cup mold with butter flavored cooking spray and layer bottom of mold with ¾ cup toasted pecans.
- Mix together cheeses, onion, mayonnaise and cayenne pepper.
- Spoon cheese mixture into mold, pat down to compact mold and allow to firm-up in the refrigerator for at least 3 hours.
- Unmold on a serving platter. Garnish with fresh parsley and sprinkle with remaining ¼ cup pecans.
- Add strawberry preserves to space in center of unmolded cheese ring.
- Serve with butter crackers.
- Cook's Tip: For a smaller cheese carousel, recipe may easily be halved.

A Chef's View

Shape cheese balls into different shapes to fit the season—a Christmas tree or giant star. Decorate with cuts of pimiento, green pepper, and olives.

A Chef's View

Plan a cheese-tasting party so you and your guests can get acquainted with a number of cheeses. Plan about one-fourth pound of cheese per person, including a balance of strong and mild cheeses as well as textures ranging from soft to hard. Serve with an assortment of crackers that will enhance the flavor of the cheeses.

A Show-Me Specialty

Southwestern Guacamole Dip is famous at Andrea's Restaurant in Poplar Bluff, Missouri. Founded by a mother-daughter team, Andrea Greer, the daughter and a professional chef, creates her own menus and cuts her own meat. Bjaye Parkin Greer is host and business manager.

Andrea's Restaurant
2216 North
Westwood Boulevard
Poplar Bluff
573-776-1701

A Chef's View

Firm-textured raw fruits and vegetables make excellent containers for dips. Try pineapple, grapefruit, cantaloupe, green pepper, turnip or a large cucumber. First, cut a narrow slice from bottom so the container sits flat; then, carve out the center and fill the cavity.

Andrea's Southwestern Guacamole

Level: Easy
Yield: 3 cups
Preparation Time: 1 hour

3 medium ripe avocados
4 tablespoons fresh lime juice
½ teaspoon ground cumin
¼ teaspoon garlic salt
¼ teaspoon Cajun season
¼ cup mayonnaise
1 cup sour cream
1 cup medium-hot chunky salsa, or to taste
Tortilla chips

- Scoop out avocados and place pulp in glass mixing bowl.
- Stir in lime juice, cumin, garlic salt, Cajun seasoning, mayonnaise, sour cream and salsa without completely mashing avocados and keeping chunky appearance.
- Chill to combine flavors.
- Serve with tortilla chips.
- Cook's Tip: Add avocado pit to dip to prevent darkening, if refrigerating.

Apples N' Almond Toffee Brickle Dip

Level: Easy
Yield: 2 cups
Preparation Time: 8 hours

1 (46-ounce) can pineapple juice
6 Granny Smith apples, unpeeled, cored and thinly sliced
¾ cup brown sugar, firmly packed
½ cup granulated sugar
1 teaspoon vanilla extract
1 (8-ounce) package cream cheese, softened
6 ounces bit-o-brickle almond toffee pieces, divided

- Soak apples overnight in pineapple juice. Refrigerate and keep chilled in juice until ready to serve.
- Mix sugars, vanilla extract and cream cheese until smooth. Fold in bit-o-brickle pieces, reserving 1 tablespoon of candy.
- Pour cream cheese mixture into a decorative crystal bowl. Sprinkle with remaining bit-o-brickle.
- Drain apples and serve with dip.
- Cook's Tip: Dip can be refrigerated.

Chinese Ginger Garlic Dip

Level: Quick and Simple
Yield: 2 cups
Preparation Time: 15 minutes

¼ cup finely chopped fresh ginger
3 garlic cloves, minced
1 cup mayonnaise
1 cup sour cream
¼ cup chopped fresh parsley
¼ cup finely chopped water chestnuts or peeled jicama
1½ tablespoons soy sauce
Fresh vegetables

- Combine ginger, garlic, mayonnaise, sour cream, parsley, water chestnuts and soy sauce. Mix well.
- Chill to blend flavors.
- Serve with fresh vegetables.

A Chef's View

Using garlic in your dishes depends on how strong you want the garlic flavor. Garlic has a high oil content; the fresher the bulb, the more oil it contains and the stronger the flavor. For the most intense flavor, finely chop or mash cloves to release more of the oils. For a milder taste, cloves may be used whole, often unpeeled and removed prior to serving.

Cottage Spinach Dip

Level: Easy
Yield: 2 cups
Preparation Time: 12 hours

1 (10-ounce) package frozen chopped spinach, thawed and drained
½ cup sour cream
½ cup mayonnaise
1 cup chopped green onion, white and green parts
½ cup small-curd cottage cheese
½ tablespoon Worcestershire sauce
½ tablespoon lemon juice
Dash garlic salt
Black pepper, to taste
Assorted chips, crackers or bread rounds

- Mix spinach, sour cream, mayonnaise, green onion, cottage cheese, Worcestershire sauce and lemon juice. Season with garlic salt and black pepper.
- Refrigerate in an airtight container for 12 hours.
- Serve chilled with assorted chips or crackers.
- Cook's Tip: Serve in a hollowed out bread round with bread pieces.

A Chef's View

Don't stick to the same old dip or spread forever. Experiment and collect your own seasoning secrets - a few drops of Worcestershire or a favorite seasoning added to a recipe will give it a new life. Start with a party-proven recipe and let your imagination take it from there.

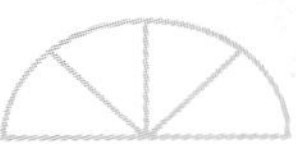

A Chef's View

Create an antipasto platter starring cheese to whet the appetites of your guests. Start with a variety of very thinly sliced cold meats, such as garlic salami, mortadella, cappicola, or prosciutto. Next, add a wedge of Gorgonzola or Parmigiano-Reggiano cheese and shaving of aged provolone or slice of fresh mozzarella cheese. Complete the tray with a variety of olives, pickled peppers, marinated artichoke hearts, fresh vegetables and perhaps some cantaloupe slices, strawberries, or sliced fresh figs.

A Missouri Window

Missouri's motto: 'Salus Populi Suprema Lex Esto' - translated from Latin, becomes, 'Let the welfare of the people be the supreme law.'

Cucumber Yogurt Dip

Level: Easy
Yield: 2 cups
Preparation Time: 8 hours

2	(8-ounce) cartons unflavored yogurt
1	(1-pound) cucumber, peeled, seeded, finely chopped and squeezed dry
2	teaspoons finely chopped fresh dill weed
3	garlic cloves, minced
1	tablespoon extra-virgin olive oil
1	tablespoon fresh lemon juice
	Salt, to taste
	Dill weed sprigs, for garnish
	Pita bread rounds, cut into wedges and toasted

- Place yogurt in a fine sieve set over a bowl. Cover and chill for 6 hours allowing yogurt to drain.
- Stir together drained yogurt, prepared cucumbers, chopped dill weed, garlic, oil, lemon juice and salt.
- Cover and chill dip, for at least 2 hours and up to 8 hours, to allow the flavors to develop.
- Stir dip, garnish with dill weed sprigs and serve with pita wedges.

Fiesta Dip

Level: Quick and Simple
Serves 8
Preparation Time: 20 minutes

1	(16-ounce) can refried beans
1	(4.5-ounce) can chopped green chiles
1	(16-ounce) carton sour cream
1	tomato, chopped
2	(6-ounce) cartons frozen avocado dip, thawed
½	cup chopped green onion, white and green parts
1	(4-ounce) can chopped ripe olives
1	cup (4 ounces) grated Cheddar cheese
	Large tortilla chips

- Layer ingredients in order listed on a 12-inch round platter.
- Chill and serve with large tortilla chips.

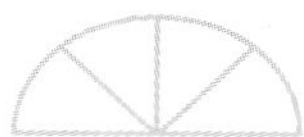

Hummus

Level: Quick and Simple
Yield: 2 cups
Preparation Time: 30 minutes

- 5 garlic cloves, minced
- 2 cups canned chickpeas, rinsed and drained
- ⅓ cup tahini
- ⅓ cup fresh lemon juice
- ½ teaspoon salt
- ½ teaspoon ground cumin
- ⅓ cup unflavored yogurt
- ⅓ cup chicken broth
- ⅓ cup olives, optional
- ⅓ cup roasted red peppers, optional
- Minced garlic, optional
- Pita chips or crackers

- ◆ Combine garlic, chickpeas, tahini, lemon juice, salt, cumin and yogurt in a food processor or blender. Blend until smooth.
- ◆ Add chicken broth for desired consistency.
- ◆ Give additional flavor to hummus by folding in olives, roasted red peppers or additional minced garlic.
- ◆ Serve with pita chips or crackers.
- ◆ Cook's Tip: For homemade tahini, toast ⅓ cup sesame seeds then add ⅛ cup canola oil. Blend into a paste.

Spinach Tofu Dip

Level: Quick and Simple
Yield: 1½ cups
Preparation Time: 15 minutes

- 2 green onions, coarsely chopped, white and green parts
- 1 garlic clove, peeled
- 1 (10-ounce) package frozen chopped spinach, thawed and squeezed dry
- ½ teaspoon cayenne pepper
- ¼ pound silken tofu
- 2 tablespoons lemon juice
- Splash sesame oil
- 1 tablespoon soy sauce
- Assorted raw vegetables

- ◆ Combine green onions, garlic, spinach, cayenne pepper, tofu, lemon juice, sesame oil and soy sauce in a food processor. Process until smooth.
- ◆ Serve with raw vegetables.

A Chef's View

Try this healthy Kid Friendly snack. More people grow tomatoes in their backyard gardens than any other crop. Use a small round tomato and slice off the very top and scoop out the seeds and pulp with a spoon. Fill the cavity with ⅓ cup cottage cheese or stuff the tomato with hummus. Sprinkle chopped nuts on top for crunch.

A Chef's View

Tofu, a soybean curd made from soy milk, is packed with protein and vitamin B, low in sodium and saturated fat, and is cholesterol-free. Although virtually tasteless by itself, tofu easily absorbs other flavors and lends itself to many different cooking techniques. Soft tofu is good for whipping, blending, and crumbling, and a good substitute for creamy ingredients in dips, puddings, soups, and salad dressings. Silken tofu can be stirred into soups, stews, and creamy pasta dishes and will virtually disappear. Firm tofu can be cubed, sliced or crumbled for use in salads, stir-frying, and pasta. Extra-firm tofu is a good choice for stir-frying.

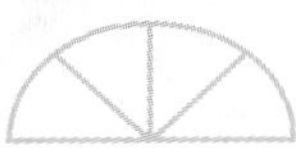

A Chef's View

Olive oil is so popular today that you can buy just about any variety in your local grocery store. Olive oils are graded according to the amount of acid they contain. The lower the acid is the better the oil. Cold-pressed extra-virgin olive oil has the finest and fruitiest flavor. The deeper the color, the more intense the flavor. Light olive oil is not lighter in calories, but lighter in flavor. It should be used in recipes where a strong olive oil taste is not desirable. It has a higher smoking point than other olive oils, and so it should be used for high heat frying. Extra-virgin olive oil is made from the first pressing of the olives, during which time no heating of the fruit occurs and no chemicals are used. It has almost no acidity and is thick and rich in color. Extra-virgin is generally considered to be the finest and fruitiest of all the oils, and therefore, the most expensive.

Summer Tomato Relish

Level: Quick and Simple
Yield: 4 cups
Preparation Time: 30 minutes

4	large fresh tomatoes, peeled and chopped
½	cup chopped celery
1	medium red onion, chopped
¼	cup chopped green bell pepper
1	(4-ounce) can chopped green chiles
2	tablespoons red wine vinegar
¼	cup mild olive oil
1	teaspoon mustard seeds
1	teaspoon crushed coriander seed
½	teaspoon salt
	Dash black pepper
	Dash hot pepper sauce
	Large corn chips or tortilla triangles

- Layer ingredients in a 11x7x2-inch glass dish in the following order: tomatoes, celery, red onion, green pepper and chopped green chiles.
- Combine the vinegar, olive oil, mustard seed, coriander, salt, black pepper and hot pepper sauce. Mix well.
- Pour marinade over vegetables. Cover and refrigerate until ready to serve.
- Stir vegetables before serving. Serve with corn chips or tortilla triangles.
- Cook's Tip: For a refreshing taste, serve relish over grilled fish.

Peanut Butter Yogurt Dip

Level: Quick and Simple
Yield: 1 cup
Preparation Time: 10 minutes

½ cup creamy peanut butter
½ cup vanilla yogurt
¼ teaspoon ground cinnamon
¼ cup raisins
2 cups miniature pretzel twists, apples or banana slices

- Combine peanut butter, yogurt, cinnamon and raisins in a small bowl. Mix well.
- Refrigerate in a covered container.
- Serve with pretzel twists, apples or banana slices.

Asian Vegetable and Beef Turnovers

Level: Easy
Yield: 48 pieces
Preparation Time: 1 hour

½ pound ground chuck
1 envelope beef-flavored mushroom soup mix
1½ cups canned bean sprouts, drained
½ cup chopped onion
½ cup sliced water chestnuts, drained and chopped
3 (8-ounce) packages refrigerated crescent rolls
1 egg white, beaten
Sesame seeds

- Brown ground chuck in a large skillet. Add soup mix, bean sprouts, onion and water chestnuts. Simmer. Drain excess liquid.
- Separate rolls as directed. Cut each one in half lengthwise and flatten with hand.
- Spoon a teaspoonful of beef mixture in center of each triangle. Fold over and seal edges with fork tines.
- Place on ungreased cookie sheet, brush with beaten egg white and sprinkle with sesame seeds.
- Bake or freeze turnovers at this time. After freezing store in a freezer bag for later use.
- Preheat oven to 375 degrees.
- Bake frozen or partially thawed turnover on ungreased cookie sheet.
- Bake 15 minutes or until lightly browned.

A Chef's View

Make a simple after-school snack by peeling a banana and cutting it into coin-size pieces. Use vanilla wafers to make sandwiches, with a banana coin between two wafers. Add peanut butter and raisins between the wafers for an added treat.

A Missouri Window

Missouri was named after a tribe called the Missouri Indians meaning 'town of the large canoes.'

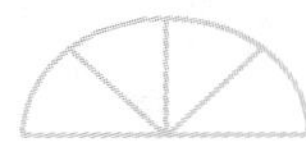

A Chef's View

Before measuring honey, coat the cup or spoon with vegetable cooking spray. The honey will slide off easily. Try the same technique with peanut butter, syrup or molasses.

A Chef's View

The pecan, a native American nut, is a member of the Hickory family and has a fat content of more than 70 percent. Unshelled pecans can be stored in a cool, dry place for up to 6 months. Refrigerate shelled pecans in an airtight container for up to 3 months, or freeze up to 6 months. Care must be taken when storing pecans because their high fat content invites rancidity.

Chinese Chicken Wings

Level: Easy
Serves 12
Preparation Time: 1½ hours

3 pounds chicken wings, tips removed
2 tablespoons canola oil
Salt and black pepper, to taste
1 cup honey
½ cup soy sauce
2 tablespoons ketchup
1 garlic clove, minced
Parsley, for garnish
Cherry tomatoes, for garnish

- Preheat oven to 375 degrees. Coat a 13x9x2-inch baking dish with cooking spray.
- Halve chicken wings, brush with oil and place in baking dish. Sprinkle with salt and black pepper.
- Bake 30 minutes. Drain.
- Combine honey, soy sauce, ketchup and garlic. Stir and brush honey mixture over chicken, coating evenly.
- Bake an additional 50 minutes or until bubbly.
- Garnish with parsley and cherry tomatoes.
- Cook's Tip: To make ahead, wrap wings in heavy-duty aluminum foil after first baking and refrigerate. Increase final baking time by 20 minutes.

Pecan Stuffed Dates

Level: Easy
Yield: 36 pieces
Preparation Time: 1 hour

1 pound pitted dates
½ pound pecan halves
1 pound sliced bacon, cut in half width-wise
1 cup brown sugar, firmly packed

- Preheat oven to 400 degrees. Coat a broiler pan and its grill with cooking spray.
- Stuff each date with a pecan half.
- Wrap a half slice of bacon around each date, securing with a wooden pick.
- Place wrapped dates on broiler pan and sprinkle with brown sugar. Bake until crisp, approximately 12-15 minutes, turning once.
- Serve warm.

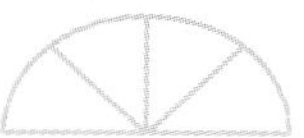

Dried Cherry and Almond Chicken Salad in Wonton Cups

Level: Easy
Serves 24
Preparation Time: 2 hours

2 cups finely chopped cooked chicken breast
¼ cup mayonnaise
¼ cup dried cherries, chopped
¼ cup smoked almonds, chopped
3 green onions, minced, white and green parts
24 wonton wrappers

- Combine chicken, mayonnaise, cherries, almonds and green onion in a medium bowl. Cover and refrigerate until ready to serve in wonton cups.
- Preheat oven to 350 degrees.
- Cut the wontons into circles with a cookie cutter. To create cups, coat a miniature muffin tin with cooking spray and press the wonton circles into each tin.
- Coat wonton circles with butter-flavored cooking spray. Bake for 7 minutes or until lightly browned.
- Remove from oven and cool.
- Fill wonton cups with the chicken salad and serve.
- Cook's Tip: Wonton cups can be prepared, cooled and stored in an airtight container until ready to use.

Bleu Cheese Fingers

Level: Easy
Serves 10
Preparation Time: 45 minutes

10 ounces Roquefort cheese
5 tablespoons heavy cream
15 slices whole wheat sandwich bread, crusts removed
2 Bartlett pears, cored and thinly sliced into wedges
1 cup pecan pieces, toasted

- Heat oven to 350 degrees.
- Combine cheese and heavy cream in a small bowl until mixture is soft enough to spread. Set side.
- Cut bread in half crosswise and place on a baking sheet. Toast in oven, 10-15 minutes per side, until golden. Remove from oven.
- Spread 1 heaping teaspoon cheese mixture on each bread finger. Top each finger with a pear slice, at an angle. Garnish with pecans.
- Serve at room temperature.

A Show-Me Specialty

Dried Cherry and Almond Chicken Salad in Wanton Cups is a specialty of Colleen Miner, a food presentation specialist from Minnesota.

A Chef's View

There are two main groups of cherries, sweet and sour. The larger of the two are firm, heart-shaped sweet cherries. They're delicious for eating out of hand and can also be cooked. The most popular varieties range from the dark red to purplish black Bing, Lamert, and Tartarian, to the golden, red-blushed Royal Ann. Sour cherries are small, softer, and more globular than the sweet varieties. Most are too tart to eat raw, but make excellent pies and preserves.

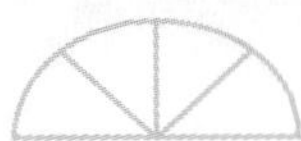

A Chef's View

For a quick appetizer overlap kasseri or scamorza cheese slices, or other meltable cheese, in a shallow baking dish. Sprinkle with sliced ripe olives, snipped fresh oregano, minced garlic, and crushed red pepper. Heat in a 450 degree oven about 10 minutes or until cheese just begins to melt. Serve on crackers or French bread slices; rewarm as needed.

Hallelujah Ham Loaves

Level: Easy
Yield: 60 sandwiches
Preparation Time: 30 minutes

½	pound (2 sticks) butter, softened
3	tablespoons poppy seeds
1	teaspoon Worcestershire sauce
3	tablespoons prepared mustard
1	medium onion, minced
1	pound cooked ham, minced
3	cups shredded Swiss cheese
60	small party bread rolls

- Preheat oven to 400 degrees.
- Cream butter, poppy seeds, Worcestershire sauce and mustard.
- Add onion, ham and Swiss cheese. Mix well.
- Halve rolls lengthwise and place bottom cut side up in a jelly-roll pan or on a cookie sheet.
- Spoon ham mixture on top and cover with top of roll. If desired, seal six sandwiches in aluminum foil and freeze.
- To bake, sprinkle lightly with water and cover with foil.
- Bake 10 minutes or until heated through.

Baja Shrimp Nachos

Level: Easy
Yield: 40 pieces
Preparation Time: 20 minutes

1½	cups (6-ounces) grated Cheddar cheese
1	(4.5-ounce) can chopped green chiles
1	(2.25-ounce) can sliced ripe olives, drained
¼	cup sliced green onion, white and green parts
¼	cup mayonnaise
¼	pound tiny precooked shrimp, patted dry
40	round tortilla chips

- Combine cheese, green chiles, olives, onion and mayonnaise in a large bowl.
- Gently fold shrimp into cheese mixture.
- Top each chip with a rounded teaspoon of shrimp mixture.
- Microwave shrimp nachos on high until cheese is melted.
- Nachos may also be broiled in oven. Avoid browning chips.

Petite Crab Cakes

Level: Easy
Serves 4
Preparation Time: 30 minutes

2 tablespoons chopped fresh parsley
1 teaspoon dry mustard
Dash hot pepper sauce
1 teaspoon Worcestershire sauce
2 eggs, beaten
2 tablespoons mayonnaise
1 cup fresh bread crumbs
1 pound crabmeat, flaked or broken
All-purpose flour, for dredging
Salt and black pepper, to taste
Oil, for frying

- Combine parsley, dry mustard, hot pepper sauce, Worcestershire sauce, eggs and mayonnaise together. Mix well.
- Fold in bread crumbs and crabmeat
- Divide mixture into 8 cakes and dredge in flour.
- Deep-fry cakes at 375-380 degrees for 2-3 minutes or until golden brown on both sides.
- Optional: Pan-fry on both sides in butter.
- Cook's Tip: To make fresh bread crumbs, remove crusts from bread, place in food processor and pulse, chopping quickly. Use immediately.

A Chef's View

There are more than 4,000 varieties of fresh and saltwater crabs, the latter being the most plentiful. The major catch on the Pacific coast is the Dungeness crab; from the North Pacific come the king crab and snow crab; along the Atlantic and Gulf coasts it's the blue crab; and the Florida waters give us the stone crab.

Gingered Shrimp

Level: Easy
Yield: 40 pieces
Preparation Time: 2½ hours

1½ pounds medium shrimp, cooked, peeled and deveined
¼ cup soy sauce
2 teaspoons finely chopped gingerroot
¼ cup white vinegar
2 tablespoons sugar
2 tablespoons apple juice
1½ teaspoons salt
3 tablespoons thinly sliced green onion, white and green parts

- Arrange shrimp in single layer in a shallow glass container.
- Heat soy sauce to boiling in saucepan; add gingerroot. Reduce heat; simmer 5 minutes or until most of the liquid is absorbed.
- Stir in vinegar, sugar, apple juice and salt. Pour over shrimp.
- Cover with plastic wrap and refrigerate for 2-3 hours.
- Remove shrimp from marinade; arrange on serving plate. Sprinkle with onions.

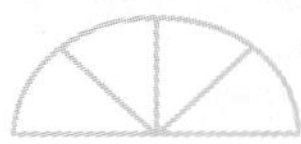

A Chef's View

Phyllo (FEE-loh) literally translated from Greek means 'leaf.' Culinarily, it refers to tissue-thin layers of pastry dough used in various Greek and Near Eastern sweet and savory preparations, the best known being baklava and spanakopita. Unopened, phyllo can be stored in the refrigerator for up to a month. Once opened, use within 2-3 days. Frozen phyllo can be stored for up to 1 year.

Phyllo Lobster Triangles

Level: Expert Cook
Yield: 60 pieces
Preparation Time: 1 hour

- 1 pound thawed phyllo pastry, follow package directions to keep fresh
- 1 pound (4 sticks) unsalted butter, melted and divided
- 6 green onions, finely chopped, white and green parts
- ¾ pound lobster meat, steamed and flaked
- ¼ cup white wine
- 2 tablespoons all-purpose flour
- ¼ cup heavy cream
- ⅛ teaspoon cayenne pepper
- Salt and black pepper, to taste

- Sauté green onions over high heat in 2 tablespoons melted butter.
- Add lobster meat and wine, stirring quickly to combine.
- Drain mixture, reserving liquid.
- Add 2 tablespoons melted butter and flour to another sauté pan to make a roux. Cook slowly over medium heat for 3-5 minutes. Do not brown roux.
- Pour reserved wine mixture and heavy cream into roux. Stir constantly until mixture thickens.
- Add lobster meat and cayenne pepper. Season to taste with salt and black pepper. Cool.
- Place one sheet of phyllo on work surface and brush with butter. Top with two additional sheets, buttering each sheet.
- Cut buttered sheets in half lengthwise. Cut each half crosswise into 6 equal parts.
- Spoon a teaspoon of lobster filling onto the end of each phyllo strip. Form a triangle by folding the right-hand corner of the phyllo to the opposite side as you would a flag. Keep folding in triangle shape until at end of strip.
- Repeat process with remaining strips and remaining phyllo until all of lobster filling is used.
- Unbaked triangles can be frozen on a cookie sheet and stored in an airtight bag for future use. Thaw 10 minutes before baking.
- To bake phyllo triangles, preheat oven to 400 degrees.
- Place triangles on a buttered baking sheet. Brush tops of triangles with butter and bake for 10 minutes or until golden brown.

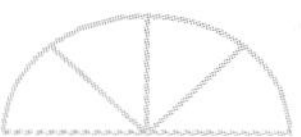

Mushroom Pinwheel Fingers

Level: Easy
Yield: 48 pinwheels
Preparation Time: 30 minutes

1	pound fresh button mushrooms, chopped
12	ounces cream cheese, softened
¼	teaspoon black pepper
½	teaspoon Worcestershire sauce
½	teaspoon seasoned salt flavor enhancer
½	teaspoon garlic salt
¾	cup chopped white onion
1	(16-slice) loaf fresh white sandwich bread
4	tablespoons butter, melted

- Combine mushrooms, cream cheese, black pepper, Worcestershire sauce, seasoned salt, garlic salt and onion in a food processor. Blend until smooth.
- Cut crust off bread, roll bread flat and spread with cream mushroom mixture.
- Roll jelly-roll fashion. Freeze 2 hours, seam sides down in an airtight covered container.
- Preheat oven to 400 degrees.
- Remove rolls from freezer. Before baking, slice in thirds and brush with melted butter.
- Bake 15 minutes.
- Serve warm.

A Chef's View

Morel mushrooms, native to Missouri, are found in the spring sprouting from hillsides. They are highly prized wild mushrooms with black spongy heads. They are great in cream sauces. Porcini, usually sold dried, is native to Italy. Reconstitute them in hot soups, sauces, and stews. Portobello mushrooms may measure up to six inches in diameter and are known for their flat open tops. Grill them whole, then cut into thick slices for sandwiches or salads. Shiitake is a dark capped mushroom that originated in Asia and they are now grown in the United States. They can withstand longer cooking times. Enoki are pin-headed mushrooms, often floated in clear soups, and are favored chiefly for their shape rather than their flavor.

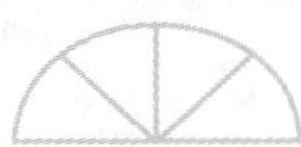

A Show-Me Specialty

Savory Palmiers is a specialty of Colleen Miner, a food presentation specialist from Minnesota.

A Chef's View

Also called palm leaves, a palmier is a crispy delicacy made of puff pastry dough that is sprinkled with granulated sugar, folded, and rolled several times, then cut into thick strips. After baking, these golden brown, caramelized pastries are served with coffee or tea or as a dessert accompaniment. Made with a variation of spices, a palmier can be served as side dish with dinner.

Savory Palmiers

Level: Easy
Serves 20
Preparation Time: 1 hour

1 sheet puff pastry, thawed
2 tablespoons prepared mustard
6 shaved honey-baked ham slices
2 ounces fresh basil or baby spinach leaves, stems removed
6 Swiss cheese slices

- Spread mustard over entire sheet of thawed puff pastry.
- Place ham on top of pastry and top with basil or spinach and Swiss cheese.
- Begin rolling pastry at the long side and continue until roll reaches middle of pastry sheet. Roll the other side until both rolls meet in the middle.
- Turn so rolled side is down before cutting dough into ½-inch slices using a bread knife and a sawing motion.
- Preheat oven to 425 degrees.
- Place cut slices on a parchment lined cookie sheet and bake for 15 minutes or until golden. Serve hot.
- Cook's Tip: Palmiers may be cut, sealed with plastic wrap and refrigerated until ready to bake. Any appropriate combination of meat and cheese may be substituted for the ham and Swiss cheese.

Lobster Deviled Eggs

Level: Easy
Yield: 48 pieces
Preparation Time: 45 minutes

2 dozen eggs
2 cups chopped steamed lobster meat
1 tablespoon mustard
3 shallots, minced
2 tablespoons mayonnaise
2 tablespoons capers
3 tablespoons minced chives plus additional for garnish
Salt and pepper, to taste

- Simmer eggs in lightly salted water for 12-15 minutes. Run under cold water until eggs are cool, then crack and peel cleanly.
- Split eggs neatly and remove yolks.
- Blend yokes, lobster, mustard, shallots, mayonnaise, capers and 3 tablespoons chives. Season with salt and pepper.
- Fill eggs with lobster mixture and garnish with chives.

Baked Italian Artichoke Spread

Level: Easy
Serves 12
Preparation Time: 45 minutes

- 1 (8-ounce) package nonfat cream cheese product, softened
- ½ cup nonfat sour cream alternative
- ¼ teaspoon garlic powder, divided
- ⅛ teaspoon cayenne pepper
- Dash hot pepper sauce, optional
- ½ cup no-salt added tomato sauce, optional
- ¼ teaspoon ground oregano
- ⅛ teaspoon onion powder
- ½ cup frozen artichoke hearts, thawed and chopped
- ¼ cup chopped green onion, white and green parts
- ¼ cup chopped red bell pepper
- ¼ cup sliced ripe olives
- ½ cup (2-ounces) shredded part-skim mozzarella cheese
- ½ teaspoon dried Italian seasoning
- Shredded wheat crackers or garlic Melba rounds

- ◆ Preheat oven to 350 degrees. Coat a 9-inch pie plate with cooking spray.
- ◆ Combine cream cheese, sour cream, ⅛ teaspoon garlic powder, cayenne pepper and optional hot pepper sauce in a small bowl. Cream until smooth.
- ◆ Spread cream cheese mixture in pie plate.
- ◆ Stir together tomato sauce, oregano, ⅛ teaspoon garlic powder and onion powder in a small bowl.
- ◆ Pour tomato sauce mixture over seasoned cream cheese.
- ◆ Layer artichokes, green onion, bell pepper, olives, mozzarella cheese and Italian seasoning in order given over tomato sauce.
- ◆ Bake uncovered for 15-20 minutes or until thoroughly heated.
- ◆ Serve with shredded wheat crackers or garlic Melba rounds.

A Chef's View

An artichoke is actually an edible thistle that dates back to when ancient Romans prized it as a food of the nobility. It is a flower bud of a large thistle-family plant. Purchase an artichoke that is heavy for its size, has a tight leaf formation, and a deep green color. The leaves should squeak when pressed together. When preparing whole artichokes for cooking, slice off the stem to form a flat base and snap off the tough outer leaves closest to the stem. Trim about ½ inch off the pointed top. Simmer, covered, in an inch of water in a stainless steel pan. They are done when the bottoms can be pierced with a knife tip, about 20-30 minutes depending on the size and number of artichokes.

A Chef's View

Christopher Columbus brought back from the New World a member of the Capsicum genus, the chile. Today, this pungent pod plays an important role in the cuisines of many dishes. There are more than 200 varieties, more than 100 of which are indigenous to Mexico. As a general rule, the larger the chile the milder it is. The seeds and membrane can contain up to 80 percent of a chile's capsaicin, the potent compound that gives chiles their fiery nature. Since neither cooking nor freezing diminishes capsaicin's intensity, removing a chile's seeds and membrane is the only way to reduce its heat.

Green Chile Artichoke Spread

Level: Easy
Yield: 2½ cups
Preparation Time: 30 minutes

1 (14-ounce) can artichoke hearts, drained and coarsely chopped
1 cup mayonnaise
1 cup freshly grated Parmesan cheese
½ teaspoon garlic powder
½ teaspoon Worcestershire sauce
2 drops hot pepper sauce
1 (4-ounce) can chopped green chiles, or to taste
Ground paprika, chives, parsley or green onion, for garnish
Assorted crackers or chips

- Preheat oven to 350 degrees. Lightly coat a 3-cup baking dish with cooking spray.
- Mix together artichoke hearts, mayonnaise, Parmesan cheese, garlic powder, Worcestershire sauce, hot pepper sauce and green chiles.
- Spread artichoke mixture into a baking dish.
- Bake for 15-20 minutes.
- Sprinkle with paprika or garnish with chives, parsley or green onion.
- Serve with assorted crackers.

Shiitake Mushroom Spread

Level: Easy
Yield: 2 cups
Preparation Time: 30 minutes

- 4 tablespoons unsalted butter
- 1¼ pounds shiitake mushrooms, finely chopped
- 2 shallots, minced
- ¼ teaspoon ground white pepper
- ¾ teaspoon salt
- 2 tablespoons all-purpose flour
- ½ cup dry sherry
- 1 cup chicken stock
- 1 tablespoon chopped fresh tarragon
- ¼ cup sour cream
- Chopped green onion or tarragon, for garnish
- Melba toast, butter crackers or toasted crostini

- Melt butter in a large pan over medium-high heat.
- Add mushrooms and shallots. Sauté until mushrooms release moisture, approximately 6-8 minutes.
- Stir in white pepper and salt.
- Sprinkle mushroom mixture with flour, stirring to coat mushrooms. Cook 1 minute.
- Add sherry, stock and tarragon. Simmer, uncovered, 10-15 minutes or until liquid is absorbed. Stir occasionally.
- Remove from heat. Stir in sour cream.
- Spoon mixture into a serving bowl. Garnish with green onion or tarragon.
- Spread on Melba toast rounds, butter crackers or crostini.

A Chef's View

Originally from Japan and Korea, the delicious shiitake mushroom is now being cultivated in the United States. The cap is dark brown and can be as large as 8-10 inches across. The meat flesh has a full-bodied, some say steak-like, flavor. The stems are usually very tough and should be removed. Do not discard. They add wonderful flavor to stocks and sauces. Choose plump mushrooms with edges that curl under. Avoid any with broken or shriveled caps. The versatile mushroom is suitable for almost any cooking method including sautéing, broiling, and baking.

A Chef's View

Parsley is one of the most popular herbs, which may be used in many ways. It is a favorite garnish because of its color. Fresh parsley can be frozen by first washing and patting it dry then chopping it up and putting it in a zip locking freezer bag. Freeze it and when you need some parsley, just take out what you need.

A Chef's View

Salsa is the Mexican and Spanish word for 'sauce,' which can signify cooked or fresh mixtures. Salsa cruda is uncooked salsa and salsa verde is green salsa. The main ingredient in salsa verde is the tomatillo, a small, Mexican green tomato. Salsas can range in spiciness from mild to mouth-searing.

Clam and Cheese Dip

Level: Easy
Yield: 2 cups
Preparation Time: 15 minutes

3 tablespoons butter
½ green bell pepper, chopped
1 small onion, chopped
1 (4.25-ounce) jar chopped pimiento, drained
1 (8-ounce) can minced clams, drained
1 tablespoon Worcestershire sauce
1 tablespoon milk
4 tablespoons ketchup
¼ teaspoon cayenne pepper
¼ pound sharp processed cheese spread
Hot pepper sauce, to taste
Chopped fresh parsley or green onion tops, for garnish
Chips or crackers

- Melt butter in a large skillet over medium heat. Stir-fry pepper, onion and pimiento.
- Add clams, Worcestershire sauce, milk, ketchup, cayenne pepper and processed cheese spread to saucepan; stir.
- Mix in hot pepper sauce, to taste.
- Simmer over low heat and stir until cheese melts.
- Serve in a chafing dish surrounded by corn chips or crackers.
- Garnish top of dip with chopped fresh parsley or green onion tops.

Corn and Black Bean Salsa

Level: Easy
Yield: 4 cups
Preparation Time: 10 minutes

1 (15-ounce) can black beans, drained and rinsed
1 cup frozen corn kernels, thawed
½ cup chopped red bell pepper
½ cup chopped fresh cilantro
8 green onions, sliced, white and green parts
3 tablespoons lime juice
2 tablespoons balsamic vinegar
½ teaspoon ground cumin seeds
¼ teaspoon salt

- Combine all ingredients. Stir.
- Store in an airtight container for up to 3 days.
- Serve with chips or as a relish over grilled or baked fish.

Not Just for New Year's Day Black-Eyed Peas

Level: Easy
Yield: 4 cups
Preparation Time: 1 hour

1 (16-ounce) package black-eyed peas, thawed
1 cup minced onion, divided
1 teaspoon garlic salt
Salt and pepper, to taste
1 tablespoon diced jalapeño pepper
1 tablespoon jalapeño juice
1 teaspoon seasoned salt
1½ cups grated sharp Cheddar cheese
4 tablespoons butter, melted
1 (3-ounce) can deviled ham
3 ounces grated mozzarella cheese

- Cover peas with water in a saucepan with ¼ cup onion. Simmer for 30 minutes, or until just tender. Drain.
- Season peas with garlic salt, and salt and pepper, to taste.
- Mash peas lightly and stir in jalapeño pepper, jalapeño juice, seasoned salt, Cheddar cheese, butter and ham.
- Spoon mixture into a 9-inch round baking dish and top with mozzarella cheese. Dip may be covered and refrigerated at this time until ready to use.
- Preheat oven to 350 degrees.
- Bake dip for 30 minutes or until bubbly.
- Serve warm with crackers or as a side dish.

Jezebel Sauce

Level: Quick and Simple
Yield: 4 cups
Preparation Time: 10 minutes

1 (18-ounce) jar apple jelly
1 (18-ounce) jar pineapple preserves
1 (5-ounce) jar prepared horseradish
1 teaspoon dry mustard
Cream cheese, optional
Assorted crackers

- Combine apple jelly, pineapple preserves, horseradish and dry mustard. Mix well.
- Refrigerate in an airtight container.
- Spoon sauce over softened cream cheese on a flat serving dish.
- Serve with assorted crackers or on poultry.
- Cook's Tip: Sauce will keep indefinitely if kept in a tightly sealed jar or container.

A Chef View

Salt is a terrific flavor enhancer, helping to reduce bitterness and acidity, and bringing out other flavors in the food. Most recipes that call for salt are referring to table salt. Salt connoisseurs often prefer to use Kosher salt for cooking, and sea salt for table use. They claim that both have a softer flavor than table salt. Should you by accident put extra salt into any food, add one teaspoonful of brown sugar or a slice of potato, and the salty taste will disappear.

A Chef's View

Mustard, whole or ground, gives good flavor to a variety of dishes. Use alone in small amounts in various soups, meat dishes, pastries, dumplings, and even in some puddings and sweet dishes.

A Culinary Reflection

I was about 7 or 8 years old when my mother's sister, Aunt Rose to me, and her friend Rose would spend their Saturday mornings teaching me to cook and bake. Mom was always afraid to let me in her kitchen because I might hurt myself or mess it up. Friend Rose's husband was a professional chef, and they had every imaginable cooking utensil and oh-so-many recipes in my eyes. I was always my Aunt Rose's favorite niece and she spoiled me rotten when it came time to cooking. My love of cooking and baking brings back fond memories of the times spent in the kitchen with the two Roses.

- Carol Jean DeFeo

Orange Pecans

Level: Quick and Simple
Yield: 2 cups
Preparation Time: 35 minutes

2 tablespoons unsalted butter
4 teaspoons finely grated orange peel
2 teaspoons ground cinnamon
½ teaspoon ground cloves
¼ teaspoon cayenne pepper
2 cups pecans
3 tablespoons granulated sugar
1 teaspoon salt

- Preheat oven to 300 degrees.
- Melt butter in saucepan over low heat.
- Add orange peel, cinnamon, cloves and cayenne pepper and stir 30 seconds or until aromatic.
- Add pecans, then sugar and salt. Stir until pecans are evenly coated.
- Place nut mixture on a baking sheet. Bake 20-30 minutes until nuts are toasted, stirring occasionally. Watch carefully.
- Cool and store in an airtight container at room temperature.
- Cook's Tip: For best flavor, use within three days.

White Cheddar and Bleu Cheese Fondue

Level: Easy
Serves 2
Preparation Time: 40 minutes

½ pound sharp white Cheddar cheese, grated
½ pound bleu cheese, crumbled
1 cup beer
Coarse kosher salt and ground pepper, to taste
¼ loaf cubed French bread, for dipping
1 quartered fig, for dipping
2 stalks blanched asparagus, for dipping
1 cut and cored apple, for dipping
1 cut and cored pear, for dipping

- Melt cheeses with beer in a fondue pot or slow cooker. Add seasonings to taste. Keep warm over a small flame.
- Arrange cubed bread, fig slices, asparagus, apple and pear on platter.
- Cook's Tip: Provide individual long handled forks or skewers for dipping.

Santa Fe Salsa

Level: Easy
Yield: 7 cups
Preparation Time: 15 minutes

- 1 (16-ounce) can crushed tomatoes, undrained
- 2 (14.5-ounce) cans diced tomatoes, undrained
- 1 (4.5-ounce) can chopped green chiles, undrained
- 1 medium onion, chopped
- 2 large jalapeño peppers, seeded and chopped
- 2 garlic cloves, minced
- ½ cup chopped fresh cilantro
- 2 tablespoons lime juice
- 1 tablespoon granulated sugar

- ◆ Combine all ingredients in a large glass bowl.
- ◆ Store in the refrigerator for up to 3 days in an airtight non-reactive container.
- ◆ Cook's Tip: Serve with chips, over fish or with tacos or burritos.

Tangy Ranch Snack Mix

Level: Easy
Yield: 12 cups
Preparation Time: 45 minutes

- 9 cups crispy corn, wheat and rice cereal squares
- 2 cups bite-size bagel chips, garlic-flavored
- 1 cup bite-size pretzels
- ⅓ cup canola oil
- 1 teaspoon dried dill weed
- ¼ teaspoon lemon and herb seasoning
- ⅛ teaspoon garlic powder
- 1 (1-ounce) package ranch salad dressing mix

- ◆ Combine cereals, bagel chips and pretzels in a large microwave-safe bowl.
- ◆ Mix canola oil, dill weed, lemon and herb seasoning and garlic powder in a small bowl.
- ◆ Slowly pour oil mixture over cereal mixture, stirring until all pieces are evenly coated.
- ◆ Microwave on HIGH for 3-4 minutes, stirring thoroughly every minute with a spatula and scraping sides and bottom of bowl.
- ◆ Sprinkle salad dressing mix gradually over cereal mixture. Stir until all pieces are evenly coated.
- ◆ Spread on absorbent paper to cool.
- ◆ Store in an airtight container.
- ◆ Cook's Tip: Due to differences in microwave ovens, cooking time is approximate.

Avocado Feta Salsa

Level: Easy
Yield: 2 cups
Preparation Time: 15 minutes

1 large avocado, seeded, peeled and chopped
2 plum tomatoes, chopped
¼ cup chopped red onion
1 garlic clove, minced
1 tablespoon chopped fresh parsley
½ teaspoon chopped fresh oregano
1 tablespoon olive oil
½ teaspoon red wine vinegar
¼ cup crumbled feta cheese

◆ Combine all ingredients except feta cheese in a small bowl.
◆ Fold in feta cheese.
◆ Serve immediately.
◆ Cook's Tip: Serve this tangy version of guacamole with grilled chicken, fish, pasta or as an appetizer served with chips.

A Chef's View

Herbs should be used with discretion. More is never better! A good rule of thumb is to use ¼ teaspoon of a dried herb for a recipe that serves 4. You can then increase this amount according to your taste.

A Chef's View

Last-minute entertaining can go full speed ahead with these easy appetizers made from seemingly simple supplies that might be in your pantry or refrigerator or quickly purchased at the local market.

- *Fill hollow cucumber cups with a mixture of chopped honey-roasted peanuts, cilantro, and ground red pepper. Top with a carrot quill.*
- *Belgian endive leaves transport an equal blend of mascarpone cheese and purchased salmon roe dip, capers, and lemon peel.*
- *Layer mini-bagel crisps with bite-size slices of smoked salmon. Top the tower with sour cream and snipped fresh dill.*
- *Sprinkle bleu cheese crumbles on Italian bread brushed with olive oil; broil until cheese melts. Nest slivers of red onion on top.*

A Missouri Window

In 1812 Missouri was organized as a territory and later admitted as the 24th state of the Union on August 10, 1821.

Cool Cucumber Sauce

Level: Easy
Yield: 3 cups
Preparation Time: 3 hours

2	cups sour cream
3	tablespoons white wine vinegar
3	tablespoons dried dill weed, or to taste
1	tablespoon fresh lemon juice
2	teaspoons grated onion
1	teaspoon salt, or to taste
½	teaspoon cayenne pepper
1	large cucumber, peeled, seeded and chopped

- Combine sour cream, vinegar, dill weed, lemon juice, onion, salt and cayenne pepper. Blend well.
- Stir in cucumber.
- Cover and chill.
- Cook's Tip: Use as a dip with crackers or vegetables or drizzle over *Windows'* Sophisticated Salmon Mousse.

Apple Cider Spritzer

Level: Quick and Simple
Serves 12
Preparation Time: 10 minutes

½	gallon apple cider
½	liter seltzer water
½	liter lemon-lime flavored carbonated beverage
	Apple slices, for garnish

- Mix first 3 ingredients and serve over ice.
- Garnish with sliced apples dipped in a solution of lemon juice and water to prevent discoloration.

Children's Fruit Juicy Punch

Level: Quick and Simple
Yield: 1 gallon
Preparation Time: 15 minutes

4 cups pineapple juice, chilled
1 quart orange juice, chilled
1 quart lemonade, chilled
1 (33.8-ounce) bottle ginger ale, chilled
Orange or pineapple slices, for garnish

- Combine first 3 ingredients.
- Stir in ginger ale just before serving.
- Serve over crushed ice.
- Garnish with orange wedges or pineapple slices.

Honey Nectar Shake

Level: Easy
Serves 4
Preparation Time: 2 hours

1 cup pineapple juice
1 cup peach nectar
1 (10-ounce) package frozen sliced strawberries, slightly thawed
2 ripe bananas
1 tablespoon honey

- Combine pineapple juice, peach nectar and strawberries in a blender at high speed until well mixed.
- Break bananas into chunks and add to blender.
- Add honey. Blend until smooth and thick.
- Chill until ready to serve. Do not freeze. Stir before serving.

A Missouri Window

Missouri: ?muh ZOOR ee? or ?muh ZOOR uh?

Missourians and visitors alike have a common problem: they can't agree on how to pronounce the state's name. The question has been discussed, argued about and fought over - but never resolved. The eastern half of the state leans toward the 'ee' sound at the end, yet many western Missourians say they live in either 'Missourah' or 'Missouree.' A great majority of residents under the age of 45 say 'Missouree,' but there's more difference of opinion among older Missourians.

A Chef's View

Always use the freshest fruits when preparing fruit drinks. Try to use fruit at the peak of its season. Don't despair when fresh fruit isn't available. Many types of fruit can be purchased frozen and are just as flavorful.

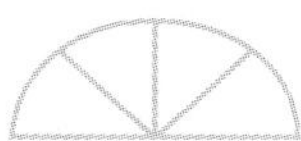

A Chef's View

Easy to prepare, nourishing, and delicious blended fruit drinks, smoothies are the quintessential beverage, healthy and indulgent at the same time. They know no gender, age, or lifestyle limit. Use fruit juices, yogurts, sorbets, sherbets, tofu, soy milk, whole milk, or rice with fresh fruit to prepare a smoothie. They are a healthy food choice that provides essential nutrients in the form of a deliciously indulgent drink.

Cranapple Frostee

Level: Easy
Serves 8
Preparation Time: 1 hour

3 cups cranberry juice
¾ cup apple juice
1 pint raspberry sherbet
8 mint sprigs, for garnish

- Mix cranberry and apple juices. Refrigerate.
- Pour into chilled glasses to serve.
- Top each serving with a scoop of sherbet and stir twice.
- Garnish with a sprig of mint.

Iced Almond Tea

Level: Easy
Yield: 2½ quarts
Preparation Time: 2 hours

4 orange-pekoe tea bags, regular size
2 cups boiling water
1½ cups granulated sugar
⅓ cup lemon juice
1 teaspoon vanilla extract
1 teaspoon almond extract
2 quarts water

- Add tea bags to 2 cups boiling water. Steep for 10 minutes.
- Remove tea bags.
- Add sugar, lemon juice and flavorings. Stir well.
- Add 2 quarts water and stir.
- Chill thoroughly and serve over ice.

English Custard Float

Level: Good Cook
Serves 8
Preparation Time: 3 hours

1	cup granulated sugar
1	heaping tablespoon all-purpose flour
⅛	teaspoon salt
1	quart whole milk, divided
3	egg yolks
1	teaspoon vanilla extract
2	tablespoons pasteurized egg white mix
6	tablespoons warm water

- Combine sugar, flour and salt in a large bowl.
- Add enough milk to make a paste mixture, reserving remainder of milk.
- Stir egg yolks into paste mixture and beat with an electric mixer.
- Add reserved milk slowly while beating on low speed of mixer.
- Pour mixture into a double boiler and cook over medium heat for 15-20 minutes or until custard coats spoon. Stir frequently.
- Strain custard mixture if lumpy. Cool.
- Mix in vanilla extract.
- Beat pasteurized egg white mix with water until very stiff.
- Fold into cooled custard. Refrigerate in a covered pitcher.
- Prior to serving, put custard-filled pitcher into freezer for 20-30 minutes.
- Remove from freezer and stir gently, scraping sides and bottom, to remove ice crystals.
- Pour into small punch cups or brandy snifters. Serve chilled.
- Cook's Tip: Recipe may be doubled.

A Culinary Reflection

When it snowed, my family enjoyed a homemade 'float.' My mother would make a dessert beverage of eggs, milk, sugar, flour, and vanilla, called boiled custard or 'float.' She poured it in a pitcher and put it on the back porch steps in the snow to get cold. When very cold, she stirred in two cups of fresh snow and poured it into glasses to drink. My father always added a teaspoon of 'flavoring' to his, which I discovered later was bourbon. My sister, Robin Till, also a physician's spouse, and I continue to serve the English Custard Float to our families (minus the snow and bourbon) at Christmas. However, we now put the pitcher in the freezer 20-30 minutes prior to serving, then stir it slightly to get the ice crystals off the sides and bottom of a pitcher.

~ Iris Hunt

A Missouri Window

Lithiated Lemon was the creation of Charles Griggs from Missouri, who introduced the lemon-lime drink in 1929. Four years later, he renamed it 7-Up. Sales increased significantly.

A Chef's View

Layer edible flowers face down in the bottom of a metal mold or fluted pan. Add 1½ inches of distilled water. Freeze until firm. Continue to add layers of flowers and water to the mold, freezing each layer before adding another. Place briefly in a bowl of hot water and invert to remove from the mold. Ice cubes can be prepared n the same manner. Freezing in layers keeps the flowers from floating to the top, which becomes the bottom when inverted. The distilled water ensures that the ice will freeze clear.

Edible flowers include pesticide-free chive, chamomile, lavender, lemon, mimosa, orange, peach, plum, and squash blossoms, as well as chrysanthemums, daisies, geraniums, jasmine, lilacs, marigolds, and violets.

Pineapple Octopus Bubbles

Level: Quick and Simple
Serves 2
Preparation Time: 5 minutes

1 cup pineapple juice
1 cup club soda
Pineapple slices, for garnish

- Pour ½ cup pineapple juice in each of two glasses.
- Add ½ cup club soda to each glass. Stir.
- Serve immediately, garnished with a pineapple slice.

Raspberry Punch

Level: Quick and Simple
Serves 20
Preparation Time: 15 minutes

1 (8-ounce) can crushed pineapple, chilled
1 (10-ounce) package frozen red raspberries, partially thawed
1 (12-ounce) can frozen lemonade concentrate, thawed
2 quarts lemon-lime flavored carbonated beverage, chilled
Lemon, orange slices or fruit ice ring, for garnish

- Process pineapple and raspberries in a blender or food processor until smooth.
- Pour into a punch bowl and stir in lemonade.
- Add the carbonated beverage slowly to the punch bowl.
- Decorate with lemon and orange slices.
- Cook's Tip: Float a flowered or fruited ice ring in punch.

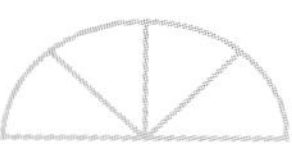

Summer Orange Smoothie

Level: Quick and Simple
Serves 2
Preparation Time: 5 minutes

1½ cups orange juice
¾ cup milk
½ cup granulated sugar
½ teaspoon vanilla extract
1 cup crushed ice
1 banana, optional
Orange slices, for garnish

- Combine orange juice, milk, sugar, vanilla, ice and banana in a blender.
- Blend until frothy.
- Serve in frosty glasses. Garnish each with an orange slice.

A Chef's View

For the best orange smoothie, use a seedless orange, such as the navel in winter or the Valencia in the spring or summer. Select oranges that are heavy for their size and avoid any with soft or spongy spots or blemishes. Oranges are available year-round, although different varieties have different peak seasons.

Cranberry Tea

Level: Quick and Simple
Serves 10-12
Preparation Time: 15 minutes

2 cups brewed tea
½ cup granulated sugar
¼ cup lemon juice
½ teaspoon ground cinnamon
¼ teaspoon ground cloves
½ gallon (64-ounces) cranberry juice cocktail

- Mix tea with sugar, lemon juice, cinnamon and cloves.
- Add cranberry juice and heat thoroughly.
- Serve hot.

A Chef's View

From orange to cranberry, juices are the perfect ingredient to flavoring teas. You can squeeze your own for maximum flavor or use a concentrate mixed with water for convenience. When buying ready-made juices, check the actual fruit juice content because many can contain as little as 10 percent real juice, the rest being a variety of additives.

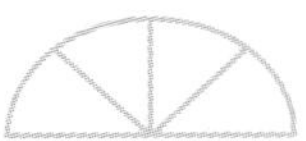

A Chef's View

Different varieties of coffee and milk can create delicious combinations:

- *Café au Lait: ⅓ coffee and ⅔ steamed milk*
- *Café Cubano: very sweet espresso*
- *Cappuccino: ⅓ espresso, ⅓ steamed milk, ⅓ froth*
- *Espresso: strong, rich coffee*
- *Latte: ⅓ espresso and ⅔ steamed milk*
- *Macciato: espresso with a dollop of frothed milk*
- *Mocha: ⅓ espresso, ⅔ steamed milk, a shot of chocolate syrup, and a topping of whipped cream*

Knowing the language of ordering your favorite coffee drink is essential:

- *Shot: one small espresso cupful*
- *Double or Tall: a double-size drink or a double shot of espresso*
- *Skinny: a drink of nonfat milk in place of whole milk*

Café Con Leche

Level: Quick and Simple
Serves 6
Preparation Time: 10 minutes

½ cup heavy cream
⅛ teaspoon ground nutmeg
1 tablespoon confectioners' sugar
1 pot brewed coffee

- Combine heavy cream, nutmeg and confectioners' sugar. Mix well. Refrigerate.
- Brew coffee.
- Whip cream mixture until stiff just before serving coffee.
- Top six cups strong, hot coffee with flavored whipped cream.

White Hot Chocolate

Level: Easy
Yield: 9 cups
Preparation Time: 20 minutes

12 ounces white chocolate, chopped
1¾ cups heavy cream, divided
6 cups milk
2 tablespoons plus 1 teaspoon freshly grated orange peel, divided
¼ cup granulated sugar
½ teaspoon vanilla extract
⅛ teaspoon ground nutmeg
Freshly grated orange peel, for garnish
White chocolate curls, for garnish

- Melt white chocolate in top of double boiler over gently boiling water; upper pan should not touch water. Set aside.
- Combine 1 cup cream, milk, 2 tablespoons orange peel and sugar in a large saucepan.
- Bring cream mixture just to a boil, stirring often. Reduce heat and simmer 2 minutes.
- Add 1 cup milk mixture to white chocolate in double boiler. Stir well with a wire whisk.
- Pour white chocolate into milk mixture in saucepan. Simmer over low heat until warmed, stirring gently.
- Beat remaining ¾ cup cream, 1 teaspoon orange peel, vanilla extract and nutmeg until soft peaks form for whipped cream.
- Pour hot chocolate into warmed mugs. Spoon dollop of whipped cream onto hot chocolate. Garnish with orange peel and white chocolate curls.

Holiday Wassail

Level: Easy
Serves 24
Preparation Time: 3½ hours

3	oranges
3	lemons
2	quarts water
1	(1-ounce) box cinnamon sticks, broken into 1-inch pieces
1	tablespoon whole allspice
1½	cups granulated sugar
1	gallon apple cider
	Orange slices, for garnish
	Cinnamon sticks, for garnish

- Squeeze juice from oranges and lemons. Set juice aside.
- Cut up orange and lemon peels. Simmer in a pan with water, cinnamon sticks and allspice for 3 hours. Spices may be adjusted to taste. Strain and discard liquid.
- Place pulp in a large saucepot. Add sugar, cider and fruit juices.
- Bring juice and pulp to a boil before serving.
- Serve wassail in warm clear glass mugs with a cinnamon stick stirrer and an orange slice.

A Chef's View

'Wassail,' Norse for 'be in good health,' is an old toast. Wassail is a drink consisting of ale or wine sweetened with sugar and flavored with spices.

For a good toast, know the history behind it. From their ancient Greek origins, some toasts have long enjoyed an important place in international diplomacy. Herald the New Year with the ancient custom of drinking to 'your good health' in languages reflecting the heritage of family and friends.

- *American: Cheers*
- *Russian: Na zdorovia*
- *Chinese: Kan bei*
- *French: A Votre Santé*
- *Swedish: Sköal*
- *German: Prosit*
- *Spanish: Salud*
- *Irish & Scottish: Slainte*
- *Japanese: Kampai*
- *Israeli: L'Chaim*

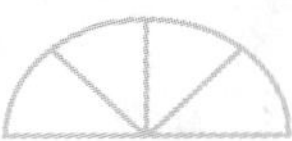

A Chef's View

Use a large electric coffeepot without the coffee basket to keep hot drinks hot during a large gathering. Prepare the recipe as directed, pour into the coffeepot and then plug in the cord.

A Chef's View

Children can prepare Spicy Mocha Mix, pour it into an airtight container, decorate the container with ribbon, and give it as a gift to their teachers or grandparents. A handmade card with the instructions for making the warm drink and individual greetings can round out this thoughtful and special gift.

Russian Tea

Level: Easy
Yield: 2 gallons
Preparation Time: 3 hours

1½	cups water
¼	cup loose tea or 4 regular-size orange-pekoe tea bags
1	(32-ounce) can pineapple juice
1	(16-ounce) can frozen orange juice, prepared according to directions
1	(16-ounce) can frozen lemonade, prepared according to directions
3	tablespoons whole cloves, tied in cheesecloth
4	cinnamon sticks
¾-1½	cups granulated sugar

- Make strong tea base with 1½ cups water and tea.
- Add all other ingredients to tea base and let simmer 2-3 hours. Do not boil.
- Serve piping hot or store in refrigerator until ready to use.
- To serve, bring to simmer but do not boil.

Spicy Mocha Mix

Level: Quick and Simple
Yield: 3 cups
Preparation Time: 10 minutes

1	cup granulated sugar
1	cup nonfat dry milk
½	cup powdered cream
3	tablespoons instant coffee
¼	teaspoon ground cinnamon
½	teaspoon ground allspice
	Dash salt

- Combine all ingredients and mix well.
- Store in an airtight container large enough to hold 3 cups.
- Make single serving by adding 1 cup hot water to 3 tablespoons of the mocha mix in a warm cup. Stir until blended.
- Cook's Tip: Top with whipped topping and chocolate shavings.

Visions of Plenty

Breads & Breakfast

A Missouri Window

Mark Twain

The most famous stretch of the Mississippi River lies along the Mark Twain area in northeast Missouri. The boyhood home of Samuel Clemens, this region is rich in river and outdoor history. It was in the town of Hannibal that Clemens began his writing career under the pen name of Mark Twain. Stomping grounds for Tom Sawyer and Huck Finn, downtown Hannibal features many attractions and activities for families to experience a bit of the lifestyle portrayed in the stories of Twain, including Injun Joe's cave.

Nearby, Mark Twain Lake has earned the reputation for outstanding fishing, sailing, and boating. South of Hannibal is Clarksville, on the Mississippi River, known for its large numbers of wintering bald eagles. In Athens, at the Battle of Athens State Historic Site, the northernmost location of a Civil War battle fought west of the Mississippi River, Union troops defeated the pro-South Missouri State Guard in 1861.

Photos: The Mark Twain Home/Museum & Tom Sawyer Whitewashing Contest, Hannibal

Alliance Members At Large

Missouri has 11 county medical society Alliances, organized and thriving throughout the state. Alliance Members-At-Large are those dues-paying members who are involved in health advocacy activities espoused on the state and national levels, but who do not have the benefit of a county Alliance available to them. Members-At-Large are very active in the communities of Sedalia, Mexico, Hannibal, and others.

The following Members-At-Large have served as MSMA Alliance presidents: Mrs. W. M. Bickford, 1927-28, Saline County; Mrs. David Long, 1932-33, West Central Medical Alliance; Mrs. Robert Haynes, 1943-44, Saline County; Mrs. J.B. McCubbin, 1944-45, Callaway County; Mrs. W.E Koppenbrink, 1946-47, Lafayette-Ray Counties; Mrs. W.L. Alee, 1947-48, Miller-Morgan-Moniteau Counties; Helen McBurney, 1953-54, Saline County; Ravena Martin, 1954-55, Lafayette-Ray Counties; Esther Bauman, 1958-59, Nodaway-Atchinson-Gentry-Worth Counties; Ruth Kelling, 1960-61, Lafayette-Ray Counties; Mildred Bohnsack, 1965-66, Grand River Medical Alliance; Pat Reid, 1969-70, Saline County; Ruthanne Wise, 1972-73, Johnson County; Janet Campbell, 1978-79 Pettis County; Jan Meyer-Simon, 1981-82, Lafayette-Ray Counties. Mrs. Kelling, Mrs. Wise, Mrs. Campbell, and Mrs. Simon also served as presidents of the Southern Medical Association Auxiliary

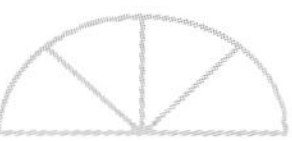

Glazed Citrus Loaf

Level: Good Cook
Yield: 1 loaf
Preparation Time: 1½ hours

1	cup granulated sugar
½	cup low-fat milk
6	tablespoons unsalted butter, softened
2	eggs
1½	cups all-purpose flour
1	teaspoon baking powder
3	teaspoons freshly grated lemon peel
3	teaspoons freshly grated orange peel
1	teaspoon freshly grated lime peel
½	cup plus 1 tablespoon granulated sugar
2	tablespoons lemon juice
2	tablespoons orange juice
2	tablespoons fresh lime juice
1	sliced lemon, for garnish
1	sliced orange, for garnish
1	sliced lime, for garnish

- Preheat oven to 350 degrees. Grease and flour a 9x5x3-inch loaf pan.
- Combine granulated sugar, milk, butter and eggs. Mix well.
- Blend in flour and baking powder.
- Add peels; mix well.
- Pour batter into loaf pan and bake for 50-60 minutes, or until a tester inserted in the center comes out clean.
- Remove from oven; let cool slightly. Remove from pan.
- Set cake on a piece of foil, prick top with a fork.
- Mix together ½ cup plus 1 tablespoon granulated sugar and citrus juices in a saucepan.
- Cook over low heat, stirring constantly, until sugar dissolves and mixture becomes thickened.
- Pour citrus glaze over top of cake.
- Garnish with fresh fruit slices in a decorative design on top of cake.
- Serve warm or at room temperature.

A Chef's View

To zest citrus fruits, it's always a good idea to use fruit that is fresh, cold, dry, and firm enough to peel or grate easily. The zest can be removed in strips or grated off the whole fruit. To take off zest in strips, use a vegetable peeler and remove the colored part of the rind only, without any of the bitter white pith. The pieces of zest may be used as is, cut into julienne strips or chopped.

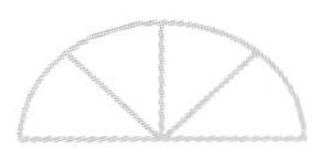

A Chef's View

Try these flavored butters on your special breads, bagels or pancakes for a festive and tasty touch.

Each one requires 1 stick (½ cup) of softened unsalted butter plus the additions.

- *Maple Butter: Add ¾ cup pure maple syrup and mix until fluffy.*
- *Cinnamon Butter: Add 1 tablespoon brown sugar and 1 teaspoon cinnamon.*
- *Citrus Butter: Add ½ teaspoon fresh orange or lemon zest.*
- *Strawberry Butter: Add two large, fresh, ripe, hulled strawberries with confectioners' sugar to taste.*
- *Honey-Pecan Butter: Toast ⅓ cup pecans in a shallow pan for about 8 minutes. Remove and finely chop. Beat butter until fluffy, than beat in 2 tablespoons of honey. Mix in the pecans.*

Date Nut Loaf

Level: Good Cook
Yield: 1 loaf
Preparation Time: 1½ hours

1	cup chopped dates
1	teaspoon baking soda
1	cup boiling water
1½	cups sifted all-purpose flour
¼	teaspoon salt
½	cup brown sugar, firmly packed
½	cup pecans or walnuts, coarsely chopped
1	egg, beaten
1	tablespoon canola oil
1	(8-ounce) package cream cheese, softened and whipped
1	tablespoon granulated sugar
1	tablespoon freshly grated lemon peel

- Preheat oven to 325 degrees. Coat a 9x5x3-inch loaf pan with cooking spray.
- Place dates in a large bowl, sprinkle baking soda over dates and pour boiling water over top. Set aside to cool for 10 minutes.
- Mix flour, salt, sugar and nuts in a small bowl.
- Beat egg with oil and add to cooled date mixture.
- Stir in flour mixture. Mix well.
- Pour batter into prepared pan.
- Bake for 50-60 minutes or until bread begins to pull away from side of pan or cake tester inserted into the center comes out clean.
- Set aside to cool for 10 minutes in pan. Remove bread from pan and cool on a wire rack.
- Combine whipped cream cheese with sugar and lemon peel in a medium-size bowl.
- To serve, slice bread and top with a spoonful of cream cheese mixture.
- Cook's Tip: Serve with whipped topping garnished with a half pecan.

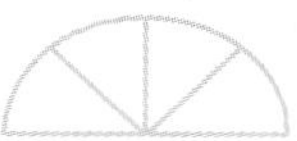

Missouri State Fair Blue Ribbon Zucchini Bread

Level: Good Cook
Yield: 2 loaves
Preparation Time: 1½ hours

- 3 medium zucchini
- 2¼ cups granulated sugar, divided
- 6 teaspoons ground cinnamon, divided
- 3 eggs
- 1 cup canola oil
- 3 teaspoons vanilla extract
- 3 cups all-purpose flour
- 1 teaspoon salt
- 1 teaspoon baking powder
- 1 teaspoon baking soda
- 1½ cups English or black walnuts, chopped
- ½ cup raisins, optional

- ◆ Preheat oven to 325 degrees.
- ◆ Prepare zucchini by partially peeling, grating and draining in a colander. End result should equal 2 cups. Set aside.
- ◆ Combine 4 teaspoons cinnamon and ¼ cup sugar. Set aside.
- ◆ Coat two 9x5x3-inch loaf pans with cooking spray. Dust pans with the cinnamon-sugar mixture, reserving 2 tablespoons for top of bread.
- ◆ Beat eggs until foamy.
- ◆ Fold oil, 2 cups sugar and vanilla extract into eggs. Mix well. Add prepared zucchini.
- ◆ Sift together flour, salt, baking powder, baking soda and 2 teaspoons cinnamon. Gradually add to zucchini mixture. Blend well after each addition.
- ◆ Fold in nuts and raisins, if desired.
- ◆ Pour into the prepared loaf pans. Sprinkle 1 tablespoon cinnamon-sugar mixture over top of each loaf.
- ◆ Bake for 50-60 minutes or until a cake tester inserted into the center comes out clean.
- ◆ Cool in pan for 10 minutes. Remove bread to wire rack to cool completely.

A Chef's View

To freeze or store a sweet bread wrap in plastic wrap first then in aluminum foil, especially if the bread contains any type of nut. Nuts will react with the foil over time.

A Chef's View

Poppy seeds are small, dried, bluish-gray seeds of the poppy plant that measure less than 1/16 inch in diameter and it takes about 900,000 to equal 1 pound. Poppy seeds have a crunchy texture and a nutty flavor. They're used as a filling in various cakes, pastries, coffee cakes, and as a topping for many baked goods. Because of their high oil content, poppy seeds are prone to rancidity. They can be stored, airtight, in the refrigerator for up to 6 months.

Orange Glazed Poppy Seed Bread

Level: Good Cook
Yield: 2 loaves
Preparation Time: 1½ hours

3	cups all-purpose flour, unsifted
1½	teaspoons salt
1½	teaspoons baking powder
1½	tablespoons poppy seeds
3	eggs, slightly beaten
1⅛	cups canola oil
2¼	cups granulated sugar
1½	cups milk
2	teaspoons almond extract, divided
2	teaspoons butter flavoring, divided
2	teaspoons vanilla extract, divided
¼	cup orange juice
¾	cup confectioners' sugar

- Preheat oven to 350 degrees. Grease and flour two 9x5x3-inch loaf pans.
- Sift flour, salt, baking powder and poppy seeds together. Set aside.
- Combine eggs, canola oil, sugar and milk in order given. Add 1½ teaspoons each of almond extract, butter flavoring and vanilla extract. Mix well.
- Add flour mixture to liquid mixture a little at a time. Mix well with electric beaters at least 2 minutes.
- Divide batter between the 2 loaf pans.
- Bake for 50-60 minutes or until a cake tester inserted into the center comes out clean.
- Prepare orange glaze while bread is baking.
- Combine orange juice and ½ teaspoon each of almond, butter and vanilla extracts. Set aside.
- Sift confectioners' sugar after measuring. Gradually add orange juice liquid mixture to confectioners' sugar and mix well. Mixture will be thin.
- Remove loaves from oven and immediately insert tines of fork or cake tester several times across the top of loaves.
- Spoon glaze over bread while hot.
- Cool loaves and then remove from pans.

Pumpkin Bread

Level: Easy
Yield: 2 loaves
Preparation Time: 1½ hours

3	cups granulated sugar
1	cup canola oil
2	eggs
1	cup water
1	cup canned solid pack pumpkin
1	teaspoon vanilla extract
3½	cups sifted all-purpose flour
½	teaspoon baking powder
2	teaspoons baking soda
1	teaspoon salt
½	teaspoon cinnamon
½	teaspoon ground nutmeg
½	cup English walnuts, chopped, optional
1	cup raisins, optional

- Preheat oven to 325 degrees. Grease two 9x5x3-inch loaf pans.
- Blend sugar and oil together in a mixing bowl.
- Add eggs, water, pumpkin and vanilla extract. Beat well.
- Sift flour, baking powder, baking soda, salt, cinnamon and nutmeg together. Add to pumpkin mixture. Mix well.
- Add nuts and raisins, if desired.
- Pour batter into loaf pans.
- Bake for 65-75 minutes or until a cake tester inserted into the center comes out clean.
- Cool in pan for 10 minutes. Remove to a wire rack to cool completely.

A Chef's View

Place a paper doily on top of a loaf of uncut sweet bread before serving and sift confectioners' sugar on top. Carefully remove the doily and the result will be an attractive design adding to the beautiful presentation of food on the dessert or tea table.

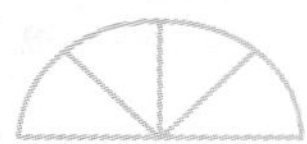

A Chef's View

Don't throw overripe bananas away. Peel, mash, and freeze for later use in breads, muffins, pancakes, waffles, milk shakes, and fruit salad dressings.

Chocolate Chip Banana Muffins

Level: Good Cook
Yield: 24 muffins
Preparation Time: 1 hour

2	eggs, well-beaten
1	cup granulated sugar
3-4	large ripe bananas, mashed
2	cups all-purpose flour
½	teaspoon salt
1	teaspoon baking soda
½	cup canola oil
1	cup miniature chocolate morsels
2	teaspoons vanilla extract

- Preheat oven to 375 degrees. Line a muffin pan with liners.
- Add sugar slowly to eggs while beating constantly.
- Combine bananas and egg mixture. Mix well.
- Sift flour, salt, and baking soda into the banana mixture.
- Add oil and lightly stir.
- Fold in chocolate morsels and vanilla extract.
- Pour batter ⅔ full into muffin cups.
- Bake muffins for 20-25 minutes.
- Cool muffins in tins 2-3 minutes.
- Serve muffins warm.
- To reheat muffins, enclose loosely in aluminum foil and heat approximately 5 minutes in a preheated 450 degree oven.
- Cook's Tip: For banana bread pour batter into 2 greased 8½x4½x2½-inch loaf pans. Bake bread for 1 hour or until done in a preheated 350 degree oven. Cool in pans for 10 minutes and then remove to a wire rack to complete cooling.

M M M M M Muffins

Level: Quick and Simple
Yield: 24 muffins
Preparation Time: 30 minutes

4½ cups wheat-bran flakes cereal with raisins
1½ cups granulated sugar
2½ cups all-purpose flour
2½ teaspoons baking soda
1 teaspoon salt
2 eggs, beaten
¼ pound (1 stick) margarine, melted
2 cups buttermilk

- Preheat oven to 400 degrees.
- Coat 2 muffin tins with butter-flavored cooking spray.
- Combine cereal, sugar, flour, baking soda and salt in a large bowl.
- Add eggs, melted margarine and buttermilk to cereal mixture. Stir lightly.
- Fill muffin cups ¾ full.
- Bake for 15-20 minutes.
- Batter will keep in an airtight container for up to 1 week.
- Cook's Tip: Muffins do not freeze well.

A Chef's View

The secret of good muffins is in the mixing. Combine all the dry ingredients in a bowl, and form a well in the center of the mixture. Add the liquid all at once and stir only enough to moisten the dry ingredients. The mixture will be lumpy, but further mixing will make the muffins tough.

A Missouri Window

The honeybee was designated as the state insect on July 3, 1985.

Sour Cream Corn Muffins

Level: Easy
Yield: 12 muffins
Preparation Time: 30 minutes

1 cup sour cream
¼ cup milk
1 egg
1 teaspoon salt
2 tablespoons butter, melted
¾ cup yellow cornmeal
1 cup all-purpose flour
¼ cup granulated sugar
2 teaspoons baking powder
½ teaspoon baking soda

- Preheat oven to 375 degrees.
- Grease muffin cups.
- Beat sour cream with milk, egg, salt and butter.
- Add cornmeal, flour, sugar, baking powder and baking soda. Mix until moistened.
- Divide batter between muffin cups. Bake for 20 minutes.
- Cool muffins in cups for 5 minutes. Serve warm.

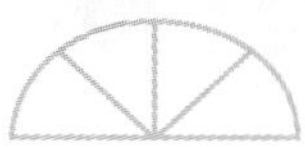

A Missouri Window

It's been said that Missouri is where everything comes together. It's the top of the south, the bottom of the north, the end of the east and the beginning of the west. Take a trip through Missouri's history and you, too, will agree that it all meets right here.

Onion Shortcake

Level: Easy
Serves 9-12
Preparation Time: 1½ hours

4	tablespoons butter
2	large sweet onions, chopped
1	(8-ounce) carton sour cream
½	teaspoon dry dill weed
¼	teaspoon salt
2	cups (8-ounces) grated sharp Cheddar cheese, divided
1	(16-ounce) can cream-style corn
⅓	cup milk
1	(8.5-ounce) box corn muffin mix
1	egg, beaten
4	drops hot pepper sauce

- Preheat oven to 425 degrees and coat a 13x9x2-inch glass baking dish with cooking spray.
- Melt butter, and sauté onion until softened.
- Combine onion mixture with sour cream, dill weed, salt and 1 cup cheese. Set aside.
- Combine corn, milk, muffin mix, egg and hot pepper sauce.
- Pour corn mixture into baking dish.
- Spread onion mixture on top and cover with remaining 1 cup cheese.
- Bake 30-40 minutes until cheese is melted and begins to brown.
- Serve warm.

Bevo Mill Famous Cheddar Cheese and Chive Biscuits

Level: Quick and Simple
Yield: 30 biscuits
Preparation Time: 30 minutes

6	cups sifted all-purpose flour
2	teaspoons salt
4½	tablespoons baking powder
⅔	cup granulated sugar
¼	cup dried chives
¾	cup grated Cheddar cheese
¼	pound (1 stick) plus 3 tablespoons butter, melted
½	cup canola oil
2¾	cups milk

- Combine flour, salt, baking powder, sugar, chives and cheese.
- Add butter and oil mixing until both are incorporated.
- Pour in milk and stir with a fork just until mixture pulls away from side of the bowl. Do not over mix.
- Preheat oven to 400 degrees.
- Drop biscuit mixture from a large spoon onto an ungreased 15x10x1-inch jelly-roll pan. Each biscuit should weigh approximately 2 ounces.
- Bake for 20 minutes or until done and lightly browned.
- Serve warm.

A Show-Me Specialty

Bevo Mill, located in the heart of downtown St. Louis, was built in 1916 by August A. Busch, Sr., as an authentic windmill, in Flemish architectural style. The location was approximately halfway between the Anheuser Busch Brewery and Grant's Farm, his home. When Prohibition was the controversy of the day, it served only Bevo, a nonalcoholic drink that tasted like beer, regular beer, and wine to its clientele. The drinks were served only at the tables, a novel idea back then. Built by the stones gathered by Mr. Busch from Grant's Farm, Bevo Mill also follows the German and Dutch tradition with a pair of storks mounted on the top of the chimney to ensure good luck. The vaulted ceilings end in stone-carved gnomes, originally exhibited at the Paris exposition of 1889.

Bevo Mill
4749 Gravois
St. Louis
800-288-2386

A Chef's View

Basil, called the royal herb by ancient Greeks, is an annual member of the mint family. Fresh basil has a pungent flavor that some describe as a cross between licorice and cloves. It's a key herb in Mediterranean cooking and essential to the delicious Italian pesto. When choosing fresh basil, watch for evenly colored leaves with no sign of wilting. Refrigerate basil, wrapped in barely damp paper towels and then in a plastic bag for up to 4 days. To preserve fresh basil, wash and dry the leaves and place layers of leaves, then coarse salt, in a container that can be tightly sealed.

Flaky Tomato Basil Biscuits

Level: Easy
Yield: 1½ dozen
Preparation Time: 25 minutes

1¾	cups all-purpose flour
2	teaspoons baking powder
½	teaspoon salt
¼	teaspoon granulated sugar
4	tablespoons unsalted butter
⅓	cup half-and-half
2	ripe tomatoes, peeled, seeded and chopped
⅓	cup chopped fresh basil

- Preheat oven to 425 degrees.
- Combine flour, baking powder, salt and sugar.
- Cut butter into dry mixture until it resembles coarse crumbs.
- Add half-and-half, tomatoes and basil. Stir until moistened.
- Transfer dough to floured surface. Knead 30 seconds.
- Roll out dough to ½-inch thickness and cut into desired shapes.
- Bake for 12-15 minutes or until golden.

Yorkshire Popovers

Level: Easy
Serves 6
Preparation Time: 50 minutes

2	eggs
1	cup milk
1	cup all-purpose flour
½	teaspoon salt
	Fresh cracked pepper, to taste
¼	cup beef drippings or melted butter

- Preheat oven to 450 degrees. Place a popover or large muffin pan in the preheated oven for 10 minutes to heat it up.
- Beat eggs until foamy and light in a mixing bowl.
- Whisk in milk until combined.
- Add flour, salt and pepper. Beat just until batter is smooth.
- Pour beef drippings in bottom of hot pan. Pour batter over drippings.
- Bake for 10 minutes at 450 degrees. Reduce temperature to 350 degrees and continue baking for 15-20 minutes more until popovers are puffy and brown.
- Serve immediately, as popovers deflate rapidly.

Dill Bread

Level: Good Cook
Yield: 3 loaves
Preparation Time: 6 hours

1¼	cups warm water, divided
1	(¼-ounce) package active dry yeast
6½	tablespoons honey, divided
2	cups fat-free small-curd cottage cheese
⅛	cup dill seed
3	eggs, beaten
3	tablespoons dried minced onion
1	tablespoon salt
¾	teaspoon baking soda
9	cups all-purpose flour
3	tablespoons oil

- Combine ⅛ cup warm water, yeast and ½ tablespoon honey in a small bowl. Let stand until mixture bubbles, approximately 4-6 minutes.
- Mix cottage cheese, dill, eggs, onion, salt and baking soda together in a large bowl.
- Add yeast mixture, after it has bubbled, to cottage cheese mixture.
- Stir in flour, 2 cups at a time, and oil, 1 tablespoon at a time. Mix until dough forms a ball but is still tacky. Dough hooks for an electric mixer can be used for this step.
- Place in a large greased bowl and turn to coat all surfaces lightly with oil.
- Cover with plastic wrap and let rise in a warm place until doubled.
- Preheat oven to 350 degrees.
- Punch dough down, divide into 3 equal portions. Form each into a loaf. Place in 3 oiled 9x5x3-inch loaf pans. Let rise again.
- Bake loaves for 45-60 minutes, or until golden brown.
- Bread should sound hollow when thumped on side or bottom when removed from pan. If not, return to oven for additional baking.
- Remove bread from pans and cool on a rack.

A Chef's View

Thought by first century Romans to be a good luck symbol, dill has been used in many ways for thousands of years. The annual herb grows to a height of about 3 feet and has feathery green leaves called dill weed, marketed in both fresh and dried forms. Dill weed quickly loses its fragrance during heating, so it should be added toward the end of the cooking time in a recipe. Dill weed is used to flavor many dishes such as salads, vegetables, meats, and sauces. The tan flat dill seed is actually the dried fruit of the herb and heat brings out the flavor of the seed, which is stronger and more pungent than that of the weed. It's most often used in the United States for the brine in which dill pickles are cured.

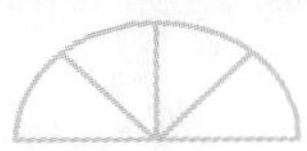

A Chef's View

Focaccia (foh-KAH-chyah) is a large, flat Italian bread that is liberally brushed or drizzled with olive oil and sprinkled with salt. Slits cut into the dough's surface may be stuffed with fresh rosemary before the bread is baked.

Use these spreads on various baked breads:

- *Herbed Cheese Spread: Mix 2 tablespoons minced fresh herbs of choice, 2 tablespoons minced sun-dried tomatoes, 1 minced garlic clove and 8 ounces softened cream cheese. Chill and serve.*
- *Garlic Spread: Mix 8 ounces softened cream cheese and ¼ cup sour cream until smooth. Add 2 crushed garlic cloves, ¼ cup sliced green onions with tops and ¼ teaspoon salt. Serve at room temperature with warm bread.*

Store spreads in an airtight container in the refrigerator.

Quick Focaccia

Level: Easy
Serves 6-8
Preparation Time: 1 hour

¼	cup extra-virgin olive oil
3	garlic cloves, crushed
1	pound frozen white bread dough, thawed
2	tablespoons dried Italian herbs
	Coarsely ground salt, to taste
	Freshly ground black pepper, to taste

- Mix olive oil and garlic. Coat a 15x10x1-inch rectangular pan with half of seasoned oil.
- Stretch dough into a rectangle, approximately 10x12-inches. Place on the coated pan.
- Coat dough with remaining oil. Sprinkle with dried herbs, salt and black pepper.
- Preheat oven to 375 degrees.
- Allow dough to rise approximately 20 minutes.
- Bake bread in the bottom third of oven for 10-15 minutes or until golden brown.
- Break or tear into pieces.
- Pour extra-virgin olive oil on to a saucer and top with fresh coarsely ground black pepper. Dip focaccia in olive oil.
- Cook's Tip: Other seasonings can be added to unbaked dough. Add any of the following alone or in combination: fresh or sun-dried tomatoes, brine-cured olives, sliced green onion, roasted peppers, Romano or Parmesan grated cheese.

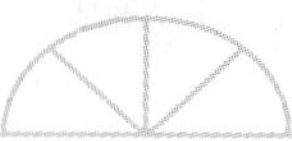

Refrigerator Dinner Rolls

Level: Good Cook
Yield: 3 dozen
Preparation Time: 5 hours

- 2 cups boiling water
- 1 cup granulated sugar
- 1 cup solid vegetable shortening
- 1 teaspoon salt
- 2 cakes yeast or 2 packages dry yeast
- 1 cup lukewarm water
- 1 tablespoon granulated sugar
- 3 large eggs, beaten
- 8 cups all-purpose flour, unsifted and divided
- 4 tablespoons butter, melted

- Pour boiling water over sugar, shortening and salt in a lightly greased Dutch oven or large bowl. Stir until dissolved. Cool to lukewarm.
- Place yeast in 1 cup warm water activated with 1 tablespoon sugar. Set aside until bubbly.
- Combine yeast mixture, eggs and cooled shortening mixture. Mix well.
- Add 5 cups flour and blend well. Add remaining flour, one cup at a time and knead until dough pulls away from sides of bowl.
- Cover bowl with damp cloth and allow dough to rise in the refrigerator for at least 4 hours. Dough may be kept for 4-5 days.
- To bake, roll dough to ¼-inch thick on a floured surface.
- Cut into rounds with a large drinking glass dipped into flour. Fold ½ of each circle of dough over onto the other half and place on an ungreased baking sheet. Top half of roll should overlap bottom to allow both sides to rise evenly.
- Cover rolls with a light weight cloth and let rise several hours (2-4 hours) before baking.
- Preheat oven to 325 degrees.
- Bake 10-12 minutes or until slightly brown.
- Brush tops of rolls with butter after removing from oven.

A Chef's View

In making bread, the rising dough needs the ideal temperature - 85 degrees for yeast bread. A gas oven with a pilot light on, an electric oven with the oven light on or containing a large pan of hot water should provide this temperature as well as a draft-free environment. Place the dough in a greased bowl, turning it to coat the top surface. Cover the bowl with plastic wrap. Rising is complete when the dough has doubled in bulk, unless your recipe specifies otherwise. To test, lightly press a finger ½ inch into the dough. If the indention remains, the dough has risen enough and is ready to shape.

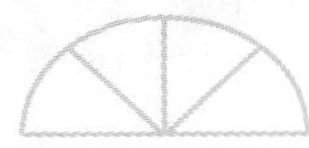

A Chef's View

Sally Lunn bread is a rich, slightly sweet yeast bread that was brought to the Colonies from England. It became a favorite in the south. There are several tales as to its origin, the most popular being that Sally Lunn, an 18th-century woman from Bath, England, created this delicate cakelike bread in her tiny bakery for her prominent patrons' tea parties. Those original Sally Lunns were baked as large buns, slit horizontally and slathered with thick clotted cream.

Clotted cream is a specialty of Devonshire, England, and is made by gently heating rich, unpasteurized milk until a semisolid layer of cream forms on the surface. After cooling, the thickened cream is removed. Clotted cream can be spread on bread or spooned atop fresh fruit or desserts. It can be refrigerated, tightly covered, for up to 4 days.

Sally Lunn Bread

Level: Easy
Serves 6-8
Preparation Time: 4 hours

1	cup milk
½	cup solid vegetable shortening
¼	cup water
4	cups all-purpose flour, sifted and divided
⅓	cup granulated sugar
2	teaspoons salt
2	(¼-ounce) packages active dry yeast
3	eggs

- Heat milk, shortening and water until warm (120 degrees).
- Blend 1⅓ cups flour, sugar, salt and dry yeast in large mixing bowl.
- Mix warm liquids into flour mixture. Beat with electric mixer on medium speed for 2 minutes, scraping sides of bowl.
- Add, gradually, ⅔ cup flour and eggs. Beat an additional 2 minutes.
- Mix in remaining flour until incorporated. Batter will be thick but not stiff.
- Cover, let rise in a warm place until dough is double in size, approximately 1¼ hours.
- Beat dough down with spatula or on low speed of mixer.
- Grease a 10-inch tube pan. Turn dough into pan. Cover and let rise until increased ⅓-½ in bulk.
- Bake 40-50 minutes.
- To cool, turn out on plate after baking.

Tuscan Bread

Level: Good Cook
Yield: 1 loaf
Preparation Time: 4 hours

1	tablespoon active dry yeast
2	cups lukewarm water, divided
4¼	cups all-purpose flour, divided
⅓	cup whole wheat flour
	Dash salt

- Make sponge by combining dry yeast with ½ cup lukewarm water in a bowl until yeast dissolves. Let stand 10 minutes until foamy.
- Add ¾ cup unbleached all-purpose flour and stir until combined.
- Cover bowl loosely with waxed paper and let rise in a warm place until doubled, approximately 1½ hours.
- Stir 3½ cups unbleached all-purpose flour, whole wheat flour and salt together in a large bowl.
- Make a well. Pour in sponge and then 1½ cups lukewarm water.
- Mix together with a wooden spoon, beating vigorously for 10-12 minutes or until smooth and elastic. Dough will bounce back slightly when pressed with fingertip.
- Form dough into a ball and dust lightly with flour. Place in a large well-greased bowl and cover loosely with a kitchen towel.
- Let rise in warm place until doubled, approximately one hour.
- Transfer dough to a well-floured surface, flatten into an oval and form into a large rectangular loaf.
- Place loaf on a floured baking sheet and dust lightly with flour. Cover loaf with kitchen towel and let rise again in warm place until doubled, approximately one hour.
- Preheat oven to 400 degrees.
- Bake loaf for 45-55 minutes or until bread loaf sounds hollow when taped lightly on the side.
- Let cool on a wire rack before serving.

A Chef's View

All the following flavored butters require 1 stick (½ cup) of softened unsalted butter.

- *Chive Butter: Add 2 heaping tablespoons minced fresh chives, salt, and freshly ground black pepper.*

- *Herb Butter: Add 2 tablespoons minced fresh herb leaves of choice, 1 teaspoon fresh lemon juice, salt, and freshly ground black pepper.*

- *Lemon Butter: Add the juice of ½ lemon, 1 tablespoon minced fresh lemon zest, salt, and freshly ground white pepper.*

- *Pecan Butter: Add ⅓ cup toasted and minced pecans, salt, and freshly ground black pepper.*

After adding the seasonings of choice and blend in the flavorings with a wood spoon. Place the butter on a sheet of waxed paper or aluminum foil, fold the top half over it, and form the butter into a 6-inch log by rolling in the paper. Twist the ends and chill until firm or freeze for several months. When ready to use, slice medallions of butter on to bread plate.

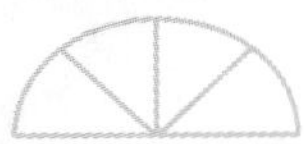

A Chef's View

Puff pastry is made by placing pats of chilled butter between layers of pastry dough, then rolling it out, folding it in thirds and letting it rest. This process, which is repeated 6 to 8 times, produces a pastry comprising hundreds of layers of dough and butter. When baked, the moisture in the butter creates steam, causing the dough to puff and separate into hundreds of flaky layers.

A Chef's View

'Fines herbes' is not misspelled. It's pronounced FEEN erb or FEENZ erb. It is a mixture of very finely chopped herbs made from chervil, chives, parsley, and tarragon. Burnet, marjoram, savory, and watercress can be used as part of the blend. Because they quickly loose their flavor, fines herbes should be added to a cooked mixture shortly before serving.

Puffed Cheese Twists

Level: Easy
Serves 18
Preparation Time: 1 hour

½ cup grated Parmesan cheese
¾ teaspoon seasoned pepper
¾ teaspoon dried parsley flakes or dill weed
¼ teaspoon garlic powder
Dash paprika
1 (17-ounce) package frozen puff pastry sheets, thawed
1 egg white, lightly beaten

- Mix cheese and seasonings in a small bowl.
- Unfold pastry sheet and brush lightly with egg white.
- Sprinkle pastry with ¼ of the seasoned mixture, lightly pressing the mixture into the pastry.
- Turn pastry over and repeat the procedure.
- Cut pastry sheet in half and cut each half into nine 1-inch strips and twist each strip into a spiral shape.
- Repeat this procedure with other puff pastry sheets.
- Coat a baking sheet lightly with cooking spray.
- Preheat oven to 350 degrees.
- Place twists on baking sheet. Bake for 15 minutes.
- Cook's Tip: Use a very sharp knife for cutting puff pastry. Thaw for 20 minutes at room temperature. Keep thawed pastry in refrigerator until ready to use.

Seasoned Pita Crisps

Level: Easy
Yield: 48 pieces
Preparation Time: 30 minutes

½ pound (2 sticks) butter, softened
2 garlic cloves, minced
½ teaspoon fines herbes
1 package (6 rounds) pita bread
¾ cup grated freshly grated Parmesan cheese

- Cream butter, garlic and fines herbes.
- Split pita bread. Place rounds inside down on a cookie sheet.
- Spread rounds with butter mixture and then sprinkle with freshly grated Parmesan cheese
- Place cookie sheet under broiler for 10-12 minutes.
- Serve hot or at room temperature. Break into 4 pieces.
- Cook's Tip: Serve with gazpacho, potato soup or salsa.

Apple Gruyère Tart

Level: Good Cook
Serves 4-6
Preparation Time: 2 hours

2	cups all-purpose flour
1	teaspoon dry mustard
	Salt
8	tablespoons unsalted butter, softened and divided
1	(6-ounce) brick Gruyère cheese, divided
	Cold water
1	large onion, finely chopped
2	small eating apples, peeled, cored and grated
2	large eggs
⅔	cup heavy cream
¼	teaspoon fines herbes
½	teaspoon prepared mustard
	Black pepper, to taste

- Sift flour, dry mustard and pinch of salt into a large bowl.
- Cut in 6 tablespoons softened unsalted butter and 6 tablespoons of grated cheese until mixture forms soft crumbs.
- Add cold water, a tablespoon at a time, and mix to form pastry ball. Chill, covered, for 30 minutes.
- Make filling by melting 2 tablespoons unsalted butter in a skillet. Add onion. Cook and stir for 10 minutes or until onion is softened but not brown.
- Stir in grated apple and cook for 3 minutes. Remove from heat to cool.
- Preheat oven to 400 degrees.
- Roll out pastry ball. Line a lightly greased 8-inch fluted tart pan with pastry. Chill for 20 minutes.
- Place parchment paper on top of pastry. Fill with pie weights or dried beans. Bake for 20 minutes.
- Beat together eggs, cream, fines herbes, prepared mustard and season with salt and black pepper. Add to apple-onion mixture.
- Grate ¾ of the remaining cheese and stir into mixture. Slice remaining cheese. Set aside.
- Take pastry out of oven, remove pie weights or dried beans and parchment paper. Cool slightly.
- Pour filling in cooled pastry shell and arrange sliced cheese over top of tart.
- Reduce oven heat to 375 degrees.
- Return tart to the oven and cook for 20 minutes or until filling is just firm.
- Cook's Tip: Serve warm with a crisp mixed-greens salad.

A Chef's View

Pie weights are small pelletlike metal or ceramic weights used when baking an unfilled pie or tart crust to keep it from shrinking. The weights (1-2 cups) are poured into a foil- or parchment-lined unbaked pie crust. The shell is then partially baked, the foil and weights are lifted out, and the baking is finished. Pie weights can be found in gourmet shops. Heavy dried beans may also be used.

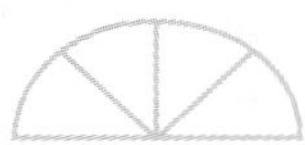

A Missouri Window

Missouri's theme is "Where the Rivers Run," and for good reason. The Mississippi, the Missouri, the Osage, the Gasconade, and more than 120 other rivers flow through the state where one can follow the water routes that launched Lewis and Clark or first settlers through the Gateway to the West. Missouri has more miles of navigable rivers than any other state.

A Chef's View

Eggs should be at room temperature before using in recipes. If refrigerated, set out for 30 minutes before use. To determine whether an egg is fresh, immerse it in a pan of cool, salted water. If it sinks, it is fresh. If it rises to the surface, discard egg. When making scrambled eggs, add a little water when scrambling, the eggs will be light and fluffy. Just as your scrambled eggs are finishing cooking, add a splash of cold milk and the cooking process will stop, keeping your eggs moist.

Bacon Apple Toast

Level: Easy
Serves 6
Preparation Time: 45 minutes

1	pound thick sliced bacon
3	Jonathan apples, unpeeled, cored and sliced ¼-inch thick
12	Jarlsberg cheese slices, ⅛-inch thick
	Sourdough bread, round, sliced and toasted on both sides

- Fry bacon in a large skillet until crisp. Drain on paper towels.
- Cook apple segments until tender in bacon drippings.
- Place toast on a jelly-roll pan. Cover toast completely with sliced cheese.
- Cook under broiler until cheese melts over sides of bread and is slightly golden. Remove from oven.
- Top each slice of bread and cheese with two slices of bacon and then with 4-5 overlapping slices of sautéed apples.
- Serve immediately.
- Cook's Tip: Sourdough toast can be spread with butter and mustard, topped with cooked ham, a pineapple slice, a sprinkle of brown sugar, slices of Jarlsberg cheese and broiled until cheese is golden and melting.

Italian Brunch Casserole

Level: Easy
Serves 8
Preparation Time: 1 hour

1	(8-ounce) tube crescent rolls
1	pound mild pork or Italian sausage
1	(8-ounce) package shredded mozzarella cheese
6	large eggs
¾	cup milk
¼	teaspoon dried Italian seasoning

- Preheat oven to 435 degrees.
- Press crescent dough in bottom of a greased 13x9x2-inch glass baking dish.
- Brown sausage over medium heat until it crumbles and is no longer pink. Drain.
- Spoon sausage over dough.
- Sprinkle cheese over sausage.
- Whisk together eggs, milk and Italian seasoning. Pour over cheese.
- Bake 20 minutes or until eggs are set and cheese is lightly browned.
- Remove from oven and let stand at room temperature 5-10 minutes before serving.

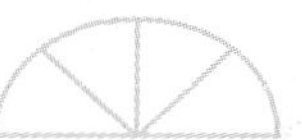

Kentucky Hot Browns

Level: Expert Cook
Serves 2
Preparation Time: 45 minutes

- ¼ pound (1 stick) butter
- ½ cup all-purpose flour
- ¾ cup half-and-half
- ¾ cup heavy cream
- ⅓ cup freshly grated Romano cheese
- ¼ cup freshly grated Parmesan cheese
- ½ cup dry sherry, heated, to cook off alcohol
- 2 egg yolks, beaten
- 4 toast points, 2 slices halved, cut diagonally with crust removed
- 4 cooked turkey breast slices, cut ⅛-inch thick
- 4 slices bacon, fried
- 4 tomato wedges
- Parsley sprigs, for garnish
- Ground nutmeg, for garnish

- ◆ Melt butter in a heavy skillet. Sprinkle flour into butter, stirring to make a roux of moderately thick consistency. Cook until roux is golden brown.
- ◆ Whisk in half-and-half and heavy cream gradually. Cook until flour taste is gone.
- ◆ Stir in cheeses. Add sherry and continue stirring until sauce has thin consistency and cheese is melted.
- ◆ Strain sauce into a saucepan.
- ◆ Add beaten egg yolks and blend completely.
- ◆ Sauce may be gently reheated. Do not boil.
- ◆ Assemble Hot Browns by placing 2 toast points in an ovenproof serving dish. Cover with turkey and a generous amount of sauce. Repeat for second serving.
- ◆ Brown under broiler.
- ◆ Remove from oven. Place bacon and tomato wedges across each portion.
- ◆ Garnish with parsley and sprinkle with nutmeg.

A Culinary Reflection

The first Saturday in May was Derby Day for my family. Grandpa T was a horse trader who always had horses and wanted to be at the Derby if he could. But in lieu of Kentucky, he would plan a party for family and friends, then watch the Derby with his own betting game. Our Derby Day began with an early morning ride followed by breakfast and a late lunch just before the Derby. Lunch was country ham on rolls, pecan tassies, chocolate dip with strawberries, cheese grits, marinated vegetables, mock champagne or asti spumanti, and finally mint juleps. Decorations were our family silver, white cloths, and roses. I still try to keep his traditions by giving mint julep mix to friends.

~ Millie Bever

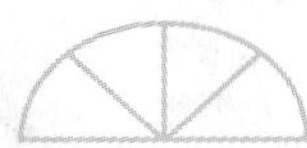

A Chef's View

Refrigerated or frozen egg substitutes are easy to use, readily available, and enable anyone on a cholesterol-restricted diet to enjoy great-tasting egg dishes. These products are based mostly on egg whites, contain less fat than whole eggs, and have no cholesterol. Use ¼ cup of either the refrigerated or thawed frozen egg product for each whole egg in scrambled egg dishes, omelets, quiches, and stratas. They can even be used to replace hard-cooked eggs in salads and other recipes, cook the egg product as you would cook an omelet and cut it into bite-size pieces.

Peppered Shrimp and Eggs

Level: Easy
Serves 4-6
Preparation Time: 45 minutes

3 slices bacon
½ cup chopped onion
¾ cup diced red, green or yellow bell pepper
½ pound shrimp, cooked and peeled
½ teaspoon salt
¼ teaspoon cayenne pepper
6 eggs, beaten
¼ cup heavy cream
½ teaspoon Worcestershire sauce
Fresh parsley and/or seafood sauce, for garnish

- Fry bacon until crisp in a large skillet. Drain on paper towels. Crumble and set aside.
- Cook onion and peppers in bacon fat until tender.
- Add precooked shrimp and seasonings to bell pepper mixture.
- Combine eggs, cream, Worcestershire sauce and crumbled bacon in a small bowl.
- Add egg mixture to shrimp and vegetables and cook until done.
- Cook's Tip: Can be baked in oven if made in an iron skillet or placed in a greased baking dish. Bake for 10-15 minutes or until eggs are set.
- Garnish each serving with parsley and/or a spoonful or two of seafood sauce.

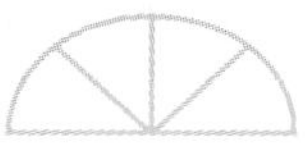

Sausage and Egg Strata

Level: Easy
Serves 12
Preparation Time: 3 hours

9 eggs
1½ teaspoons dry mustard
3 cups milk
2 pounds sausage and/or ham
6 slices white bread, cubed or 3 cups herbed-seasoned croutons
1½ pounds sharp cheese, grated
3 green onions, thinly sliced, white and green parts
5 large mushrooms, finely chopped
Chopped green bell pepper or jalapeño peppers, optional

- Beat eggs, mustard and milk together.
- Remove sausage casings, crumble into bite-size pieces. Scramble sausage in a fry pan until warmed through but not browned.
- Place bread or seasoned croutons in a buttered 3 quart glass baking dish.
- Combine sausage, cheese, green onion and mushrooms and optional green peppers or jalapeño peppers. Spoon over bread or croutons.
- Pour eggs over bread and sausage mixtures. Cover, refrigerate and let stand 2 hours or overnight.
- Bake in a preheated 350 degree oven for 1 hour or until set. Cover with aluminum foil, if necessary, to prevent excess browning.
- To serve cut in squares and sprinkle with parsley.
- Cook's Tip: Can be doubled easily and freezes well for future use.

Sausage, Egg and Potato Casserole

Level: Easy
Serves 6-8
Preparation Time: 1 hour

1½ pounds pork sausage
2½ cups frozen hash browns
8 eggs, slightly beaten
8 ounces processed cheese loaf, cubed
1 cup cream of celery soup
¾ cup evaporated milk

- Preheat oven to 350 degrees. Butter a 13x9x2-inch baking dish.
- Brown and drain sausage.
- Combine hash browns, eggs, cheese loaf cubes, cream of celery soup and evaporated milk in a large bowl.
- Add sausage and mix.
- Pour into baking dish and bake 40-45 minutes.

A Chef's View

Substitute whole wheat bread, sour dough bread, English muffins or French bread for white bread in stratas or other egg casseroles requiring bread.

A Missouri Window

The Katy Trail, flat and as wide as a train, meanders through a wide variety of Missouri's most scenic landscape. The Katy Trail State Park is open for 225 miles from St. Charles to Clinton and is operated by the Department of Natural Resources as part of the state park system. It begins in St. Charles on the eastern side of Missouri and with only about a three percent grade winds its way through the vineyards on the bluffs of the Missouri river, through the state capitol Jefferson City and up through Columbia. Rocheport, a Missouri river town, features majestic bluffs and many antique shops and stops. Dipping south, the Katy has stops in Sedalia, home of Missouri's State Fair and the Scott Joplin Ragtime Festival.

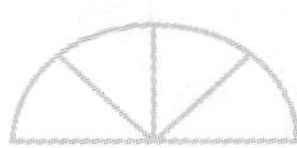

A Missouri Window

'Sail away from the safe harbor. Catch the trade winds in your sails. Explore, dream, discover.'

- Mark Twain, Hannibal, Missouri

Caramel Soaked French Toast

Level: Easy
Serves 4-5
Preparation Time: 9 hours

1½	cups brown sugar, firmly packed
½	pound (2 sticks) butter or margarine, divided
¼	cup plus 2 tablespoons light-colored corn syrup
10	French bread slices, 1¾-inch thick
4	eggs, beaten
2½	cups milk, half-and-half or skim milk
1	tablespoon vanilla extract
¼	teaspoon salt
3	tablespoons granulated sugar
1½	teaspoons ground cinnamon

- Combine brown sugar, 1½ sticks butter and corn syrup in a saucepan. Cook over low heat for 5 minutes, stirring to prevent burning.
- Pour mixture into a greased 13x9x2-inch baking dish. Distribute evenly over bottom.
- Place French bread slices over melted butter-sugar mixture.
- Combine eggs, milk, vanilla extract and salt. Mix well and pour over bread.
- Cover and chill at least 8 hours or overnight.
- Preheat oven to 350 degrees.
- Mix granulated sugar and cinnamon. Sprinkle over bread.
- Melt remaining ¼ cup butter and drizzle over top.
- Bake, uncovered, for 50 minutes or until golden brown.

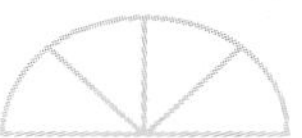

Orange Pecan French Toast

Level: Easy
Serves 4
Preparation Time: 20 minutes

4	eggs, beaten
¼	cup orange juice concentrate
½	cup milk
½	cup pecans, finely ground
½	teaspoon vanilla extract
⅛	teaspoon ground cinnamon
	Dash ground nutmeg
8	French bread slices, cut 1-inch thick
3	tablespoons butter
	Butter, syrup and confectioners' sugar, for garnish

- Beat together eggs, orange juice concentrate, milk, pecans, vanilla extract, cinnamon and nutmeg in a shallow bowl.
- Dip bread into egg mixture, coating both sides. Soak for 30 seconds on each side.
- Melt 1 tablespoon butter in a flat skillet and fry bread on both sides over medium heat for 2-3 minutes or until each side is golden brown.
- Serve with butter, syrup and confectioners' sugar.

Sweet and Gooey Bubble Bread

Level: Easy
Serves 12
Preparation Time: 8-10 hours

18	frozen dinner rolls
1	(3.4-ounce) package butterscotch pudding mix, not instant
1	cup brown sugar, firmly packed and divided
1	teaspoon ground cinnamon
½	cup pecans
¼	pound (1 stick) margarine or butter

- Butter a fluted tube pan. Arrange dinner rolls in bottom.
- Mix together dry pudding mix and ¾ cup brown sugar. Sprinkle over rolls.
- Combine ¼ cup brown sugar, cinnamon and pecans. Sprinkle over rolls.
- Melt margarine or butter and pour over all.
- Let rise 8 hours or overnight.
- Bake for 25-30 minutes in a preheated 350 degree oven.
- Invert pan on a plate to serve.

A Culinary Reflection

Forty-five years ago, I was active in a Swedish - Lutheran Hospital Auxiliary and one year we put on a Swedish Smorgasbord (huge!). The highlight was the homemade Swedish Limpa Bread. Wanting to do my part, I said I would bake a couple of loaves. I spent an entire day kneading and mixing and kneading some more. When I finally brought my treasure out of the oven, instead of looking light, brown and luscious, exuding heavenly odors, my Limpa bread looked like a big flat stone and weighed just as much. I cried, and then I laughed, and we used it as a door stop. I never made bread again. (Swedish Limpa Bread is a moist rye bread that is flavored with fennel or anise, cumin, and orange peel. The result is an immensely flavorful, fragrant loaf of bread.)

- Geraldine Hill

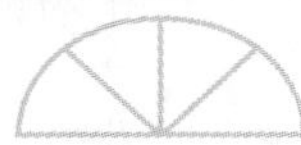

A Chef's View

Cinnamon is the inner bark of a tropical evergreen tree. The bark is harvested during the rainy season when it's more pliable. When dried, it curls into long quills, which are either cut into lengths and sold as cinnamon sticks, or ground into powder.

Cinnamon Apple Bars

Level: Easy
Yield: 24 bars
Preparation Time: 1 hour

2¼	cups all-purpose flour, divided
1¼	cups granulated sugar, divided
1	teaspoon baking powder
½	teaspoon salt
1	cup (2 sticks) butter
2	egg yolks, beaten
4	cups peeled apple slices
1	egg white, slightly beaten
1	cup confectioners' sugar
¼	cup milk
½	teaspoon vanilla extract or butter flavoring

- Preheat oven to 350 degrees. Lightly coat a jelly-roll pan with butter-flavored cooking spray.
- Combine 2 cups flour, ½ cup sugar, baking powder and salt in a large mixing bowl.
- Cut in butter, using a fork or mixer, until dough forms crumbs.
- Add egg yolks and mix until a dough ball just begins to form. Do not overmix.
- Mold ¾ of dough evenly into a jelly-roll pan, reserving remainder for topping.
- Mix apples, ¼ cup flour, ¾ cup sugar and cinnamon together. Spoon over molded dough in jelly-roll pan.
- Top apple mixture with remaining crumbled dough. Brush with beaten egg white.
- Bake for 40 minutes, or until edges are brown.
- Remove from oven and cool slightly.
- Drizzle with butter icing made from confectioners' sugar, milk and vanilla extract or butter flavoring.
- Cut into bars and serve.

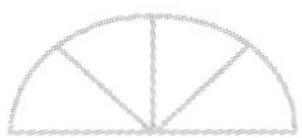

Cinnamon Pecan Coffee Cake

Level: Easy
Serves 18
Preparation Time: 1 hour

2	cups granulated sugar
½	pound (2 sticks) margarine
2	eggs
1	cup lite sour cream
1	tablespoon vanilla extract
2	cups all-purpose flour
¼	teaspoon salt
1¼	teaspoons baking powder
1	tablespoon ground cinnamon
¾	cup brown sugar, firmly packed
½	cup pecans, chopped

- Preheat oven to 325 degrees. Grease a 13x9x2-inch baking pan.
- Cream sugar and margarine in a large mixing bowl.
- Add eggs, sour cream and vanilla. Mix well.
- Sift together flour, salt and baking powder. Fold into egg mixture.
- Mix cinnamon, brown sugar and pecans in a small bowl. Set topping aside.
- Pour ½ of batter into greased pan.
- Sprinkle ½ of topping mix over batter.
- Add remaining batter and sprinkle with remaining topping.
- Bake for 45-50 minutes or until a cake tester inserted into the center comes out clean.
- Cool for 10 minutes and serve warm.

A Culinary Reflection

When I think of my grandmother, I see her in her kitchen where she was always making the food my family loved. She raised eleven children, and after they were grown, they still stopped by to pick up homemade chicken soup with noodles, dumplings, and a variety of other home-baked goods. Her kitchen was spotless. No one could wear nail polish while cooking, and our hair had to be covered with a hair net, as was hers. She wore the ever-present apron, of which I still have a few. As my mom and her sisters were growing up, they were not interested in learning to cook the 'old-fashioned' way. As they got married and had families of their own, they did try to learn to make some of our favorite foods. They tried to measure how much flour my grandmother's hand held, so they could write down the recipes to follow. They soon found that the only way to learn is to do it, and to know the feel of the dough when it is right.

- JoAnn Fioretti

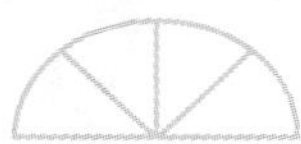

A Chef's View

The two types of commercial yeast available are baker's yeast, as used as a leavener, and active dry yeast, in the form of tiny, dehydrated granules. The yeast cells are alive but dormant because of lack of moisture. When mixed with a warm liquid, the cells once again become active. Active dry yeast is available in two forms, regular and quick-rising, of which the latter takes about half as long to leaven bread. Leaveners are those that lighten the texture and increase the volume of baked goods such as breads, cookies, and cakes. Yeast, but also baking powder and baking soda, are the most common leaveners used today.

Decadent Cinnamon Rolls

Level: Expert Cook
Yield: 3-4 dozen
Preparation Time: 4 hours

2	(¼-ounce) packages active dry yeast
2½	cups lukewarm water
1	(18.25-ounce) box yellow cake mix
6-7	cups all-purpose flour, divided
3	eggs
⅓	cup canola oil
1½	teaspoons salt
½	pound (2 sticks) butter, softened
	Cinnamon and granulated sugar, to taste
	Raisins and chopped pecans, optional
1	pound confectioners' sugar
4	tablespoons butter, melted
1½	teaspoons vanilla extract
½-¾	cup milk

- Dissolve yeast in warm water in the large mixing bowl of an electric mixer.
- Add cake mix, 1 cup flour, eggs, oil and salt. Beat well until bubbles appear.
- Add 5¼ cups flour, slowly, changing to dough hook as mixture becomes dough-like. Mix until all flour is absorbed.
- Turn dough out on well-floured board, kneading approximately 5 minutes. Place in greased bowl and let rise until double in bulk.
- Punch down dough and divide into 2 parts.
- Preheat oven to 350 degrees.
- Using a well-floured rolling pin and lightly-floured board, roll each dough round until ⅓-inch thick and rectangular in shape.
- Spread dough with softened butter. Sprinkle with cinnamon and sugar. Top with raisins and chopped pecans, if desired.
- Roll each rectangle up jelly-roll fashion from long side.
- Cut 1-inch thick rolls with the back of a table knife or dental floss. Place rolls in a greased baking pan and allow to rise until doubled.
- Bake for 25-35 minutes.
- Combine confectioners' sugar, 4 tablespoons melted butter, vanilla extract and milk until smooth. Drizzle over rolls while still hot.
- A brown sugar or caramel topping may be substituted for glaze.
- Cook's Tip: Freeze individual rolls in zip-top sandwich bags. To reheat, remove from sandwich bag and microwave on full power for 30 seconds.

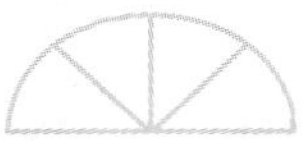

Chunky Apple Pancakes with Cinnamon Butter

Level: Easy
Serves 4-6
Preparation Time: 30 minutes

¼ pound (1 stick) butter or margarine, softened
¼ cup confectioners' sugar
½ teaspoon ground cinnamon
5 medium-size apples
2 cups all-purpose flour
4 teaspoons baking powder
2 teaspoons salt
½ cup granulated sugar
2 eggs
⅓ cup milk
2 teaspoons canola oil

- Blend butter or margarine, confectioners' sugar and cinnamon in a small bowl for cinnamon-butter. Cover and keep refrigerated until ready to use.
- Peel, core and cut apples into thinly cut ½-inch long slices.
- Mix together flour, baking powder, salt and sugar in a large bowl.
- Beat eggs, milk and oil together in a second bowl.
- Combine liquid and dry ingredients. Stir to just moisten dry ingredients.
- Fold in apples.
- Coat a hot griddle with butter-flavored cooking spray.
- Pour ¼ cup of batter for each pancake on griddle and cook on medium heat until bubbles form on top. Turn and brown on second side. Pancakes are thick and cook slowly.
- Serve with reserved cinnamon butter.

A Chef's View

Use a bulb baster to 'squeeze' your pancake batter onto the hot griddle for perfect pancakes every time. As the pancakes cook, bubbles form on the surface. The moment they start to break (1 to 2 minutes depending on thickness), use a pancake turner to lift one edge and peek underneath. If it is golden brown, flip the cake.

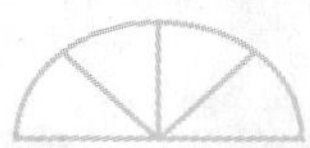

A Missouri Window

In 1889, Aunt Jemima pancake flour, invented in St. Joseph, Missouri, was the first self-rising flour for pancakes and the first ready-mix food ever to be introduced commercially.

A Chef's View

Oats are by far the most nutritious of the cereal grasses. Humans don't usually consume oats until after they have been cleaned, toasted, hulled and cleaned again after which time they become oat groats. Rolled oats, also called old-fashioned oats are steamed and flattened with huge rollers. Quick-cooking rolled oats are groats that have been cut into several pieces before being steamed and rolled into thinner flakes. Instant oats are not interchangeable with old-fashioned or quick-cooking oats.

Gourmet Waffles

Level: Quick and Simple
Serves 1
Preparation Time: 15 minutes

½ cup all-purpose flour, sifted
½ teaspoon baking powder
1/16 teaspoon salt
1 egg yolk, beaten
½ cup milk
1 tablespoon canola oil
1 egg white, stiffly beaten

- Combine flour, baking powder and salt.
- Mix egg yolk and milk in a large bowl.
- Stir dry ingredients into milk mixture.
- Blend in canola oil.
- Fold in egg white, leaving a few fluffs.
- Heat waffle iron. Coat iron surface with butter-flavored cooking spray.
- Pour batter onto waffle iron and bake according to iron directions.
- Makes one large waffle to be served with your favorite topping.

Nutty Granola

Level: Easy
Yield: 5 cups
Preparation Time: 1 hour

2 cups old-fashioned rolled oats, uncooked
1 cup rice cereal
¾ cup rice bran
¾ cup raisins
⅓ cup slivered almonds
1 tablespoon ground cinnamon
⅓ cup honey
1 tablespoon margarine, melted

- Preheat oven to 350 degrees. Coat a cookie sheet with cooking spray.
- Combine oats, cereal, bran, raisins, almonds and cinnamon in a large bowl.
- Drizzle honey and margarine over oat mixture. Stir to coat.
- Spread oat mixture on the greased baking sheet.
- Bake for 8-10 minutes. Let cool.
- Cook's Tip: Serve granola as a topping for fresh fruit, yogurt or ice cream; as a snack; or as a cereal with milk.

A Garden Panorama

Salads

A Missouri Window

Heart of Missouri

In the heart of Missouri lies the metropolis of Columbia, considered one of the USA's most liveable cities, and the state Capitol of Missouri, Jefferson City. Visitors and residents of the area are frequently found biking on the Katy Trail, the Kansas-Arkansas-Texas railroad bed, which stretches nearly the length of Missouri, spelunking in the caves of Rock Bridge State Park, wining and dining in quaint nearby river towns, and experiencing theatrical or visual arts. Home to the University of Missouri - Columbia, the oldest University west of the Mississippi River, all of Boone County is worth exploring.

Rolling hills and valleys to the south lead the way to Jefferson City, which is also the county seat for Cole County, bounded on the north by the Missouri River and the east by the Osage River. The state Capitol was moved to Jefferson City from St. Charles in 1826, and is named for U.S. President Thomas Jefferson. Noted murals by Thomas Hart Benton and Sir Frank Brangwyn can be found in the Capitol as well as the large fountain of Centaurs situated on the grounds. The nearby Governor's Mansion also contains paintings by Benton and George Barnett. Jefferson City is the site of Lincoln University, founded in 1866 by black veterans of the American Civil War.

Photos: The Katy Trail, Missouri River Bluffs & the Missouri River in Winter

In the fall of 1924, the Boone County Auxiliary was formed with 15 founding members. The group continued to grow and contribute to the welfare of mid-Missouri, and by 1928, the Auxiliary had established a scholarship fund for medical students at the University of Missouri - Columbia School of Medicine.

Boone County Medical Society Alliance

Today, with more than 85 members, the Boone County Medical Society Alliance awards scholarships to a medical or nursing student at UMC. An additional scholarship fund was established in 1973 by the Alliance when Dr. R. S. Battersby gave the initial monies in honor of his wife, Ann Anderson Battersby, who served as BCMSA's president from 1942-43. This award recognizes a student's contribution to the community through volunteerism.

While the Alliance recognizes student volunteerism, the members also take great pride in their many efforts to promote good health in the community. Alliance members frequently can be found volunteering with Columbia public schools using the *Organella Doll*, the *Bones Puzzle* project, and *Sensory Bags*; doing clerical work at the local family health center; serving on committees for the Health Adventure Center; and making contributions to the Coyote Hill foster community. BCMSA is also actively involved in several *Stop America's Violence Everywhere Campaign - SAVE* projects such as organizing child constructed banners and poster contests as well as participating in local health fairs to promote antiviolence tactics. The Alliance continues to support its medical community as well as the citizens of Boone County while providing mutual support to one another.

The following Boone County Alliance members have served as MSMA Alliance presidents: Mrs. M. P. Ravenal, 1929-30; Mrs. M. Pinson Neal, 1935-36; Sue Wilson, 1976-77; Pattye Barbee, 1989-90; and Beverly Murrell, MD, 1999-2000.

The Cole County Medical Auxiliary was founded in 1927 and has grown steadily over the years. As time went by, members focused on community involvement, especially in the areas of health awareness and education.

Cole County Medical Alliance

Today, the physician spouses of Cole County are involved in a variety of activities. Some of these projects include: working on antiviolence campaigns with elementary school children; participating in high school health fairs and talking about teen stress; promoting awareness of organ donation; providing schools with supplies to help deter pregnancies and teen drinking; supporting the local Rape and Abuse Crisis Center; furnishing teen hotline labels for placement on school ID cards; and offering scholarships to high school seniors desiring to pursue a health career.

Things have, indeed, changed over the years, and the Cole County Medical Alliance is committed to providing health resources and continuing to make contributions to the community.

The first president of Cole County was Mrs. S. P. Howard, who later became the Missouri State Medical Association Auxiliary president in 1940. In 1994, Jean Wankum became the second MSMA Alliance president to serve from Cole County.

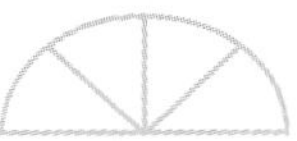

Fresh Apple Fruit Salad with Pecans

Level: Easy
Serves 4
Preparation Time: 45 minutes

4	cups tart red apples, unpeeled, cored and chopped
1	(20-ounce) can pineapple chunks, drain and reserve juice
2	cups seedless green grapes
4	tablespoons butter
¼	cup granulated sugar
1	tablespoon lemon juice
2	tablespoons cornstarch
2	tablespoons water
1	cup mayonnaise
1	teaspoon poppy seeds
1½	cups pecans, chopped and toasted

- Combine apples, pineapple and grapes in a large bowl.
- Bring pineapple juice, butter, sugar and lemon juice to a boil in a saucepan.
- Whisk cornstarch and water together. Add to pineapple juice mixture. Cook and stir until thickened. Cool.
- Stir in mayonnaise.
- Pour mayonnaise mixture over fruit and toss to coat fruit.
- Stir in poppy seeds and sprinkle with pecans.
- Cook's Tip: Cut calories by using ½ cup low calorie mayonnaise and ½ cup unflavored yogurt instead of mayonnaise.

A Missouri Window

The Jefferson Landing State Historic Site in Jefferson City is significant as a rare surviving Missouri River landing. The Lohman Building, built in 1839, is a sturdy stone structure that served as a tavern and hotel, and in its heyday also housed one of the city's largest warehouse and mercantile businesses. Today, the main floor contains a visitor center with exhibits featuring the city's history. The building also serves as the support facility for the Missouri State Museum, located on the ground floor of the Capitol. Across the street from the Lohman Building is the Union Hotel, built in 1855. Today, the hotel houses the Elizabeth Rozier Gallery with its program of rotating exhibits emphasizing Missouri art and culture. The building also houses the city's Amtrak station.

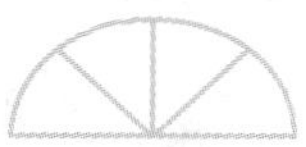

A Chef's View

A papaya is native to North America, and when ripe, has a vivid golden-yellow skin. The similarly colored flesh is juicy and silky smooth, with an exotic sweet-tart flavor. The rather large center cavity is packed with shiny, grayish-black seeds, which are edible, but are usually discarded. Look for richly colored papayas that give slightly to palm pressure. Ripe papaya is best eaten raw.

A Missouri Window

The town of Boonville, right on the Missouri River, was the site of the first actual clash of arms between Union and pro-Confederate Missouri State Guard troops. The town has long been rumored to have had ties to the underground railroad. It is believed that a station existed in a cellar attached to one of the old houses in town.

South Seas Fruit Salad

Level: Easy
Serves 4-6
Preparation Time: 35 minutes

1 papaya, peeled, seeded and cut into 1-inch chunks
2 bananas, peeled and sliced ½-inch thick
1 mango, peeled, pitted and cut into 1-inch chunks
1 pint strawberries, hulled and halved
1 cup pineapple chunks
2 tablespoons fresh lemon juice
2 tablespoons fresh lime juice
2 tablespoons granulated sugar, or to taste
¼ cup fresh mint leaves, coarsely chopped
Mint sprigs, for garnish

- Combine all fruits in a large glass serving bowl and toss very gently to mix.
- Sprinkle with lemon juice, lime juice, sugar and mint and toss again.
- Garnish top with tiny mint sprigs before serving.
- Cook's Tip: Fruit may be refrigerated. Serve in stemmed wide-mouth wine glasses. Add a small scoop of lime or pineapple sherbet or a sorbet for a dessert alternative. Garnish with mint.

Circus Salad

Level: Quick and Simple
Serves 3
Preparation Time: 10 minutes

3 oranges
½ cup shelled peanuts
Iceberg lettuce, leaves and shredded
Animal crackers

- Peel oranges, cut away pith and cut into small pieces.
- Chop peanuts into small pieces. Add to orange sections and mix well.
- Place orange mixture in lettuce cups with shredded lettuce.
- Decorate with animal crackers around edge of salad plate and top of salad.

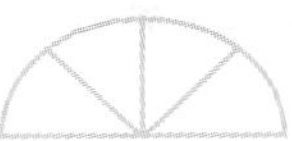

Stephenson's Apple Farm Frozen Fruit Salad

Level: Easy
Serves 6-8
Preparation Time: 6 hours

- 1 (3-ounce) package cream cheese, softened
- ⅓ cup mayonnaise
- 1 teaspoon lemon juice
- 2 egg whites
- ⅓ cup granulated sugar
- 1 cup heavy cream
- 6 large marshmallows, each cut into 4 pieces
- ¼ cup Mandarin orange slices, drained
- 1 (16-ounce) can fruit cocktail, drained
- 2 tablespoons chopped maraschino cherries
- 1 tablespoon chopped walnuts
- Lettuce leaves

- Mix cream cheese, mayonnaise and lemon juice.
- Whisk egg whites until foamy. Beat in sugar, a tablespoon at a time, until stiff peaks form.
- Beat heavy cream until stiff. Fold whipped cream into egg whites.
- Fold egg-white mixture into cheese mixture.
- Stir marshmallows, Mandarin orange slices, fruit cocktail and walnuts into cheese mixture.
- Pour into an 8-inch square pan.
- Freeze. Cut into squares to serve.
- Serve on green lettuce leaves.

A Show-Me Specialty

Frozen Fruit Salad is a specialty of Stephenson's Apple Farm Restaurant in Lee's Summit, Missouri. In 1870, the Stephenson fruit and vegetable farm sold produce to folks traveling between Lee's Summit and Independence. In 1946, a restaurant was opened in the original stone produce building called the Apple Farm. The orchard surrounding the area produces fresh apples, peaches, and berries. Hickory smoked meats, homemade apple butter, preserves, and relishes are prepared the way they were back in the 1880s.

Stephenson's
Apple Farm Restaurant
40 Highway
Lee's Summit Road
Kansas City

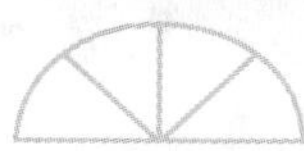

A Chef's View

Great Salad Greens

◆ *Select salad leaves that look vibrant and crisp, with no wilted, decayed, or blemished spots. The peppery taste of greens becomes bitter with age. Stems on loose greens should appear freshly cut.*

◆ *Store greens by removing any wilted or decayed leaves and bands or ties that bind greens together. Place greens in perforated plastic bags because they retain moisture while allowing air circulation. Store in crisper drawer of the refrigerator.*

◆ *Wash leaves in a large basin of cold water when ready to prepare a salad. This may have to be done several times. Spin or pat dry with paper towels.*

Mandarin Orange Salad

Level: Easy
Serves 4
Preparation Time: 3-8 hours

¼	cup sliced almonds or pecan halves
10	teaspoons granulated sugar, divided
2	tablespoons apple cider vinegar
1	tablespoon fresh chopped parsley
½	teaspoon salt
	Dash black pepper
⅓	cup canola oil
1	head iceberg lettuce, torn into bite-size pieces
¼	head romaine lettuce, torn into bite-size pieces
1	cup chopped celery
2	green onions, chopped, white and green parts
1	(11-ounce) can Mandarin oranges, drained

◆ Toast almonds with 4 teaspoons sugar over low heat in a heavy skillet. Stir constantly until sugar is just melted and almonds are coated. Cool and break apart. Store at room temperature.

◆ Add vinegar, 6 teaspoons sugar, parsley, salt, black pepper and oil to a jar with tightly fitted lid. Shake well to mix. Refrigerate 3-8 hours.

◆ Combine lettuces, celery, green onion and oranges. Toss with salad dressing.

◆ Sprinkle almonds over top of salad and toss lightly.

◆ Cook's Tip: Mandarin orange liquid may be added to dressing, adjusting seasonings, if needed.

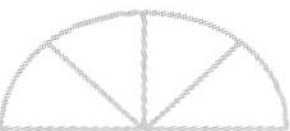

Orange Oriental Salad

Level: Easy
Serves 8
Preparation Time: 30 minutes

2	cups radicchio lettuce, cored, rinsed, dried and finely shredded
2	Belgian endive lettuce heads, separated into leaves and rinsed
4	large seedless oranges, peeled and sliced into ¼-inch rounds
2	bunches watercress, rinsed and woody stems discarded
1	(6-ounce) can frozen orange juice concentrate, unsweetened
	Freshly grated peel and juice of 1 large orange
⅓	cup light soy sauce
⅓	cup rice wine vinegar
1	tablespoon minced fresh ginger
1½	teaspoons sesame oil
4	green onions, chopped, white and green parts
¼	cup flat leaf parsley, chopped
1	cup light olive oil or peanut oil
1	thinly sliced sweet red onion, separated into rings

- Place a mound of radicchio on 8 chilled plates.
- Arrange endive, orange slices and watercress attractively.
- Process orange juice concentrate, peel and juice of orange, soy sauce, vinegar, ginger, sesame oil, green onion and parsley in a blender until smooth.
- Whisk in oil separately, being careful not to emulsify.
- Drizzle dressing around and over salad. Place onion rings on top.
- Store any unused dressing in the refrigerator up to 2 weeks.

A Missouri Window

Winston Churchill, former Prime Minister of England, delivered his "Iron Curtain" speech at Westminster College in Fulton in 1946.

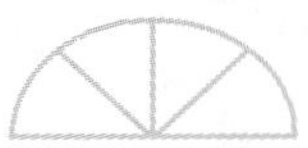

A Chef's View

When making a large tossed salad, place the dressing in the bottom of the bowl. Then add the ingredients that taste best marinated, like cucumbers, artichokes, green onions, peppers, etc. Top with salad greens. Cover and refrigerate. Toss before serving.

A Chef's View

Wash and trim strawberries right before serving or they will not retain their shape, especially if sliced. To keep strawberries fresh, arrange them in a single layer on a paper towel-lined plate and place them in the refrigerator.

Raspberry Spinach Salad

Level: Quick and Simple
Serves 8
Preparation Time: 15 minutes

2	tablespoons raspberry vinegar
2	tablespoons raspberry jam
⅓	cup canola oil
8	cups spinach, rinsed, stemmed and dried
¾	cup macadamia nuts, coarsely chopped
1	cup fresh raspberries
3	kiwi, peeled and sliced

- Combine vinegar and jam in a blender or small bowl.
- Add oil in a thin stream, blending well.
- Toss spinach with half each of nuts, raspberries and kiwi with the dressing in a large flat bowl.
- Divide salad between 8 chilled plates and top immediately with remaining fruits and nuts.
- Serve.

Strawberry Romaine Salad

Level: Easy
Serves 8
Preparation Time: 3¼ hours

1	cup canola oil
¾	cup granulated sugar
½	cup red wine vinegar
2	garlic cloves, minced
½	teaspoon salt
½	teaspoon ground paprika
¼	teaspoon ground white pepper
1	large head Romaine lettuce
1	head Boston lettuce
1	pint strawberries, rinsed, stemmed and sliced
1	cup (4-ounces) Monterey Jack cheese, shredded
½	cup chopped walnuts, toasted
	Fresh spinach, optional

- Whisk together oil, sugar, vinegar, garlic, salt, paprika and ground white pepper.
- Store in a container with an airtight lid for several hours in the refrigerator.
- Tear lettuces and place in a large bowl.
- Add strawberries and cheese.
- Toss with salad dressing and sprinkle with walnuts just before serving.

Chicken Fruit Toss

Level: Easy
Serves 6-8
Preparation Time: 2-3 hours

4	whole chicken breasts, skinned and boned
2	cups red or green seedless grapes
1	(16-ounce) can pineapple chunks, drained or fresh pineapple
1	(11-ounce) can Mandarin orange slices, drained and cut in half
2	small red apples, unpeeled, cored and diced
1	(8-ounce) can sliced water chestnuts, drained
1	cup sliced celery, cut on the diagonal
¾	cup mayonnaise
1	teaspoon soy sauce, or to taste
1	tablespoon granulated sugar
½	teaspoon curry powder
1	cup slivered almonds, toasted
	Leafy lettuce, sliced oranges or apples, for garnish

- Poach chicken. Cool and cube.
- Combine chicken, grapes, pineapple chunks, orange pieces, diced apples, water chestnuts and celery.
- Whisk together mayonnaise, soy sauce, sugar and curry.
- Toss chicken and mayonnaise mixture together.
- Adjust seasonings to taste.
- Refrigerate. Serve on lettuce leaves on chilled plates.
- Garnish with toasted almonds and/or orange or apple slices.
- Cook's Tip: Serve in pita bread pockets lined with lettuce.

A Chef's View

To poach a chicken means to cook it gently in liquid just below the boiling point when the liquid's surface is beginning to show some quivering movement. The amount and temperature of liquid used depends on the food being poached. Meats and poultry are usually simmered in stock. Poaching produces a delicate flavor in foods, while imparting some of the liquid's flavor to the ingredient being poached.

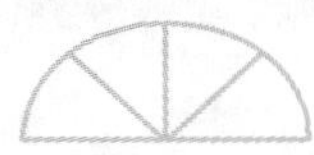

A Chef's View

To pit and peel an avocado, cut it in half lengthwise around the pit with a stainless steel knife. Carbon steel will discolor the fruit. Rotate the two halves to separate them. The pit will stay in one half. If you are not using the whole fruit, set aside the half with the pit. Remove the pit gently with a spoon or gently hit the pit with the blade of a knife, and, while grabbing hold of the fruit, gently rotate the pit out with the knife. Place the avocado cut side down and peel the skin off with a knife or your fingers. Sprinkle cut surfaces with lemon juice, lime juice or white vinegar to keep it from darkening.

To soften unripe avocados, cut the avocado in half, remove the pit, wrap each half tightly in microwave-safe plastic wrap, and place in the microwave at high for 1 minute. Run immediately under cold water to stop the cooking and unwrap.

Mexican Stack Buffet Salad

Level: Easy
Serves 8
Preparation Time: 30 minutes

2	pounds ground beef
1	(8-ounce) can tomato sauce
2	teaspoons garlic powder
½	teaspoon salt
1	(14.5-ounce) can diced tomatoes
2	tablespoons chili powder
1	(14.5-ounce) can ranch-style beans
1	(14.5-ounce) package round corn chips
3	cups cooked rice
1	pound Cheddar cheese, shredded
4	tomatoes, diced
1	head iceberg lettuce, shredded
1	large onion, diced
2	(10-ounce) cans sliced ripe olives, drained
1	(16-ounce) carton lite sour cream
1	(4-ounce) package chopped pecans
1	(4-ounce) can flaked coconut
1	(24-ounce) jar picante sauce

- Brown ground beef in a large skillet. Drain.
- Add tomato sauce, garlic powder, salt, diced tomatoes, chili powder and beans.
- Stir and simmer until warmed through.
- Place remaining ingredients in separate bowls.
- Serve buffet style and let each guest take a plate and 'stack' their own salad as tall as they like.

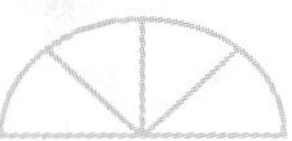

Artichoke Rice Salad

Level: Easy
Serves 4
Preparation Time: 40 minutes

2	cups chicken stock
1	cup white rice, uncooked
¼	cup chopped green onion, white and green parts sliced on the diagonal
¼	cup chopped red bell pepper
¼	cup chopped green bell pepper
¼	cup sliced pimiento-stuffed olives
1	(6-ounce) jar marinated artichoke hearts, drained and halved
½	cup mayonnaise
½	teaspoon dried dill weed
½	teaspoon salt
⅛	teaspoon black pepper
	Lettuce leaves, for garnish
	Sliced pimiento-stuffed olives, for garnish

- Bring stock to a boil in a medium-size saucepan. Stir in rice.
- Return to a boil, reduce heat and simmer, covered, for 20 minutes or until done.
- Cool.
- Stir in onion, peppers, olives, artichoke hearts, mayonnaise, dill weed, salt and black pepper.
- Chill.
- Spoon salad into a lettuce-lined bowl and garnish with additional olives, if desired.
- Cook's Tip: Salad may be served individually on lettuce-lined plates.

A Missouri Window

Ha Ha Tonka State Park, Indian for 'laughing waters,' is a geological wonderland: sinkholes, caves, a huge natural bridge, soaring bluffs, and Missouri's ninth largest spring. Fifteen miles of trails traverse the park, leading visitors to spectacular scenery, natural wonders and the famous castle ruins. Accessible, paved walkways and rugged, rocky trails provide every hiking experience, from a casual boardwalk stroll to an overnight backpack trip. Looming over all is the ruin of the turn-of-the-century stone castle built by a wealthy businessman. The empty shell of this great mansion overlooks Ha Ha Tonka Spring and Lake of the Ozarks from atop a 250-foot bluff.

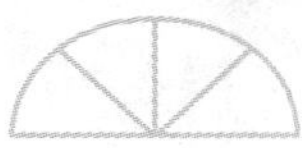

A Chef's View

In its infinite variety, Chinese cookery is one of the most sophisticated in the world. It is wider in scope than the French and more imaginative in its creative techniques and ingredients than the Italian. An authentic Chinese bill of fare begins with clear soup. A leaf of watercress, a sliver of scallion, or a shave of carrot to beguile the eye may join the clearest of broth. Next comes firm, flaky rice and a favorite mixed vegetable dish, or one combined with small amounts of shrimp or chicken.

There are three objectives all Chinese chefs have for their food. It must have visual appeal, impart a fragrant aroma, and taste good. Every meal is a feast to a Chinese chef.

Asian Chicken Salad

Level: Easy
Serves 8-10
Preparation Time: 35 minutes

1 pound chicken breasts, skinned, boned and diced
½ cup plus 2 tablespoons canola oil, divided
3 tablespoons sesame seeds
¼ cup slivered almonds
2 packages coleslaw mix
2 packages chicken-flavored oriental noodles
6 green onions, chopped, white and green parts
3 tablespoons soy sauce
4 tablespoons granulated sugar
2 teaspoons salt
1 teaspoon ground white pepper
6 tablespoons white wine vinegar
Dry seasoning mix from oriental noodles, optional
Radicchio lettuce leaves, optional

- Cook and stir chicken in a skillet in 2 tablespoons oil until fully cooked.
- Remove chicken, drain and set aside.
- Preheat oven to 375 degrees.
- Toast sesame seeds and almonds on a jelly-roll pan for 5-10 minutes. Mix and turn at least once. Watch carefully. Cool.
- Mix together coleslaw mix, lightly crushed oriental noodles, chicken and green onion. Cover and refrigerate until ready to serve.
- Prepare salad dressing by whisking together soy sauce, sugar, salt, white pepper, ½ cup oil, vinegar and seasoning mix, if desired, in a small bowl.
- Add the toasted sesame seeds, toasted almonds and salad dressing to noodle mix just before serving. Toss.
- Cook's Tip: Place each salad serving on top of the red leaves of radicchio lettuce leaves for a color contrast.

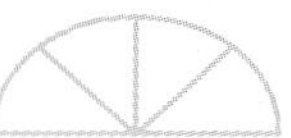

Greek Pasta Salad

Level: Easy
Serves 6
Preparation Time: 8-12 hours

1	pound bow-tie pasta
1	large red onion, chopped
4	Roma tomatoes, chopped
1	medium cucumber, skinned, seeded and chopped
1	medium zucchini, skinned, seeded and chopped
1	green bell pepper, diced
½	cup sliced ripe olives
4	tablespoons dry parsley flakes
1	teaspoon black pepper
3	teaspoons garlic salt
1	teaspoon fresh basil
¾	cup olive oil
5	tablespoons lemon juice
2	cups (12-ounces) feta cheese, crumbled

- Cook pasta to al dente and drain.
- Add vegetables to cooked pasta.
- For dressing, whisk together parsley flakes, black pepper, garlic salt, basil, olive oil and lemon juice.
- Pour dressing over mixture and toss.
- Stir in cheese.
- Chill 8-12 hours to blend flavors. Toss before serving.

A Chef's View

Decorate the tops of salads with various vegetable garnishes. Using a vegetable cutter, cut thin lengthwise strips of carrot to create carrot curls. Roll each carrot strip up and secure with a wooden pick. Place in ice water for several hours to curl. Just before garnishing, remove wooden picks.

Create cherry tomato roses by scoring an "X" on the blossom end of each cherry tomato. Using a sharp knife, carefully peel back the skin partway down the side of the tomato to make four petals. Nestle in sprigs of parsley for leaves.

A Chef's View

Roasted red bell peppers can be prepared in your own kitchen. Cut each pepper in half lengthwise. Remove the stem, seeds, and white membrane. Flatten each half with the palm of your hand. Place pepper halves, skin side up, on a foil-lined baking sheet. Broil 15 minutes or until blackened, charred and blistered. Remove from the oven and fold the foil around the peppers to seal in the steam. Let stand for about 10 minutes. Remove the peppers and the blistered skin will peel off easily with a knife.

Tortellini and Vegetable Medley

Level: Easy
Serves 8-10
Preparation Time: 30 minutes

2 (12-ounce) packages cheese tortellini, fresh or frozen
1 (8.5-ounce) can artichoke hearts, drained and quartered
1 red bell pepper, roasted and chopped
1 pint cherry tomatoes, halved
1 cup feta cheese, crumbled
1 (5.75-ounce) can ripe olives, drained and halved
7 green onions, white and green parts sliced on the diagonal
1 (13.5-ounce) can black beans, drained and rinsed
1 large avocado, peeled, pitted and cut in chunks
1 medium cucumber, peeled, seeded and cut into chunks
¼ cup white wine vinegar
3 garlic cloves, minced
3 tablespoons chopped fresh basil
1 teaspoon Dijon mustard
½ cup extra-virgin olive oil
Dash salt
Dash sugar

- Cook tortellini according to package directions.
- Drain and transfer to a large bowl.
- Add artichoke hearts, red pepper, tomatoes, cheese, olives, onion, beans, avocado and cucumber.
- To make dressing, whisk together vinegar, garlic, basil, mustard, olive oil, salt and sugar.
- Toss salad gently with dressing.
- Flavors are best when served at near room temperature.
- Cook's Tip: Keeps well in refrigerator for several days.

Crab Louie Salad

Level: Quick and Simple
Serves 4-6
Preparation Time: 15 minutes

1	large head lettuce, any type
3	eggs, hard-boiled and chopped
3	cups flaked crabmeat
1	cup mayonnaise
¼	cup heavy cream
¼	cup seafood cocktail sauce
1	teaspoon Worcestershire sauce
	Quartered artichoke hearts, optional
	Sliced water chestnuts, drained, optional
3	tomatoes, quartered, for garnish
½	cup pitted ripe olives, drained, for garnish

- Tear lettuce into bite-size pieces.
- Combine lettuce, eggs, crabmeat and optional ingredients.
- Whisk together mayonnaise, cream, cocktail sauce and Worcestershire sauce.
- Pour over salad and gently toss to coat.
- Garnish with tomatoes and ripe olives.

Tempura Roasted Peppers

Level: Good Cook
Serves 4
Preparation Time: 35 minutes

4	large red bell peppers, roasted, peeled, seeded and stemmed
	Salt, to taste
	Freshly ground black pepper, to taste
⅔	cup all-purpose flour
½	cup cornstarch
1	large egg, beaten
1	cup ice-cold soda water
½	teaspoon salt

- Preheat deep-fat fryer with oil to 350 degrees. Cut roasted peppers into 1-inch strips. Season with salt and pepper. Set aside.
- Combine flour, cornstarch, egg, soda water and ½ teaspoon salt in a mixing bowl and mix well.
- Dip each slice of pepper in batter, coating completely and letting excess drip off.
- Lay pepper strips carefully in hot oil. Fry until crispy and slightly golden, about 2 minutes. Fry in batches. Drain on paper towels. Season with salt. Serve with *Windows'* Crab Louie Salad.

A Chef's View

Lettuce is not always green.

- *Boston lettuce has a tightly packed head with green outer leaves and light yellow inner leaves. It offers a subtle, sweet taste and is soft and tender.*
- *Bibb lettuce has a deep, rich green color and is whitish green toward the core. It has a delicate and buttery flavor and is slightly crisper than Boston.*
- *Belgian endive offers a white to whitish-green color with a snappy texture and tone and somewhat bitter taste. The leaves can also serve as a pretty garnish.*
- *Arugula is bunches of oak-shaped leaves in a light-to-dark green color, with long stems. It's pungent, peppery, and crisp.*
- *Radicchio adds purple-red color to any salad. A variety of endive, its hearty texture holds up well with chicken salad, imparting a slightly bitter taste.*

A Missouri Window

The state musical instrument, the fiddle, was brought to Missouri by fur traders and settlers in the late 1700s.

Shrimp Pasta Salad

Level: Easy
Serves 6
Preparation Time: 4 hours

3	cups water
1	pound unpeeled medium-size fresh shrimp
6-8	ounces seashell macaroni
½	medium green bell pepper, diced
½	medium red bell pepper, diced
1	cup thinly sliced celery
½	small red onion, coarsely chopped
3	green onions, chopped, white and green parts
1	tablespoon chopped fresh parsley
¼	cup mayonnaise
¼	cup Italian salad dressing
1	tablespoon lemon juice
½	teaspoon dried oregano leaves
¼	teaspoon salt
	Dash black pepper
	Hard-boiled egg slices, for garnish
	Fresh parsley, for garnish

- Bring water to boil. Add shrimp and cook 3-5 minutes or until shrimp are pink.
- Drain well and rinse with cold water.
- Chill, peel and devein shrimp and return to refrigerator.
- Cook macaroni al dente. Drain, rinse with cold water and drain again.
- Add peppers, celery, onions and parsley. Toss.
- Whisk together mayonnaise, salad dressing, lemon juice, oregano, salt and black pepper.
- Add to macaroni mixture and toss. Fold in shrimp.
- Chill before serving.
- Garnish with sliced hard-boiled eggs and fresh parsley.

Corn Relish

Level: Easy
Serves 6-8
Preparation Time: 2 hours

2	(15¼-ounce) cans whole kernel corn, drained
1	(15-ounce) can sliced carrots, drained
1	green bell pepper, chopped
1	medium Vidalia onion, chopped
2	celery ribs, sliced
½	cup canola oil
¼	cup apple cider vinegar
¼	cup water
1	teaspoon granulated sugar
1	teaspoon celery seeds
	Salt and black pepper, to taste

- Pour drained corn and carrots into a container with an airtight cover.
- Add green pepper, onion and celery.
- Combine canola oil, vinegar, water, sugar and celery seed in a large bowl. Mix well. Season to taste with salt and black pepper.
- Pour dressing over vegetables and toss.
- Refrigerate in covered container at least 2-3 hours to blend flavors.
- Cook's Tip: For an extra special flavor, roast 4 ears of corn on the grill. Cool and cut from cob and use in salad. Frozen corn, slightly thawed, can also be used but decrease water to ⅛ cup.

A Missouri Window

Members of the Hall of Famous Missourians

- *Josephine Baker - dancer, human rights activist*
- *Thomas Hart Benton - painter, muralist*
- *Susan Elizabeth Blow - established first public kindergarten*
- *Omar N. Bradley - World War II general*
- *George Washington Carver - scientist, botanist, educator*
- *Samuel Langhorne Clemens - author Mark Twain*
- *Walter Cronkite - television reporter, anchor*
- *Walt Disney - film and animation pioneer*
- *Joyce C. Hall - founder of Hallmark Cards, Inc.*
- *Scott Joplin - ragtime composer, pianist*
- *Charlie Parker - jazz musician, composer*
- *James Cash Penney - founder of department store chain*
- *John J. Pershing - World War I general*
- *Sacagawea - guide - interpreter for Lewis and Clark*
- *Harry S Truman - U.S. President*
- *Laura Ingalls Wilder - 'Little House' series author*

A Chef's View

A little distilled white vinegar goes a long way. Keep it on hand for the following uses:

- *Remove spaghetti sauce stains from plastic.*
- *Make vinegar ice cubes to clean and deodorize garbage disposal.*
- *Cut grease during cleanup.*
- *Clean sponges.*

German Potato Salad

Level: Easy
Serves 8
Preparation Time: 1⅓ hours

2 pounds red potatoes
2 (14.5-ounce) cans chicken broth
4 teaspoons salt
8 slices bacon
8 teaspoons chopped onion
3 tablespoons all-purpose flour
⅓ cup boiled potato stock
1 cup apple cider vinegar
1 teaspoon dry mustard
2 tablespoons Dijon mustard
½ cup granulated sugar
½ teaspoon black pepper
½ cup chopped fresh parsley
½ teaspoon dried rosemary leaves, crumbled

- Boil potatoes in skins in chicken broth and salt until tender. Drain, reserving potato stock. Dice potatoes.
- Fry bacon in a small skillet until crisp. Drain and crumble. Set aside.
- Discard ⅔ of the bacon drippings. Cook onion in remaining bacon fat in skillet.
- Begin preparing potato salad dressing by whisking together flour and potato stock in a small bowl. Set aside.
- Add apple cider vinegar, mustards, sugar and black pepper to onion in skillet. Mix well.
- Stir reserved potato stock mixture into skillet. Continue stirring until dressing reaches medium consistency.
- Pour dressing over potatoes, sprinkle reserved bacon, parsley and rosemary leaves. Toss carefully to avoid mashing potatoes.
- Cook's Tip: Garnish with radish roses and sprigs of fresh parsley for leaves.

Green Bean and Feta Salad with Walnuts

Level: Easy
Serves 6
Preparation Time: 1 hour

- 1½ pounds fresh green beans, strings removed and halved crosswise
- ¾ cup olive oil
- ½ cup loosely packed fresh mint leaves
- ¼ cup white wine vinegar
- 1 garlic clove, minced
- ¾ teaspoon salt
- ¼ teaspoon black pepper
- 1 cup chopped walnuts, toasted
- ½ cup chopped red onion
- 1 cup crumbled feta cheese

- Cook beans in a small amount of boiling water for 5 minutes or until crisp tender.
- Drain and plunge into ice water. Drain and pat dry. Cover and chill.
- Combine oil, mint, vinegar, garlic, salt and pepper in a food processor or blender. Process 20 seconds or until well blended. Refrigerate.
- Transfer beans to a serving bowl. Top with walnuts, onion and cheese.
- Pour dressing over salad, toss and serve immediately.

Mango Broccoli Salad

Level: Easy
Serves 6
Preparation Time: 8-12 hours

- 2 bunches fresh broccoli, cut into florets or 1 (16-ounce) package frozen
- ½ cup low-fat mayonnaise
- 2 tablespoons rice wine vinegar
- 2 teaspoons granulated sugar
- 2 mangoes, peeled, seeded and chopped
- ½ cup walnut pieces

- Steam or microwave broccoli until crisp-tender. Drain.
- Stir together mayonnaise, vinegar and sugar.
- Pour over broccoli and toss to coat all pieces.
- Add mango and nuts and stir to combine.
- Chill 8-12 hours to enhance flavors.

A Chef's View

Do not buy the larger, nobby green beans. They are old and tougher than young beans. To see if beans are fresh, break a bean in half and it should snap with a crispy feel. One pound of fresh beans will serve 4 people.

A Missouri Window

The present Capitol completed in 1917 and occupied the following year is the third Capitol in Jefferson City and the sixth in Missouri history. The first seat of state government was housed in the Mansion House, Third and Vine Streets, St. Louis; the second was in the Missouri Hotel, Maine and Morgan Streets, also in St. Louis. St. Charles was designated as temporary capital of the state in 1821 and remained the seat of government until 1826 when Jefferson City became the permanent capital city. Jefferson City was named for Thomas Jefferson, the third President of the United States.

A Missouri Window

Missouri takes its name from one of its earliest settlers, the Missouri Indians. Other Indian nations living in the state before Europeans include the Osage, the Sacs, Foxes, Otos, Iowas, Miamis, Kickapoos, Delewares, Shawnees and Kansas.

Green Bean and Onion Salad with Bleu Cheese

Level: Easy
Serves 4-6
Preparation Time: 4 hours

1	pound fresh green beans
1	cup water, boiling
4	cups ice water
1	small red onion, sliced and separated into rings
⅓	cup red wine vinegar
¾	cup canola oil
1	teaspoon onion powder
1	garlic clove, minced
3	teaspoons freshly grated lemon peel
6-12	leaves radicchio lettuce
1	cup Gorgonzola or Stilton cheese crumbles
1	cup chopped pecans, toasted

- Wash green beans; trim ends and remove strings.
- Add beans to 1 cup boiling water. Cover and cook 5 minutes at low heat. Stir occasionally.
- Drain and immediately add beans to ice water. Let stand 5-10 minutes, then drain well.
- Toss beans and onion together in a container with an airtight lid.
- Whisk vinegar, oil, onion powder, minced garlic and lemon peel.
- Pour over beans and onion and chill 2-3 hours.
- Remove beans and onion with a slotted spoon. Place on individual serving plates lined with lettuce leaves.
- Pour remaining marinade in a sauce bowl for table use.
- Garnish salad with cheese of choice and pecans. Drizzle with additional marinade, if desired.
- Cook's Tip: Use a prepared Caesar, Italian, raspberry or red wine vinaigrette salad dressing, regular or low-fat, for even easier preparation.

Asparagus Aspic with Horseradish

Level: Easy
Serves 10-12
Preparation Time: 8 hours

1	(16-ounce) can asparagus pieces, drain and reserve liquid
1	(¼-ounce) envelope unflavored gelatin
1	(3-ounce) package lemon gelatin
1	(3-ounce) package cream cheese, softened and cut into chunks
1	tablespoon grated onion
1	tablespoon white wine vinegar
¼	teaspoon salt
1	cup mayonnaise
½	cup milk
	Dash ground white pepper
	Lettuce leaves
	Prepared horseradish

- Add enough water to the asparagus liquid to make one cup. Boil.
- Dissolve gelatins in the boiled liquid. Cool.
- Pour cooled gelatin liquid into bowl of food processor.
- Add cream cheese, onion, vinegar, salt, mayonnaise, milk and white pepper. Process until creamy.
- Arrange asparagus pieces in bottom of oiled mold.
- Pour gelatin liquid gently on top of asparagus pieces. Chill until firm.
- Unmold salad on a lettuce-lined plate and serve with horseradish.
- Cook's Tip: Present individual appetizer servings on a lettuce leaf with a dollop of horseradish.

A Chef's View

Aspic is a savory jelly, usually clear, made of meat, fish or vegetable stock and gelatin. Tomato aspic, made with tomato juice and gelatin, is opaque. Clear aspics may be used as a base for molded dishes, or as glazes for cold dishes for fish, poultry, meat, and eggs. They may also be cubed and served as an accompaniment relish with cold meat, fish or fowl.

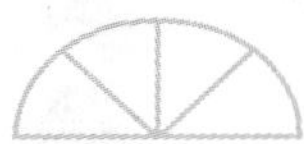

A Chef's View

Load a garlic press and storer with peeled garlic cloves, and refrigerate. It's odor free and ready to use. With a simple twist, press out exactly the amount of garlic you need. It crushes and stores shallots and chopped onions, too.

A Chef's View

After your shaped dish is completely congealed, carefully unmold. To break the suction, run a knife around the edge of the mold. If the mold has fluted sides, press the edge of the salad lightly with your finger and gently pull away from the sides. Also unmold the salad using the hot towel method. Wet a dish towel with hot water, and wring it out. Wrap the towel around the bottom and sides of the container, and let it stand for 1-2 minutes. Then place a serving platter on top of the mold and invert. If it doesn't unmold, repeat the process.

Tangy Green Bean and Pea Salad

Level: Easy
Serves 4
Preparation Time: 8-12 hours

2 celery ribs, sliced
¾ cup chopped green onion, white and green parts
1 medium cucumber, peeled, seeded and chopped
1 large green bell pepper, chopped
1 (14.2-ounce) can early peas, drained
2 (14.5-ounce) cans French style green beans, drained
1 (4-ounce) jar sliced pimientos
½ cup canola oil
1 cup tarragon vinegar
1 cup granulated sugar
2 garlic cloves, minced
Salt and black pepper, to taste

- Combine celery, green onion, cucumber, bell pepper, peas, green beans and pimiento in a large bowl. Toss.
- Whisk together canola oil, tarragon vinegar, sugar and garlic until sugar dissolves.
- Season to taste with salt and black pepper.
- Pour salad dressing over vegetables and toss. Refrigerate.
- Cook's Tip: Salad dressing should be prepared 1-2 days in advance to enhance flavor.

Blushing Cherry Mold

Level: Easy
Serves 6-8
Preparation Time: 1 day

1 (3-ounce) package black cherry gelatin
½ cup boiling water
1 tablespoon lemon juice
1 (16-ounce) can pitted black or Bing cherries, drain and reserve juice
½ cup dry red wine
1 (11-ounce) can Mandarin oranges, drained
½ cup pecan halves
Lettuce leaves

- Dissolve gelatin in boiling water. Cool for 10 minutes.
- Add lemon juice, cherry juice and wine.
- Pour into a 3-cup mold.
- Add drained fruit and nuts.
- Chill until set.
- Unmold on a bed of lettuce leaves. Serve.

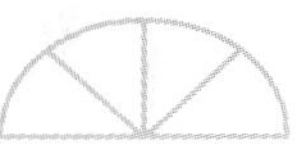

Cranberry Fruit Salad

Level: Easy
Serves 6-8
Preparation Time: 1 day

- 1 (6-ounce) package lemon gelatin
- 2 cups boiling water
- 1 (12-ounce) package cranberries, rinsed
- 2 cups granulated sugar
- 1 cup seedless grapes, any color
- 1 cup pecans, chopped
- 2 cups miniature marshmallows
- ½ pint heavy cream, or 1 (8-ounce) carton whipped topping mix
- Lettuce leaves

- ◆ Dissolve gelatin in hot water in a large bowl. Chill until slightly set.
- ◆ Chop cranberries with sugar in a blender.
- ◆ Mix grapes, pecans and marshmallows with cranberries.
- ◆ Whip heavy cream until stiff and fold into fruit mix.
- ◆ Pour into two 4-cup ring molds.
- ◆ Chill until firm.
- ◆ Unmold on lettuce-lined plate.

Coconut Pecan Apricot Salad

Level: Easy
Serves 12
Preparation Time: 8 hours

- 1 (20-ounce) can crushed pineapple
- 2 (3-ounce) packages apricot gelatin
- 2 cups buttermilk
- 1 (3.5-ounce) can flaked coconut
- 1 cup chopped pecans
- 1 (8-ounce) carton frozen whipped topping, thawed
- Lettuce leaves, for garnish
- Whipped topping, for garnish
- Mint sprigs, for garnish

- ◆ Mix pineapple and gelatin together in a saucepan. Bring to a boil. Let cool completely.
- ◆ Add buttermilk, coconut, pecans and whipped topping to gelatin mixture. Mix thoroughly.
- ◆ Pour into a 13x9x2-inch glass dish. Refrigerate overnight.
- ◆ Serve 3x3-inch squares on a lettuce leaf. Top with a dollop of whipped topping and garnish with a mint sprig.

A Culinary Reflection

The day before Thanksgiving and Christmas, I can remember my mother getting out the food chopper and clamping it onto the table to make cranberry salad. My dad would help and as they ground the cranberries, apples and oranges, juice ran everywhere in spite of the fact that a bowl was there to catch the ground fruit. Juice not only ran into the bowl, but out the handle of the grinder, and onto the table. It was a mess, but the final product was worth the effort. We all looked forward to Mom's cranberry salad at Thanksgiving and Christmas.

~ Jean Kruse

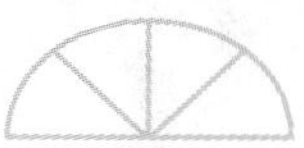

A Culinary Reflection

Every holiday for as long as I can remember, my mother made a congealed salad with lime gelatin, pineapple, pecans, and cream cheese, which was a favorite of mine. I am sure it had a formal name, but as a small child, I just called it 'green stuff.' Over the years, the name I gave it as a child survived, and I'm not sure anyone now remembers the correct name. My mom is in her eighties, and it warms my heart to hear my children, in their late teens and early twenties, to request some of Grandma's 'green stuff.'

~ Liz Kagan

Pineapple Surprise Salad

Level: Easy
Serves 18
Preparation Time: 8 hours

1 (3-ounce) package lemon gelatin
1 (3-ounce) package lime gelatin
2 cups boiling water
1 (20-ounce) can crushed pineapple, drained
1 (16-ounce) carton small-curd cottage cheese
1 cup mayonnaise
1 cup sweetened condensed milk
1 cup walnuts, coarsely chopped
2 teaspoons prepared horseradish

- Dissolve gelatins in boiling water. Cool and refrigerate until slightly thickened.
- Add pineapple, cottage cheese, mayonnaise, sweetened condensed milk, walnuts and horseradish. Mix well.
- Pour into a 13x9x2-inch glass dish or two 8x8x2-inch dishes.
- Refrigerate until set.
- Cook's Tip: This large salad keeps well in the refrigerator and can be prepared well in advance.

Avocado Dressing

Level: Quick and Simple
Yield: 1 cup
Preparation Time: 10 minutes

1 ripe avocado
¼ cup loosely packed fresh basil leaves
1 small garlic clove, peeled
Juice of 2 limes
3 tablespoon red-wine vinegar
½ cup extra-virgin olive oil
Salt and freshly ground black pepper, to taste

- Slice avocado lengthwise. Remove and discard pit. Peel and place pulp in the bowl of a food processor.
- Add basil, garlic, lime juice and vinegar; process until combined.
- Add olive oil slowly through the machine's feed tube, and process until dressing is smooth. It should be thick but of pourable consistency. Add extra lime juice to adjust consistency.
- Season with salt and pepper, and use immediately to prevent dressing from turning brown.
- Serve over *Windows'* Mexican Stack Buffet Salad or other green salad.

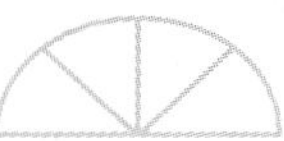

Strawberry and Pretzel Salad

Level: Easy
Serves 9
Preparation Time: 3-8 hours

2½	cups thin baked pretzels, broken into pieces
1½	sticks butter, melted, do not substitute
1	(8-ounce) package cream or Neufchâtel cheese, softened
1	cup granulated sugar
1	(8-ounce) carton frozen whipped topping, thawed
2	(3-ounce) packages wild strawberry-flavored gelatin
2	cups boiling water
2	(10-ounce) packages frozen strawberries

- Preheat oven to 350 degrees.
- Stir pretzels and butter in 13x9x2-inch baking dish, coating pretzels completely.
- Bake for 10 minutes. Stir once during baking and again when baked. Cool.
- Cream cheese and sugar together.
- Fold in whipped topping.
- Spread over cooled pretzels, completely covering surface and sealing edges.
- Mix gelatin in boiling water. Add frozen strawberries. Cool until slightly thickened.
- Pour gelatin mixture gently over cheese layer.
- Refrigerate until set.
- Cook's Tip: Salad is best made the evening before serving.

Pear Dressing

Level: Quick and Simple
Yield: 1¼ cups
Preparation Time: 10 minutes

1	(16-ounce) can pears in heavy syrup
¼	cup extra-virgin olive oil
2	tablespoons fresh lemon juice
1½	teaspoons salt
¼	teaspoon coarsely ground black pepper

- Drain pears, reserving 2 tablespoons syrup.
- Place pears in a blender with oil, lemon juice, salt, pepper and reserved syrup. Blend until smooth.
- Cook's Tip: Make dressing up to 3 days ahead and store, in an airtight container, in the refrigerator.

A Missouri Window

The first Capitol in Jefferson City burned in 1837 and a second structure completed in 1840 burned when the dome was struck by lightning on February 5, 1911.

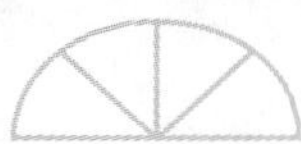

A Missouri Window

In 1841, the University of Missouri, the first state university west of the Mississippi River, began accepting students.

A Missouri Window

In 1901, the first State Fair was held in Sedalia. In 1904, the World's Fair opened in St. Louis.

Tuna Lemon Mold

Level: Easy
Serves 4-6
Preparation Time: 5 hours

1 (3-ounce) package lemon gelatin
½ cup boiling water
½ medium onion, chopped
2 (7-ounce) cans tuna, flaked
½ cup mayonnaise
1 cup heavy cream
½ teaspoon salt
½ teaspoon ground paprika
½ teaspoon garlic powder
Lettuce leaves
Lemon wedges, for garnish
Fresh parsley, for garnish
Pimiento-stuffed green olives, for garnish

- Dissolve gelatin in boiling water. Cool.
- Pour gelatin into blender and add onion. Blend on medium-speed for 30 seconds.
- Add tuna and mayonnaise. Puree until well blended, stopping several times to push ingredients into blades with spatula.
- Blend in cream, salt, paprika and garlic powder slowly into tuna mixture.
- Pour into oiled 4-cup mold.
- Chill 4-5 hours.
- Unmold on bed of lettuce leaves and garnish with lemon wedges, parsley and olives.

Honey Lemon Dressing

Level: Quick and Simple
Yield: 1¼ cups
Preparation Time: 10 minutes

½ cup sour cream
½ cup mayonnaise
1½ tablespoons lemon juice
¼ cup honey
½ teaspoon dry mustard
Celery salt, to taste

- Whisk ingredients as listed until well blended.
- Chill and serve over spinach or fruit salad.

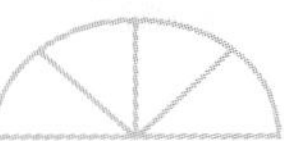

Missouri Governor's Mansion Basil Vinaigrette

Level: Quick and Simple
Yield: 2 cups
Preparation Time: 5 minutes

- 3 garlic cloves, chopped
- ½ cup granulated sugar
- ¾ cup chopped fresh basil
- ½ teaspoon salt
- ½ teaspoon black pepper
- ½ cup apple cider vinegar
- 1 cup canola oil

- Using a food processor, blend garlic, sugar, basil, salt and black pepper until basil is finely chopped.
- Add vinegar and blend.
- Pour oil slowly into the feeding tube and blend until smooth.
- Store in a tightly sealed container in the refrigerator.
- Use on any green salad.

Hoonoono Lau Ai Palani

Level: Easy
Yield: 3 cups
Preparation Time: 10 minutes

- 1 (10¾-ounce) can tomato soup
- 1 teaspoon chopped green onion
- 1 garlic clove, minced
- 2 tablespoons Worcestershire sauce
- ½ teaspoon dry mustard
- 1 cup canola oil
- ⅔ cup granulated sugar
- ⅔ cup apple cider vinegar
- 2 teaspoons salt
- ¼ teaspoon black pepper

- Place all ingredients in a quart size jar and shake well.
- Store in the refrigerator.
- Cook's Tip: This is a French dressing from Hawaii.

A Show-Me Specialty

Basil Vinaigrette is served with salads at the Missouri Governor's Mansion. The Mansion is the living home for Missouri's Governor and First Lady. The home is open for tours and special events. Groups may eat in one of the famous rooms with portraits of the First Ladies looking on surrounded by opulent window dressings and state antiques.

Missouri Governor's Mansion
100 Madison Street
Jefferson City
573-751-4141

A Chef's View

White vinegar can be a helpful cleaner in the kitchen. Use it to:

- *Make crystal glasses sparkle.*
- *Remove coffee and tea stains from pots and cups.*
- *Loosen burned food from pans.*

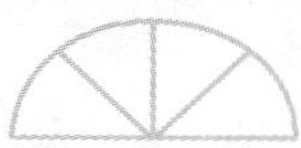

A Missouri Window

One of the earliest centers of industry in central Missouri, Boone's Lick is the site of the salt-manufacturing business once owned and operated by Daniel Boone's sons, Daniel M. and Nathan Boone. Visitors to the 51-acre historic site may follow a self-guided, wooded trail that leads down the hillside to the salt springs where the Boone brothers began their business in 1805.

Mayfair Dressing

Level: Easy
Yield: 4 cups
Preparation Time: 10 minutes

1 garlic clove, sliced
1 celery rib, sliced
½ medium onion, sliced
1 (2-ounce) can flat anchovies
1 teaspoon black pepper, freshly ground
1 teaspoon seasoned salt flavor enhancer
½ teaspoon granulated sugar
2 tablespoons prepared mustard
1 tablespoon lemon juice
3 eggs
2 cups canola oil

- Process garlic, celery, onion, anchovies, black pepper, seasoned salt flavor enhancer, sugar, mustard and lemon juice in a blender.
- Add 3 whole raw eggs and blend.
- Drizzle oil through feed tube, a quarter of a cup at a time, blending after each addition.
- Refrigerate in an airtight container.
- Cook's Tip: The use of raw eggs can cause health problems with certain individuals.

Sapsago Dressing

Level: Easy
Yield: 5 cups
Preparation Time: 10 minutes

1 quart mayonnaise
2 tablespoons dried parsley
2 tablespoons dried onion flakes
2 tablespoons grated sapsago cheese
1 teaspoon garlic salt
1 teaspoon onion powder
½ teaspoon black pepper
1½ cups buttermilk

- Mix all ingredients except buttermilk.
- Blend in buttermilk.
- Store in an airtight container in the refrigerator.
- Cook's Tip: Makes a great vegetable dip.

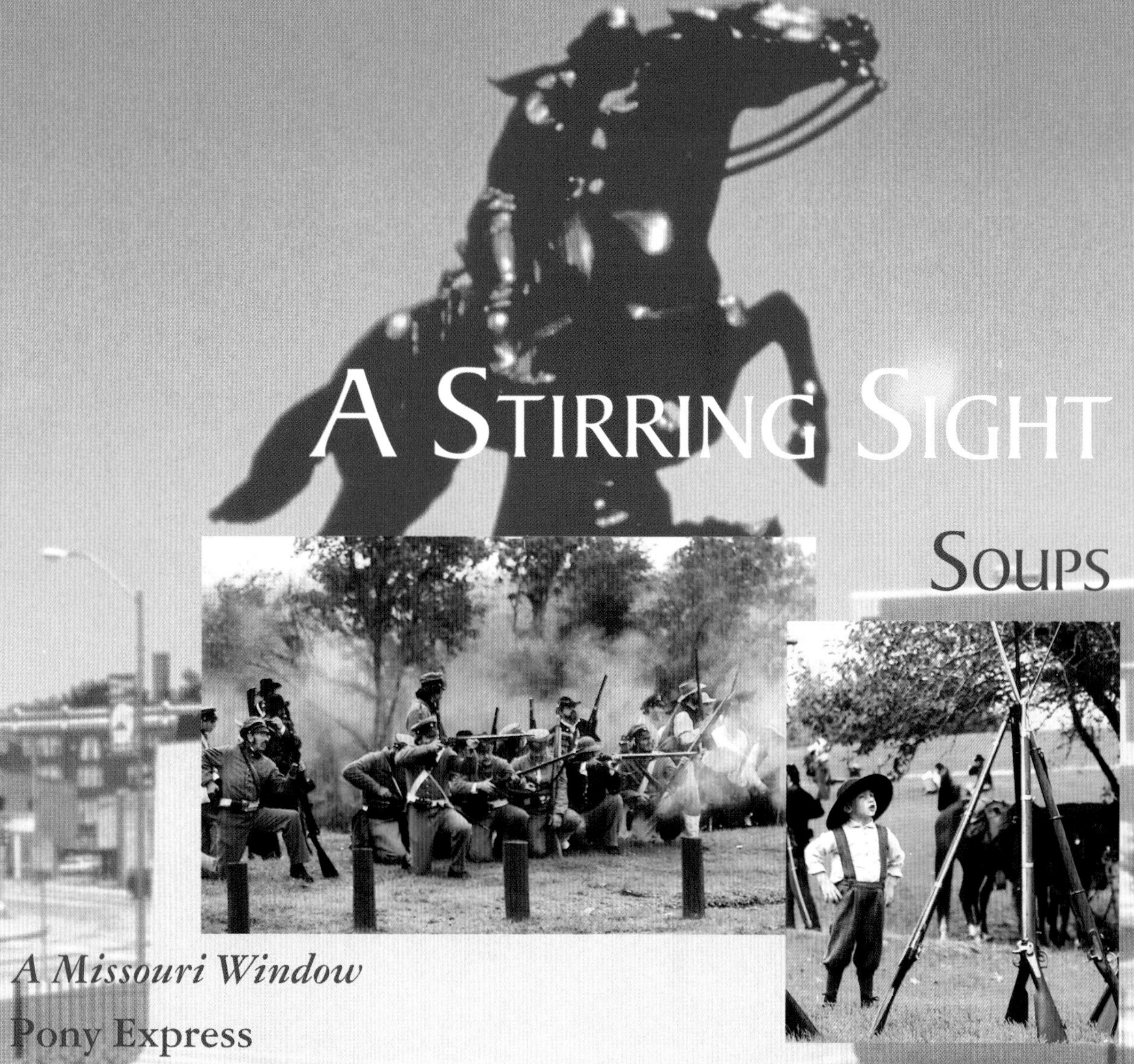

A Stirring Sight

Soups

A Missouri Window

Pony Express

Missouri's first and last frontier is situated in northwest Missouri. Squarely in the middle is St. Joseph, a town rich in history, famous for being the origin of the Pony Express, and where Jesse James met his demise. Nestled on scenic river bluffs overlooking the Missouri River, St. Joseph played an important role in the development of the west.

In the summer of 1804, Meriwether Lewis and William Clark camped on the banks of the Missouri River in what is now St. Joseph. In 1826, St. Joseph was established as an early Indian trading post, which quickly expanded into a major trade center. The city served as the starting point for wagon trains filled with pioneers and outfitted thousands of '49ers when gold was discovered in California. In fact, during the Gold Rush of the mid-1800s, more travelers left from St. Joseph than from any other river town. A variety of architectural styles, including Victorian and Italianate, can be found in both commercial and residential construction symbolizing the prosperity and optimism of the time.

In 1860, St. Joseph's most daring adventure sent the first Pony Express rider to Sacramento, California, carrying mail to the western frontier. Although the Pony Express lasted only 18 months, its legend lives on with the preservation of the stables and headquarters. In the nearby town of Lexington, folks can experience a Civil War reenactment.

Photos: The Pony Express Museum Monument, St. Joseph & Civil War Reenactment Battle of Lexington

The Buchanan County Medical Auxiliary was organized at the Missouri Methodist Hospital, September 1924, under the direction of Mrs. James F. Owens, the first president of the Auxiliary, with 16 charter members. In 1931-32, Buchanan County Auxiliary was honored to have Anna McGlothan preside as national president of the Women's Auxiliary of the American Medical Association at its tenth annual meeting in New Orleans. Mrs. Owens was national Corresponding Secretary that same year.

Buchanan County Medical Society Alliance

The Auxiliary was organized to promote health in the community with the first health issue addressing prevention and treatment of tuberculosis. Throughout the years, the Alliance has addressed the health needs of the citizens of St. Joseph. In the '40s, it was preparing for a fight on polio. In the '50s, air raid warning sirens were purchased with Auxiliary funds. In the '60s, members presented civil defense programs in schools. During the '90s, breast cancer awareness and an ambitious *Stop America's Violence Everywhere Campaign - SAVE* project were promoted.

The following members have served as MSMA Alliance presidents: Anna McGlothan, 1926-27; Mrs. C. H. Werner, 1937-38; Lillian Butler, 1968-69; Helen Willman, 1973-74; Eileen Dyer, 1988-89; and Rhonda Wade, 2001-2002.

Apricot Soup

Level: Easy
Serves 2
Preparation Time: 1 hour

1 (28-ounce) can apricots with juice
1 cup light cream or milk
1 tablespoon fresh lemon juice
Fresh mint leaves, for garnish

- Process apricots and juice in a blender.
- Mix with cream and lemon juice.
- Refrigerate until chilled.
- Serve cold soup in chilled bowls garnished with fresh mint leaves.

Cantaloupe Soup

Level: Easy
Serves 4-6
Preparation Time: 2 hours

1 (3-pound) cantaloupe, peeled, seeded and diced
5 tablespoons butter
1 tablespoon granulated sugar
¼ teaspoon ground ginger
Grated lemon peel
Dash salt
2½ cups milk
Lemon juice or white wine, to taste, optional
Cantaloupe curls, for garnish
Fresh mint leaves, for garnish

- Cook cantaloupe in butter with sugar, ginger, lemon peel and salt until soft. Stir frequently.
- Add milk and, if desired, lemon juice or white wine, to taste.
- Bring to a boil.
- Turn heat to low and simmer for 10-15 minutes.
- Cool.
- Blend, in batches, in a food processor. Pour into a bowl, cover and chill.
- Serve cold and garnish with cantaloupe curls and mint leaves.

A Missouri Window

Missouri is sometimes called the Mother of the West because it once lay at the frontier of the United States. The state supplied many of the pioneers who settled the vast region between Missouri and the Pacific Ocean. The cities of St. Louis, St. Charles, Independence, St. Joseph, and Westport Landing (now Kansas City) served as jumping-off places for the westbound pioneers.

A Chef's View

Nutritious soup may precede a meal as an appetizer, may be a substantial meal in itself, or may be the grand finale after an outing.

A Chef's View

When serving cold soup as a first course, improvise a chiller to keep soup cold on a warm night. Mount a glass custard cup or other small cup for the soup in a gaily-colored bowl filled with crushed ice. If both your soup and dishes are white, add food color to the ice trays before freezing and crushing.

A Missouri Window

Squaw Creek National Wildlife Refuge in Mound City is home to thousands of migrating waterfowl.

Chilled Apple Soup

Level: Easy
Serves 4
Preparation Time: 1 hour

4	cups apple juice
4	Gala apples, peeled, cored and diced
½	teaspoon cinnamon
1	teaspoon fresh lemon juice
½	cup brown sugar, packed
	Cinnamon sticks, optional

- Simmer apple juice, apples, cinnamon, lemon juice and brown sugar in a large stockpot until apples are barely tender.
- Refrigerate soup in a covered container.
- Serve cold.
- Cook's Tip: This soup looks especially attractive served in a clear mug with a cinnamon stick.

Iced Strawberry Soup

Level: Easy
Serves 4
Preparation Time: 1 hour

4	(8-ounce) containers strawberry yogurt
1	cup milk
¼	teaspoon cinnamon
½	teaspoon salt
2½	cups fresh sliced strawberries
1	(8-ounce) container plain yogurt, for garnish
	Dash nutmeg
	Lemon slices, for garnish

- Combine strawberry yogurt, milk, cinnamon and salt. Stir gently.
- Fold in strawberries.
- Chill.
- Serve soup topped with a dollop of plain yogurt and dash of nutmeg in chilled bowls. Float a lemon slice on top.

EBT Gazpacho

Level: Easy
Serves 4
Preparation Time: 4 hours

4	medium vine-ripened red tomatoes, peeled, seeded and diced
1	red bell pepper, seeded and diced
1	green bell pepper, seeded and diced
1	yellow bell pepper, seeded and diced
1	jalapeño pepper, seeded and diced
¼	cup Italian parsley, chopped
¼	cup chopped fresh basil leaves
¼	cup fresh lime juice
2½	cups canned tomato juice
2	cucumbers, peeled, seeded and diced
½	teaspoon cayenne pepper
	Fresh basil leaves or edible flowers, for garnish

- Mix all ingredients into a large bowl. Chill.
- Serve chilled. Garnish with fresh basil leaves or edible flowers.

Vichyssoise

Level: Easy
Serves 6
Preparation Time: 2 hours

4	tablespoons unsalted butter
1	medium yellow onion, sliced
2	leeks, split lengthwise, cleaned and chopped
1	celery rib, chopped
1	bay leaf
⅛	teaspoon dried thyme
⅛	teaspoon cayenne pepper
	Ham bone
4	cups whole milk
1	pound red potatoes, peeled and sliced
1	large egg yolk, beaten
	Salt, to taste
1	cup heavy cream
	Chopped chives and parsley, for garnish

- Sauté onion, leeks, celery, bay leaf, thyme and cayenne in butter.
- Add ham bone. Simmer 5 minutes.
- Stir in milk and add potatoes. Simmer until potatoes are tender.
- Remove ham bone and bay leaf. Process vegetable mixture until smooth.
- Blend in egg yolk, salt and heavy cream.
- Serve chilled. Garnish with chives and parsley.

A Show-Me Specialty

Gazpacho is a specialty of Chef Leo Geismar, the General Manager/Chef from EBT Restaurant. Emery, Byrd, and Thayer Department Store was Kansas City's first department store, founded in 1863. The store served generations of Midwesterners during a century of business. During the 1960s, the advent of suburban flight and new shopping malls signaled the end to a legend. One of the features of the department store was an open Mezzanine that served as a fashionable tearoom, so in 1979, Emery, Byrd and Thayer was reborn as EBT Restaurant. An upscale, fine dining restaurant fashioned artifacts and memorabilia from the store including the columns, the chandeliers, stained glass and the original elevator cages. Today, it continues the tradition of fine food and excellent service in a beautiful setting.

EBT Restaurant
1310 Carondelet
Kansas City
816-942-8870

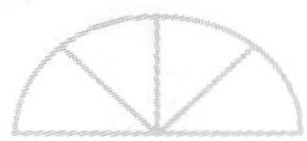

A Chef's View

Ginger is a plant from tropical and subtropical regions that's grown for its gnarled and bumpy root. Most ginger comes from Jamaica. The flavor is peppery and slightly sweet, while the aroma is pungent and spicy. Ginger must be peeled to reserve the delicate flesh just under the surface. Look for mature ginger with smooth skin. It should have a fresh, spicy fragrance. Fresh unpeeled ginger, tightly wrapped, can be refrigerated for up to 3 weeks and frozen for up to 6 months. Ground ginger is a very different from that of its fresh form and is not an appropriate substitute for dishes specifying fresh ginger. It is, however, delicious in many savory dishes such as soups, curries, and meats.

Apple Soup

Level: Easy
Serves 8
Preparation Time: 1 day

2 large Granny Smith apples, peeled, cored and diced
1 medium potato, peeled and diced
1 carrot, diced
1 celery rib, diced
1 medium onion, diced
4 garlic cloves, minced
½ inch fresh ginger, peeled and thinly sliced
1 tablespoon canola oil
1½ tablespoons curry powder
8 cups chicken stock
Seasoned salt, to taste
Black pepper, to taste
1 cup cold milk
½ cup sour cream
Fresh mint leaves, for garnish

- Cook and stir apples, potato, carrot, celery, onion, garlic, and fresh ginger in oil in a large stockpot until onion is soft.
- Add curry and chicken stock; stir.
- Simmer stock 30 minutes. Cool.
- Pour stock mixture in blender in batches to puree.
- Store and chill in a non-reactive container in the refrigerator for at least 3 hours or overnight.
- Season with salt and black pepper to taste.
- Stir in milk.
- Serve in chilled bowls garnished with a dollop of sour cream and fresh mint leaves.

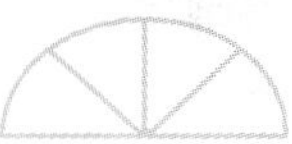

Autumn Pumpkin Bisque

Level: Easy
Serves 8
Preparation Time: 1 hour

1	pound sliced bacon, diced
1	medium onion, chopped
2	(16-ounce) cans solid pack pumpkin
2	cups half-and-half
4	cups milk
2	teaspoons ground cumin seeds
2	teaspoons salt
½	teaspoon ground white pepper
¼	cup chopped fresh parsley
	Grated Swiss cheese
	Chopped fresh cilantro
	Pine nuts, toasted

- Fry bacon in a 6-quart stockpot until crisp. Drain.
- Add chopped onion to stockpot with bacon drippings and sauté until translucent.
- Stir pumpkin and 2 cups half-and-half into stockpot.
- Pour and stir milk into pumpkin mixture until desired consistency is reached.
- Season soup with cumin, salt, white pepper and parsley. Stir.
- Heat thoroughly but do not boil.
- Top individual servings with grated Swiss cheese, chopped cilantro and pine nuts.
- Cook's Tip: For a warm winter lunch, serve bisque in a small hollowed-out pumpkin accompanied by a toasted Swiss cheese sandwich.

A Chef's View

Serve these Sweet Cinnamon Croutons with Windows' Apple Soup or Autumn Pumpkin Bisque.

Cube 8 slices of French bread and place cubes in a large zip-top plastic bag. Melt ½ cup of butter and pour over cubes in bag. Seal bag and shake to coat. Combine 1 tablespoon sugar and ¾ teaspoon ground cinnamon and sprinkle over bread. Shake again. Arrange cubes on an ungreased jelly-roll pan. Bake for 25-30 minutes in a 325 degree oven or until bread cubes are crisp and dry.

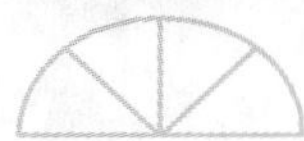

A Chef's View

To make a white roux, heat 4 tablespoons of pan drippings or butter over medium high heat. Add 4 tablespoons of all-purpose flour and whisk vigorously. Reduce heat to low when mixture thins and starts to bubble. Cook and lightly whisk until a toasty aroma is emitted. Cook 2 minutes more, stirring occasionally. Use immediately to thicken a liquid that is at or below room temperature. To thicken a hot liquid, allow roux to cool to room temperature or refrigerate. Tightly wrapped roux can be refrigerated for up to one month. Break off pieces as needed. Recipe can be doubled or tripled.

Green Beans, Potatoes and Ham in Redeye Gravy

Level: Easy
Serves 4
Preparation Time: 1½ hours

3	tablespoons canola oil
3	tablespoons all-purpose flour
1	large onion, chopped
1	boiled or smoked ham slice, ½-inch thick, cut into cubes
3	large red potatoes, peeled and cut in 1-inch cubes
1	(14.5-ounce) can whole green beans
1	tablespoon ground paprika
¼	teaspoon cayenne pepper
1	tablespoon salt
3-4	cups water

- Heat oil in a stockpot over medium heat. Add flour and chopped onion, stirring constantly until a golden roux forms.
- Add ham, potatoes, green beans and seasonings to stockpot.
- Stir in 3-4 cups of water and simmer over medium-low heat for 1 hour.
- Adjust seasonings.
- Cook's Tip: Serves 4 as a main dish with French bread or 8 as a side dish.

Asian Egg Drop Soup

Level: Easy
Serves 4
Preparation Time: 30 minutes

4	cups plus 2 tablespoons prepared chicken stock
1	tablespoon soy sauce
1	tablespoon cornstarch
2	eggs, lightly beaten
3	green onions, chopped, white and green parts
	Salt and white pepper, to taste

- Bring 4 cups soup stock and soy sauce to a boil. Make a slurry by combining cornstarch and 2 tablespoons of chicken stock. Stir until dissolved. Add cornstarch mixture slowly into stock, stirring stock constantly until thickened. Reduce heat to a simmer.
- Pour eggs slowly into stock while stirring soup in the same direction. The egg will spread and feather. Turn off heat and add green onions. Season with salt and pepper, and serve immediately.
- Cook's Tip: A slurry is a thin paste of water and flour, which is stirred into hot preparations such as soups, stews and sauces as a thickener. After the slurry is added, the mixture should be stirred and cooked for several minutes in order for the flour to lose its raw taste.

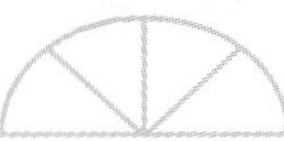

Maytag White Cheddar Cheese Soup

Level: Good Cook
Serves 4
Preparation Time: 30 minutes

¼ pound apple-smoked sliced bacon, cut in 1-inch pieces
2 tablespoons unsalted butter
½ cup chopped sweet onion
¼ cup chopped celery
¼ cup all-purpose flour
12 ounces pale ale
4 cups chicken stock
½ pound Maytag white Cheddar cheese, grated
Salt and black pepper, to taste
Toasted croutons, for garnish
Parsley or chives, for garnish

- Brown bacon in a stockpot and pour off excess drippings.
- Add butter, onion and celery to pot with bacon and cook over medium heat for 5 minutes.
- Sprinkle stockpot mixture with flour. Cook and stir constantly for 3 minutes. Whisk in pale ale and then chicken stock.
- Bring soup to a boil, reduce heat and simmer an additional 10 minutes.
- Add grated cheese and season with salt and black pepper, to taste.
- Do not boil soup after cheese is added.
- Ladle into bowls. Garnish with toasted croutons, parsley or chives.

Basil Tomato Soup

Level: Easy
Serves 6-8
Preparation Time: 1 hour

1 large red onion, diced
Canola oil
1 tablespoon minced fresh ginger
1 tablespoon brown sugar
4 cups whole Roma tomatoes, diced
5 cups chicken stock
1 cup packed basil leaves
Salt and black pepper, to taste

- Caramelize onion, ginger and sugar in a large saucepan with a little oil.
- Add tomatoes and bring to a simmer over medium heat.
- Season with salt and pepper.
- Pour stock into tomato mixture. Simmer on low heat approximately 20 minutes. Add basil and puree. Check for seasoning.
- Serve with *Windows'* Flaky Tomato Basil Biscuits.

A Missouri Window

In 1809, Joseph Charless founded the first newspaper in Missouri, the "Missouri Gazette."

A Culinary Reflection

My father prepared most of our meals while I was growing up. His favorite was a large pot of goulash with lots of spices. My three siblings and I would sit at the table with huge bowls of goulash steaming in front of us. At that time only my brother could appreciate the wonderful taste of my Dad's goulash. As soon as my Dad left the room, my sisters and I would pile our goulash in our brother's bowl. Now, I would give anything for a bowl of my Dad's goulash.

- Kelly O'Leary

A Chef's View

Top your Taco Soup with Chili-Cheese Croutons. Cut a French bread loaf into 16 slices and place on a baking sheet. Bake at 375 degrees for 5 minutes, turning slices once. Stir together ½ cup finely shredded Monterey Jack cheese, ⅓ cup butter and 3 teaspoons of chili powder and spread cheese mixture onto the toasted bread. Bake an additional 7 minutes. Use a pizza cutter to cut into cubes.

Spicy Black-Eyed Peas and Sausage

Level: Easy
Serves 6
Preparation Time: 1¼ hours

1 pound medium or hot ground pork sausage
1 small onion, chopped
2 garlic cloves, minced
2 (16-ounce) packages frozen black-eyed peas
4 cups chopped fresh tomatoes, or 2 (16-ounce) cans whole tomatoes, chopped with juices
½ cup water
1 teaspoon chili powder, or seasoned to taste
Black pepper, to taste

- Brown pork sausage until cooked in a skillet, stirring to crumble.
- Drain sausage, reserving 1 tablespoon drippings in skillet.
- Stir in onion and garlic and sauté 5 minutes.
- Return sausage to skillet and add black-eyed peas, tomatoes, water, chili powder and black pepper.
- Cover and simmer for 1 hour or until peas are tender. Serve warm.

Taco Soup

Level: Easy
Serves 6
Preparation Time: 1½ hours

1 pound ground beef or ground venison
2 large onions, chopped
1 (1-ounce) package taco seasoning
1 (10-ounce) can chopped tomatoes with chiles
1 (14.5-ounce) can diced tomatoes
1 (4-ounce) can tomato sauce
1 (14.5-ounce) can whole kernel corn, drained
1 (15-ounce) can chili beans
1 (15-ounce) can water
1 cup shredded Cheddar cheese

- Brown meat and onion in a large skillet. Drain.
- Stir in taco seasoning, tomatoes with chiles, diced tomatoes, tomato sauce, corn, chili beans and water.
- Add one can of water and stir.
- Simmer chili for 1 hour, stirring occasionally.
- Adjust seasonings, if necessary.
- Sprinkle with cheese before serving.
- Cook's Tip: Serve with corn chips or cornbread.

White Chili

Level: Easy
Serves 8-10
Preparation Time: 1 hour

1	(3-pound) chicken
1	tablespoon olive oil
2	medium onions, chopped
4	garlic cloves, minced
2	teaspoons ground cumin
¼	teaspoon ground cloves
¼	teaspoon cayenne pepper
1	teaspoon dried oregano leaves
2	(4-ounce) cans chopped mild or hot green chiles, to taste
2	(15-ounce) cans great Northern beans, drained and rinsed
4	cups chicken stock, from cooked chicken
3	cups shredded Monterey Jack cheese
	Sour cream, for garnish
	Shredded Cheddar cheese, for garnish
	Sliced jalapeño peppers, drained, for garnish

- Place chicken in a large pot. Cover with water and cook.
- Remove chicken to platter, bone when cool and dice into bite-size pieces.
- Reserve cooking liquid.
- Heat oil in a large stockpot. Sauté onion and garlic until translucent.
- Stir in cumin, cloves, cayenne pepper and oregano. Add chiles, chicken, beans and stock. Mix well.
- Simmer on medium-low heat for 30 minutes, stirring occasionally.
- Add Monterey Jack cheese and stir. Serve.
- Garnish bowls of chili with sour cream, Cheddar cheese and jalapeño peppers, as desired.

A Chef's View

Choose individual chiles rather than chili powders for a fresher taste. Anchos, with their sweet raisiny flavor are the most common mild chiles for a chili con carne. Like the chile taste but not the heat? Add New Mexico Reds and California chiles for a more complex flavor without turning up the heat. For extra fire, you may want to consider guajillo, de Arbol, pequín, japanais, jalapeños, habaneros or cayenne. If you taste as you cook, you can build the flavor and avoid a fiery, overly hot chili.

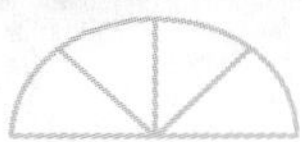

A Chef's View

Delicious and filling hot soups may stand alone as a complete meal. Never serve a hot soup warm. Warm bowls by placing in a clean dishwasher and placing the cycle on dry.

Creole Gumbo

Level: Good Cook
Serves 8
Preparation Time: 1½ hours

3	tablespoons butter
3	tablespoons all-purpose flour
1	medium onion, finely chopped
1	garlic clove, minced
1	slice cooked ham, cut into 1-inch cubes
1½	pounds fresh okra, cut into 1-inch rounds
1	(28-ounce) can tomatoes
1	teaspoon salt
¼	teaspoon black pepper
1	tablespoon Creole seasoning
2	pounds crabmeat
2	pounds raw shrimp, peeled and deveined
8	cups cooked rice

- Make a roux by melting butter in bottom of a large stockpot. Stir in flour until well blended, approximately 3-4 minutes or until the taste of flour is eliminated.
- Brown roux slowly while adding onion and garlic.
- Add ham and continue to brown but do not burn roux.
- Stir in okra, tomatoes, salt, black pepper and Creole seasoning.
- Cover and simmer at least 30 minutes over medium heat. Stir occasionally.
- Mix in crabmeat and shrimp ½ hour before serving. Cook over medium heat.
- Serve over cooked rice.

Lobster Bisque

Level: Good Cook
Serves 6
Preparation Time: 35 minutes

4	tablespoons butter, divided
2	tablespoons finely chopped fresh shallots
2	tablespoons finely chopped fresh chives
1	garlic clove, minced
½	medium onion, finely chopped
2	tablespoons all-purpose flour
3	cups skim milk
1	(10¾-ounce) can tomato soup
½	cup heavy cream
1	pound fresh or frozen lobster meat, cooked and cut into bite-size pieces
4	tablespoons light sherry
	Ground paprika, for garnish
	Ground white pepper, for garnish

- Sauté fresh shallots, chives, garlic and onion in 3 tablespoons melted butter in a medium-size skillet.
- Remove shallot mixture with slotted spoon and set aside.
- Add 1 additional tablespoon butter and flour to skillet. Stir constantly to make a roux. Cook 2-3 minutes.
- Pour milk gently into roux while stirring with a whisk.
- Add the tomato soup and continue whisking until mixture almost boils.
- Turn heat to low simmer. Stir in cream and shallot mixture.
- Fold in lobster.
- Heat thoroughly.
- Stir in sherry. Mix thoroughly.
- Pour in serving bowls.
- Garnish with paprika and ground white pepper.

A Culinary Reflection

When I was growing up, we had oyster stew every Christmas Eve at my Grandmother's house in Austin, Texas. She grew up in Missouri, so I don't know where the tradition started. It was quite awful, and I always ate a lot of crackers. When I got married and started my own family traditions, the oyster stew on Christmas Eve was not one of them. My Grandmother came to my house for Christmas when we were stationed in San Antonio (in the Air Force). I think that was the first time she realized that not everyone liked her oyster stew! By the way, I do love oysters, raw, fried or baked, just not her oyster stew!

~ Mary Ann Couch

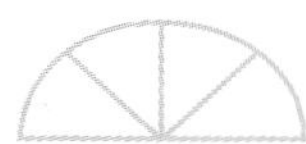

A Chef's View

To render fat is to melt animal fat over low heat so that it separated from any connective pieces of tissue, which, during rendering, turn brown and crisp and are generally referred to as cracklings. The resulting clear fat is then strained through a paper filter or fine cheesecloth to remove any residue.

To sweat vegetables is to cook them in a small amount of fat over low heat. The ingredients are covered with foil and then the pot is tightly covered. With this method, the ingredients soften without browning and cook in their own juices.

New England Clam Chowder

Level: Good Cook
Serves 8
Preparation Time: 1½ hours

¼ pound salt pork or bacon, finely minced
1 large onion, chopped
2 celery ribs, chopped
1 large leek, white and light green part only, chopped
2 tablespoons all-purpose flour
4 cups hot water
Salt and black pepper, to taste
1 pound russet potatoes, peeled and cubed
4 cups whole milk
2 (10-ounce) cans whole baby clams
Chives, for garnish
Oyster crackers

- Place salt pork or bacon in a stockpot and cook over medium-low heat to render fat.
- Add onion, celery and leeks and cook for 15 minutes over low heat to sweat vegetables without browning.
- Sprinkle vegetable mixture with flour, stirring to coat all vegetables evenly and creating a pale golden roux, approximately 2 minutes.
- Add hot water, stir to avoid lumps and season with salt and black pepper. Cook for 30 minutes at a constant simmer.
- Add potatoes and return to simmer. Allow to cook until potatoes are tender.
- Pour in milk and heat thoroughly but do not scorch or boil milk.
- Stir in clams, heat through and adjust the seasoning.
- Sprinkle with chives and serve with oyster crackers.

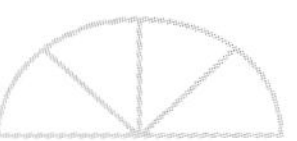

Tomato Tortellini Soup

Level: Easy
Serves 6
Preparation Time: 1 hour

4	teaspoons olive oil
½	cup chopped onion
1	cup chopped carrot
½	cup chopped fennel, optional
2	garlic cloves, minced
1	teaspoon dried basil leaves
1	teaspoon dried oregano leaves
1	bay leaf
4	cups canned whole tomatoes, in thick puree, chopped
2	cups water
2	cups chicken stock
1	(16-ounce) package dried cheese tortellini
2	cups fresh escarole or spinach, shredded
	Italian parsley, for garnish

- Heat olive oil in a large stockpot. Sauté onion, carrot, optional fennel and garlic. Cook until vegetables are crisp tender.
- Add basil, oregano and bay leaf, and cook 1 minute.
- Stir in chopped tomatoes, water and chicken stock. Cook 15 minutes.
- Add pasta, and cook until tortellini is tender, adding additional water, if necessary.
- Stir in escarole or spinach and cook 6 minutes.
- Garnish with Italian parsley.

A Missouri Window

The 'Missouri Waltz' became the state song under an act adopted by the General Assembly on June 30, 1949.

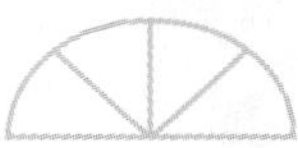

A Culinary Reflection

In true German fashion, my husband's family took a humble meal and turned it into a feast. This Christmas Eve tradition, Walterspiel Potato Soup, is served with hot bread and crisp salad before opening presents. It launches the anticipated festivities of the evening and it closes with bright-eyed children singing 'Happy Birthday Dear Jesus' over a candlelit pumpkin pie. Each child gets to blow out the candle so the last Advent candle is often used. The wax on the top of the pie isn't too bad with whipping cream and coffee.

~ Barbara Domann

Walterspiel Potato Soup

Level: Good Cook
Serves 6
Preparation Time: 1½ hours

4	slices bacon, diced
6	leeks, chopped
¼	cup chopped green onion
2	tablespoons all-purpose flour
4	cups beef bouillon
6	large red potatoes, peeled and thinly sliced
2	egg yolks, beaten
1	(16-ounce) carton sour cream
1	tablespoon minced fresh parsley
1	tablespoon minced fresh chervil

- Sauté bacon in a large deep saucepan for 5 minutes.
- Add leeks and onion and sauté an additional 5 minutes.
- Stir in flour and mix well.
- Slowly add bouillon and stir constantly.
- Add potatoes and simmer for 1 hour.
- Combine egg yolks and sour cream and slowly add to soup, stirring constantly.
- Simmer and stir for an additional 10 minutes.
- Add parsley and chervil.
- Serve with a salad and hot bread.

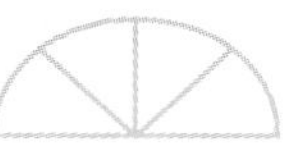

Mushroom Miso Soup

Level: Quick and Simple
Serves 6
Preparation Time: 30 minutes

½	teaspoon canola oil
4	green onions, finely chopped, reserve tops for garnish
2	garlic cloves, minced
1	teaspoon grated fresh ginger
½	cup carrots, diced
1½	cups freshly sliced shiitake mushrooms, divided
2	tablespoons miso
4	cups vegetable stock
1	tablespoon low-sodium soy sauce
2	tablespoons dry sherry, or to taste
1	teaspoon rice wine vinegar
	Dash hot pepper sauce, or to taste
1	cup diced firm tofu

- Heat canola oil in heavy saucepan over medium heat. Add green onions and garlic. Sauté until soft.
- Add fresh ginger, carrots and 1 cup mushrooms. Cook an additional 5 minutes or until vegetables are crisp tender.
- Dissolve miso in vegetable stock and add to vegetables in the saucepan along with the soy sauce, sherry and vinegar. Add hot sauce to taste.
- Add diced tofu.
- Reheat soup. Ladle into cups and garnish with green onion tops and reserved shiitake mushroom slices.

A Chef's View

Miso, also called bean paste, has the consistency of peanut butter and comes in a wide variety of flavors and colors. This fermented soybean paste has three basic categories - barley miso, rice miso, and soybean miso - all of which are developed by injecting cooked soybeans with mold cultivated in either a barley, rice or soybean base. Miso is used in sauces, soups, marinades, dips, main dishes, salad dressings and as a table condiment. It's easily digested and extremely nutritious, having rich amounts of B vitamins and protein. Miso can be found in Japanese markets and natural food stores. It should be refrigerated in an airtight container.

A Chef's View

Textured vegetable protein is a bland-tasting, dried, granular product produced from highly refined defatted soybean meal. It's used in soybean burgers and other soy meat products, and can be used as an extender in processed foods from breakfast cereal to frozen desserts. TVP can be found in bulk and 1-pound bags in natural food stores.

Textured Vegetable Protein Soup

Level: Easy
Serves 4
Preparation Time: 3 hours

1	cup textured vegetable protein (TVP), granules or chunks
3	cups water
	Ketchup or steak sauce, for flavor, to taste
2	tablespoons canola oil
4	cups assorted seasonal vegetables, chopped into bite-size pieces
4	cups tomato juice
	Salt and black pepper, to taste
	Garlic cloves, sliced or minced, to taste
	Fresh basil leaves, chopped, to taste
	Chili spice, for a chili flavor
2	cups canned red beans, optional

- Rehydrate TVP with water for 20 minutes adding dash of ketchup or steak sauce for flavor.
- Heat oil in a large stock pot. Add TVP with water and cook for 15 minutes; stirring occasionally.
- Add vegetables and cook for 10-15 minutes over medium heat, stirring occasionally. Water, in small amounts, may be added to keep moist.
- Pour tomato juice into pot. Add herbs and seasonings. Gently simmer soup for 1-2 hours.
- Stir in chili seasoning, if using.
- Stir in red beans 10-15 minutes before serving and simmer. Adjust seasonings.

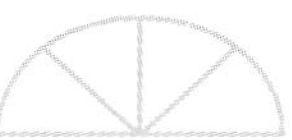

Beef Stock

Level: Easy
Yield: 1½ quarts
Preparation Time: 5 hours

- 3 pounds beef shank bones, cut into pieces
- 4 lean short ribs of beef
- 1 medium onion, quartered
- 2 carrots, quartered
- 2 celery ribs, quartered
- 2½ quarts water
- 1 (14-ounce) can tomatoes, drained
- 8 parsley sprigs
- 4 sprigs thyme, or ½ teaspoon dried
- 1 bay leaf
- 4 black peppercorns

- ◆ Preheat oven to 450 degrees.
- ◆ Place beef bones and short ribs in a large roasting pan. Brown in oven for 40 minutes, stirring once or twice.
- ◆ Add onion, carrots and celery and continue cooking until bones and vegetables are well browned, approximately 20 minutes.
- ◆ Remove roasted meat and vegetables from roasting pan and put in a large stockpot.
- ◆ Pour off all the fat in the roasting pan and add 1 cup of water. Bring to a boil, scraping the bottom of the pan to dislodge any brown bits. Add to stockpot.
- ◆ Add 9 cups water, tomatoes, parsley stems, thyme, bay leaf and peppercorns to stockpot.
- ◆ Bring to a boil and skim the foam that rises to the surface. Reduce heat and simmer stock, partially covered, for 4 hours.
- ◆ Strain. Press the bones and vegetables firmly with a rubber spatula to get all the liquid.
- ◆ Skim fat from surface of stock if using immediately.
- ◆ Refrigerate for up to one week or freeze in 1-cup containers for future use. Scrape off fat before using.
- ◆ Cook's Tip: Milder in flavor than beef stock, veal stock is made in exactly the same way, with veal bones in place of beef.

A Missouri Window

In 1881, Governor Thomas Crittenden offered a $5000 reward for the arrest and conviction of members of the Jesse James gang. The next year, Bob Ford killed Jesse James in St. Joseph. To this day, speculation exists as to whether or not Jesse James was actually killed.

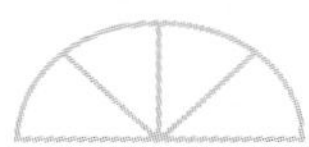

A Chef's View

Stocks made from scratch create a richer base for soups and stews as does the replacement of some of the milk in a recipe with cream.

Often times soups, sauces, and stews are seasoned by creating a bouquet garni. Place 1 small peeled and quartered onion, 1 garlic clove, 1 sprig thyme, 1 bay leaf, 4 sprigs of fresh parsley and 10 black peppercorns on a square of cheese cloth. Tie the packet with twine to enclose the ingredients.

A Chef's View

Most soups freeze well. However, cubed vegetables tend to go mealy, especially potatoes. Better results are obtained when vegetables are shredded.

Chicken Stock

Level: Easy
Yield: 3 quarts
Preparation Time: 3 hours

1	(5-pound) roasting chicken, cut into parts
1	large onion, peeled and quartered
1	large carrot, quartered
6	celery ribs, quartered
15	parsley sprigs
10	black peppercorns
4	quarts water

- Put all ingredients in a large stockpot.
- Bring to a boil and skim the foam that rises to the surface.
- Reduce heat and simmer, partially covered, for 2 hours.
- Strain. Press chicken and vegetables with a rubber spatula to get all the liquid.
- Skim fat from surface if using stock immediately.
- Refrigerate for up to a week or freeze in 1-cup containers for future use. Scrape off fat before using.

Vegetable Stock

Level: Easy
Yield: 2 quarts
Preparation Time: 1 hour

6	small onions, chopped
8	carrots, chopped
3	celery ribs, chopped
1	small bunch parsley
4	sprigs thyme, or ½ teaspoon dried
2	bay leaves
1½	teaspoons black peppercorns
6	garlic cloves, sliced
2½	quarts water

- Place all ingredients in a 6-quart stockpot.
- Bring to boil. Reduce heat and simmer stock, partially covered for 45 minutes.
- Strain. Press vegetables firmly to get all liquid.
- Refrigerate in a covered container for up to 4 days or freeze in 1-cup containers for future use.

Vistas of Bountiful Harvests

Pasta & Grains

A Missouri Window

Trails West

Kansas City is the western anchor to Missouri. The heart of the Kansas City area encompasses an all-American city with a distinctly European flavor, complementing its heartland appeal with the dazzling fountains of Rome, bold architecture of Spain, and the wide boulevards of Paris.

Shopping, dining, and nightlife are all part of Country Club Plaza, developed in the 1920s as America's first shopping center, with fountains and Moorish architecture. The historic Westport district hosts great live blues and jazz. Kansas City's famous barbecue, baseball Royals or football Chiefs, and the majestic Union Station, beautifully restored, make this western frontier a pleasure to visit.

Historically, Clay and Platte counties, located in northern part of Kansas City, awestruck Lewis and Clark on their way up the Missouri River. Its "extensive open prairies, hills and valleys, scattering trees, and handsome creeks" were documented in their journal in July 1804.

Just east of Kansas City is Independence, with the home and presidential library of Harry S Truman. The supply point for the Santa Fe, Oregon, and California Trails is situated at the National Frontier Trails Center.

Photos: The Country Club Plaza Fountains, Union Station, Kansas City & Harry S Truman Monument, Independence

During the 1920s, a group of Clay County physician spouses formed the Clay County Medical Association Auxiliary. By the 1950s, the Auxiliary was hard at work sponsoring the future nurse's club and scholarships at various Northland High Schools. Teaching good health practices in the 1960s led to fundraisers to promote vaccines for children. During the 1970s, many gowns and diapers were dispensed to various hospital pediatric units for children. In 1983, the Auxiliary expanded its borders to Platte County and became known as the Clay-Platte County Medical Society Auxiliary. In the 1990s, Alliance members provided underprivileged families with *Cash for Car Seats* to protect children. Recently, the *Stop America's Violence Everywhere Campaign - SAVE* project fully expanded. The Alliance continues to support the family shelter, Safehaven, with time and funding.

Clay-Platte Medical Society Alliance

Current and future projects include teaching middle school children the importance of non-violence. In cooperation with Synergy, a family shelter, the Alliance is commencing a new reading program for shelter children. Changes have occurred throughout the years but one thing has remained constant: this organization gives freely of its time, talent, and treasure to support the health of the citizens in Kansas City's Northland.

The following members have served as MSMA Alliance presidents: Mrs. William A. Goodson, 1934-35; Mrs. Evora Williams, 1967-68; Mary Kay McPhee, 1975-76; Ina May Fakhoury, 1980-81; Polly Bowles, 1984-85; and Gayle Vilmer, 1986-87. Mrs. McPhee also served as an American Medical Association Alliance president in 1985-86.

Medical Alliance of the Metropolitan Medical Society of Greater Kansas City

The Woman's Auxiliary to the Jackson County Medical Society was founded in May 1924 by Mrs. E. H. Skinner, who served as the first president. Eventually, the Jackson County Medical Auxiliary became the Medical Alliance of the Metropolitan Medical Society of Greater Kansas City in 1995.

For 78 years, the Alliance has worked to: 1) be informed of legislation at the state and national levels impacting the medical community; 2) raise funds for medical and nursing education; 3) promote awareness and programs for community wellness issues; and 4) provide opportunities for service and continuing education of its members. Timely information on current state and national legislation is provided for members. Funds for the AMA Foundation have been raised since 1924. In 1948, the Student Nurses Loan Fund was instituted to provide interest-free loans and grants.

Early health promotion activities began in the 1920s and '30s with issues of health and hygiene. Throughout the next 50 years, the Alliance provided funds and volunteers for many local health groups, and utilized radio and television for health promotions such as breast cancer awareness, blood drives, and health programs in school districts. The turn of a new century saw Alliance support for the Free Health Clinic of Kansas City, the *Stop America's Violence Everywhere Campaign - SAVE* project, tissue and organ donation, and osteoporosis diagnosis and prevention.

The first MSMA Alliance president was from Jackson County, Mrs. George H. Hoxie, 1924-25. She was followed by Mrs. A. W. McAlester, 1930-31; Mrs. Herbert Mantz, 1938-39; Mrs. M. Gilkey, 1945-46; Mrs. Dwight T. Van Del McLean, 1950-51; Marie Leitz, 1955-56; Jane Wade, 1961-62; Wilda Stacey, 1966-67; Vivian Lytton, 1974-75; Pat Stelmach, 1977-78; Jackie Sanders, 1983-84; Sandra Mitchell, 1987-88; Mary Hunkeler, 1991-92; and Carol Jean DeFeo, 2002-03. Mrs. Hoxie and Mrs. Mitchell also served as American Medical Association Alliance presidents.

Baked Vermicelli with Spinach and Mushrooms

Level: Easy
Serves 10-12
Preparation Time: 1 hour

1	pound fresh mushrooms, sliced
5	green onions, sliced, white and green parts
5	tablespoons butter, divided
2	tablespoons all-purpose flour
2	cups milk
2	tablespoons sherry, optional
1	teaspoon salt
⅛	teaspoon black pepper
¼	teaspoon dried basil leaves
	Dash ground nutmeg
1	(8-ounce) package vermicelli
2	cups grated mozzarella cheese
2	cups cooked fresh or frozen spinach, well-drained

- Preheat oven to 350 degrees. Coat a 12x8x2-inch baking dish with cooking spray.
- Sauté mushrooms and green onions in 3 tablespoons butter. Set aside.
- Make a white sauce by cooking 2 tablespoons butter and flour in a saucepan over low heat. Stir constantly.
- Add milk, sherry, salt, black pepper, basil and nutmeg to white sauce. Stir and keep warm.
- Cook vermicelli al dente. Drain. Keep warm.
- Assemble casserole by layering half each of the vermicelli, mushrooms, onions and cheese.
- Spread all of spinach over first layer.
- Layer remaining ingredients in order ending with cheese.
- Pour white sauce over all.
- Bake, uncovered, for 30 minutes or until warmed throughout.

A Chef's View

Al Dente is an Italian phrase meaning 'to the tooth.' It is used to describe pasta that is cooked only until it offers slight resistance when bitten into.

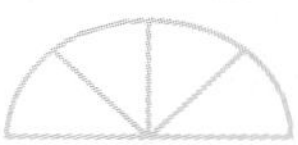

A Culinary Reflection

One of my original cooking mentors was my friend's mother, Faustina. She was a second-generation Italian American. She baked delicious homemade pizza. We didn't have a pizzeria in our town for years. So being the lucky girl with an Italian friend, I learned the love of pizza and cooking by experience. She taught me to eat first, then gave me the desire to learn how to cook it. Spaghetti, lasagna, meat and cheese ravioli - she taught it all. My favorite was making ravioli, which was an all-day session. The Old World way was to cover the beds with sheets, and dry the ravioli on them. It was great fun and kept our interest. Faustina's recipes are still some of my family favorites. She had my six-year-old daughter writing her first recipes and asking for other recipes wherever we went. The chocolate chip cookie recipe written by the hand of a six-year-old is still my favorite.

~ Millie Bever

Christmas Angel Pasta

Level: Easy
Serves 8-10
Preparation Time: 45 minutes

4	cups cooked angel hair pasta
4	eggs, separated
1	(12-ounce) can evaporated skim milk
1	cup (4-ounces) shredded reduced-fat Swiss cheese
1	(4-ounce) can chopped green chiles, drained
1	(13-ounce) can artichoke hearts, drained and quartered
½	cup chopped red bell pepper
¼	cup sliced red onion
½	teaspoon ground cumin
3	egg whites
½	cup freshly grated Parmesan cheese, grated
½	cup fresh parsley, snipped
½	cup reduced-fat sour cream
½	cup salsa

- Preheat oven to 325 degrees. Coat a 13x9x2-inch baking dish with cooking spray.
- Spread cooked angel hair pasta evenly over bottom of baking dish.
- Combine egg yolks, evaporated skim milk, Swiss cheese, green chiles, artichoke hearts, red bell pepper, red onion and cumin in a large bowl. Mix well.
- Beat egg whites until stiff peaks form. Fold beaten egg whites into egg mixture, combining gently.
- Pour over pasta.
- Top with freshly grated Parmesan cheese and parsley.
- Bake for 30 minutes or until set.
- Top with sour cream and salsa.
- Serve immediately.

Twin Oaks Country Club Linguine with Feta Cheese and Shrimp

Level: Easy
Serves 1
Preparation Time: 45 minutes

- 6 ounces linguine pasta, cooked al dente
- 6 shrimp, shelled, deveined and grilled
- 4 tablespoons extra-virgin olive oil
- 1 teaspoon chopped garlic
- 7 pieces sun-dried cherry tomatoes
- ⅛ cup chopped walnuts
- ½ ounce crumbled feta cheese
- Salt and black pepper, to taste

- Keep prepared pasta and shrimp warm.
- Heat oil in a skillet and then add garlic, sun-dried tomatoes and walnuts. Cook and stir.
- Add pasta and shrimp. Toss until pasta is well coated.
- Sprinkle with cheese. Toss.
- Season with salt and black pepper, to taste.

Linguine with Basil Tomato Sauce

Level: Easy
Serves 4-6
Preparation Time: 2½ hours

- 6 large ripe tomatoes
- 1 lemon, juiced
- 2 large garlic cloves, chopped
- 1 teaspoon salt
- ¼ teaspoon red pepper flakes
- ½ cup fresh chopped basil leaves
- ½ cup chopped fresh parsley leaves
- ½ cup extra-virgin olive oil
- 1 pound linguine, cooked al dente
- 1 cup feta cheese crumbles, for garnish
- Parsley sprigs, for garnish

- Dip tomatoes in boiling water for 2 minutes to loosen skin.
- Peel tomatoes and chop. Place in a medium-size bowl.
- Add lemon juice, garlic, salt, red pepper flakes, basil and parsley to tomatoes. Stir to coat tomatoes and then add olive oil.
- Cover and let marinate at room temperature for at least 2 hours.
- Prepare linguine according to package directions for al dente pasta.
- Pour seasoned tomatoes over hot pasta.
- Garnish with generous amounts of crumbled feta cheese and fresh parsley sprigs.

A Show-Me Specialty

Feta Cheese and Shrimp Pasta is a specialty of the Twin Oaks Country Club Restaurant in Springfield, Missouri.

Twin Oaks
Country Club Restaurant
1020 East State
Highway M
Springfield
417-881-4744

A Chef's View

There's a fine line between undercooked and overcooked pasta. Undercooked pasta is hard and raw tasting. Overcooked pasta tastes doughy and gummy. Pasta that is cooked just right is completely tender, but still firm.

A Chef's View

Can't decide which pasta to use for a particular sauce? Remember: the thinner the sauce, the longer the pasta. Long pastas include spaghetti, linguine, and vermicelli. The twists and turns of short pasta, such as penne, fusilli, and farfalle, trap the thicker sauces. Fettuccini is perfect for Alfredo sauce, while penne or ziti work well with thick tomato sauce.

Penne Spinach Casserole

Level: Easy
Serves 6
Preparation Time: 30 minutes

- 2 cups uncooked penne pasta
- 1 (10-ounce) box frozen spinach, thawed and well-drained
- ½ teaspoon dried oregano
- 1 (15-ounce) can kidney beans, drained and rinsed
- ¾ cup nonfat ricotta cheese
- ⅓ cup grated Parmesan cheese, divided
- 1 tablespoon garlic powder
- 1 (28-ounce) can crushed tomatoes
- ½ cup grated nonfat mozzarella cheese

- ◆ Cook penne pasta according to package directions. Drain and place in a large mixing bowl.
- ◆ Toss with spinach, oregano, beans, ricotta, 3 tablespoons Parmesan cheese and garlic powder.
- ◆ Coat a 13x9x2-inch casserole dish with cooking spray.
- ◆ Place ⅓ of the crushed tomatoes in bottom of casserole followed with one-half the pasta mixture. Follow with another third of the crushed tomatoes, the remainder of the pasta mixture and the last of the crushed tomatoes.
- ◆ Cover and bake in the microwave oven until heated through, approximately 10-15 minutes, depending upon the power of the microwave.
- ◆ Top with grated mozzarella cheese and microwave for 3 additional minutes or until cheese melts.
- ◆ Serve with additional grated Parmesan cheese.

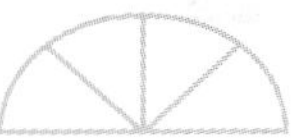

Spaghetti with Roasted Vegetable Sauce

Level: Easy
Serves 4
Preparation Time: 45 minutes

8	ounces uncooked spaghetti
2	large ripe tomatoes, cored, halved and seeded
1	small onion, chopped
1	garlic clove, sliced
½	green bell pepper
½	(6-ounce) can tomato paste
¼	cup fresh basil leaves
	Salt and freshly ground black pepper, to taste
4	tablespoons freshly grated Parmesan cheese, grated

- Preheat oven broiler.
- Cook pasta according to package directions and drain. Keep warm.
- Place tomatoes, onion, garlic and bell pepper skin side up on a flat cookie sheet.
- Roast under the broiler until vegetable skins turn brown and look blistered, approximately 10 minutes.
- Place vegetables, along with any juices, into a food processor. Add tomato paste and fresh basil; puree until smooth.
- Pour into a saucepan and heat until warm. Adjust seasoning with salt and black pepper, to taste.
- Serve over cooked spaghetti and sprinkle with freshly grated Parmesan cheese and cracked black pepper.

A Chef's View

Red pepper flakes are ground dried red chiles. They give a welcome kick to many vegetable sauces for pasta. Grind them yourself in a spice grinder from whole dried red chiles. Your taste suggests the amount to use but begin with ¼ teaspoon in a sauce for a pound of pasta.

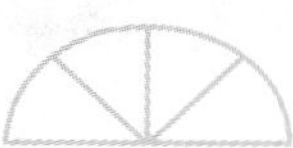

A Chef's View

The next time you make pasta, cook more than you need. Follow package directions, except omit the salt and butter or margarine. Rinse and drain well. Line custard cups or small plastic food containers with plastic wrap. Fill with pasta and freeze until firm. Remove frozen pasta from containers, wrap individually, and store in a large freezer bag. When you need pasta, simply unwrap the amount you need and drop into a pot of boiling water. Cook 1 minute. Drain and serve.

Tagliatelle with Wild Mushrooms, Peas and Prosciutto

Level: Good Cook
Serves 4
Preparation Time: 30 minutes

4	tablespoons softened unsalted butter, divided
1	tablespoon olive oil
⅓	cup minced shallots
12	ounces wild mushrooms, such as shiitake, oyster or cèpes, rinsed, trimmed and sliced
1	teaspoon minced fresh thyme
	Salt and pepper, to taste
1	cup small fresh or frozen peas, thawed
½	cup slivered prosciutto
1	cup heavy cream
12	ounces tagliatelle pasta
	Freshly grated Parmesan

- Heat 2 tablespoon of butter and oil over moderate heat. Add shallots and cook, stirring, 3 minutes, or until softened.
- Cook tagliatelle in a large pot of boiling salted water until al dente. Drain and transfer to a serving bowl. Add remaining 2 tablespoons of butter to pasta and toss to combine.
- Add mushrooms, thyme and salt and pepper, to taste, to the shallot mixture. Stir.
- Cook mushroom and shallot mixture, stirring occasionally, for 7 minutes, or until mushrooms are lightly golden.
- Stir in prosciutto and peas and cook for 2 minutes, or until heated through.
- Add cream and simmer just until lightly thickened.
- Pour sauce over buttered pasta and toss to coat.
- Serve with Parmesan cheese.

Fettuccini with Shrimp Sauce

Level: Easy
Serves 6
Preparation Time: 30 minutes

3	pounds shrimp, peeled, deveined and butterflied
3	quarts boiling water
¼	pound (1 stick) butter
¾	cup extra-virgin olive oil
1	cup chopped onion
3	garlic cloves, minced
¼	cup chopped fresh parsley
1	teaspoon dried oregano leaves
½	cup Sauterne, or sweet white wine
⅓	cup Italian salad dressing
½	cup water
4	teaspoons chicken bouillon granules
	Black pepper, to taste
1	(12-ounce) package fettuccini, cooked al dente

- Place shrimp in rapidly boiling water for 30 seconds. Drain and place in a broiler pan.
- Combine butter and olive oil in a saucepan and heat until butter melts.
- Add onion, garlic, parsley and oregano and cook over medium heat until onion is almost translucent.
- Stir in wine, salad dressing, water, chicken bouillon and black pepper. Cook until bouillon is dissolved. Reduce heat to low and simmer for 5 minutes.
- Turn on broiler element in stove.
- Pour mixture over shrimp and broil 4 inches from heat for 5 minutes.
- Turn shrimp and broil for an additional 5 minutes.
- Place warm cooked noodles on a large platter and pour shrimp sauce over to coat noodles. Arrange shrimp on top.
- Serve.

A Chef's View

The ever-popular Fettuccine Alfredo was created in the 1920s by the Italian restaurateur Alfredo di Lello. The sauce for this divine creation is made of butter, Parmesan cheese, heavy cream, and freshly ground black pepper. It is served over - what else but - fettuccine noodles.

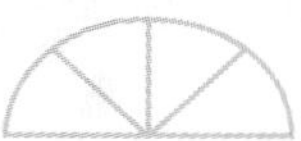

A Show-Me Specialty

Lampe Scampi and Angel Hair Pasta is a specialty of Rick's Restaurant downtown Columbia, Missouri.

Rick's
38 North Eighth
Columbia
573-442-7881

A Chef's View

There are over 200 varieties of cheese around the world. Most are made in France, Italy, Germany, Holland, Switzerland, Scandinavia, the British Isles, the United States, and Canada. Many cheeses are named for the place they were invented. Cheddar cheese was first made in England near a small town called Cheddar. Parmesan cheese was first made in Parma, Italy.

Rick's Lampe Scampi and Angel Hair Pasta

Level: Good Cook
Serves 1
Preparation Time: 40 minutes

4	ounces uncooked angel hair pasta
	Water
6	tablespoons margarine, divided
6	shrimp (16-20 count), peeled, deveined, headless and tails off
2	teaspoons minced garlic
¼	pound mushrooms, ¼-inch slices
1	tablespoon bourbon
2	tablespoons dry white wine
½	lemon, juiced
½	teaspoon Dijon-style mustard
	Chopped parsley, as desired
¼	tomato, ½-inch dice

- Cook angel hair pasta in boiling water to al dente. Keep warm.
- Melt 2 tablespoons margarine in a skillet while pasta is cooking.
- Sauté shrimp, garlic and mushrooms.
- Add bourbon and flambé by adding flame to inside of sauté pan with a fireplace match.
- Stir carefully until flame subsides.
- Add wine and lemon juice, reduce by ½ volume.
- Stir in remaining 4 tablespoons margarine, mustard, parsley and tomato.
- Place pasta in center of serving plate. Surround with shrimp.
- Pour sauce over pasta and shrimp. Serve hot.

Elegant Pesto

Level: Quick and Simple
Yield: 1 cup
Preparation Time: 10 minutes

1 garlic clove, peeled
3 tablespoons pine nuts
½ cup extra-virgin olive oil
2 cups fresh basil, medium packed
1 tablespoon butter, melted
1 tablespoon water
½ cup freshly grated Romano cheese

- Crush the garlic in a food processor. Add pine nuts and olive oil. Pulse until nuts are chopped.
- Add basil and process until smooth.
- Melt butter, add water and cheese to basil mixture and process until well-blended.
- Cook's Tip: Serve over cooked pasta or grilled fish.

Pasta with Smoked Salmon

Level: Easy
Serves 4
Preparation Time: 45 minutes

1 cup heavy cream
1 cup sour cream
2 cups flaked smoked salmon
4 tablespoons tomato paste
4 tablespoons *Windows'* Elegant Pesto
1 sprig fresh rosemary
3 tablespoons chopped garlic
6 tablespoons minced garlic chives
3 tablespoons lemon juice, freshly squeezed
2 tablespoons freshly grated lime peel
2 pounds pasta, any type
1 cup grated Parmesan cheese

- Heat heavy cream and sour cream together in a large saucepan.
- Add all remaining ingredients except pasta and cheese. Cover and simmer ½ hour.
- Cook pasta and ladle sauce over.
- Sprinkle with cheese and serve.

A Chef's View

Pesto comes from the Italian word 'Pestare' which means to pound or to bruise. The classic way to make pesto is with a mortar and pestle, but today it is easier to use a blender or food processor. Ingredients can include a variety of herbs, garlic, nuts, salt, olive oil, and cheese, along with black and red beans and sun-dried tomatoes. Pesto can be kept in the refrigerator and used as a dip or to enhance sauces, soups or stews. Pesto can be frozen in ice cube trays, then transferred to plastic bags and stored in the freezer.

Pine nuts, also called piñon or pignoli, are derived from the pine cones of several varieties of pine trees. The process of retrieving these nuts is very labor intensive, which accounts for their expense. Because they are high in fat, pine nuts turn rancid quickly. They should be stored in an airtight container in the refrigerator for up to 3 months or frozen for up to 9 months. To toast pine nuts, cook in a dry frying pan over medium heat for 1 to 2 minutes until lightly golden.

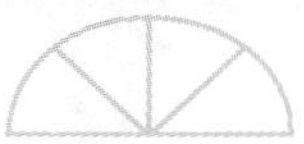

Chicken and Noodle Casserole

Level: Easy
Serves 15
Preparation Time: 1½ hours

5	whole chicken breasts, with skin
2	ribs celery, chopped
1	(12-ounce) package frozen noodles
5	cups chicken stock
2	chicken bouillon cubes
1	(8-ounce) package cream cheese, cubed
1	small white onion, chopped
¼	teaspoon garlic powder
½	teaspoon salt, optional
1	(10¾-ounce) can cream of mushroom soup
1	(10¾-ounce) can cream of celery soup
1	cup sour cream
1	cup buttered bread crumbs, or 1 cup shredded Cheddar cheese

- Add chicken breasts and celery to a large pot. Cover with water and cook until tender or approximately 1 hour. Drain and cool.
- Remove bone, skin and shred chicken.
- Line bottom of a greased 13x9x2-inch casserole dish with shredded chicken.
- Prepare frozen noodles in 5 cups of chicken stock with bouillon cubes. Cook according to packages directions until noodles are tender.
- Add cream cheese, onion, garlic powder, optional salt, soups and sour cream.
- Pour over chicken in casserole dish.
- Refrigerate or freeze at this time. Wrap tightly with aluminum foil when freezing.
- Preheat oven to 350 degrees.
- Top with bread crumbs or Cheddar cheese before baking.
- Bake for 1 hour uncovered or until cheese melts and casserole is bubbly.
- Cook's Tip: If frozen, partially thaw in the refrigerator and then bake for an additional 10-15 minutes, or until heated through. Tent with foil, if needed, to prevent cheese from excess browning.

A Chef's View

Try these different ways to use Windows' Elegant Pesto.

- *Stir 2 tablespoons pesto into an 8-ounce carton of commercial sour cream for an instant dip.*
- *Serve warmed pesto as a topper for baked potatoes. Allow about 1 tablespoon per potato.*
- *Spread a small amount of pesto over slices of French bread, and then toast them before serving.*
- *Stir about 3 tablespoons pesto into a can of tomato soup, dilute as the can directs.*
- *Try pesto as an omelet filling. Spoon about 2 tablespoons over half of a 3-egg omelet, fold it over, and serve.*
- *Stir 2 tablespoons pesto into ½ cup softened unsalted butter. Serve the pesto butter as a bread spread or toss it with hot vegetables. Melt the butter for dipping shrimp or lobster.*

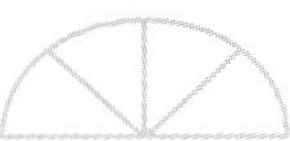

Macaroni with Turkey Marinara Sauce

Level: Easy
Serves 4
Preparation Time: 2½ hours

- 2 pounds turkey thighs or drumsticks
- 1 (15½-ounce) jar spaghetti sauce with mushrooms
- ½ cup red wine
- 1 (4-ounce) can mushroom pieces, undrained
- 1 green bell pepper, chopped
- 1 onion, cut into wedges
- 10 ounces macaroni, uncooked
- Fresh parsley, for garnish
- Freshly grated Parmesan or Romano cheese, for garnish

- ◆ Rinse turkey.
- ◆ Place in a large Dutch oven and cover with spaghetti sauce, wine, mushrooms, green pepper and onion.
- ◆ Bring to a boil.
- ◆ Reduce heat, cover and simmer for 2 hours.
- ◆ Remove turkey and bone. Continue to cook sauce an additional 10-15 minutes on medium to reduce and thicken.
- ◆ Cook macaroni according to package directions. Drain and place in large bowl.
- ◆ Return turkey to sauce and heat through. Pour over macaroni and garnish with fresh chopped parsley and freshly grated Parmesan or Romano cheese.

A Chef's View

Pasta Cooking Tips

◆ *Start with fresh of good-quality dried pasta and use ample water - 6 quarts for up to 1 pound of pasta.*

◆ *Salt water just before adding pasta - 3½ tablespoons per 6 quarts of water.*

◆ *Prevent pasta from sticking together by stirring frequently not by adding oil.*

◆ *Undercook pasta by a minute or two if adding pasta to a sauce, as it will simmer in the sauce.*

◆ *Serve the pasta the moment it's done.*

◆ *Heat serving bowls to keep pasta and its sauce warm.*

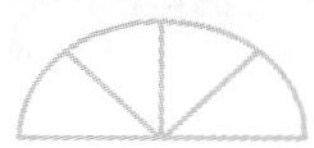

A Culinary Reflection

When I was growing up my family would visit my immigrant Italian grandparents every Sunday afternoon. My mother's stepfather, Theodore, greeted us as soon as we entered the kitchen with a tiny glass of his full-bodied, very dry red wine. His cheeks and the tip of his nose were rosy red, and his bewhiskered face showing his pride as each little tike raised a tiny glass of wine and shouted, "Salud!" The kitchen was always the heart of family celebrating. Plates were laden with hard-crusted bread baked in an outdoor stone oven, olives of all kinds, freshly grated cheese, red sauce to accompany meatballs, and slow-cooked chicken; and, of course, we ate every tasty bite. After appetites were happily satisfied, the adults moved into the living room for coffee, cordials, pipes, cigars, and grown-up conversation. A couple of the mothers would attend to the kids for dessert with ice cream, cake, and all kinds of Italian cookies and sweets. Now these foods are tangible only through my lingering childhood memories.

– Mary Catherine Heimburger

Noodles with Beefy Three Cheese Sauce

Level: Easy
Serves 8
Preparation Time: 50 minutes

1	pound ground beef
½	teaspoon garlic salt, or to taste
¼	teaspoon black pepper, or to taste
2	(8-ounce) cans tomato sauce
1	cup small-curd cottage cheese
1	(8-ounce) package cream cheese, softened and cubed
½	cup sour cream
½	cup chopped green onion, white and green parts
1	(8-ounce) package medium-wide egg noodles
½	cup grated Parmesan cheese
2	tablespoons butter, melted

- Preheat oven to 350 degrees. Coat a 13x9x2-inch casserole dish with cooking spray.
- Brown ground beef. Drain and then season beef with garlic salt and black pepper.
- Stir tomato sauce into ground beef.
- Combine cottage cheese, cream cheese, sour cream and onion in a saucepan. Cook and stir over low heat until warm.
- Cook noodles to al dente. Drain and rinse noodles.
- Place noodles in the bottom of casserole dish and pour meat mixture over noodles.
- Sprinkle with Parmesan cheese.
- Pour heated cheese mixture over meat and drizzle with melted butter.
- Bake for 30 minutes or until bubbly.

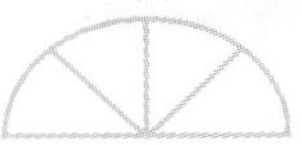

Penne with Asparagus and Shaved Ham

Level: Easy
Serves 4-6
Preparation Time: 30 minutes

4	tablespoons butter
½	onion, finely chopped
1	pound asparagus, trimmed of tough end stems
½	pound shaved ham
1	cup heavy cream
	Salt and black pepper, to taste
1	pound penne pasta
	Romano cheese, freshly grated

- Sauté onion and asparagus in butter until asparagus is tender and onion is translucent, approximately 10 minutes.
- Add ham and sauté for an additional 3-4 minutes.
- Stir in cream and simmer for 10-15 minutes. Season with salt and black pepper, to taste.
- Prepare pasta according to package directions. Drain.
- Pour cream mixture over cooked pasta and toss. Generously sprinkle with freshly grated Romano cheese.
- Serve immediately.

Coconut Ginger Rice

Level: Easy
Serves 6
Preparation Time: 30 minutes

2	tablespoons canola oil
¼	cup peeled julienned fresh ginger
2	cups long-grain white rice, rinsed
4	cups water
½	cup canned coconut milk, stirred well
4	green onions, white and green parts, divided
1½	teaspoons salt, or to taste
¼	teaspoon cracked black peppercorns, or to taste

- Heat oil in a skillet over medium heat until hot, but not smoking.
- Cook and stir ginger for 2 minutes, or until fragrant.
- Add rice and cook, stirring for 1 minute, or until rice crackles.
- Pour water and coconut milk into rice mixture. Stir in 2 chopped green onions, salt and pepper.
- Reduce heat to low, cover and cook for 20-25 minutes, or until the rice is cooked through.
- Serve hot rice garnished with the 2 remaining thinly sliced green onions.

A Missouri Window

In 1865, slavery was abolished in Missouri by an ordinance of immediate emancipation, making Missouri the first slave state to emancipate its slaves before the adoption of the 13th Amendment to the U.S. Constitution.

A Chef's View

Rice tips:

- *To keep rice grains separate, add a tablespoon of butter or oil to the water.*
- *To avoid gummy rice, do not stir simmering rice, as this mashes the grains.*
- *To prevent scorching, simmer rice in a heavy pan.*
- *To keep rice warm before serving, place it in a covered baking dish in a warm oven.*
- *To add more flavor, simmer rice in broth or broth mixed with water.*
- *To salvage watery rice, fluff it with a fork over low heat to evaporate the water.*

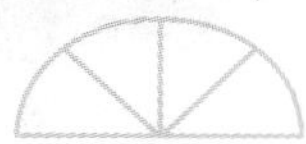

A Chef's View

A few drops of lemon juice added to simmering rice will keep the grains separate.

A Chef's View

Parmesan is the most useful of pasta cheeses. It is an aged cow's milk cheese and is nutty and brown-buttery with a hint of orange peel. Parmesan keeps for several weeks if properly stored. To prevent it from drying out, wrap it tightly in waxed paper or butcher paper, then overwrapping with aluminum foil before refrigerating. Always grate Parmesan freshly for each use.

Armenian Rice

Level: Good Cook
Serves 10
Preparation Time: 1½ hours

3	garlic cloves, minced
¼	pound (1 stick) butter
1	cup (1-inch) vermicelli pieces
1	cup uncooked white rice
1	green bell pepper, cleaned and chopped
1	(8-ounce) can sliced water chestnuts, drained
1	(2½-ounce) can sliced ripe olives, drained
1	(4-ounce) can mushroom pieces and stems, drained
2	cups chicken broth
	Salt, to taste

- Preheat oven to 350 degrees. Coat a 2-quart baking dish with cooking spray.
- Sauté garlic in butter in a large skillet over medium-low heat.
- Remove garlic and add vermicelli. Stir and cook slowly until dark brown.
- Spread vermicelli mixture, rice, green pepper, water chestnuts, olives and mushrooms in baking dish.
- Pour chicken broth over all. Season with salt, to taste.
- Cover with aluminum foil and bake for 1 hour or until rice in center is done.
- Cook's Tip: Bake ahead, refrigerate (covered) and reheat (covered) the next day with an additional ¼ cup broth poured over top, at 325 degrees for 30 minutes.

Parmesan Wine Rice

Level: Easy
Serves 4
Preparation Time: 35 minutes

1	tablespoon butter
1	medium onion, chopped
1	garlic clove, minced
1	cup chicken broth
1	cup uncooked rice
1	cup dry white wine
½	cup grated Parmesan cheese

- Melt butter in a heavy skillet over medium heat.
- Add onion and garlic. Stir and cook 8-10 minutes or until translucent.
- Stir in broth, rice and wine. Bring to a boil.
- Reduce heat to low. Cover and cook 25 minutes or until liquid is absorbed.
- Stir in grated Parmesan cheese and serve warm.

Fruity Wild Rice

Level: Good Cook
Serves 6-8
Preparation Time: 3 hours

1 cup wild rice, washed
5 cups chicken stock, divided
1 cup brown rice
1 cup pecans, chopped
1 cup dried currants
1 cup dried apricot halves
4 green onions, chopped, white and green parts
½ cup chopped fresh parsley
1 tablespoon freshly grated orange peel
Freshly ground black pepper, to taste
2 tablespoons orange juice concentrate
¼ cup olive oil

- Bring 2⅓-cups chicken stock and wild rice to boil in a heavy saucepan. Reduce to medium heat, cover and simmer 45 minutes or until tender. Add water, if needed. Drain and set aside in a large bowl.
- Boil remaining 2⅔-cups chicken stock and brown rice in another heavy saucepan. Reduce heat, cover and simmer 45 minutes or until tender. Add water, if needed. Drain and add to the wild rice.
- Combine the pecans, currants, apricots, green onions, parsley, orange peel and black pepper. Add to rice mixture and fluff.
- Whisk together orange juice concentrate and olive oil.
- Pour over rice mixture and toss.
- Let seasoned rice sit at room temperature for 2 hours to allow flavors to blend.
- Serve at room temperature.
- Cook's Tip: A great Autumn or holiday side dish when served with pork or beef tenderloin.

A Chef's View

Arborio rice is a specialty of Italy's Piedmont and Lombardy regions. It has short, round grains that cook to a pleasantly chewy texture while developing their own creamy sauce which are the distinctive characteristics of risotto.

Basmati is highly aromatic, long-grained variety of rice prized for its sweet, nutlike flavor and perfume. White and brown basmati are wonderful to use when making pilaf.

Jasmine rice is grown in Thailand and is a long-grained variety with a sweet, floral scent similar to that of basmati.

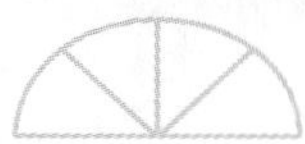

A Missouri Window

Rose O'Neill was the creator of the world renowned Kewpie Doll. She suffered through two unsuccessful marriages and suffered from a severe depression. During this time of pain and sorrow, the small people comforted her in a dream. She drew her mental pictures in pen and ink to honor the little spirits that helped ease her through her rough times. She called them her "Sweet Monsters". In 1913 Rose copyrighted her invention and started a worldwide Kewpie Craze. The Kewpie's worldwide success restored her life and made Rose a millionaire. Doll collectors around the world still search high and low for a cherished Kewpie Doll.

Pine Nut Wild Rice Salad

Level: Easy
Serves 10
Preparation Time: 1 hour

1	(7-ounce) box long-grain wild rice, cooked and cooled
1	(9-ounce) box yellow saffron rice, cooked and cooled
10	ounces crumbled feta cheese
½	cup chopped red bell pepper
½	cup chopped green bell pepper
⅔	cup chopped Vidalia or green onion
1	cup pine nuts, toasted
1	(2-ounce) jar diced pimientos, drained
1	(8-ounce) bottle vinaigrette salad dressing
	Lettuce leaves and parsley sprigs

- Combine long-grain and saffron rice, cheese, bell peppers, onion, pine nuts and pimientos in a large bowl. Mix well.
- Pour vinaigrette over salad and toss, using enough dressing to coat.
- Refrigerate until ready to serve.
- Adjust salad dressing, to taste.
- Serve on lettuce leaves and garnish with fresh parsley sprigs.
- Cook's Tip: Add cooked chicken or ham for a main dish salad. Serve with a fruit muffin.

Nutty Couscous

Level: Easy
Serves 4
Preparation Time: 45 minutes

1¾	cups chicken broth
1	cup couscous
⅓	cup toasted walnuts, chopped
2	tablespoons finely diced red bell pepper
1	tablespoon minced Italian parsley
	Ground black pepper, to taste

- Bring chicken broth to a boil in a small saucepan.
- Add couscous, walnuts, bell pepper, parsley and black pepper, to taste. Stir to blend. Cover and remove from heat.
- Let mixture stand for 5-10 minutes or until all the liquid has been absorbed.
- Fluff couscous mixture with fork before serving.
- Cook's Tip: Couscous requires little attention and works well with a number of complementary ingredients such as tomato, peppers, herbs and pesto.

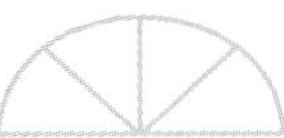

Polenta

Level: Easy
Serves 6-8
Preparation Time: 40 minutes

9 cups water
1 tablespoon salt
3 cups coarse-grain cornmeal

- Bring water to a boil over high heat in a large heavy pot. Add salt and reduce heat until water is simmering.
- Add cornmeal, slowly in a steady stream by the handfuls through your fingers, into the simmering water. To avoid lumps, stir quickly and constantly with a wooden spoon while adding cornmeal.
- Stop adding cornmeal from time to time, if necessary, to beat mixture vigorously.
- Cook, stirring constantly, 20-30 minutes. Polenta will become very thick while cooking. It is done when it comes away cleanly from the sides of the pot.
- Pour polenta onto a large wooden board or into a jelly-roll pan. Wet your hands and evenly smooth out until approximately 2 inches thick.
- Let polenta cool 5-10 minutes or until it solidifies.
- Cut cooled polenta into 1-inch wide slices 6 inches long. A biscuit cutter or greased glass may be used to cut rounds.
- Place polenta slices in individual bowls and serve with your favorite warmed sauce.
- Cook's Tip: For fried polenta, polenta frittata, prepare as above. Heat approximately 1-inch of canola oil in a deep skillet until a 1-inch cube of bread turns brown immediately when fried. Fry polenta on both sides until golden, drain and serve hot.

Crockery Cooker Polenta

Level: Easy
Serves 8-10
Preparation Time: 2-3 hours

3 tablespoons melted butter
¼ teaspoon paprika
Dash cayenne pepper
6 cups boiling water
2 cups cornmeal
1 teaspoon salt

- Use 1 tablespoon butter to lightly grease wall of crockery cooker.
- Sprinkle paprika and cayenne inside pot. Turn cooker to high.
- Add water, cornmeal, salt and remaining butter to pot. Stir well until smooth with no lumps.
- Cover cooker and cook on high for 2-3 hours or on low for 6-9 hours, stirring occasionally.
- Cook's Tip: For a delightful variation, add chopped red bell peppers, chopped spinach or Parmesan cheese, to taste.

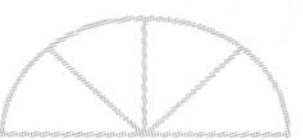

A Chef's View

Risotto (rih SAW toh, ree ZAW toh) is an Italian rice dish made by stirring hot broth into a mixture of rice and sometimes, sautéed onion. It is made usually from Arborio rice, which is an Italian-grown rice with high starch kernels that are shorter and fatter than any other grained rice, and traditionally used for risotto because of the creaminess it gives to the dish. For the perfect risotto, do not rinse the rice before cooking it. The starch that coats each grain lends to the creaminess of the dish. Both the broth and the rice should be kept at a lively simmer throughout preparation.

Risotto

Level: Expert Cook
Serves 6
Preparation Time: 1 hour

9	cups chicken stock
6	tablespoons olive oil
1	medium onion, minced
1	carrot, minced
2	celery ribs, minced
1	cup white wine
2	cups Arborio rice
½	cup grated freshly grated Parmesan cheese

- Bring chicken stock to a boil in a stockpot, reduce heat and simmer.
- Heat olive oil in another heavy stockpot. Add onion, carrot, celery and wine. Cook over low heat until vegetables are soft and wine reduces by half.
- Add rice and cook, stirring an additional 3 minutes.
- Pour 1 cup of stock into rice. Stir and simmer. After stock is absorbed, add another cup of stock, stir and simmer. Repeat until all stock has been added and absorbed.
- Serve on a warm platter and garnish with freshly grated Parmesan cheese.

Mango Sticky Rice

Level: Easy
Serves 4
Preparation Time: 40 minutes

1	cup jasmine rice
¾	cup canned coconut milk
¼	cup packed light-brown sugar
1	ripe mango, peeled and diced
2	tablespoons finely chopped crystallized ginger

- Cook or steam rice in water according to package directions. Let cool and transfer to a mixing bowl.
- Mix coconut milk and brown sugar. Pour over rice.
- Add mango and mix well.
- Sprinkle rice and mango mixture with crystallized ginger and mix again.
- Serve.

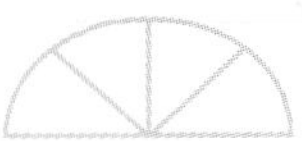

Skillet Rice with Tomatoes

Level: Easy
Serves 4
Preparation Time: 40 minutes

1	tablespoon olive oil
3	tablespoons minced shallots
3	tablespoons chopped green bell pepper
½	cup uncooked rice
1	cup canned tomatoes, undrained
1	cup chicken stock
¼	cup apple juice
1	teaspoon ground ginger
1	teaspoon dried tarragon
4	dashes hot-pepper sauce
2	tablespoons minced fresh parsley

- Heat oil in a skillet until hot. Sauté shallots and bell pepper in oil until wilted but not browned, stirring constantly.
- Add rice and stir. Sauté for 1 additional minute.
- Stir in tomatoes, stock, apple juice, ginger, tarragon and hot-pepper sauce. Cover and simmer for 20 minutes, stirring once after the first 10 minutes.
- Remove from heat and let stand for 5 minutes.
- Fluff with fork, sprinkle with parsley and serve.

Wild Rice with Apples and Sun-Dried Cherries

Level: Easy
Serves 2
Preparation Time: 45 minutes

2	tablespoons olive oil
2	tablespoons finely minced onion
1	tablespoons curry powder
1	apple, peeled, cored, and cut into small cubes
1	cup chopped white button mushrooms
¼	cup sun-dried cherries
1½	cups cooked wild rice
	Salt and freshly ground black pepper, to taste

- Heat a sauté pan. Add olive oil and sauté minced onions and curry powder until translucent.
- Add chopped apple, mushrooms and sun-dried cherries. Stir until mushrooms are cooked through.
- Add cooked wild rice and stir-fry until rice is hot and tender. Add salt and pepper to taste. Serve warm.

A Chef's View

Often recipes call for removing tomato skins and seeds.

To remove skins:

- *Fill a saucepan ¾ full of water. Bring to a boil.*
- *Cut a shallow X in the skin at the tomato's base.*
- *Submerge each tomato in boiling water for 20-30 seconds.*
- *Remove from boiling water using a slotted spoon and submerge tomato in a bowl of ice cold water.*
- *Core tomato from stem end.*
- *Peel the tomato, starting at the X, using your fingertips and, if necessary, the knife edge.*

To remove tomato seeds:

- *Cut the tomato in half, crosswise.*
- *Hold each half over bowl, squeezing gently to force out the seed sacs.*

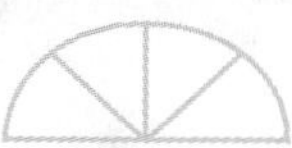

A Chef's View

The term grits actually refers to any coarsely ground grain such as corn, oats or rice. Most grits come in a choice of grinds and are cooked with water or milk. They are usually boiled or baked and eaten as hot cereal or served as a side dish flavored with cheese, sausage, bacon or vegetables.

White Cheddar Cheese Grits

Level: Easy
Serves 6
Preparation Time: 40 minutes

3	cups water
¾	cup grits, not quick-cooking
1½	teaspoons minced garlic
2	tablespoons butter
1½	cups (6-ounces) grated white Cheddar cheese
¼	cup freshly grated Parmesan cheese
¼	cup heavy cream
	White pepper, to taste
6	slices bacon, fried and crumbled

- Preheat oven to 350 degrees.
- Butter a 1½-quart baking dish.
- Bring water to a boil and slowly stir in grits. Reduce heat, cover and simmer for approximately 15 minutes or until grits are slightly soupy. Stir frequently.
- Sauté garlic in butter until tender while grits are simmering. Add to grits.
- Add white Cheddar cheese, freshly grated Parmesan cheese, heavy cream and white pepper. Stir until cheese melts.
- Pour mixture into baking dish.
- Bake 30-35 minutes or until edges are slightly browned.
- Remove from oven and top with crumbled bacon. Serve immediately.

A Sight to Behold
Fruits & Vegetables

A Missouri Window

Water Wilderness

Missouri's water wilderness region abounds in the southeast corner of the state with scenic views of crystal-clear rivers, bubbling springs, wildlife, lakes, forests, and Missouri's highest point, Taum Sauk Mountain. Underground rivers formed many caves, including the Ononodaga Cave near Leesburg, helping to make Missouri the "Cave State."

The region's largest town, Poplar Bluff, is located on the Black River. Near Piedmont, the Black River widens into scenic Clearwater Lake, the 1,650-acre lake offering beaches, lodges, fishing, and campgrounds. North of Poplar Bluff is Wappapello Lake, a U.S. Army Corps of Engineers lake, known for some of the best fishing in southeast Missouri. Hikers and backpackers enjoy national hiking trails in the Mark Twain National Forest nearby.

Miles of canoeing rivers, including the Jack's Fork and Current, America's first national scenic riverways, take paddlers and tubers through picturesque woods and bluffs. Farther downstream is Big Springs, one of the two largest single outlet springs in the U.S. with an output of 277 million gallons of water per day.

West of Thayer is Grand Gulf State Park, which resembles a mini-Grand Canyon. In Rolla, a small version of England's Stonehenge exists and a segment of old Route 66 passes through town. St. James is well known for its wineries with the Meremec State Park and Meremec River nearby. Near Ironton, giant red boulders perch atop Ozark hills forming Elephant Rocks State Park.

Photos: The Current River, Carter County, Alley Spring, Shannon County & Johnson Shut-Ins, Reynolds County

Quad County Medical Alliance (Butler-Wayne-Ripley-Carter Counties)

From 1961 until the present, the health of this four-county area has been the main focus of the Quad County Medical Alliance. The promotion of local health efforts by medical professionals has been its primary goal. In the early days, many spouses donated time individually to various charitable activities. Over time, many began to enjoy a closer relationship with other physician spouses and began to contribute more to the community in the spirit of positive volunteerism as an organized group.

First comprised of Butler, Wayne and Ripley counties, the Alliance added Carter county in 1975. Activities and fundraisers were popular, when in 1984, the Alliance focused their attention on a safe house for women, called Haven House, in Poplar Bluff. The first large fundraiser was an international dinner taking advantage of the excellent cooking skills of the diverse cultural makeup of the membership. Subsequent fundraisers have continued to share proceeds with the original Haven House project. Honoring physicians with 40 years of service is a local tradition at the Doctors' Day celebration. The Alliance also provides a health-related scholarship to Three Rivers Community College each year.

Members make an effort to keep abreast of legislative activities on the state and national levels and contact their lawmakers on a frequent basis. *The Stop America's Violence Everywhere Campaign - SAVE* project has also brought awareness through public service announcements, making the area a safer place to live. The Alliance membership continues to be family- and community-oriented, and remains committed to health care education endeavors.

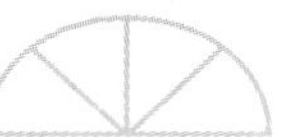

Apple Volcanoes

Level: Quick and Simple
Yield: 4 apples
Preparation Time: 10 minutes

- 4 medium apples
- ½ cup peanut butter
- ½ cup raisins
- ½ cup granola

- Cut top off apple and core. Do not cut through to bottom. Discard core.
- Fill center of apple with peanut butter.
- Sprinkle with raisins, granola or topping of your choice.
- Serve as an after school snack or as a healthy dessert.

Baked Apricots with Gingersnap Crumbles

Level: Easy
Serves 4-6
Preparation Time: 45 minutes

- 2 (17-ounce) cans apricot halves, drain and reserve ⅓ cup juice
- 3 tablespoons brown sugar
- ½ teaspoon ground cinnamon
- ½ teaspoon ground ginger
- 3 tablespoons butter, divided
- ½ cup *Windows'* Gingersnap cookies, crumbled

- Preheat oven to 375 degrees. Butter a 1½-quart round baking dish.
- Layer half the apricots on bottom of baking dish.
- Combine sugar, cinnamon and ginger.
- Sprinkle sugar mixture over apricots and then add remaining apricots.
- Dot top with 1½ tablespoons butter.
- Pour the ⅓ cup reserved juice over the apricots.
- Crumble gingersnaps over top and dot with remaining butter.
- Bake uncovered for 40-45 minutes.
- Cook's Tip: Serve warm to accompany pork tenderloin or spoon over French vanilla ice cream topped with a dollop of ginger or cinnamon-flavored whipped topping. See *Windows'* Gingersnaps recipe.

A Missouri Window

In 1812, the first general assembly of the Territory of Missouri met. The five original counties were organized: Cape Girardeau, New Madrid, St. Charles, St. Louis, and Ste. Genevieve.

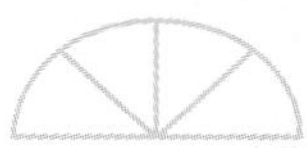

A Chef's View

What's your favorite summer fruit? If you can't decide on just one, then create a kebab that you'll love tasting your way through the various fruits.

A Chef's View

Use the fresh fruits of summer by making fruited herb vinegars to use on fresh green salads. Try this Peach-Mint Vinegar: Combine 2 peeled, chopped peaches, ¼ cup chopped fresh mint leaves, 2 tablespoons honey, and 1½ cups white wine vinegar in a jar. Cover and let stand at room temperature 2 weeks. Pour through a wire-mesh strainer into a container; discard solids. Yield: 1½ cups.

Summer Fruit Kebabs

Level: Quick and Simple
Serves 6
Preparation Time: 15 minutes

12 large strawberries, rinsed and stemmed
12 seedless green grapes, washed
12 (1-inch) fresh pineapple pieces
12 red or black seedless grapes, washed
12 orange sections, peel and white pith removed
1 (3-ounce) package cream cheese, softened
3 tablespoons sour cream
3 tablespoons confectioners' sugar
¼ teaspoon almond extract

- Place fruit pieces on skewer in the following order: strawberry, green grape, pineapple, red or black grape and orange. Repeat.
- Combine cream cheese, sour cream, confectioners' sugar and almond extract.
- Cream for 2 minutes or until smooth.
- Refrigerate until ready to use.
- Serve dip in hollowed-out orange halves, placed in center of a platter surrounded by fruit kebabs.

Marinated Fruits of Summer

Level: Easy
Serves 10-12
Preparation Time: 2½ hours

¼ cup orange marmalade
1 (6-ounce) can frozen lemonade concentrate
2 tablespoons orange-flavored liqueur, optional
3 cups melon: watermelon, honeydew and cantaloupe, cut-up
1 cup halved fresh strawberries
1½ cups cubed fresh pineapple
1 (15-ounce) can Mandarin oranges, drained
1 pint raspberries or blueberries or combination, washed
½ cup flaked coconut

- Mix marmalade, lemonade and orange-flavored liqueur together.
- Combine the melons, strawberries, pineapple and Mandarin oranges.
- Pour lemonade mixture over fruit, tossing gently.
- Cover and chill for at least 2 hours.
- To serve, spoon fruit and juices into round-bowl red wine glasses. Top with raspberries and/or blueberries and sprinkle with coconut.

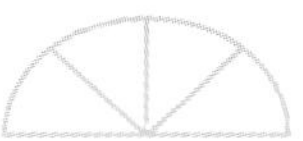

Oranges in Red Wine Sauce

Level: Easy
Serves 8
Preparation Time: 2 hours

2	cups dry red wine
2	cups water
1¼	cups granulated sugar
1	lemon, sliced
6	whole cloves
¾	teaspoon ground cinnamon
8	oranges, peeled, white pith removed and sectioned
8	amaretto-flavored cookies, lightly crumbled
	Windows' Buttery Pound Cake, optional
	Whipped topping, optional

- Bring wine, water, sugar, lemon, cloves and cinnamon to a boil in a saucepan.
- Boil until reduced by half.
- Remove cloves and pour sauce over sectioned oranges.
- Refrigerate until well chilled.
- To serve, spoon into wide-mouth stemmed glasses and sprinkle with crumbled amaretto-flavored cookies.
- Cook's Tip: Oranges can also be spooned over sliced pound cake and topped with a dollop of amaretto-flavored whipped topping. See *Windows'* Buttery Pound Cake recipe.

A Missouri Window

Missouri's earthquake activity has been concentrated under the southeast town of New Madrid. The first written account was by a French missionary on a voyage down the Mississippi River, who reported feeling a distinct tremor on Christmas Day 1699 while camped in what is now Memphis, Tennessee. On December 16, 1811, the first tremor of the most violent series of earthquakes in the U.S. history struck the area. In New Madrid, residents felt their houses rock, heard timbers crack and breaking, and saw chimneys and trees fall. Large fissures in the area suddenly opened and swallowed large quantities of river and marsh water. On January 23, 1812, a second major shock, seemingly more violent than the first, occurred. A third great earthquake, perhaps the most severe of the series, struck on February 7, 1812. Chimneys were knocked down in Cincinnati, Ohio, and bricks were reported to have fallen from chimneys in Georgia and South Carolina. The first shock was felt distinctly in Washington, D.C., New Orleans, Detroit, and Boston.

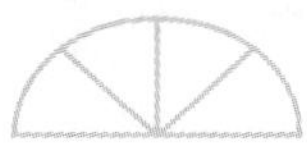

A Chef's View

A garnish can dress up a dish to fit almost any occasion. Make a strawberry fan by using a fresh strawberry with its green top still attached. Slice the berry from the tip almost all the way to the stem end. Carefully, fan out the berry slices.

Or create sugared fruit by using a clean brush to apply a mixture of water and meringue powder over cranberries or miniature bunches of grapes. Immediately sprinkle with granulated sugar to give a frosted look to fruit.

A Missouri Window

'Missouri is a resplendent mosaic of nature's gifts.'

~ Senator Thomas Eagleton

Sherried Fruit Compote

Level: Easy
Serves 4
Preparation Time: 1 hour

- ⅓ cup dry sherry
- ¼ cup lemon juice, freshly squeezed
- ¼ cup granulated sugar
- 1½ cups fresh blueberries, washed
- 1 cup sliced strawberries
- 2 fresh peaches, pitted and sliced
- 1 large banana, sliced
- Yogurt or custard
- Whipped cream

- Combine sherry, lemon juice and sugar. Stir until sugar dissolves.
- Toss with fruit to coat.
- Cover and chill.
- Divide between four stemmed glasses.
- Top with yogurt or custard and then with whipped cream.

Strawberry Blooms

Level: Easy
Serves 6
Preparation Time: 20 minutes

- 12 large fresh strawberries, rinsed and dried
- 1 (3-ounce) package cream cheese, softened
- 2 tablespoons confectioners' sugar
- 1 tablespoon sour cream

- Remove stems from strawberries to form a flat base.
- Place strawberries on cutting surface, pointed end up.
- Slice each strawberry in half vertically to within ¼-inch of base with a sharp knife.
- Cut each half into 3 wedges to form 6 petals. Do not slice through base.
- Combine cream cheese, confectioners' sugar and sour cream; beat until light and fluffy.
- With a pastry bag and star tip or small spoon, fill strawberries with cream cheese mixture.
- Cook's Tip: Serve as an appetizer on a silver tray or crystal-footed platter. To serve as a dessert, place two or three strawberries on a small plate drizzled with chocolate. Garnish with fresh mint.

Strawberries Romanoff

Level: Quick and Simple
Serves 8
Preparation Time: 15 minutes

- 2 pints fresh medium-size strawberries, washed, hulled and patted dry
- ⅔ cup granulated sugar, divided
- ⅓ cup plus ½ tablespoon orange-flavored liqueur, divided
- 1 teaspoon freshly grated orange peel
- ¾ cup heavy cream
- Mint sprigs, for garnish

◆ Toss strawberries with ⅓ cup sugar and ⅓ cup orange-flavored liqueur in a bowl.
◆ Fold in orange peel.
◆ Whip heavy cream with remaining ⅓ cup sugar until soft peaks form. Add ½ tablespoon orange-flavored liqueur to whipped cream for additional flavor.
◆ Divide berries among stemmed red-wine glasses and top with whipped cream and a mint sprig.
◆ Serve immediately.

Winter Fruit Compote

Level: Easy
Yield: 5 cups
Preparation Time: 1½ hours

- 1 (21-ounce) can cherry pie filling
- 1 (20-ounce) can pineapple chunks
- 1 (6-ounce) package dried mixed fruit
- 1 (12-ounce) package dried pitted prunes
- 2 (11-ounce) cans Mandarin oranges

◆ Preheat oven to 350 degrees.
◆ Mix together all ingredients in a large bowl.
◆ Pour into a large greased casserole dish and cover with foil.
◆ Bake 1 hour.
◆ Cook's Tip: Use as a side dish, a condiment for ham, or a topping for cake or ice cream.

A Culinary Reflection

Many years ago, when we moved to the farm, I felt compelled to be a good farm wife and mother. My first project was to pick blackberries and make jelly. Following the instructions, I got to the step that said 'place cooked blackberries in a cheesecloth and place over a large pan,' so the juice would strain through. After it dripped for a while, I became impatient and thought I would speed up the project. I gathered up the cheesecloth and twisted it. Great amounts of blackberry juice came forth. Instead of stopping, I continued to twist, when on the last turn, the cloth ruptured and blackberry pulp machine-gunned across the kitchen! It sprayed everything in its path, including the cookie jar, a canister set, and the coffeepot. They were all outlined on the wall, even the knob of the lid on the coffeepot. What a mess! That was farm lesson number one. To this day, I do not make jelly.

~ Mary Eleanor Farrell

A Missouri Window

Missouri's oldest community, Saint Genevieve, was founded as early as 1735.

A Chef's View

Use a stiff vegetable brush to scrub vegetables rather than peel them. Peeling causes a loss of vitamins found in and just under the skin. Sand and dirt can be removed from fresh vegetables by soaking in warm salted water for 5 minutes.

Buttery Lemon Asparagus

Level: Easy
Serves 6
Preparation Time: 30 minutes

4	tablespoons butter
1½	pounds fresh asparagus, sliced in 1-inch diagonal pieces
1	medium onion, chopped
1	garlic clove, minced
1	teaspoon instant chicken bouillon granules
¼	cup sliced almonds, lightly toasted
2	teaspoons freshly grated lemon peel
2	tablespoons freshly squeezed lemon juice

- Melt butter in a large skillet.
- Add asparagus, onion, garlic and bouillon granules.
- Cook and stir until asparagus is crisp tender.
- Add almonds, lemon peel and lemon juice.
- Serve immediately.

Roasted Asparagus and Mushrooms with Rosemary

Level: Easy
Serves 4
Preparation Time: 30 minutes

1	pound fresh asparagus, trimmed
½	pound fresh shiitake or white button mushrooms, cleaned and trimmed
2	teaspoons olive oil or canola oil
¼	teaspoon dried rosemary, crushed
	Black pepper, freshly ground
	Garlic powder, to taste, optional

- Preheat oven to 500 degrees.
- Place asparagus spears and mushrooms in a large plastic bag with a tight-fitting seal.
- Drizzle oil and rosemary over vegetables.
- Seal tightly and shake gently to coat vegetables with oil.
- Arrange vegetables in a single layer on a large baking sheet.
- Season with black pepper and garlic, if desired.
- Roast approximately 10 minutes or until asparagus is crisp-tender.

Grilled Acorn Squash

Level: Easy
Serves 1
Preparation Time: 1 hour

1 acorn squash
2 tablespoons brown sugar
2 tablespoons butter
Garlic salt, to taste, optional

- Wash squash, cut in half and remove seeds.
- Using a large fork, pierce the inside fruit of the squash along bottom and sides.
- Sprinkle each half with 1 tablespoon brown sugar or garlic salt.
- Fill each center with 1 tablespoon butter.
- Wrap in foil and place on the barbecue grill for approximately 50-60 minutes.

Hobo Beans

Level: Easy
Serves 6-8
Preparation Time: 1½ hours

8 ounces lean ground beef
½ pound thick sliced bacon, diced
1 small onion, chopped
⅓ cup brown sugar, firmly packed
⅓ cup ketchup
½ cup barbecue sauce
1 tablespoon prepared mustard
2 tablespoons molasses
½ teaspoon chili powder
1 (16-ounce) can red beans, with liquid
1 (16-ounce) can butter beans, with liquid
1 (16-ounce) can pinto beans, with liquid
1 (16-ounce) can pork and beans

- Preheat oven to 350 degrees. Lightly coat an 13x9x2-inch baking dish with cooking spray.
- Brown beef, bacon and onion together in a skillet.
- Add brown sugar, ketchup, barbecue sauce, mustard, molasses and chili powder to meat. Mix well.
- Stir beans and their liquid into meat mixture.
- Pour into baking dish.
- Bake for 45-60 minutes until bubbly.
- Cook's Tip: Serve as a side dish or a main dish with a salad.

A Missouri Window

Taum Sauk Mountain State Park is located in the St. Francois Mountains, one of the most rugged and scenic areas of the state. Almost 1.5 billion years ago, volcanic eruptions of hot ash settled and cooled to form rhyolite. Erosion has left only the roots of these mountains behind, now dotted by oak-hickory forest and rocky glades. Taum Sauk Mountain literally stands above others as the highest point in Missouri, rising to 1,772 feet. An easy walk leads visitors to the top. From there, the moderately rugged three-mile Mina Sauk Falls Trail continues to the tallest wet-weather waterfall in Missouri. Mina Sauk Falls drops 132 feet over a series of rocky ledges. A portion of this trail also serves as part of the Taum Sauk Section of the Ozark Trail. Farther down the trail lies Devil's Tollgate, an eight-foot-wide passage through volcanic rhyolite standing 30 feet high.

A Chef's View

The adzuki or azuki bean is a small dried, russet-colored bean with a sweet flavor. Adzuki beans can be purchased whole or powdered at Asian markets. They are particularly popular in Japanese cooking where they're used in confections.

Adzuki Bean Burgers

Level: Good Cook
Yield: 12 burgers
Preparation Time: 20 minutes

1	cup brown rice
1	medium onion, chopped
2	garlic cloves, crushed
1	small green bell pepper, seeded and chopped
1	medium carrot, coarsely grated
2	tablespoons sunflower oil
4	tablespoons butter
1	(14-ounce) can adzuki beans, drained
1	egg, beaten
½	cup grated hard cheese
1	teaspoon dried thyme
½	cup toasted nuts or flaked almonds
	Salt and black pepper, to taste
	Whole-wheat flour or cornmeal, for coating
	Oil, for deep-frying
	Hamburger buns, toasted
	Lettuce
	Pickle relish

- Cook rice according to package instructions, allowing to slightly overcook so it is softer. Drain and transfer to large bowl.
- Fry onion, garlic, green pepper and carrot in oil and butter until vegetables are softened, approximately 10 minutes.
- Mix vegetable mixture into rice, together with adzuki beans, egg, cheese, thyme and nuts or almonds.
- Season to taste. Cover and chill.
- Shape into 12 burgers. Dredge with flour or cornmeal.
- Heat ½ inch oil in a large, shallow skillet. Fry burgers in batches until browned on each side, approximately 5 minutes total.
- Remove and drain burgers on paper towels.
- Serve on toasted hamburger buns with lettuce and relish.
- Cook's Tip: To freeze burgers, cool after cooking then open-freeze before wrapping and bagging. Cook frozen burgers by baking in a preheated 350 degree oven for 20-25 minutes.

Orange Beets

Level: Easy
Serves 6
Preparation Time: 35 minutes

20	small beets
2	tablespoons cornstarch
1	cup light brown sugar, firmly packed
1	(6-ounce) can frozen orange juice concentrate
¾	cup apple cider vinegar
1	teaspoon ground cinnamon, optional
½	teaspoon ground cloves, optional
2	tablespoons butter

- Cut beet tops leaving 1 inch of stem and root intact. Wash beets.
- Cover beets with water and bring to a boil. Lower heat, cover and simmer until beets are tender, approximately 30-35 minutes.
- Drain, reserving 1 cup cooking liquid.
- Plunge beets in cold water and squeeze to peel. Set aside.
- Combine cornstarch, brown sugar, orange juice, vinegar, optional cinnamon and ground cloves and reserved liquid in a saucepan. Whisk. Heat liquid until thickened and clear, stirring often.
- Add butter and whole beets.
- Heat thoroughly before serving.

A Chef's View

It's best to peel cooked beets under a running faucet so the beet juice is rinsed away before it can stain. Because of their color, beets can bring color to the food in a recipe.

Create a red beet rose by cooking a large red beet in water to cover until tender. Peel in a spiral strip about ¾-inch wide with a sharp knife. Begin by rolling up the strip tightly for the center of the rose, then loosening at the outer edge. Soak in cold water to freshen and set the color, and use as a garnish.

Tomato Pie

Level: Easy
Yield: 1 pie
Preparation Time: 45 minutes

3	large tomatoes
1	(9-inch) *Windows'* Never Fail Pie Crust
2	green onions, thinly sliced
6	leaves chopped fresh basil
	Garlic salt, to taste
	Ground black pepper, to taste
¼	cup finely grated Swiss cheese
¼	cup Parmesan cheese
¾	cup mayonnaise
1	cup grated sharp Cheddar cheese

- Preheat oven to 350 degrees.
- Peel tomatoes. Slice ½-inch thick. Arrange one layer in pie shell.
- Sprinkle tomatoes with onion, basil, garlic salt, pepper, Swiss cheese and Parmesan cheese. Repeat with second layer of tomatoes.
- Mix mayonnaise and Cheddar cheese together and spread over pie.
- Bake for 30 minutes or until lightly browned.

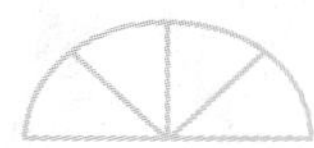

A Culinary Reflection

When I was a child, I lived with my grandparents. We had a large family and our house was the gathering place for our family and friends. In our back yard we had a cherry tree and an apple tree. Each spring we eagerly awaited the ripening of the cherries because my grandmother made delicious pies. These were served with vanilla ice cream that my granddad prepared in a hand-cranked ice cream maker in the back yard. In the fall we would harvest the apples and make apple butter in a very large copper-lined black kettle over an open fire. Of course we always put silver dollars in the bottom of the kettle to keep the apples from sticking. When the apple butter was ready, it was great fun to see who could find the silver dollars. It was the gathering of family and friends and the sharing which made my childhood so special.

~ Sharan Leslie Klingner

Red Cabbage and Apples

Level: Easy
Serves 6
Preparation Time: 2 hours

1	head red cabbage, cored and outer leaves removed
1	medium onion, chopped
¼	cup bacon drippings
½	cup red wine
½	cup water
¼	cup red wine vinegar
3	tablespoons brown sugar
2	tart apples, peeled, cored and sliced

- Shred cabbage.
- Sauté onion in bacon drippings until tender.
- Add shredded cabbage and toss.
- Combine wine, water, vinegar and brown sugar; mix well. Pour over cabbage.
- Add sliced apples and cook over low heat, covered for 1½ to 2 hours.
- Check occasionally to be sure that all liquid has not boiled away; add more red wine or water, if necessary.
- Toss before serving. The apples will have dissolved into the cabbage.
- Cook's Tip: Serve with *Windows'* Killer Brats and Crispy Potato Pancakes.

Carrot Ring

Level: Easy
Yield: 1 carrot ring
Preparation Time: 1 hour

7	carrots
½	cup butter or margarine, softened
¾	cup packed brown sugar
1	egg, slightly beaten
1¼	cup all-purpose flour
½	teaspoon salt
1	teaspoon baking powder
1	teaspoon baking soda
1	teaspoon lemon juice
1	(10-ounce) package frozen baby green peas

- Cut carrots into thin slices and cook until soft. Drain.
- Preheat oven to 350 degrees. Coat a 7-cup smooth-sided ring mold with cooking spray.
- Mash carrots with butter or margarine and brown sugar.
- Add egg to carrot mixture and mix well.
- Sift together flour, salt, baking powder and baking soda.
- Combine carrot mixture, dry ingredients and lemon juice. Mix well.
- Pour into ring mold. Batter will be heavy, its texture more like a sticky bread dough than a cake mix.
- Set mold in a roasting pan filled with hot water so water reaches ¾ of the way up mold.
- Bake for 45 minutes or until a cake tester inserted into the center comes out clean.
- Prepare frozen peas, according to package directions, five minutes before removing vegetable ring from oven.
- Remove vegetable ring from oven and let set for 3 minutes. Unmold onto a round platter and fill center with steamed peas.
- Cook's Tip: Additional seasonings such as nutmeg, cinnamon or pumpkin pie spice may be added.

A Culinary Reflection

My mother always made a carrot ring for our Thanksgiving dinners. It was a favorite of our family, so I wanted to carry on that tradition when I had my own family. My husband and children always check that I am planning to make the vegetable dish - and often request it for Thanksgiving and Christmas. My oldest son loves to cook and tried to serve it at a dinner he prepared for the family. It was a bit soft and mushy - so he now has a little more respect for what it takes to turn out a great carrot ring! What is a carrot ring? It's a dish of cooked carrots, flour, and seasonings baked in a ring pan and served hot with steamed green peas to fill the center. A pretty dish.

- Eileen Dyer

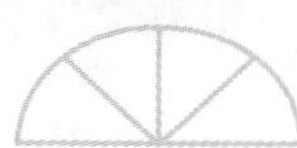

A Chef's View

It's easy to glaze vegetables. Simmer carrots, winter squash, apples or other produce until just tender, and remove from the cooking liquid. Add sugar or brown sugar to liquid, and boil until the mixture is syrupy. Return the vegetables or fruits to the syrup, stirring until they are glazed and warm. For an instant glaze, melt a small amount of jelly or preserves and pour over cooked, drained vegetables. Try orange marmalade over carrots or winter squash, or apple jelly over onions.

Copper Pennies

Level: Easy
Serves 6-8
Preparation Time: 1 day

2	pounds frozen crinkle cut carrots
1	medium onion, chopped
1	green bell pepper, chopped
1	(10¾-ounce) can tomato soup
½	cup white wine vinegar
¾	cup canola oil
1	tablespoon Worcestershire sauce
1	teaspoon prepared mustard
½	teaspoon dried basil leaves
1	teaspoon celery seeds
1	teaspoon salt
¾	cup granulated sugar

- Cook carrots crisp tender in water. Do not overcook. Drain and cool.
- Layer ½ of carrots, onion and green pepper in a large bowl. Repeat layers with remaining ingredients.
- Combine tomato soup, vinegar, canola oil, Worcestershire sauce, prepared mustard, basil, celery seed, salt and sugar in a saucepan and bring to a boil, stirring occasionally.
- Pour mixture over layered vegetables.
- Let stand covered, 8-12 hours or overnight, at room temperature.
- Toss before serving.
- Serve at room temperature.

Baked Cauliflower and Swiss Cheese

Level: Easy
Serves 8-10
Preparation Time: 45 minutes

- 2 (2-pound) cauliflower heads, broken into florets
- ¼ cup green bell pepper, diced
- 1 (7.3-ounce) jar sliced mushrooms, drained
- 4 tablespoons butter
- ⅓ cup all-purpose flour
- 2 cups milk
- 1 cup (4-ounces) shredded Swiss cheese
- 2 tablespoons diced pimientos
- ½ teaspoon salt
- Ground paprika

- Preheat oven to 325 degrees.
- Cook cauliflower in a saucepan in a small amount of water for 6-7 minutes or until crisp tender. Drain.
- Cook and stir green pepper and mushrooms in butter in a large saucepan for 2 minutes.
- Add flour to mushroom mixture then gradually stir in milk. Bring to boil. Boil for 2 minutes, stirring constantly.
- Remove from heat and stir in cheese until melted. Add pimientos and salt. Stir.
- Place cauliflower in a greased 13x9x2-inch glass baking dish. Top with sauce.
- Bake, uncovered, for 25 minutes or until bubbly.
- Sprinkle with paprika. Serve immediately.

A Chef's View

To prevent darkening, add any kind of citrus juice to the cooking water of lightly colored vegetables, such as cauliflower, turnips or potatoes.

A Chef's View

Cauliflower is an accommodating vegetable that adapts to many seasonings and preparations. Look for cauliflower that is firm and relatively unblemished, and with a compact, not spreading, surface. Cauliflower leaves are perfectly edible. You can cook them, chop them up and add them to your stockpot for soup.

Italian Oven Fried Cauliflower

Level: Easy
Serves 8
Preparation Time: 1¼ hours

1½	cups reduced-fat mayonnaise
1	medium head cauliflower, trimmed, cut into florets
2	cups Italian-seasoned bread crumbs

- Preheat oven to 350 degrees. Lightly coat a jelly-roll pan with butter-flavored cooking spray.
- Spoon mayonnaise into a large freezer zip-top plastic bag.
- Add cauliflower. Seal and coat florets.
- Pour bread crumbs into a flat bowl.
- Add ⅓ of the cauliflower florets and coat with bread crumbs. Spread florets in a single layer on greased jelly-roll pan.
- Repeat with remaining cauliflower mixture and bread crumbs.
- Bake for 1 hour. Serve immediately.

A Chef's View

Eggplants are either male or female. Look at the blossom end - if it's indented, it's a female; if it's smooth, it's a male. Males have fewer seeds, which sometimes taste bitter. To remove most of the bitterness, slice eggplant, and sprinkle with salt; let stand 30 minutes. Rinse and pat dry with paper towels.

Select eggplants that are firm, unblemished, and heavy for their size. Use them within one to two days of purchase, or place them in a plastic bag and store them in the refrigerator up to five days.

Mozzarella Baked Eggplant

Level: Easy
Serves 4
Preparation Time: 30 minutes

1	large eggplant, unpeeled
3-4	tablespoons olive oil, divided
	Salt and black pepper, to taste
3	large plum tomatoes, sliced
4	ounces mozzarella cheese, cut into 8 slices
	Fresh basil leaves, shredded

- Preheat oven to 375 degrees. Lightly coat a jelly-roll pan with butter-flavored cooking spray.
- Trim eggplant and cut lengthwise into 4 slices so they lay flat. Arrange eggplant on baking sheet.
- Brush eggplant liberally with olive oil and season with salt and black pepper.
- Alternate tomato and cheese slices along eggplant, starting and ending with a tomato slice.
- Brush with additional olive oil and sprinkle with shredded basil.
- Bake for 15 minutes, or until the eggplant is tender and the cheese is bubbling and golden.

Ants on a Log

Level: Quick and Simple
Serves 8
Preparation Time: 10 minutes

4 celery ribs, washed
¾ cup peanut butter
½ cup raisins

- Dry celery ribs with a paper towel and cut into 5-inch pieces.
- Spread peanut butter in the well of each celery rib.
- Press raisins gently into the peanut butter.
- Cook's Tip: Substitute any cream cheese filling or soft spreadable cheese for peanut butter.

Mexicorn Corn Soufflé

Level: Easy
Serves 8
Preparation Time: 1 hour

1 (16-ounce) can cream style corn
1 (16-ounce) can corn with pimiento
1 (8½-ounce) box corn muffin mix
3 eggs, beaten
1 cup sour cream
½ cup chopped onion
1 green bell pepper, finely chopped
1 garlic clove, minced
¼ pound (1 stick) butter or margarine
Salt and black pepper, to taste
2 cups shredded Cheddar cheese

- Preheat oven to 350 degrees. Coat a 3-quart casserole dish with cooking spray.
- Combine corns, muffin mix, eggs and sour cream.
- Sauté onion, bell pepper and garlic in butter. Season with salt and pepper.
- Add hot mixture to corn mixture and blend together.
- Pour mixture into the casserole dish and top with cheese.
- Bake for 45 minutes.

A Chef's View

Children's Cooking Hints

A special reminder to all young people who cook: Always! Always! Always!

- *Check with your Mom and Dad before you start to cook.*
- *Wash your hands before you start cooking.*
- *Check with your Mom and Dad when using a knife.*
- *Cut away from yourself when using a knife or vegetable peeler.*
- *Be careful with anything hot. Use a potholder.*
- *Turn the handles of saucepans inward on the stove so no one can bump the handles.*
- *Plug in electrical cords with dry hands.*
- *Use paper towels to wipe up spills right away.*
- *Turn the oven, burners, and lights on the stove off as soon as you finish cooking.*

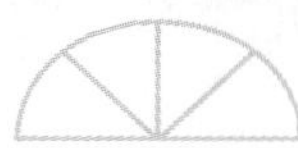

A Chef's View

There is nothing better than the smoky flavor of grilled corn. Husk the ear of corn, soak it in cold water, butter it, rewrap it in the husk, and then grill it. Another way is to simply cook the shucked ears directly over the coals. To remove the corn kernels from the cob, hold the cob vertically over a wide bowl or pan. Slice straight down the kernels with a knife. After the kernels have been removed, turn the knife over and with its dull side scrape the cob on all sides to extract the 'milk.' For a creamier texture, score the kernels by slicing through the middle of each row before cutting them off the ear. Use milk and sugar to bring out the sweetness of day-old corn when cooking it.

Green Chile Corn Squares

Level: Easy
Serves 8
Preparation Time: 1¼ hours

¼	cup chopped onion
¼	cup chopped green or red bell pepper
1	tablespoon margarine
2	eggs
1½	cups milk
1	(16-ounce) package frozen corn
1½	cups (6-ounces) shredded sharp Cheddar cheese, divided
¼	cup diced green chiles
	Pinch red pepper flakes
¾	cup buttered bread crumbs

- Preheat oven to 325 degrees. Butter an 11x7x2-inch glass baking dish.
- Cook and stir onion and bell pepper in margarine until onion is translucent. Set aside.
- Beat eggs until foamy in a very cold greaseless bowl.
- Fold in milk, corn, 1 cup cheese, chiles, cooked onion and bell pepper.
- Add pepper flakes and stir to blend well.
- Pour into prepared baking dish and bake for 45 minutes.
- Combine bread crumbs and remaining ½ cup cheese.
- Sprinkle over top of corn mixture and bake an additional 15 minutes.
- Cut in squares. Serve.

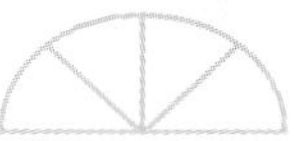

Jalapeño Corn

Level: Easy
Serves 4
Preparation Time: 45 minutes

¼	pound (1 stick) butter
2	(3-ounce) packages cream cheese
¼	cup milk
1	garlic clove, minced
3	cups fresh white corn, or 2 (12-ounce) cans shoepeg corn, drained
2	jalapeño peppers, seeded and minced
	Salt and black pepper, to taste

- Preheat oven to 350 degrees. Butter a 1½-quart glass baking dish.
- Combine butter, cream cheese, milk and garlic in a saucepan.
- Stir over low heat until smooth.
- Add corn, jalapeño peppers, salt and black pepper, to taste.
- Pour into buttered baking dish and bake 30 minutes or until lightly browned at edges.

A Chef's View

Jalapeño peppers can sting and irritate the skin. Wear plastic disposable gloves when handling peppers and do not touch eyes. To seed, cut peppers in half lengthwise. Remove seeds, membranes and stems with small paring knife.

Mushroom Veggie Burgers

Level: Easy
Serves 8
Preparation Time: 1 hour

½	pound (1½ cups) fresh mushrooms, finely chopped
1	large onion, chopped
1	medium zucchini, chopped
2	medium carrots, chopped
⅓	cup unsalted cashew pieces
4	cups fresh bread crumbs, include crusts
4	tablespoons chopped fresh parsley
	Salt and black pepper, to taste
	All-purpose flour, for shaping burgers
	Oil, for frying

- Cook mushrooms in a nonstick skillet, stirring for 10-12 minutes, until all moisture is removed.
- Process onion, zucchini, carrots and cashews in a food processor until beginning to bind together.
- Stir in bread crumbs, mushrooms, parsley and season to taste with salt and black pepper.
- Flour hands and shape mixture into 8 burgers and chill until firm.
- Cook burgers in a nonstick skillet with very little oil for 8-10 minutes, turning once, until golden brown.
- Serve hot.
- Cook's Tip: Serve on a toasted bun with fresh tomatoes, lettuce and onion.

A Chef's View

Cultivated mushrooms are grown indoors in a controlled environment, so they are available the year around. Look for firm, not spongy, mushrooms with smooth, unblemished caps. The caps should be tightly closed underneath, with no gills showing. Mushrooms do not keep well; if you can't use them the day you buy them, refrigerate them in a paper bag.

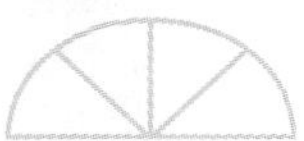

A Chef's View

Ethiopian slaves brought the okra plant to America's South. The green okra pods have a ridged skin and a tapered, oblong shape. Fresh okra is firm and brightly colored with the pod under 4 inches long. Okra can be prepared in a variety of ways and when cooked gives off a viscous substance that serves to thicken any liquid in which it is cooked. Okra can also be braised, baked, and fried.

A Chef's View

Balsamic vinegar is made from the newly pressed juice of selected white grapes. The juice is boiled until reduced to a third of its original volume. The syrup is then aged over a period of years in a series of wooden barrels until it becomes very dark and concentrated, mellow, and aromatic. It is best used sparingly, not as a regular vinegar, but more as a condiment.

Fried Okra

Level: Easy
Serves 4
Preparation Time: 20 minutes

1	pound okra, 1 to 2-inches long
2	eggs, beaten
½	cup milk
1	teaspoon salt
	Canola oil, for frying
1	cup crushed crackers or seasoned bread crumbs
	Salt and freshly ground black pepper, to taste

- Wash and dry okra. Remove stems.
- Mix beaten eggs, milk and salt.
- Heat 1 inch of canola oil in a large skillet.
- Dip okra into the egg mixture, then into crumbs, coating thoroughly.
- Fry okra in the hot oil until crisp, lightly browned and just tender. Drain on paper towels.
- Serve sprinkled with salt and black pepper.
- Cook's Tip: Okra may be cut into ½-inch pieces before coating and then fried.

Glazed Pearl Onions

Level: Quick and Simple
Serves 4-6
Preparation Time: 15 minutes

1	pound pearl onions, peeled
2	tablespoons butter or margarine
1	tablespoon brown sugar
½	teaspoon cornstarch
¼	teaspoon salt
¼	teaspoon dry mustard
	Dash black pepper
1	tablespoon apple cider or balsamic vinegar

- Combine onions and butter in a 1½-quart glass baking dish.
- Cover and microwave onions on HIGH for 6-8 minutes, or until tender, stirring once.
- Drain. Reserve liquid.
- Combine brown sugar, cornstarch, salt, mustard and black pepper.
- Stir in vinegar and reserved cooking liquid.
- Microwave on HIGH for 45-60 seconds, or until clear and thickened.
- Pour sauce over onions. Toss to coat.

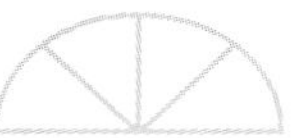

Crispy Potato Pancakes

Level: Easy
Yield: 2 dozen
Preparation Time: 40 minutes

2	pounds russet or Yukon gold potatoes
1	medium sweet white onion
½	cup chopped green onion, white and green parts
1	large egg, beaten
	Salt and freshly ground black pepper, to taste
	Canola oil, for frying
	Sour cream, sweetened with confectioners' sugar, to taste
	Applesauce

- Peel potatoes and cover with cold water. Using a grater or a food processor coarsely grate potatoes and sweet white onion.
- Place grated potatoes and grated onion in a fine mesh strainer or tea towel and squeeze out all liquid over a bowl.
- Allow potato starch to settle to bottom of bowl. Reserve starch by carefully pouring off water.
- Mix grated potato and grated onion with potato starch. Add green onions, egg, salt and pepper. Toss.
- Heat a griddle or non-stick pan and coat with a thin film of canola oil.
- Flatten 2 tablespoons of potato mixture in the palm of your hand.
- Place potato mixture on griddle, flatten again with a large spatula and fry until golden.
- Flip pancake over and brown other side.
- Remove to paper towels to drain.
- Serve potato pancakes immediately or freeze. Crisp frozen pancakes in a 350 degree oven at a later time.
- Serve with applesauce and sweetened sour cream.

A Chef's View

Here are some 'tater tricks:

- *Store potatoes in a slightly raised bin in a cool, dark, well-ventilated place - never in a plastic bag or a refrigerator.*
- *Don't squander the skins. The cortex of the potato, just below the peel, holds one-third of its nutrients.*
- *Always prick the skin before baking to avoid a dangerous buildup of steam.*
- *Don't wrap baking potatoes in foil or they'll be soggy and steamed.*
- *Do oil the potato skin before baking for better flavor and appearance.*

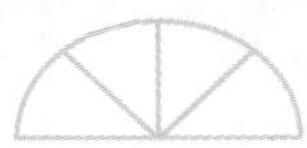

A Chef's View

Special Spuds

- *New potatoes and boiling potatoes hold their shape better than russets do.*
- *Cook potatoes unpeeled to lock in their flavor and nutrients. Once they're boiled, you can slip the skins off easily, if you wish.*
- *The potato cooking water makes a delicious soup base or a liquid in moist, nutritious breads.*
- *Potatoes for salads absorb more flavors if you dress them while they're hot, then chill them.*
- *Keep a box of dried instant potato flakes on hand to thicken sauces and soups. Potato flakes thicken without masking or changing flavors.*

Holiday Party Potatoes

Level: Easy
Serves 8
Preparation Time: 1 hour

5	pounds red potatoes, peeled
1	cup sour cream
1	(8-ounce) package cream cheese, softened
¼	teaspoon black pepper
⅛	teaspoon garlic salt
1	teaspoon salt, or to taste
¼	teaspoon onion salt
2	tablespoons butter, cut into cubes
	Ground paprika, for garnish

- Preheat oven to 350 degrees. Butter a 2-quart glass casserole dish.
- Cook potatoes in boiling salted water until tender. Drain and mash until smooth.
- Add sour cream, cream cheese, black pepper and flavored salts. Beat until light and fluffy. Adjust seasonings.
- Spoon potatoes into casserole dish. Swirl potato mixture with the back of a spoon to make a circular pattern.
- Dot potatoes with butter and bake for 30 minutes.
- Garnish with paprika and place under broiler for a brief time, if desired.
- Cook's Tip: Potatoes may be covered and refrigerated for two days before baking or frozen for two weeks. Bring to room temperature before baking.

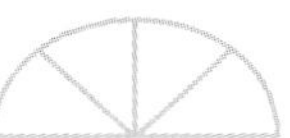

Potato Cheese Puff

Level: Easy
Serves 4-6
Preparation Time: 1½ hours

2½	cups hot mashed potatoes, do not use instant
1	cup cream-style cottage cheese
1	cup sour cream
2	teaspoons salt
	Dash black pepper
1	garlic clove, minced
3	tablespoons finely chopped onion
3	tablespoons finely chopped pimiento
4	tablespoons butter, divided
3	egg yolks, well-beaten
3	egg whites

- Preheat oven to 350 degrees. Butter a 2-quart glass baking dish.
- Combine potatoes, cottage cheese, sour cream, salt, black pepper, garlic, onion, pimiento, melted butter and egg yolks.
- Beat potato mixture until light and fluffy.
- Beat egg whites in a clean bowl with grease-free beaters until stiff.
- Fold egg whites into the potato mixture.
- Pour into the casserole, swirl top and dot with remaining 2 tablespoons of butter.
- Bake for 1 hour.
- Cook's Tip: Low-fat ricotta cheese, low-fat sour cream and decreasing the butter to only 2 tablespoons can lower the fat content of this dish.

A Culinary Reflection

I grew up in a large family (nine children), and my mother is an excellent cook. However, once when I was eight years old, she decided to make instant mashed potatoes. My older sister had tasted the potatoes and put the word out to the rest of us that they tasted terrible. So when it was time to eat, she brought a large coffee mug to the table and hid it in her lap. While mom was distracted with the baby in the high chair, the mug was passed from kid to kid and the potatoes were disposed of into the mug. We sat in the order of our ages around the table from the oldest to the youngest with the baby next to mom. Our potato disposal system worked well until it got to Linda who was two at the time. She passed it to mom. We all had to eat our mashed potatoes, but she never made instant again.

~ Marilyn Underwood

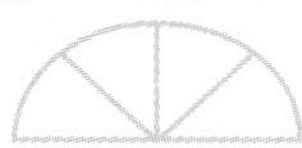

A Chef's View

Sweet Potato or Yam? A yam is generally grown in South and Central America, the West Indies and parts of Asia and Africa. The sweet potato is generally grown in the tropical areas of the Americas. Sweet potatoes and yams are not the same, even though they are frequently mistaken for one another. Yams contain more natural sugar and have higher moisture content. The sweet potato is richer in vitamins A and C. Yams and sweet potatoes may be used one for the other in most recipes.

Tomato and Mozzarella Stuffed Peppers

Level: Good Cook
Serves 6
Preparation Time: 1 hour

3 red bell peppers
1½ teaspoons olive oil
1½ tablespoons balsamic vinegar
1 garlic clove, minced
Salt and black pepper, to taste
3 large tomatoes, seeded and chopped
½ cup loosely packed fresh basil leaves, cut into thin strips
1 cup shredded Mozzarella cheese

- Preheat oven to 375 degrees. Coat a 13x9x2-inch rectangular baking dish with cooking spray.
- Cut peppers in half length-wise; remove stems, seeds and ribs.
- Place pepper halves in baking dish cut side up.
- Whisk together olive oil, vinegar, garlic, salt and black pepper in a large bowl.
- Add tomatoes, basil and mozzarella. Gently toss.
- Fill each pepper with tomato-cheese stuffing.
- Bake 40 minutes or until peppers are tender. Cover with aluminum foil if cheese begins to brown.

Apple Yams

Level: Easy
Serves 6-8
Preparation Time: 1½ hours

6 medium yams
4 tart apples, peeled, cored and sliced
Ground cinnamon, to taste
½ cup brown sugar, firmly packed
4 tablespoons butter, melted

- Cover yams with water in a stockpot and cook until fork tender. Cool and remove skins. Slice 1-inch thick.
- Preheat oven to 350 degrees. Coat a 13x9x2-inch glass baking dish with cooking spray.
- Alternate layers of yams and apples; sprinkle each layer with cinnamon, sugar and butter. Finish with a layer of apples.
- Bake covered 30 minutes.
- Uncover and bake an additional 30 minutes or until apples are fork tender.

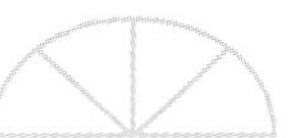

Sweet Potato Casserole with Praliné Topping

Level: Good Cook
Serves 8
Preparation Time: 1 hour

1	cup all-purpose flour
⅔	cup brown sugar, firmly packed
¼	cup chopped pecans, toasted
4	tablespoons margarine, melted
½	teaspoon ground cinnamon
4	medium sweet potatoes, peeled and quartered
½	cup granulated sugar
1½	teaspoons vanilla extract
1	large egg, white only, beaten
1	(5-ounce) can fat-free evaporated milk
1	cup flaked coconut, optional

- Combine flour, brown sugar, pecans, margarine and cinnamon, stirring to form a streusel. Set aside.
- Place potatoes in a Dutch oven; add water to cover. Bring to a boil; cover, reduce heat and simmer 30 minutes or until very tender. Drain.
- Preheat oven to 350 degrees. Coat a 2-quart casserole dish with cooking spray.
- Mash potatoes in a large bowl. Stir in 1 cup streusel, granulated sugar, vanilla extract, egg white and milk. Spoon into the casserole dish and top with remaining streusel. Bake for 45 minutes.
- Cook's Tip: Add 1 cup coconut to the streusel mix.

Rosemary Hollandaise

Level: Easy
Yield: ⅔ cup
Preparation Time: 30 minutes

2	tablespoons white vinegar
¼	teaspoon white pepper
¼	cup hot water
3	egg yolks
¾	cup (1½ sticks) butter, clarified
1½	teaspoons lemon juice
1	tablespoon ground rosemary
	Salt and black pepper, to taste

- Combine vinegar and white pepper in a saucepan and cook until reduced by one half. Cool to room temperature and add hot water and stir.
- Add egg yolks and whisk vinegar mixture until tripled in volume.
- Stir in clarified butter, whisking constantly while adding butter.
- Mix in lemon juice and rosemary. Season with salt and pepper to taste.

A Chef's View

Sweet potatoes are at their best during the months of August through October. When choosing sweet potatoes, look for those that are firm, heavy, and without bruises or cuts. The darker the skin, the sweeter and moister the pulp of the potato.

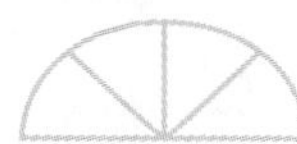

A Chef's View

Squash are welcomed in any kitchen. Thin-skinned summer zucchini can be broiled or grilled with olive oil and garlic; simmered in tomato sauce; or braised in butter with spring herbs before tossing with pasta. Add diced butternut squash and leeks to a rice-shaped pasta, drizzle with extra-virgin olive oil and sprinkle with a few hot-pepper flakes.

Summer Squash Casserole

Level: Easy
Serves 6
Preparation Time: 45 minutes

2 pounds yellow summer squash or zucchini
½ cup water
Salt, to taste
4 eggs
½ cup milk
½ cup fresh parsley, chopped
3 tablespoons all-purpose flour
2 teaspoons baking powder
1 teaspoon salt
1 (4-ounce) can diced green chiles
8 ounces ricotta or small-curd cottage cheese
8 ounces sharp Cheddar cheese, grated
3 cups small fresh bread cubes
4 tablespoon butter

- Preheat oven to 325 degrees.
- Cube or slice squash. Place in a medium-size saucepan or skillet with no more than ½ cup water and salt to taste.
- Cover and cook until barely tender, approximately 3 minutes. Drain well, then set aside to cool.
- Beat eggs in a medium-size bowl. Mix in milk, parsley, flour, baking powder, salt, green chiles and both cheeses.
- Add cooked squash.
- Butter an 11x8x2-inch baking dish. Sprinkle bottom with ½ of bread cubes.
- Pour in squash mixture. Top with rest of bread then dot with butter.
- Bake, uncovered, for 30 minutes.

Blender Hollandaise Sauce

Level: Quick and Simple
Yield: ½ cup
Preparation Time: 5 minutes

3 egg yolks
½ teaspoon salt
1 tablespoon lemon juice, freshly squeezed
¼ pound (1 stick) butter, melted

- Combine egg yolks, salt and lemon juice in a blender.
- Add melted butter and blend on high until butter is absorbed.
- Serve immediately over vegetables.

Garlic and Orange Baked Tomatoes

Level: Easy
Serves 8
Preparation Time: 40 minutes

6	tablespoons unsalted butter, softened
2	large garlic cloves, minced
2	teaspoons finely grated orange peel
	Salt and black pepper, to taste
4	large beefsteak tomatoes, or any sweet tomato
	Fresh basil leaves or cilantro, for garnish

- Mix butter with garlic, orange peel, salt and black pepper.
- Roll butter into a log and wrap in plastic or foil. Chill.
- Preheat oven to 400 degrees.
- Halve tomatoes crosswise and trim bases so they stand alone. Place tomatoes in a greased ovenproof dish.
- Slice flavored butter log in coin-size pieces and place on top of tomato halves, dividing equally.
- Bake tomatoes for 15-25 minutes or until they are just tender.
- Serve garnished with fresh basil or cilantro.
- Cook's Tip: Sprinkle grated Parmesan or Asiago cheese on top of tomatoes for an additional taste treat.

A Chef's View

Marinate sliced tomatoes over night in the refrigerator by overlapping on a platter with a lip. Combine olive oil, red wine vinegar, fresh basil, fresh parsley, minced red onion, crushed garlic and salt and pepper, to taste, in a bowl. Mix well and drizzle over tomatoes. Cover.

Spinach Soufflé

Level: Easy
Serves 6-8
Preparation Time: 1½ hours

1	(10-ounce) package frozen chopped spinach, thawed and drained
3	eggs, beaten
4	tablespoons butter, melted
4	tablespoons all-purpose flour
	Salt and black pepper, to taste
1	cup shredded Cheddar cheese
1	cup shredded American cheese
1	(16-ounce) carton small-curd cottage cheese

- Preheat oven to 350 degrees. Coat a 10x8x2-inch glass baking dish with cooking spray.
- Combine spinach, beaten eggs, melted butter, flour, salt and black pepper. Stir to blend.
- Fold in the three cheeses.
- Spoon into baking dish and bake for one hour.
- Cook's Tip: For an additional touch of flavor substitute garlic salt for regular salt and 1 (6-ounce) roll jalapeño process cheese instead of the American cheese. Add 1 teaspoon Worcestershire sauce.

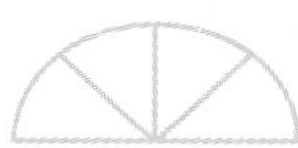

A Chef's View

Green tomatoes have a pleasant acidity that makes them perfect for frying. The best tomatoes for this dish are ones that have just started to change color. They are a little less tart then the fully green ones. Fully green tomatoes will begin to develop a pretty blush after a few days at room temperature.

Fried Green Tomatoes

Level: Easy
Serves 4
Preparation Time: 30 minutes

4	green tomatoes, sliced ½-inch thick
½	cup bacon drippings
½	cup all-purpose flour
1	tablespoon granulated sugar
	Salt and black pepper, to taste
1	tablespoon cayenne pepper
3	eggs, beaten
1	tablespoon milk
⅛	cup chopped fresh chives, optional, for garnish

- Drain sliced tomatoes on paper towels, turning once.
- Heat bacon drippings in a large cast-iron skillet over medium heat.
- Mix flour, sugar, salt, black pepper and cayenne pepper in a shallow bowl.
- Beat eggs with milk in a separate shallow bowl.
- Dip each tomato slice in egg-milk liquid and dredge in flour mixture.
- Place tomato slices in hot bacon drippings and cook over medium heat until crispy, turn to cook both sides. Do not crowd tomato slices.
- Serve topped with fresh chives, if desired.

Vegetable Tofu Stir Fry

Level: Easy
Serves 2
Preparation Time: 20 minutes

2	tablespoons sesame oil, or enough to stir fry
3	cups assorted vegetables, onion, garlic, carrots, celery, bean sprouts, bell peppers, zucchini and mushrooms, cut into bite size pieces
½	pound firm tofu, drained and cubed into ½-inch pieces
	Soy sauce
1	tablespoon granulated sugar
	Cooked rice, optional

- Heat oil in a deep skillet or wok until hot. Add garlic and onion, if using, and stir-fry for 1-2 minutes.
- Add remaining vegetables and tofu to skillet. Stir-fry briskly for 3-4 minutes or until vegetables are crisp, yet crunchy and colorful.
- Drizzle soy sauce and sprinkle sugar over vegetables and tofu. Stir-fry until coated, approximately 2 minutes.
- Divide the stir-fry between 2 warmed serving plates. Can be served over rice, if desired.

Photos: The Prairie State Park, Barton County & the White River, Branson

Ozark Mountain

America's new live-entertainment capital of Branson, crystal-blue lakes surrounded by forested hills, and attractions based on colorful native lifestyles are all part of southwest Missouri's Ozark Mountain area. Family fun highlighted by music and variety shows, shepherd's tales, and turn of the century craftspeople are all part of the entertaining and cultural Ozarks.

On river-like Lake Taneycomo, cold waters support an excellent trout fishery. Sprawling Table Rock Lake delights anglers, boaters, scuba divers, and other water recreationists. Equally big and fun is Bull Shoals Lake, while the upper end of Norfork Lake provides the region with yet another sparkling jewel.

Springfield, the state's third-largest city, offers one of Missouri's most popular attractions, Bass Pro Shops Outdoor World and the Wonders of Wildlife Museum. Just outside of Springfield, Civil War history at Wilson's Creek National Battlefield becomes alive.

Farther south, the Joplin area is rich in history with a colorful past in local mining operations. Joplin is Missouri's fourth largest metropolitan area, filled with friendly Ozark hospitality.

Other attractions include the home of *Little House* author Laura Ingalls Wilder in Mansfield. Just south, at Diamond, is the George Washington Carver National Monument, highlighting the life and career of the renowned African-American agronomist.

The Greene County Medical Society Alliance began as the Woman's Auxiliary to the Greene County Medical Society in May 1924 with Mrs. C. Bryant Elkins as president and 10 charter members. Founded on the belief that the spouse of a physician could make a difference through health awareness and education of issues affecting the community, the women's Auxiliary membership soon grew to 32 with an annual dues of one dollar. Accomplishments throughout the soon-to-be eight decades echo these beliefs in the GCMS Alliance program today.

Greene County Medical Society Alliance

Recent charitable endeavors have benefited BodyWorks, a hands-on state-of-the-art health education program at the Discovery Center of Springfield, offering classes for preschool through eighth grade students. An annual luncheon and auction fundraiser provides health scholarships; medical schools and students benefit through proceeds from a holiday sharing card. The *40 and Forever* breast cancer screening project educated the community regarding the importance of early mammograms. The Alliance continues to work in coalition with Violence-Free Families through public awareness campaigns. Currently, the GCMSA has introduced and is working closely with the *Hands Are Not For Hitting* program in the Springfield Public Schools at the elementary level. Community health-related projects benefit from the main fundraiser, the annual Society and Alliance golf tournament.

Greene County is proud of its leadership with seven of its past presidents serving as MSMA Alliance presidents: Erma Busiek, 1931-32; Nora Cole, 1939-40; Anne Cheek, 1951-52; Marjorie Peterson, 1959-60; Pat Walker, 1970-71; Joan M. H'Doubler, 1996-97; and Judy Corry, 1998-99. Today Mrs. Cheek, at 109 years of age, is the oldest living Alliance member in the United States.

The Jasper-Newton Metropolitan Medical Alliance was founded in February 1950, in Joplin by Mrs. John D. Maddox. The object of this organization was "to stimulate the spirit of fellowship and promote health-related charitable endeavors through the common bond of friendship."

Jasper-Newton Metropolitan Medical Alliance

To this end, the Jasper-Newton Metropolitan Medical Alliance has participated in many health-related endeavors, the most recent being the *Baby, Think It Over* project. This project increases awareness of infant care and support with baby mannequins containing computer programs that record and mimic infant and participant behavior. The Alliance also launched the Generation Prepared project, educating all Joplin public and private high school students in CPR by the American Heart Association standards.

The Alliance members in the foothills of the Ozarks are dedicated to ensuring the delivery of the finest health care and health education to the citizens of the four-state region. Joplin has the only free, volunteer-staffed community clinic in the United States administered and staffed by local physicians, dentists, nurses, and clergy that is solely supported by private donations and grants. Joplin also hosts the Mercy Health Resource Library, which offers free Internet, medical journals, books, and periodical resources to area citizens seeking information relating to health problems and issues.

The following Alliance members from Jasper-Newton have served as MSMA Alliance presidents: Jane Crispel, 1963-64; Lillian Gaston, 1982-83; and Becky Moore, 1997-98.

Deep Fried Catfish and Onion Rings

Level: Easy
Serves 4
Preparation Time: 2 hours

1	cup all-purpose flour
1	teaspoon salt
2	tablespoons melted butter
2	eggs, beaten
1	cup beer
2	egg whites
	Vegetable oil, for deep-frying
4	(6-ounce) catfish fillets
2	large onions, thinly sliced and separated into rings
	Windows' Tartar Sauce

- Sift flour and salt in a bowl. Stir in melted butter and eggs.
- Add beer gradually and stir until batter is smooth.
- Let batter stand in a warm place for 1 hour.
- Beat egg whites until stiffened. Fold into beer batter.
- Fill a deep heavy skillet halfway with oil and heat to 350 degrees.
- Dip fish fillets in beer batter and cook 2 at a time in hot oil for 3-4 minutes per side, or until fish is golden and flakes easily when tested with a fork. Drain on paper towels.
- Dip onion rings in the batter and fry in batches until golden, approximately 2 minutes per side. Drain on paper towels and sprinkle with salt.
- Serve immediately with *Windows'* Tartar Sauce.

Tartar Sauce

Level: Quick and Simple
Yield: 3 cups
Preparation Time: 15 minutes

2	cups mayonnaise
¼	cup dill pickle relish, drained
⅓	cup finely chopped green bell pepper
¼	cup finely chopped green onion, white and green parts
2	tablespoons finely chopped fresh parsley
1	tablespoon finely chopped capers
1-2	tablespoons lemon juice, freshly squeezed
	Salt and freshly ground black pepper, to taste

- Add all the chopped ingredients to mayonnaise. Mix well.
- Season with lemon juice, salt and black pepper to taste.
- Refrigerate in an airtight container. Sauce will thicken as it chills. Keeps well.

A Culinary Reflection

The Gasconade River is a favorite "float" of mine. Hadley, our guide in the john boat, would help us to fill a stringer of "keepers" including bass, perch, goggle-eye, and crappie. When we had enough fish for lunch, Hadley would pull onto a gravel bar and collect wood for a small fire. He would clean the fish at the rivers' edge, removing only the heads and fins, never the bones or tail, and cutting them into chunks. As a big opened can of pork and beans nestled in the ashes of the fire, Hadley would spoon some "previously used" solid shortening and bacon grease into an old iron fry pan and set it on the fire. Once melted, he placed a big wooden "farmers" match to float on the surface. When the match ignited, he knew the grease was hot enough to fry fish. He shook the fish in a brown paper bag with a mix of flour and cornmeal and dropped them into the hot grease. The fish were soon ready to eat, along with the beans, rye bread, and a cold brew - a feast indeed! Never before and never since has fried fish ever equaled those cooked by Hadley on a gravel bar while "floating" the Gasconade!

- Joan M. H'Doubler

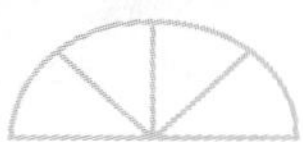

A Chef's View

The catfish gets its name from its long, whisker-like barbels which hang down from around the mouth. Most catfish are freshwater fish and the majority in the market are farmed. The channel catfish is considered the best eating. Catfish have a tough, inedible skin that must be removed before cooking. The flesh is firm, low in fat, and mild in flavor. Catfish can be fried, poached, steamed, baked or grilled. To tone down fishy flavor, soak fillets in milk for about an hour.

Catfish with Yogurt Horseradish Glaze

Level: Easy
Serves 6
Preparation Time: 30 minutes

2	pounds catfish fillets
	Salt and black pepper, to taste
½	cup yogurt
1	teaspoon cornstarch
2	tablespoons prepared horseradish
4	teaspoons dry mustard
¼	cup freshly grated Parmesan cheese
2	tablespoons lemon juice
1½	teaspoons dried dill weed
2	tablespoons capers, drained
	Lemon slices, for garnish
	Parsley sprigs, for garnish

- Preheat oven to 350 degrees. Lightly coat a glass baking dish with cooking spray.
- Season fillets with salt and black pepper.
- Combine yogurt, cornstarch, horseradish, mustard, cheese and lemon juice.
- Coat both sides of fish with yogurt mixture.
- Place fillets in baking dish. Sprinkle with dill weed and capers.
- Bake 10-12 minutes or until fish begins to flake.
- Garnish with twisted lemon slices and parsley sprigs.

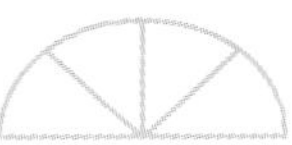

Grilled Trout with Apple Horseradish Sauce

Level: Easy
Serves 4
Preparation Time: 1 hour

4	(12-ounce) whole brook trout, cleaned with heads and tails on
3	tablespoons olive oil
	Salt and black pepper, to taste
	Windows' Apple Horseradish Sauce
2	lemons, halved

- Prepare a barbecue grill with medium-hot coals.
- Brush trout generously with olive oil. Salt and pepper to taste.
- Place trout on grill and cook until browned and fish flakes easily when tested with a fork at the thickest point, approximately 5 minutes per side.
- Serve immediately with *Windows'* Apple Horseradish Sauce and lemon halves.

Apple Horseradish Sauce

Level: Easy
Yield: ½ cup
Preparation Time: 10 minutes

8	teaspoons prepared horseradish, drained and squeezed dry
3	tablespoons mayonnaise
1	tablespoon apple cider vinegar
2	teaspoons whole-grain mustard
1	teaspoon Dijon mustard
1¼	teaspoons granulated sugar
½	teaspoon salt
	Dash cayenne pepper
¼	Granny Smith apple with peel, diced
2	tablespoons finely chopped red onion

- Whisk all ingredients except apple and onion in a large bowl until well blended.
- Fold in apple and onion.
- Refrigerate for several hours to allow the flavors to blend.
- Cook's Tip: This sauce works well with any white fish. The recipe makes only ½ cup of sauce and may need to be doubled.

A Chef's View

Look for these characteristics when choosing fish for eating: bright, clear, full, and often protruding eyes; bright-red or pink gills; firm elastic flesh which springs back when gently pressed with a finger; shiny skin; firmly attached scales; fresh mild odor; and fresh-cut appearance for fillets.

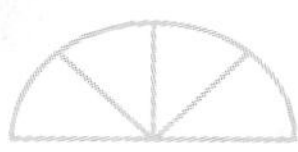

A Chef's View

Careful handling of fresh trout is the first step in preparing a great recipe. Here are some tips:

- *Do not keep your catch in a wicker creel more than three hours on a warm day.*
- *Clean trout quickly and put it in a watertight plastic bag or container to keep trout cool and dry until you reach home.*
- *Prepare trout at cleaning time according to the way you'll be cooking it.*
- *Freeze trout in a quantity suitable for one meal. Place fish in large container and cover with water, then freeze.*
- *Thaw frozen trout under cold running water. Thaw quickly but never at room temperature in warm water. Do not refreeze.*

Italian Baked Trout

Level: Easy
Serves 1
Preparation Time: 35 minutes

1 trout, per person
Greek seasoning
1 bottle nonfat Italian salad dressing
Italian seasoned bread crumbs

- Preheat oven to 350 degrees. Coat a baking dish with cooking spray.
- Clean, bone, and cut off trout's head, leaving skin on.
- Sprinkle fish with Greek seasoning.
- Dip fish in salad dressing and then in the seasoned bread crumbs.
- Place in baking dish and bake for 20-30 minutes.

Grilled Fish Steaks

Level: Quick and Simple
Serves 2
Preparation Time: 30 minutes

1 pound walleye, pike or salmon steaks
1 teaspoon soy sauce
¼ cup prepared mustard
¼ cup mayonnaise

- Preheat a barbecue grill on high for 10 minutes; decrease temperature to medium.
- Brush both sides of steaks with soy sauce.
- Combine mustard and mayonnaise and brush on steaks.
- Place fish on grate and grill 5 minutes to a side, or until fish begins to flake.

Tilapia Almondine

Level: Quick and Simple
Serves 4
Preparation Time: 30 minutes

½	cup sliced almonds
4	tablespoons butter or margarine, melted
4	large tilapia fillets, or other white fish
	Salt and black pepper, to taste
	Dried thyme, to taste
	Milk
	Self-rising flour
½	cup canola oil
1	tablespoon minced fresh parsley
	Lemon wedges

- Sauté almonds in butter in a large skillet until golden brown; do not allow butter to burn.
- Transfer almonds to a bowl and set aside.
- Sprinkle fillets with salt, black pepper and thyme. Dip in milk and dredge in flour.
- Fry fillets in hot oil and butter remaining in skillet over medium heat until golden brown, turning once, approximately five minutes per side. Drain on paper towels.
- Transfer fillets to serving platter and sprinkle with almonds and parsley; drizzle with any remaining brown butter. Serve with lemon wedges.

Tuna Jackstraws

Level: Easy
Serves 4
Preparation Time: 45 minutes

1	(7½-ounce) can water-packed tuna, drained
1	(10¾-ounce) can cream of mushroom soup
⅔	cup evaporated milk
1	(12-ounce) can shoestring potatoes
½	cup frozen peas, lightly thawed and patted dry

- Preheat oven to 350 degrees. Lightly coat a 11x7x2-inch casserole dish with cooking spray.
- Combine all ingredients in a bowl and mix well.
- Spoon into the casserole dish.
- Bake 30 minutes or until bubbly.

A Chef's View

Tilapia (tuh-LAH-pee-uh), an important food fish in Africa for centuries, has spread around the world to be found in most mass markets today. The low-fat flesh is white, sweet, and fine-textured. It's suitable for baking, broiling, grilling, and steaming.

A Chef's View

Tuna is a member of the mackerel family of fish and is found in temperate marine waters throughout the world. It is one of the most popular fish used for canning today. Canned tuna is precooked and is sold as albacore, or white meat tuna, and light meat. It can be purchased canned as solid, chunk, and flaked or grated, packed in water or oil.

A Show-Me Specialty

Blackened Red Drum Fish is a specialty of Glenn's Café in downtown Columbia, Missouri. Glenn's specializes in Cajun and New Orleans style dishes using fresh seafood and vegetables in all of their recipes.

Glenn's Café
29 South Ninth Street
Columbia
573-443-3094

A Missouri Window

Hermann, Missouri, is a storybook German village with a rich winemaking and riverboat history that is proudly displayed in area museums. Built in 1836 as the 'New Fatherland' for German settlers, the town has achieved national recognition because of its quality wines and distinctive heritage.

Glenn's Café Blackened Red Drum Fish

Level: Easy
Serves 8
Preparation Time: 30 minutes

- 1 tablespoon sweet paprika
- 1 teaspoon salt
- 1 teaspoon onion powder
- 1 teaspoon garlic powder
- 1 teaspoon cayenne pepper
- ¾ teaspoon ground white pepper
- ¾ teaspoon black pepper
- ½ teaspoon dried thyme leaves
- ½ teaspoon dried oregano leaves
- 8 (10-ounce) red drum fish fillets
- ½ cup (1 stick) butter, melted and divided

- ◆ Heat a cast iron skillet until hot.
- ◆ Prepare spice blend by combining paprika, salt, onion and garlic powders, peppers, thyme and oregano.
- ◆ Coat fillets thoroughly with melted butter and season heavily with spice blend.
- ◆ Add some melted butter to skillet.
- ◆ Place fillets carefully into a skillet. Pan fry in batches. Skillet will smoke heavily.
- ◆ Cook a ½-inch thick fillet approximately 3 minutes on each side.
- ◆ Serve with additional melted butter.

Grilled Salmon Chardonnay

Level: Easy
Serves 1
Preparation Time: 1½ hours

- 1 (16-ounce) salmon fillet, with skin
- 2 tablespoons lemon juice, freshly squeezed
- 2 tablespoons Chardonnay or other dry white wine
- 2 large garlic cloves, slivered
- 1 teaspoon Cajun spice seasoning

- ◆ Marinate salmon, skin side up, in lemon juice and wine for ½ hour in the refrigerator. Use a glass dish.
- ◆ Preheat a grill or oven broiler with rack 6 inches from heat.
- ◆ Push garlic slivers into flesh of salmon from skin side.
- ◆ Sprinkle with Cajun spice seasoning and return to marinade, skin side up, while grill heats.
- ◆ Grill 6-8 minutes, skin side down until done. Baste every 2 minutes with marinade.

Rick's Salmon Napoleon

Level: Good Cook
Serves 1
Preparation Time: 35 minutes

- 1 (8-ounce) salmon, skinned and boned
- 1 (5x5-inch) puff pastry square
- ½ ounce spinach leaves, washed and dried
- ¼ Red Delicious apple, peeled, cored and chopped
- 3 ounces dry white wine, divided
- ¼ teaspoon fresh minced garlic
- 1 teaspoon finely minced shallots
- 4-6 tablespoons margarine, divided
- ½ ounce apple cider vinegar
- 1½ tablespoons fresh lemon juice
- 2 ounces heavy cream

- Grill salmon on cooking oil-sprayed rack 6 inches from coals. Grill until flesh is opaque approximately 4-6 minutes per side depending upon temperature of coals and thickness of salmon steak.
- Brush puff pastry square with egg wash and bake until golden brown according to package directions.
- Sauté spinach, apple and 1 ounce of wine while salmon is grilling. Reduce until just moist.
- Sauté garlic and shallots in 1 tablespoon margarine until translucent.
- Add vinegar, lemon juice and 2 ounces of wine and reduce to ¼ the volume.
- Stir in cream and reduce by ½ the volume. Remove from heat.
- Whisk in additional margarine 1 tablespoon at a time until sauce is creamy.
- Split puff pastry lengthwise. Position bottom half of pastry in the center of serving plate. Spoon spinach mixture on puff pastry.
- Place salmon on top of spinach. Put top half of pastry on salmon.
- Ladle sauce over all. Serve hot.

A Show-Me Specialty

Salmon Napoleon is a specialty of Rick's Restaurant downtown Columbia, Missouri.

Rick's
38 North Eighth
Columbia
573-442-7881

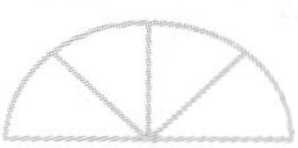

A Missouri Window

During the American Civil War (1861-1865), Missourians were torn between loyalties to the South and to the Union. After the war, manufacturing developed rapidly, and St. Louis and Kansas City grew into industrial giants. Agriculture also expanded, and Missouri became a great farming state.

Poached Salmon with Spinach

Level: Easy
Serves 4
Preparation Time: 25 minutes

1	pound salmon fillets
1½	cups water
½	cup dry white wine or water
2	green onions, white and green parts, diagonally sliced
1	bay leaf
½	(10-ounce) package frozen chopped spinach
⅛	teaspoon ground nutmeg
¼	cup shredded part-skim mozzarella cheese
	Freshly ground black pepper
	Lemon slices, optional, for garnish

- Cut salmon into 4 pieces, rinse and pat dry. Set aside.
- Combine water, wine, green onions and bay leaf in a large skillet. Bring just to a boil over high heat.
- Add salmon and return to a boil. Reduce heat, cover and simmer 8-10 minutes or until fish flakes easily with a fork.
- Remove fish with a spatula and pat dry with paper towels. Tent with aluminum foil and keep warm.
- Cook spinach according to package directions. Drain, squeeze out moisture and add nutmeg.
- Preheat broiler.
- Place salmon on a broiler-proof serving platter or on the rack of an unheated broiler pan.
- Top with spinach mixture, sprinkle with cheese and season with black pepper.
- Broil 4 inches from the heat for 1-2 minutes or until cheese melts.
- Garnish with lemon slices, if desired.

Carolina Crab Cakes with Rémoulade Sauce

Level: Easy
Yield: 24 cakes
Preparation Time: 2 hours

6	saltine crackers, crushed
¼	teaspoon cayenne pepper
½	teaspoon celery seed
1	teaspoon mustard powder
2	cups fresh bread crumbs
2	egg whites, beaten
2	cups mayonnaise
1	teaspoon freshly squeezed lemon juice
2	pounds lump crabmeat, cleaned
	Butter
	Canola oil, for frying
	All-purpose flour, for dredging
	Windows' Rémoulade Sauce

- Combine saltines, cayenne pepper, celery seed, dry mustard and bread crumbs.
- Fold saltine mixture into egg whites.
- Mix mayonnaise, lemon juice and crabmeat to egg white mixture. Mixture will appear too soft.
- Form 24 (2-ounce) patties by weight or size and place on a cookie sheet.
- Refrigerate crab cakes for approximately 45 minutes.
- Melt butter and a small amount of cooking oil in a sauté pan.
- Dredge crab cakes in flour.
- Fry cakes quickly until golden on each side. Do not crowd. Drain on paper towels.
- Place cakes on a clean cookie sheet and bake in 350 degree oven, 10-15 minutes or until springy to the touch.
- Serve with *Windows'* Rémoulade Sauce.

Rémoulade Sauce

Level: Easy
Yield: 4 cups
Preparation Time: 1 hour

4	cups mayonnaise
⅓	cup capers, drained and finely chopped
6	green onions, finely chopped, white and green parts
⅓	cup finely chopped fresh parsley
1½	tablespoons fresh lemon juice
2	tablespoons tarragon vinegar

- Combine all ingredients.
- Chill at least 1 hour.

A Chef's View

If you like your seafood with a red sauce, give this one a try.

Red Seafood Sauce: Combine 1 (12-ounce) bottle chili sauce, 2 tablespoons prepared horseradish, and 1 tablespoon lemon juice; cover and chill. Yield: 1¼ cups.

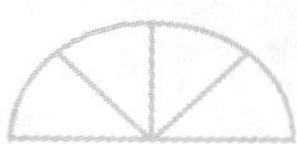

A Chef's View

Shrimp are versatile and suited to all methods of cooking. They carry other flavors well while maintaining their own sweet, tender character. Buy only as much shrimp as you need. However, if you must store them follow these tips: Rinse raw shrimp under cold running water, and drain. Store in an airtight container or heavy-duty zip-top plastic bag in the refrigerator up to two days. Freeze shrimp in airtight containers or heavy-duty zip-top freezer bags. Frozen shrimp start to lose quality after three months. Thaw them under cold running water or in the refrigerator overnight. Drain and pat dry with paper towels.

Seafood Medley

Level: Good Cook
Serves 12
Preparation Time: 2 hours

2 cups dry white wine, or vegetable stock
½ cup chopped white onion
1 cup fresh parsley, chopped and divided
½ pound (2 sticks) butter, divided
1 pound shrimp, cleaned
1 pound bay scallops
1½ pounds cooked lump crabmeat
2 (7-ounce) cans sliced mushrooms, drained
1 cup chopped celery
4 green onions, chopped, white and green parts
1 green bell pepper, chopped
1 red bell pepper, chopped
6 tablespoons all-purpose flour
2 cups half-and-half
1½ cups shredded Swiss cheese
2 tablespoons fresh lemon juice
1½ teaspoons lemon pepper
2 cups seasoned bread crumbs
½ cup sliced almonds, toasted
½ cup freshly grated Parmesan cheese

- Combine wine, white onion, ½ cup parsley and 2 tablespoons butter in a stockpot. Bring to boil.
- Add shrimp and scallops. Cook 3-5 minutes or until shrimp turns pink.
- Drain. Reserve stock. Set both aside.
- Melt 3 tablespoons butter in a skillet. Sauté mushrooms, celery, ½ cup parsley, green onions and peppers until heated through. Set aside.
- Make a roux by melting 6 tablespoon butter over low heat in a Dutch oven. Add flour, stirring constantly until smooth.
- Cook roux an additional 2 minutes, stirring constantly, to remove flour taste. Do not brown.
- Pour and stir 2 cups half-and-half gradually into roux. Cook over medium heat, stirring constantly until mixture is thickened and bubbly.
- Add Swiss cheese to half-and-half mixture. Stir until melted.
- Stir in 1⅓ cups of reserved stock, lemon juice and lemon pepper seasoning into creamed sauce.
- Fold in vegetable mixture, shrimp, scallops and crab. Do not break up seafood.
- Spoon into a lightly greased 14x10x2-inch baking dish or two 11x7x2-inch baking dishes.
- Cover with foil, bake in a preheated 350 degree oven for 40-50 minutes. Casserole should be bubbly around edges.

continued on next page

Seafood Medley continued

- Melt remaining butter and combine with bread crumbs, almonds and Parmesan cheese. Sprinkle over uncovered casserole.
- Bake an additional 10 minutes.
- Let stand 10 minutes. Serve over cooked rice.

Seafood in Sunny Lime Butter Sauce

Level: Easy
Serves 4
Preparation Time: 30 minutes

1 cup white rice
2 cups water
4 tablespoons butter, divided
1 medium onion, sliced
1 green bell pepper, sliced
1 garlic clove, pressed
1 tomato, chopped
2 tablespoons white wine vinegar
2 tablespoons lime juice
1 tablespoon Dijon mustard
½ teaspoon thyme
1 tablespoon fish base
4 ounces conch, canned/frozen, chopped and sautéed in butter
4 large shrimp
8 scallops
Salt and black pepper, to taste
Dash hot pepper sauce, or to taste

- Add rice to water in a 2-quart saucepan and bring to boil. Reduce heat, cover and simmer until water is absorbed. Set aside.
- Melt butter and sauté onion, green pepper and garlic.
- Add tomato, vinegar, lime juice, mustard, thyme and fish base.
- Simmer 10 minutes or until vegetables are soft.
- Add seafood and cook 5 minutes more or until shrimp are pink.
- Season with salt, black pepper and hot sauce to taste.
- Ladle over hot rice.
- Cook's Tip: If conch is unavailable, any other seafood may be substituted.

A Chef's View

Conch is a mollusk encased in a beautiful, brightly colored spiral shell. Conch is found in southern waters and is particularly popular in Florida and the Caribbean. Summer is the peak season for fresh conch. Store fresh conch, tightly wrapped, in the refrigerator up to 2 days. Conch can also be canned or frozen. It can be eaten raw in salads, or tenderized by pounding, then quickly sautéing. Conch is often chopped and used in chowders.

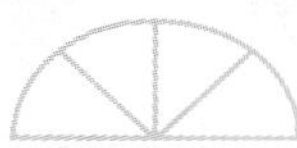

A Chef's View

An egg wash is egg yolk or egg white mixed with a small amount of water or milk. It's brushed over breads, pastry, and other baked goods before baking to give them color and gloss.

Crab Strudel

Level: Good Cook
Serves 12
Preparation Time: 1 hour

½	pound (2 sticks) unsalted butter, softened
½	cup finely chopped fresh parsley, divided
¼	cup finely chopped fresh chives
1	tablespoon lemon juice
½	cup chopped shallots, chopped
¼	cup chopped celery
1	cup Chardonnay wine, or other dry white wine
¾	pound lump crabmeat
4	ounces cream cheese, softened
1	tablespoon golden lemon thyme, chopped
½	teaspoon ground white pepper
4	egg yolks
16	sheets phyllo pastry, thawed
1	egg, beaten, for egg wash
	Lemon thyme sprigs, for garnish

- Prepare herb butter by creaming unsalted butter until soft and stir in ¼ cup parsley, chives and lemon juice. Set aside.
- Cook and stir shallots and celery in ½ cup melted herb butter in a small saucepan over medium heat for 5 minutes.
- Add wine and bring to a boil.
- Lower heat and reduce mixture to ½ cup.
- Stir in crabmeat, cream cheese, ¼ cup parsley, lemon thyme, ground white pepper and egg yolks. Mix well.
- Melt remaining herb butter in a small saucepan.
- Brush 1 phyllo pastry sheet (14x18-inches) with herb butter, top with another pastry sheet and butter until 8 layers deep.
- Spread last layer of phyllo with ½ the crab filling. Roll, jelly-roll fashion, from long end with seam to bottom.
- Repeat with second roll of phyllo pastry.
- Brush each roll with egg wash. Bake on ungreased baking sheet in a preheated 400 degree oven for 12-15 minutes or until golden brown.
- Cut each strudel roll into six pieces using a serrated knife.
- Garnish each serving with a lemon thyme sprig.
- Cook's Tip: Cut into smaller pieces and serve as an appetizer.

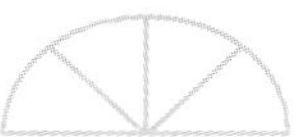

Scalloped Corn and Oysters

Level: Easy
Serves 6
Preparation Time: 1½ hours

- 2 (16-ounce) cans cream style corn
- 3 cups bread cubes, 1-inch cut
- ½ cup brown sugar, firmly packed
- ½ cup evaporated milk
- 2 eggs, beaten
- Salt and black pepper, to taste
- 2 (8-ounce) cans oysters, drained

- ◆ Preheat oven to 400 degrees.
- ◆ Combine ingredients, carefully stirring in oysters last.
- ◆ Bake uncovered, in a greased 2-quart baking dish for 1 hour.

Mushroom and Onion Stuffed Shrimp

Level: Easy
Serves 2
Preparation Time: 40 minutes

- ½ cup fresh mushrooms, finely chopped
- 2 tablespoons finely chopped onion
- ½ garlic clove, minced
- 4 rye crackers, finely crushed
- 1 tablespoon chopped pimiento
- 1 egg white, whipped
- 8 peeled jumbo shrimp, with tails
- ¼ teaspoon lemon pepper
- ¼ teaspoon salt
- Lemon wedges
- Parsley sprigs, for garnish
- Cooking oil

- ◆ Preheat oven to 400 degrees. Coat a jelly-roll pan with butter-flavored cooking spray.
- ◆ Sauté mushrooms, onion and garlic until tender over medium heat in a skillet coated with cooking spray.
- ◆ Remove from heat and stir in cracker crumbs, pimiento and whipped egg white.
- ◆ Cut a slit on inside of shrimp but do not cut through. Remove vein.
- ◆ Spray each shrimp with cooking oil to coat.
- ◆ Mound stuffing mixture in hollow of each shrimp. Place on jelly-roll pan and season with lemon pepper and salt.
- ◆ Bake 8-10 minutes or until hot. Shrimp will turn pink.
- ◆ Serve with lemon wedges and garnish with parsley.

A Chef's View

Though 18th-century satirist Jonathan Swift once wrote, "He was a bold man that first ate an oyster," this bivalve had been a culinary favorite for thousands of years. Live oysters should be covered with a damp towel and refrigerated, larger shell down, up to 3 days. The sooner they're used the better they'll taste. Oysters are also available canned in water or their own liquor, frozen or smoked.

A Missouri Window

Named for French settlers from the province of Gascony in southwestern France, the Gasconade River, starting as a tributary off the Missouri River south of Hermann, is reputed to be one of the crookedest rivers in the world. Entirely in Missouri, the river winds nearly 300 miles. A feeling of wilderness and serenity is created by steep bluffs with protruding boulders, caves, lazy eddies, dogwoods, wild flowers, birds, and the sighting of four-legged creatures at the water's edge. Add fishing to this float scene and the magic begins.

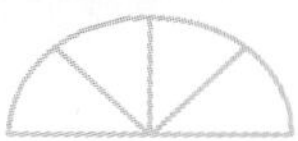

A Chef View

If you can't capture fresh flavor at the seaside, look for these seafood characteristics at your nearby landlocked supermarket when purchasing shrimp: mild odor; firm, not slippery, flesh; head closely attached to tail section; shell and flesh free of black spots.

Shrimp and Coconut Milk Curry

Level: Good Cook
Serves 6
Preparation Time: 1 hour

1	teaspoon canola oil
1	large onion, chopped
1	red bell pepper, chopped
3	garlic cloves, minced
1	jalapeño pepper, seeded and minced
2	tablespoons curry powder
1	teaspoon ground cumin seeds
1	teaspoon ground coriander
1	(12-ounce) can evaporated skim milk
¼	cup unsweetened coconut milk
1½	pounds large shrimp, peeled and deveined
1	cup frozen peas
2	tablespoons fresh lime juice
1	tablespoon cornstarch
⅓	cup fresh cilantro, chopped
	Salt, to taste
	Freshly ground black pepper, to taste
	Cooked basmati rice
	Lime wedges, optional, for garnish

- Heat oil in a Dutch oven over medium heat. Add onion and bell pepper, cook and stir until softened, approximately 5 minutes.
- Add garlic, jalapeño, curry powder, cumin and coriander and cook 1-2 minutes, stirring until fragrant.
- Reduce heat to low. Add evaporated milk and coconut milk and stir.
- Bring milk mixture to a simmer, stirring constantly. Simmer for 5 minutes.
- Add shrimp and peas and cook, uncovered, until shrimp are pink and peas warmed through, approximately 5 minutes.
- Combine lime juice and cornstarch; whisk until smooth.
- Add lime mixture to shrimp mixture and cook, stirring constantly until thickened.
- Stir in cilantro and season with salt and black pepper.
- Serve curry over brown basmati rice.
- Garnish with lime wedges, if desired.

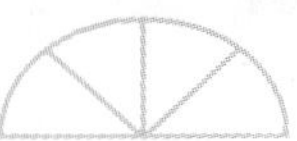

Shrimp and Rice Supreme

Level: Easy
Serves 8
Preparation Time: 45 minutes

1 cup chopped celery
½ cup green bell pepper, chopped
7 green onions, chopped, white and green parts
½ pound sliced fresh mushrooms
¼ pound (1 stick) plus 4 tablespoons butter, divided
1 pound cooked shrimp, shelled and deveined
1 (8-ounce) can sliced water chestnuts, drained
1 cup raw rice, cooked per directions
1 cup mayonnaise
1 (10¾-ounce) can cream of shrimp soup
1 tablespoon Worcestershire sauce
1 cup cornflakes cereal, crushed
1 (6-ounce) package slivered almonds

- Preheat oven to 350 degrees. Butter a 13x9x2-inch casserole dish.
- Sauté celery, green pepper, green onion and sliced mushrooms in 8 tablespoons butter.
- Mix together with shrimp, water chestnuts, cooked rice, mayonnaise, soup and Worcestershire sauce.
- Pour into buttered casserole dish.
- Melt 4 tablespoons butter and combine with crushed cornflakes.
- Sprinkle casserole with cornflake mixture and then with the slivered almonds.
- Bake for 30 minutes.

A Missouri Window

In Hermann, the Deutschheim State Historic Site features four buildings, all in Hermann's historic district, which reflect the culture of German immigrants and German Americans across Missouri. The Strehly House, furnished for the 1880s, was the site of the first German print shop west of St. Louis, and the radical newspaper Lichtfreund ("Friend of Light") and the Wochenblatt ("Weekly Paper") were produced here. The winery is used for arts, crafts, and daily life displays. The Pommer-Gentner House is furnished as in the 1840s, and its barn holds a variety of early German tools.

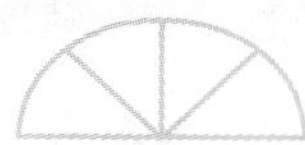

A Chef's View

Duck can be prepared in a variety of manners including roasting, braising, and broiling. Add flavor to a duck or duckling by tucking a lemon, orange, apple or onion and herbs into the body cavity before trussing and roasting. Ducks and geese should be carved before they are brought to the table. Cut through the leg joints close to the body and remove legs. Repeat with wings. Then slit the skin along either side of the breastbone. Slide the knife into the cut on one side of the breastbone and lift off meat in a single piece. Repeat on the other side. Cut the meat into serving pieces and arrange with the legs and wings on platter. It is best NOT to stuff ducks or ducklings with bread crumbs or other absorbent stuffing; it will simply sop up the fat and become greasy.

Roast Duckling à l'Orange

Level: Expert Cook
Serves 4
Preparation Time: 2 hours

1	duck, oven ready
1½	teaspoons salt, divided
¾	teaspoon black pepper, divided
1	small lemon, prick well with fork
6	garlic cloves, unpeeled
2	whole bay leaves
2	tablespoons freshly grated orange peel
⅓	cup white vinegar
¼	cup granulated sugar
⅔	cup orange juice
1¾	cups chicken stock
1	teaspoon tomato paste
½	cup dry white wine
2	teaspoons cornstarch
2	tablespoons cold water

- Preheat oven to 450 degrees.
- Remove fat from body cavity, discard and prick skin with fork.
- Sprinkle cavity with ½ teaspoon salt and ¼ teaspoon black pepper. Insert lemon in cavity along with garlic and bay leaves.
- Place duck, breast side up, on a rack in a roasting pan. Sprinkle with ½ teaspoon salt and ¼ teaspoon black pepper.
- Roast duck, uncovered 45 minutes, spoon off fat as it accumulates.
- Reduce oven temperature to 350 degrees. Roast duck until an instant-read thermometer inserted in meatiest part of thigh, but not touching bone, registers 180 degrees, approximately 35-45 minutes longer.
- Cook orange peel, for 10 minutes, in a saucepan of boiling water, drain and set aside.
- Boil vinegar and sugar without stirring, in a saucepan over moderate heat, until amber in color, approximately 4 minutes.
- Stir in orange juice, chicken stock, tomato paste, ½ teaspoon salt, ¼ teaspoon black pepper and the reserved orange peel. Set aside.
- Pour all fat from the roasting pan. Set pan over moderate heat, add wine and cook for 2 minutes, stirring constantly to loosen browned bits.
- Add to orange juice mixture, cook, uncovered, until reduced by ⅓, approximately 10 minutes.
- Blend cornstarch and water. Add to juice mixture. Cook, stirring until mixture bubbles and thickens, approximately 3 minutes.
- Carve duck into serving portions, removing breast from bone and separating legs and thighs.
- Pour sauce over duck and serve.

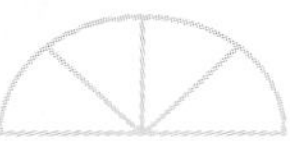

Roasted Duck Breast with Cherry Sauce

Level: Good Cook
Serves 4
Preparation Time: 1½ hours

4 (8-ounce) duck breasts
2 shallots, finely chopped
½ cup sherry vinegar
1 teaspoon granulated sugar
1 pint duck or *Windows'* Beef Demi-Glace
Salt and black pepper, to taste
4 tablespoons butter
1 cup tart cherries

- Preheat oven to 450 degrees.
- Sear duck breasts, skin side first, until crispy in an ovenproof or cast iron pan in oven.
- Turn duck breasts over and roast until juices run clear.
- Remove duck breasts from pan and let rest.
- Drain fat from pan. Add shallots, vinegar and sugar. Cook until liquid caramelizes.
- Add demi-glace and season with salt and black pepper.
- Strain hot sauce. Finish by adding butter and cherries. Warm.
- Serve each breast, sliced on a plate, with cherry sauce poured on top.

Sauce for Duck or Goose

Level: Easy
Yield: 2 cups
Preparation Time: 15 minutes

¼ pound (1 stick) butter
1 cup granulated sugar
3 ounces frozen orange juice concentrate

- Bring all ingredients to a boil. Simmer until sugar dissolves.
- Serve warm.

A Chef's View

A new cast iron skillet has to be seasoned before it can be used. Wash and dry the pan, rub the inside generously with unsalted shortening and place in a preheated 350 degree oven for about 2 hours. Once seasoned, do not clean the skillet with detergents. Use kosher salt and a nonabrasive scrubber, then rinse and wipe dry. To avoid rust, place the pan over low heat to dry thoroughly. Over time, a well-cared-for and seasoned cast iron skillet ideally will blacken, developing its own nonstick surface.

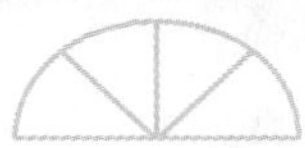

A Chef's View

Geese were bred in ancient Egypt, China, and India. The Romans revered them because it was a noisy gaggle of geese that alerted 4th-century B.C. Romans that the enemy Gauls were about to attack. Today, in the U.S., the USDA classifies the quality of geese with an A, B or C grade, with the A grade found in most mass markets. Choose a goose that is plump, with a good fatty layer and skin that is clean and unblemished. Store loosely covered in the coldest section of the refrigerator 2-3 days. Remove and store separately any giblets in the body cavity. Because geese have so much fat, they are best roasted. The fat, derived from roasting a goose, is prized by many cooks as cooking fat. Goose benefits from being served with a tart fruit sauce, which helps offset any fatty taste.

Apricot Stuffed Goose

Level: Good Cook
Serves 4
Preparation Time: 2 hours

1	wild goose, oven ready
	Salt and black pepper, to taste
2	cups dried apricots, cut in half
3	tablespoons granulated sugar
2	cups bread crumbs
½	pound (2 sticks) melted butter, divided
1	cup currant jelly
2	cups orange juice
6	tablespoons apricot brandy

- Parboil goose for 15 minutes in a large stockpot. Remove and pat dry. Rub insides and out with salt and black pepper.
- Cover apricot halves with hot water. Soak for 20 minutes. Drain.
- Combine drained apricots, sugar, bread crumbs and butter. Add enough water to moisten dressing. Lightly stuff goose. Place in a roasting pan.
- Preheat oven to 350 degrees.
- Roast goose for 20 minutes per pound. Baste with melted butter. Juices will run clear when goose is cooked.
- Mix currant jelly, orange juice and apricot brandy in a saucepan. Heat to melt jelly. Pour 1 cup glaze over goose during last 20 minutes of baking.
- Continue to baste frequently with pan juices.
- Serve goose and stuffing with remainder of heated sauce on the side.

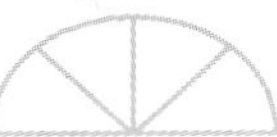

Pan Roasted Pheasant with Shiitake Mushrooms

Level: Good Cook
Serves 2
Preparation Time: 1 hour

1	(2-pound) pheasant, oven ready
	Salt and black pepper, to taste
1	tablespoon canola oil
1	cup dried figs, stems removed
2	cups raspberry-flavored wine
2	tablespoons unsalted butter, divided
2	medium shallots, thinly sliced
1	cup shiitake mushrooms, stemmed and thinly sliced
½	cup poultry stock
½	teaspoon finely chopped fresh rosemary

- Preheat oven to 400 degrees.
- Remove breast from pheasant but retain breast skin. Disjoint legs and thighs. Season pheasant pieces with salt and black pepper.
- Heat canola oil in a sauté pan over medium high heat.
- Brown legs and thighs evenly and bake in oven for 20 minutes in sauté pan.
- Bring figs and wine to a low boil in a heavy saucepan. Reduce and simmer mixture to ⅓ of original volume.
- Remove sauté pan from oven, removing legs and thighs. Return pan to stove burner for 45 seconds.
- Sear skin side of pheasant breast for 1 minute in sauté pan. Turn breast and return thighs and legs to pan. Finish in oven for 6-8 minutes.
- Remove pheasant from pan to a serving platter.
- Add 1 tablespoon butter to the pan and sauté shallots until light brown.
- Stir in shiitakes and cook until tender, approximately 1 minute.
- Mix stock and rosemary into fig and wine mixture; reduce sauce to thicken. Adjust seasonings and whisk in remaining butter.
- To serve, slice breast and arrange on serving plates with a leg and thigh. Pour fig and wine sauce over pheasant.

A Chef's View

The flavor of duck, goose, pheasant, quail, and other wild fowl is drastically affected by what the bird eats. Fish-eating fowl will often have a stronger flavor than grain- or vegetation-fed birds.

A Chef's View

Leave skin intact on most game birds during storage to act as a natural protection against freezer burn. If birds are skinned, store in water in freezer-safe containers to prevent freezer burn.

Pheasant in Sour Cream

Level: Easy
Serves 2-3
Preparation Time: 3½ hours

1	cup plus 1 tablespoon all-purpose flour, divided
1	tablespoon salt
½	teaspoon black pepper
1	tablespoon ground paprika
1	pheasant, cut into serving pieces
2	tablespoons butter
1	cup sour cream
1	cup light cream
1	(4-ounce) can whole or sliced mushrooms, drained
½	cup sherry or white wine

- Preheat oven to 300 degrees.
- Place 1 cup flour, salt, black pepper and paprika in a paper bag.
- Add pheasant and shake. Remove pheasant from bag, shaking off excess flour.
- Brown pheasant in butter in a sauté pan. Place in a buttered baking dish.
- Stir remaining 1 tablespoon flour into pan drippings. Blend in sour cream, light cream, mushrooms and sherry.
- Pour sauce over pheasant and bake for 3 hours.
- Skim off excess fat and stir sauce before serving.

Red Wine Sauce

Level: Easy
Serves 6
Preparation Time: 3 hours

1	cup shallots, sliced thin
½	teaspoon cracked black pepper
3	tablespoons butter, divided
1	cup ruby port
3	cups good quality red wine
4	cups veal stock
	Salt, to taste

- Combine shallots, pepper and 1 tablespoon butter in a non-corrosive heavy 4-quart pot. Cook over medium heat until shallots are well caramelized.
- Add ruby port and simmer until reduced to a syrup.
- Pour in red wine and reduce mixture until it is syrupy.
- Add veal stock and reduce over low heat for approximately 1½ hours.
- Strain into another pot and bring to a simmer. Whisk in 2 tablespoons cold butter. Season with salt and serve.

Quail in Madeira Wine

Level: Good Cook
Serves 4
Preparation Time: 8-12 hours

	Salt and black pepper, to taste
1½	cups all-purpose flour, for dredging
8	quail, soaked 8-10 hours in salt water and patted dry
6	tablespoons butter
2	cups sliced fresh mushrooms
1	cup Madeira wine
1	cup chicken consommé
1	celery rib, quartered
1	thinly sliced lemon
	Chopped parsley
	Wild rice, cooked according to package directions

- Preheat oven to 350 degrees.
- Season each bird with salt and pepper, to taste. Lightly dredge birds in flour.
- Melt butter in skillet.
- Brown quail until golden in melted butter. If butter burns during this process, discard and replace butter.
- Place quail in baking dish coated with cooking spray.
- Sauté mushrooms in remaining butter. Add wine and consommé; bring to a boil. Pour sauce over quail.
- Add celery and lemon slices; sprinkle with parsley.
- Bake for 1 hour or until tender.
- Remove celery and lemon slices from sauce before serving.
- Serve quail with wild rice and topped with sauce.

A Chef's View

Etiquette for quail means that you can eat as much of the breast meat as you can using your knife and fork. The rest is finger food. It is quite acceptable and almost necessary to pick up the legs and wings with your thumb and index finger. When serving quail as an entrée, allow two large birds per person. For an appetizer serving, one is appropriate. Look for quail in the frozen meat section of the grocery store.

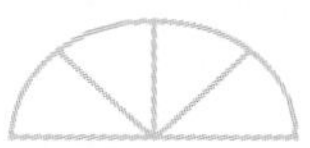

A Culinary Reflection

Over the holidays, my father went hunting and proudly returned home from the hunting trip with geese. We were going to have goose for dinner. I followed him and watched his every move, until he began 'dressing' the first goose. Now Daddy had never dressed a goose before. After a lot of trial and error he decided to singe the down off. What an odor! It was horrible! We opened up the house and went out to dinner that night.

~ Jana Wolfe

Quail with Wild Rice, Sage and Apples

Level: Good Cook
Serves 6
Preparation Time: 2½ hours

6	quail, oven ready
	Salt and black pepper, to taste
2	teaspoons grated orange peel, divided
2½	cups vegetable stock
½	cup wild rice
1	dried bay leaf
1	cup diced onion
¾	cup diced celery
½	cup minced fresh sage
1	medium green apple, peeled, cored and diced
1	egg white
⅓	cup walnuts, toasted
½	teaspoon fresh ground black pepper
¼	cup parsley, minced
½	cup chicken stock
¼	cup beef stock, optional
¼	cup fresh julienne lemon peels, blanched, for garnish
	Lemon peel, for garnish

- Preheat oven to 375 degrees.
- Wash quail and rub inside of cavities with salt and 1 teaspoon orange peel.
- Bring vegetable stock and wild rice to a boil in a saucepan. Add bay leaf and reduce heat. Simmer for 35-40 minutes or until all the liquid is absorbed.
- Heat a nonstick pan and spray with cooking oil. Sauté onion until translucent. Add celery, sage and apple. Sauté for 2 minutes and transfer to mixing bowl.
- Add egg white, remaining orange peel, walnuts, black pepper, cooked wild rice and parsley to mixing bowl; toss gently.
- Stuff quail cavities with wild rice stuffing and place into a nonstick baking pan coated with vegetable spray. Lightly season quail with salt and black pepper.
- Bake quail for 35-40 minutes.
- Remove roasted quail from baking pan. Deglaze pan with ½ cup chicken or vegetable stock and add ¼ cup beef stock if available. Allow stock to simmer for 5 minutes.
- Strain and ladle sauce over quail. Garnish as desired with lemon peel.

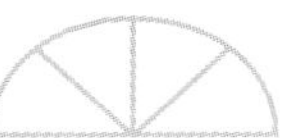

Hasenpfeffer

Level: Good Cook
Serves 4-6
Preparation Time: 1+ day

1½	cups apple cider vinegar
1¾	cups water, divided
2	large onions, sliced
1	tablespoon granulated sugar
2	teaspoons salt
¼	teaspoon peppercorns
½	teaspoon crumbled cinnamon stick
5	whole cloves
1	bay leaf
¼	teaspoon dried crushed chiles
2	rabbits, cut into serving pieces
¼	cup plus 2 tablespoons all-purpose flour, divided
	Salt and black pepper, to taste
6	tablespoons butter
¼	cup water
1	pound cooked and buttered noodles

- Mix together a marinade of cider vinegar, 1½-cups water, onion, sugar, 2 teaspoons salt, peppercorns, cinnamon stick, cloves, bay leaf and chiles in a bowl.
- Place rabbit in large glass bowl and cover with marinade. Cover with plastic wrap and let stand in the refrigerator for 24 hours or more. Turn meat occasionally.
- Remove rabbit and dry with paper towels.
- Place ¼ cup flour in a paper bag and season with salt and black pepper.
- Shake rabbit pieces in bag to cover with flour mixture.
- Heat butter in a large skillet and brown rabbit over medium heat.
- Strain marinade and add to skillet with rabbit.
- Cover skillet and simmer for 1 hour or until fork tender. Transfer rabbit to a warm serving platter.
- Mix 2 tablespoons flour and ¼ cup water, add to pan juices to make a thick gravy. Bring gravy to boil; boil for at least 1 minute.
- Serve rabbit with buttered noodles and pan gravy.

A Chef's View

To cook with peppercorns, the question is, how much pepper is enough? The answer depends on your taste. When pan-frying steak, for example, most of the peppery oils are burned off during the high heat searing process; whereas, with other cooking methods the peppercorns may infuse more peppery oils. For the best results just add the pepper according to your own taste. Reduce the amount or switch from black to white peppercorns, which are not as hot as black but very aromatic.

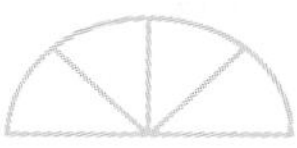

A Chef's View

Found in beef, sheep, and other animals, suet is the solid white fat found around the kidneys and loins. Many British recipes call for it to lend richness to pastries, puddings, stuffings, and mincemeat. Suet was once widely used to make tallow candles. You can ask for suet at any local meat counter.

Venison Patties with Mushroom Gravy

Level: Good Cook
Serves 4-6
Preparation Time: 40 minutes

2	pounds venison, cut into cubes
¾	pound beef suet
3-5	garlic cloves, minced, or to taste
2	tablespoons butter
¼	pound fresh mushrooms, sliced
2	tablespoons chopped onion
2	tablespoons all-purpose flour
2	cups beef bouillon
¼	teaspoon salt
⅛	teaspoon black pepper
⅛	teaspoon nutmeg
½	cup heavy cream
½	teaspoon parsley flakes, for garnish

- Grind venison adding beef suet a little at a time. Add garlic when grinding a second time.
- Form 6-8 meat patties. Salt and pepper to taste.
- Fry patties over medium heat to desired doneness. Remove to warm platter. Reserve venison juices in skillet.
- Prepare gravy by melting butter in a second medium-size saucepan. Add mushrooms and onion. Sauté over medium heat for 5 minutes until mushrooms are limp and onion translucent.
- Add flour to pan with mushrooms and onion. Blend.
- Pour bouillon slowly into mushroom mixture.
- Cook and stir until slightly thickened, approximately 5 minutes. Season with salt, black pepper and nutmeg.
- Add mushroom sauce to reserved venison juices, scraping burger juices into mushroom sauce.
- Pour cream slowly into mushroom sauce and cook over low heat. Do not boil as cream will curdle.
- Serve sauce over burgers garnished with parsley.
- Cook's Tip: Serve with mashed potatoes and string beans.

Tangy Venison Stew

Level: Good Cook
Serves 4-6
Preparation Time: 1 hour

2	pounds venison
2	cups beef stock
6	whole cloves, slightly crushed
2	teaspoons dried thyme
2	tablespoons prepared mustard
¼	cup malt vinegar
1	cup tomato sauce
	Salt and black pepper, to taste
8	medium red potatoes
4	teaspoons canola oil, divided
4	medium onions, coarsely chopped
6	garlic cloves, minced

- Cut venison into 2-inch cubes, wash and pat dry with paper towels. Set aside.
- Combine stock, cloves, thyme, mustard, malt vinegar, tomato sauce, salt and black pepper in a Dutch oven and simmer over medium heat.
- Bring potatoes to a boil in a second pot.
- Brown meat, a few pieces at a time, in a skillet with 1 tablespoon oil. After browning, add venison pieces to stock mixture.
- Add 1 teaspoon oil to skillet and sauté onion and garlic until just soft. Add to stock and meat mixture.
- Bring mixture to slow simmer, cover and keep at slow simmer for 4-6 minutes, depending on the tenderness of the meat.
- Thicken sauce by combining 1 tablespoon cornstarch mixed with ¼ cup sauce and adding to pot; or finely grate one potato and add to pot. Either will thicken the sauce.
- Cut boiled potatoes into 2-inch cubes and add to stew after meat is tender.
- Simmer for 20-30 minutes. Serve.

A Missouri Window

The state animal is the Mule. Missouri mules pulled pioneer wagons to the Wild West during the 19th century.

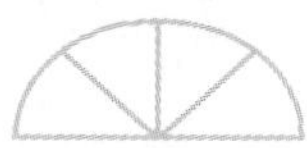

A Chef's View

Gravies rely on the drippings from meat for their rich flavor and color. The drippings called for in recipes may be extended with bouillon or milk if the volume is too low. Keep the proportions of liquid to the thickening agents the same when thickening sauces or gravies. If your sauce or gravy is not dark enough in color, add a few splashes of commercial browning and seasoning sauce. Be sure to add it before you add your other seasonings, as it does add flavor as well as color.

Venison Wellington

Level: Good Cook
Serves 4
Preparation Time: 1½ hours

1½ pounds venison steak, cut into ½-inch cubes
3 cups red potatoes, thinly sliced
½ cup finely grated carrots or rutabaga
½ cup chopped onion
½ teaspoon salt
¼ teaspoon black pepper
1 tablespoon butter
Instant unseasoned meat tenderizer
3 cups all-purpose flour
⅓ cup solid vegetable shortening
Dash salt
⅓ cup water
3 tablespoons milk

- Preheat oven to 425 degrees. Line a baking sheet with parchment paper.
- Combine venison, potatoes, carrot or rutabaga, onion, salt, black pepper, butter and a light sprinkle of meat tenderizer. Cover and set aside.
- Make crust from flour, shortening and salt gradually adding water as needed. Pat together to form a ball.
- Divide dough into 4 pieces and roll dough out to the size of an 8-inch round.
- Place 1 cup meat filling on half of the rolled crust to within ½-inch of edge; moisten edges, fold over and seal edges with tines of a fork.
- Brush with milk and bake at 425 degrees for 20 minutes. Reduce heat to 375 degrees and bake an additional 30 minutes.
- Serve with brown gravy, if desired.

Deer Jerky

Level: Easy
Yield: 18 slices
Preparation Time: 8-12 hours

- 1½ pounds venison, half-frozen
- ½ teaspoon salt
- ⅓ teaspoon garlic powder
- ½ teaspoon black pepper
- 1 teaspoon seasoned salt flavor enhancer
- 1 teaspoon onion powder
- ¼ cup Worcestershire sauce
- ¼ cup soy sauce

- Slice venison with grain of meat into ⅛-inch strips of desired lengths.
- Combine salt, garlic powder, black pepper, seasoned salt flavor enhancer, onion powder, Worcestershire sauce and soy sauce.
- Pour marinade over meat, cover and marinate 8-12 hours in a non-reactive container.
- Preheat oven to 250 degrees.
- Spread meat in a single layer on oven racks, using foil to catch drips.
- With oven door cracked open and at the lowest temperature, bake 6-8 hours.
- May be eaten immediately.

Venison Breakfast Sausage

Level: Good Cook
Yield: 1 pound
Preparation Time: 30 minutes

- 4 pounds ground venison
- ¾ pound side pork, cut in 2-inch chunks
- 3½ teaspoons ground sage
- 2½ teaspoons black pepper
- 1 teaspoon salt

- Run all meat through a grinder once, adding side pork to each pound of venison when grinding.
- Sprinkle spices over ground meat and work them with your hands.
- Shape meat into patties to fry or broil.
- Cook's Tip: Double wrap tightly and freeze for up to 3 months.

A Culinary Reflection

Raised in a family of farmers and hunters, our table was never bare of fresh beef, pork, venison, duck, goose, pheasant, fish, squirrel, homegrown vegetables and fruit. Every fall we could count on Daddy getting a deer, but one year he must have bagged the biggest and oldest buck in the woods. For all that winter and into the next summer, that never-ending supply of buck served up the toughest, gamiest, foulest-tasting venison my sisters and I ever put in our mouths. Raised in a time when you ate what was put in front of you, we shivered at the thought of having to eat what we nicknamed 'old buck' again and again. We'd had 'old buck' so much, that one day, tears rolled down our faces at the dinner table as we cried, 'Oh no! Not 'old buck' again!' With Daddy's finger pointed at us and a stern, 'you will eat what is on your plate,' we ate 'old buck' until there was no more left. To this day, we laugh and laugh at having to eat 'old buck' that year.

~ Lizabeth Fleenor

Venison Game Stock

Level: Easy
Yield: 2 quarts
Preparation Time: 5 hours

	Venison bones and meat scraps
3	celery ribs, each cut into 4 pieces
2	onions, halved
3	carrots, cut into 4 pieces
10	parsley sprigs
1	dried bay leaf
½	teaspoon dried thyme leaves
½	teaspoon peppercorns
1	cup red wine
1	gallon water

- ◆ Brown bones and scraps of venison in a roasting pan in the oven. Remove to a stockpot and deglaze pan.
- ◆ Combine roasted venison bones, deglazing liquid, vegetables and spices in a stockpot.
- ◆ Cover with water and wine.
- ◆ Simmer, slightly covered, for 5 hours. Strain and use for sauces.
- ◆ Cook's Tip: Freeze stock in ice cube trays and then store in freezer bags.

Venison Sauce

Level: Easy

Yield: 1½ cups

Preparation Time: 15 minutes

1 tablespoon olive oil

2 shallot cloves, minced

1 garlic clove, minced

½ cup Burgundy or other dry red wine

2 cups *Windows'* Venison Game Stock

½ teaspoon chopped fresh parsley or chervil

◆ Heat olive oil in a small saucepan; add shallot and garlic, and cook over medium-high heat, stirring constantly until tender.

◆ Add wine and venison stock. Bring to a boil. Reduce heat, and simmer 20 minutes.

◆ Stir in chopped parsley.

Reflections of the Fold

Beef, Veal, Lamb & Pork

A Missouri Window

Wine Country

Franklin, Warren, and Gasconade counties are situated near the Missouri River west of St. Louis - an area of rolling fields, wooded hills, and flowing streams. The small communities, farms, and crossroads settlements retain much of the character established in the 1800s by the early settlers with many of the original buildings still standing.

Much of the area's history can be traced to German and French immigrants who found the natural beauty of the Missouri River bluffs, the rolling green hills, and the deep, fertile valleys resembling the area they left behind in Germany's Rhine Valley. These immigrants discovered that this new land also resembled their homeland in its ability to support viticulture, or the harvesting of grapes, for the production of wonderful wines.

Tangible reminders of the area's wine-making heritage can be seen today in the 30 wineries and vineyards that produce more 330,000 gallons of wine annually. These wineries, some dating back to the original German immigrants, have won numerous national and international awards, and have earned the Tri-County area the title of Missouri Wine Country. While the population is growing and new businesses and industries prosper in the Tri-County area, the quiet beauty and small-town charm of the area prevail.

Photo: Missouri Wine Country, Reflected

Tri-County Medical Society Alliance

The Tri-County Medical Society Alliance celebrated fifty years of serving the needs of communities in Franklin, Warren, and Gasconade counties in the year 2000. Since the founding of the Alliance in 1950, its volunteers have generously given their time, talent, and financial resources to improve the lives of the three-county area. Some of th Alliance's programs include providing health and safety education for students in area schools and Christmas gifts to needy families during the holidays.

One of its current priorities is protecting women and children from domestic violence through the national *Stop America's Violence Everywhere Campaign - SAVE* project. Eileen Chalk, from Tri-County, served as the MSMA Alliance president in 2000-2001.

Medallions of Beef Tenderloin in Brandy Tomato Sauce

Level: Expert Cook
Serves 8
Preparation Time: 1½ hours

8	(7-ounce) center-cut beef tenderloin medallions, cut 1-inch thick
1½	teaspoons seasoned salt
¼	teaspoon black pepper, or to taste
5	tablespoons butter, divided
2	tablespoons brandy, use a quality brand
3	tablespoons all-purpose flour
2	teaspoons tomato paste
½	teaspoon fresh minced garlic
¾	cup red wine
1	cup chicken stock
½	cup beef stock
¼	teaspoon Worcestershire sauce
2	tablespoons currant jelly
2	cups sliced fresh mushrooms
	Salt

- Mix seasoned salt and black pepper. Rub on tenderloin medallions.
- Heat 1 tablespoon butter in a heavy skillet until very hot.
- Sauté tenderloin over moderately high heat until brown on both sides but raw in center.
- Arrange browned meat in a 13x9x2-inch casserole dish leaving 1-inch between slices.
- Deglaze skillet by adding brandy. Scrape up all bits from bottom of pan.
- Melt 4 tablespoons of butter until foamy in the same pan.
- Add flour. Reduce heat to low and cook, stirring constantly, until the roux mixture is golden.
- Stir tomato paste and garlic into roux. Whisk in wine, chicken stock and beef stock and bring to boil over moderate heat, stirring constantly.
- Lower heat and simmer until liquid is reduced by ⅓. Stir occasionally.
- Mix in Worcestershire sauce and currant jelly. Add mushrooms after jelly melts. Sauce should be of coating consistency. If too thick, add more liquid.
- Adjust salt and black pepper, to taste.
- Cool sauce completely. Pour over beef. Cover with foil and refrigerate over night.
- Bring beef to room temperature 2 hours before baking. Uncover.
- Preheat oven to 400 degrees.
- Bake tenderloin: Rare: 10-15 minutes; Medium Rare: 15-20 minutes; Medium-Well: 20-25 minutes.
- Spoon some sauce over tenderloin slices and additional sauce on the side.

A Chef's View

Demi-glace is a rich brown sauce that begins with a basic brown sauce. It is combined with beef stock and Madeira or sherry and slowly cooked until it's reduced by half to a thick glaze that coats a spoon. This intense flavor is used as a base for many other sauces.

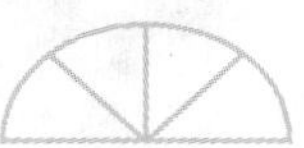

A Chef's View

Try this Green Onion Butter spread over grilled steaks. Mix ¼ cup of butter, ¼ cup of sliced green onions, ½ teaspoon of dry mustard, and ½ cup finely shredded Cheddar cheese. Spread over the steaks.

Grilled Teriyaki Marinated Filet Mignon

Level: Easy
Serves 4
Preparation Time: 8-12 hours

4	(6-ounce) filet mignon medallions
⅓	cup lite teriyaki sauce
1½	tablespoons honey
1½	tablespoons chopped fresh ginger
1½	tablespoons minced fresh garlic
1½	tablespoons chopped shallots, optional
½	tablespoon black pepper
½	tablespoon peanut oil
¾	cup shiitake mushrooms, optional

- Combine teriyaki sauce, honey, ginger, garlic, shallots, pepper and peanut oil.
- Pour marinade over filets and refrigerate steaks 8-12 hours in a tightly covered non-reactive dish. Rotate meat at least once.
- Bring meat to room temperature 30 minutes before cooking on a barbecue grill.
- Turn on gas barbecue grill or prepare coals for grilling.
- Preheat oven to 350 degrees. Coat a 15x10x1-inch rectangular pan with cooking spray.
- Clean mushrooms and place on coated pan. Bake until tender, about 10-15 minutes.
- Remove mushrooms from oven, julienne and keep warm.
- Cook filets on a barbecue grill to desired temperature by using a meat thermometer.
- Serve each filet topped with 2 tablespoons of warm mushrooms.

Paradise Grill Sirloin Peppered Steak with Armagnac

Level: Expert Cook
Serves 6
Preparation Time: 2-3 hours

6	(8-ounce) sirloin beef steaks, boned and cut 1-inch thick
1	teaspoon salt
½	cup canola oil, divided
2	tablespoons ground white peppercorns, crushed
¼	pound (1 stick) plus 2 tablespoons butter, do not substitute, divided
⅔	cup Armagnac French brandy
½	cup dry white wine
¼	cup veal or chicken stock
2	teaspoons cornstarch
½	lemon, juiced
6	watercress sprigs, for garnish

- Season steak with salt and brush generously with canola oil.
- Spread peppercorns on both sides and marinate for 2 hours.
- Brown steaks in batches in a skillet on high heat with remaining oil and 4 tablespoons butter.
- Cook to desired doneness.
- Pour off grease from skillet and add Armagnac brandy and ignite using a long fireplace match.
- Remove steaks from skillet when flame dies. Tent to keep warm.
- Add wine to skillet and bring to boil.
- Combine stock and cornstarch. Mix well. Add to wine in skillet. Cook and stir until thick.
- Pour into a saucepan and whisk in remaining 6 tablespoons butter, one tablespoon at a time. Add lemon juice and blend well. If needed, season with salt to taste.
- Pour sauce over steak and serve. Garnish with watercress.
- Cook's Tip: French fries or sautéed sliced potatoes go well with the steak.

A Show-Me Specialty

Sirloin Peppered Steak with Armagnac is a specialty of Chef Patrick Chow-Yuen of the Paradise Grill in Kansas City, Missouri.

Paradise Grill
5225 Northwest 64th Street
Kansas City
816-587-9888

A Chef's View

Rouladen is Germany's version of the French roulade, which is a thin slice of meat rolled around a filling such as mushrooms, breadcrumbs, cheese or a mixture of vegetables and meat and cheese. The rolled package is usually secured with string or a wooden pick. A roulade is browned before being baked or braised in wine or stock. Rouladen comes in many variations, including beef rolled around a pickle, onion and bacon mixture or cabbage leaves rolled around a ground beef mixture.

Beef Rouladen

Level: Good Cook
Serves 4-6
Preparation Time: 2 hours

3	(8-ounce) round steaks, cut thin and in half
¼	cup all-purpose flour, for dredging
2	tablespoons prepared mustard
¼	cup chopped fresh mushrooms
2	slices bacon, chopped and fried
2	eggs, hard-boiled, peeled and chopped
1	large onion, chopped
1	teaspoon all-purpose flour
	Salt and black pepper, to taste
	Water, divided
	Reserved cooking liquid
2-3	tablespoons all-purpose flour
	Cooked rice or noodles

- Tenderize steaks and dredge with flour.
- Spread a thin layer of mustard on one side.
- Combine mushrooms, bacon, eggs, onion, 1 teaspoon flour, and dash of salt and black pepper.
- Divide mixture between the six steaks and roll. Secure with wooden picks or tie with string.
- Brown rolls in a Dutch oven over high heat.
- Deglaze the bottom of the pan by adding ½ cup water to the browned rolls. Stir lightly until the liquid turns color.
- Add enough water to cover meat. Simmer, covered, for 1½ hours or until meat is tender.
- Make a roux with some of the cooking liquid and an equal amount of flour; add to meat. Bring to a boil, stirring constantly. Boil for at least 2 minutes.
- Serve with noodles or rice.

Tailgate Brisket

Level: Easy
Serves 10-12
Preparation Time: 8 hours

1 (5-pound) flat-end beef brisket
Liquid or dry hickory smoke, to taste
Celery salt, to taste
Onion salt, to taste
Garlic salt, to taste
Lemon juice
Black pepper
Worcestershire sauce
1 (18-ounce) bottle barbecue sauce

- Rub both sides of brisket with hickory smoke.
- Sprinkle desired amounts of celery, onion and garlic salts over both sides.
- Brush lemon juice on meat.
- Place in a glass casserole dish, cover with plastic film and refrigerate 6-8 hours.
- Remove brisket from marinade and season with black pepper and Worcestershire sauce.
- Wrap meat in foil. Place in pan, fat side up. Cover pan with foil.
- Bake in a 275 degree oven for 5 hours.
- Cool and slice.
- Return meat to roasting pan and pour barbecue sauce over meat. Cover with foil and bake an additional 45 minutes at 275 degrees.

Top Secret Marinade

Level: Easy
Yield: 2½ cups
Preparation Time: 10 minutes

1½ cups canola oil
¾ cup soy sauce
¼ cup Worcestershire sauce
⅓ cup lemon juice
2 tablespoons dry mustard
Salt, to taste
1 tablespoon black pepper
½ cup red wine vinegar
1½ teaspoons parsley flakes
2 garlic cloves, minced

- Mix all ingredients together in a glass dish.
- Use to marinate chicken, beef, lamb, pork, pheasant or vegetables before grilling.
- Turn meat or vegetables several times to marinate all sides. Keep refrigerated.
- Marinate kebabs before and while grilling.
- Cook's Tip: Always marinate in a glass dish to prevent a reaction with a metal surface.

A Missouri Window

U.S. Vice President Harry S Truman, a Missourian, became President in 1945 upon the death of Franklin Delano Roosevelt.

Okra and Ground Beef Casserole

Level: Good Cook
Serves 8-10
Preparation Time: 1½ hours

3 tablespoons canola oil, divided
¼ pound (1 stick) plus 1 tablespoon butter, divided
1 cup chopped onion
1 garlic clove, chopped
2 pounds ground beef or lamb
2 cups crushed tomatoes
1 teaspoon salt, or to taste
¼ teaspoon cayenne pepper
1 teaspoon fresh dill weed
2 eggs, beaten
1 cup grated Parmesan cheese, divided
2 pounds baby okra
Freshly ground black pepper, to taste
½ cup all-purpose flour
3 cups milk
4 egg yolks

- Preheat oven to 350 degrees.
- Melt 1 tablespoon butter with 1 tablespoon oil in a skillet. Sauté onion until soft and lightly browned.
- Add garlic and meat. Cook until meat is just cooked through. Drain.
- Stir in tomatoes, 1 teaspoon salt, cayenne pepper and dill weed. Cook over moderately high heat for 4-5 minutes to thicken. Place in a bowl to cool slightly.
- Beat 2 eggs. Stir eggs and ½ cup cheese into cooled meat. Set aside.
- Wash, dry and stem okra; cut into ¼-inch slices.
- Heat 2 tablespoons of butter and 2 tablespoons of oil in a skillet. Stirring constantly, sauté okra until very lightly browned, approximately 10 minutes. Season with salt and black pepper. Set aside.
- Melt 6 tablespoons butter in a skillet. Add flour and stir and cook for 2-3 minutes.
- Whisk in milk and bring mixture to a boil. Reduce heat and simmer for 10 minutes. Strain through a sieve if sauce is thick or lumpy.
- Beat in remaining cheese and 4 egg yolks. Season with salt and black pepper.
- Butter a 13x9x2-inch baking dish. Spread half the meat mixture in the dish. Cover with sautéed okra and top with remaining meat. Cover with sauce.
- Bake for 45-50 minutes.

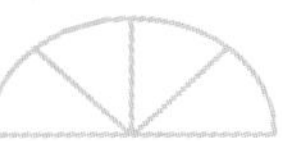

Reuben Sandwich Casserole

Level: Easy
Serves 6-8
Preparation Time: 45 minutes

1	(16-ounce) carton sour cream
1	medium onion, chopped
1	(27-ounce) can sauerkraut, drained and squeezed dry
2	cans corned beef, shredded into bite-size pieces
12	ounces Swiss cheese, shredded
	Bread crumbs from 6 slices rye bread, approximately 4 cups
¼	pound (1 stick) butter or margarine, melted

- Preheat oven to 350 degrees. Butter a 13x9x2-inch glass baking dish.
- Combine sour cream, chopped onion and sauerkraut. Spread across bottom of baking dish.
- Layer corned beef over sauerkraut mixture.
- Sprinkle Swiss cheese over corned beef.
- Cover cheese with rye bread crumbs.
- Drizzle melted margarine over bread crumbs.
- Bake for 30 minutes.
- Cook's Tip: Serve with a salad.

A Culinary Reflection

Recently, plans were made with a relative for me to bring her dinner. We both enjoy Reuben sandwiches, so I told her I would bring the sauerkraut, the corn beef, and all the fixings to grill the sandwiches at her house. The morning I was to go, I called to make certain she still planned to be home. Before hanging up, I said, 'I'll see you in a couple of hours, and I'll bring the Reubens.' Her response was, 'But, who are the Reubens?' She laughed as hard as I did when she realized what she had said.

- Nancy Thompson

Baked Stroganoff

Level: Easy
Serves 6-8
Preparation Time: 3 hours

1	(10¾-ounce) can golden cream of mushroom soup
1	(10¾-ounce) can cream of chicken soup
1	(10¾-ounce) can cream of celery soup
1	(10¾-ounce) can water
1	package onion soup mix
1½	pounds sirloin steak, cubed
1	(8-ounce) carton sour cream, optional
	Cooked buttered noodles or rice

- Preheat oven to 300 degrees. Coat a 5-quart covered casserole dish with cooking spray.
- Combine soups, water, onion soup mix and cubed steak. Pour into casserole dish.
- Bake, covered, for 3 hours.
- Remove casserole dish from oven. Stir in sour cream, if desired.
- Serve over buttered noodles or rice.

A Missouri Window

Sedalia, once the end of the trail for cattle drives, is where Scott Joplin became famous for his ragtime music. In June, fans flock to Sedalia for the Scott Joplin Ragtime Festival and in August, the Missouri State Fair draws thousands of visitors, exhibitors, and educational programs.

Cabbage Rolls in Tomato Sauce

Level: Good Cook
Serves 4
Preparation Time: 1½ hours

8	large white cabbage leaves, center veins trimmed, leaves in one piece
¼	pound ground pork
½	pound ground beef
⅓	cup chopped onion
1	cup crushed tomatoes, with juice
⅓	cup long-grain white rice, uncooked
1	tablespoon Worcestershire sauce
2	teaspoons dried oregano leaves, divided
½	cup water
	Salt and black pepper, to taste
½	cup grated white Cheddar or Swiss cheese
2	cups tomato sauce with roasted garlic
1	teaspoon granulated sugar
½	teaspoon onion powder
¼	teaspoon garlic powder

- Blanch cabbage leaves in boiling salted water for 30 seconds each and lay out to cool.
- Brown pork, beef and onion in a skillet over medium heat.
- Stir in tomatoes, uncooked rice, Worcestershire sauce, 1 teaspoon oregano, water, salt and black pepper.
- Bring mixture to a boil, reduce heat, cover and simmer for 12 minutes.
- Add cheese. Stir.
- Combine tomato sauce, sugar, 1 teaspoon oregano, onion powder and garlic powder.
- Pour half of sauce in bottom of 9x9x2-inch casserole dish.
- Place ⅓ cup of filling onto each cabbage leaf. Fold in sides, starting at an unfolded edge, roll up the leaf.
- Place, seam side down, on top of the tomato sauce mixture.
- Repeat for remaining cabbage leaves.
- Top with remaining sauce.
- Bake covered for 30-35 minutes in a 375 degree oven. Baste rolls with sauce twice during last 10 minutes
- Cook's Tip: Recipe can be doubled or made ahead and refrigerated overnight. Remove from refrigerator 30 minutes before baking.

Curried Beef Pita

Level: Easy
Serves 4-5
Preparation Time: 30 minutes

1	pound ground beef
1	medium onion, diced
1	garlic clove, chopped
1	tablespoon curry powder
1	medium zucchini, diced
¼-½	cup water
1¼	teaspoons salt
½	teaspoon granulated sugar
¼	teaspoon black pepper
1	medium tomato, diced
1	(9-ounce) package pita bread
	Shredded mozzarella cheese, optional, for garnish
	Chopped fresh parsley, for garnish

- Cook and stir ground beef, onion, garlic and curry powder in a skillet until meat is browned and onion is tender, approximately 10 minutes.
- Add zucchini, water, salt, sugar and black pepper. Heat to boiling over medium heat.
- Reduce heat to low, cover and simmer 15 minutes or until zucchini is tender. Stir occasionally.
- Stir tomatoes into ground beef and vegetable mixture. Heat through and keep warm.
- Preheat oven to 350 degrees.
- Cut each pita round in half, place on a large cookie sheet, and heat through until warm, approximately 5 minutes.
- Spoon meat mixture into pita pockets and arrange on a large platter.
- Cook's Tip: Sprinkle tops of filled pita pockets with freshly grated mozzarella cheese and chopped parsley.

A Missouri Window

The historic Santa Fe Trail from Independence led to the rich, faraway Southwest. Thousands of settlers also followed the Oregon Trail from Independence to the Pacific Northwest. Furs brought from the northwest made St. Louis the fur capital of the world.

A Missouri Window

Missouri levied a tax on bachelors on December 20, 1820.

A Missouri Window

The Missouri state folk dance is the square dance. The square dance is derived from folk and courtship dances brought to Missouri by European immigrants. Lively music and callers are the hallmarks of square dancing.

Dad's Taverns

Level: Easy
Serves 36
Preparation Time: 45 minutes

10	pounds ground beef
2	large onions, chopped
6	celery ribs, chopped
4	tablespoons prepared mustard
8	ounces ketchup
4	(10¾-ounce) cans chicken-gumbo soup
4	(10¾-ounce) cans tomato soup
4	tablespoons red wine vinegar
4	tablespoons brown sugar
	Hamburger buns

- Sauté beef, onion and celery.
- Add mustard, ketchup, soups, vinegar and brown sugar. Stir and simmer over low heat.
- Serve on buns.
- Cook's Tip: Meat sauce can be made a day before served and refrigerated or frozen in smaller quantities then thawed and reheated for a quick dinner.

Porcupines

Level: Easy
Serves 4
Preparation Time: 1½ hours

1	pound ground beef
½	cup white rice
⅓	cup chopped onion
	Salt and black pepper, to taste
1	(15-ounce) can tomato sauce
2	teaspoons Worcestershire sauce
½	cup water

- Preheat oven to 350 degrees.
- Combine beef, rice, onion, salt and black pepper in a bowl and mix well.
- Shape into balls, one tablespoon at a time. Place balls in an 8x8x2-inch baking dish.
- Mix tomato sauce, Worcestershire sauce and water in a bowl and pour over meatballs. Cover with aluminum foil.
- Bake for 45 minutes. Remove foil and bake an additional 15 minutes.

Snuggly Dogs

Level: Easy
Yield: 12 dogs
Preparation Time: 1 hour

- 2 cups all-purpose flour
- 4 teaspoons baking powder
- 4 tablespoons granulated sugar
- 1 teaspoon salt
- 5 tablespoons butter or margarine
- ¾ cups cold milk
- 12 beef wieners
- 12 slices American cheese
- Prepared mustard

- Preheat oven to 425 degrees. Lightly coat a baking sheet with cooking spray.
- Mix flour, baking powder, sugar and salt in a bowl.
- Cut in butter until crumbly.
- Add milk. Stir with fork until a ball forms. Add a bit more milk if necessary to make a soft dough.
- Knead dough 10 times on a lightly floured surface.
- Roll dough into a rectangular shape, ¼ inch thick. Cut dough into 12 rectangles.
- Heat wieners in water. Remove and wipe dry.
- Roll 1 cheese slice around wiener, place wiener on dough rectangle and dab a bit of mustard along side.
- Enclose wiener completely by dampening edges of dough to seal. Arrange on baking sheet.
- Bake for 10-15 minutes or until browned.
- Serve immediately.

A Missouri Window

The crinoid became the state's official fossil on June 16, 1989, after a group of Lee's Summit school students worked through the legislative process to promote it as a state symbol.

A Chef's View

Also called drawn butter, clarified butter is made by melting butter and allowing the milky particles which burn first in ordinary butter to fall to the bottom. Melt unsalted butter slowly, allowing milk solids to separate to the bottom. Skim off any foam that has formed on the surface. Pour off clear or clarified butter, leaving milky residue in pan. Use clarified butter for frying or sautéing foods. Its higher smoke point, a result of the mild solids being removed, allows for cooking foods at a high temperature than regular butter.

Medallions of Veal with Shiitake Mushrooms

Level: Easy
Serves 2
Preparation Time: 30 minutes

2	(5-ounce) veal medallions
½	cup all-purpose flour
2	tablespoons clarified butter
6-8	fresh shiitake mushrooms, sliced
4	canned peeled whole chestnuts
¼	cup medium dry sherry
¼	cup prepared brown gravy
	Salt and black pepper, to taste

- Flour veal medallions shaking off excess flour.
- Sauté veal in clarified butter for approximately 45 seconds on each side.
- Add mushrooms, chestnuts and sherry. Reduce liquid for approximately 1 minute.
- Stir in prepared brown gravy and bring to simmer.
- Season with salt and black pepper.
- Transfer medallions to serving platter. Pour sauce over veal.
- Serve immediately.

Green Peppercorn Sauce

Level: Good Cook
Yield: ¾ cup
Preparation Time: 30 minutes

1	tablespoon butter
2	tablespoons finely chopped shallots
¼	pound mushrooms, finely chopped
2	tablespoons minced parsley
1	teaspoon green peppercorns, rinsed and drained
	Hot pepper sauce
2	tablespoons brandy
1	cup heavy cream
	Salt, to taste

- Melt butter in a small saucepan. Add shallots and sauté over medium heat.
- Add mushrooms and sauté for 5 minutes, stirring frequently.
- Stir in parsley, peppercorns, and 3 drops of hot pepper sauce.
- Add brandy to side of saucepan and ignite it. Stir mixture until flames subside.
- Pour cream into mushroom mixture. Boil sauce, stirring constantly until it thickens.
- Season with salt, to taste.

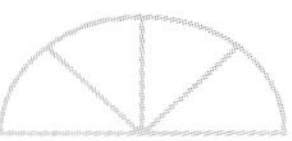

Stuffed Veal Tenderloin

Level: Good Cook
Serves 6-8
Preparation Time: 30 minutes

1½	pounds veal, cut into sixteen 1½-ounce slices
	Salt and black pepper, to taste
2	thinly sliced prosciutto ham slices, finely chopped
8	ounces Brie cheese, peeled and softened
¼	cup all-purpose flour
½	pound (2 sticks) unsalted butter
¼	pound morel mushrooms, or other mushrooms
3	shallots, finely chopped
1	cup heavy cream
1	cup parsley, chopped
	Fresh lemon juice

- ◆ Pound veal until flattened. Season lightly with salt and black pepper.
- ◆ Combine prosciutto and Brie. Spread mixture on veal slices. Roll up. Secure with a wooden pick. Dust rolls with flour.
- ◆ Melt butter over medium-high heat in a large skillet.
- ◆ Brown veal rolls on all sides and cook through. Remove to a warm covered plate.
- ◆ Sauté mushrooms and shallots in remaining butter in same pan in which rolls were browned.
- ◆ Add cream to mushroom mixture. Bring to boil. Lower heat and reduce sauce to desired consistency. Add parsley.
- ◆ Season to taste with lemon juice and salt.
- ◆ Spoon sauce over veal.

Roquefort Sauce

Level: Quick and Simple
Yield: ¾ cup
Preparation Time: 15 minutes

2 tablespoons butter
⅓ cup finely chopped shallots
2 teaspoons all-purpose flour
½ cup dry white wine
⅔ (3-ounces) cup crumbled Roquefort cheese
¼ cup heavy cream
Salt and black pepper, to taste

- ◆ Melt butter in a medium saucepan over medium heat.
- ◆ Add shallots and sauté for 5 minutes or until shallots are about to brown.
- ◆ Add flour. Cook for 1 minute, stirring constantly to remove flour taste.
- ◆ Stir in wine and boil for 5 minutes or until liquid is reduced to ¼ cup. Stir frequently.
- ◆ Reduce heat to low and add cheese. Cook until cheese is melted, stirring frequently.
- ◆ Add cream. Simmer, stirring constantly, for 2 minutes or until thickened to a sauce consistency.
- ◆ Season to taste with salt and black pepper.
- ◆ Cook's Tip: Serve as a sauce over filet mignons or any grilled beef.

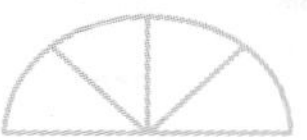

Lamb Marinade

Level: Easy

Yield: 2 cups

Preparation Time: 5 minutes

½ cup red wine

½ cup olive oil

Juice of 1 lemon

3 garlic cloves, minced

1 teaspoon dried oregano

1 teaspoon dried thyme leaves

1 teaspoon dried rosemary leaves

1 teaspoon dried marjoram leaves

- Combine all ingredients and mix well.
- Store in the refrigerator in a glass container for up to 6 weeks.
- Marinate lamb 6-8 hours in a shallow glass casserole dish, turning at least 3 times to marinate both sides of the meat.

Glazed Lamb Roast

Level: Easy
Serves 8
Preparation Time: 1 hour

1	(5-pound) leg of lamb, boned and rolled
1	(12-ounce) jar chili sauce
1	(10-ounce) jar currant jelly
¼	cup mint jelly

- Preheat oven to 475 degrees.
- Place lamb on a rack in a roasting pan. Roast for 30 minutes.
- Warm chili sauce, currant jelly and mint jelly in a small saucepan over low heat.
- Reduce oven temperature to 325 degrees and baste lamb with warmed sauce.
- Roast for 20 minutes per pound, basting occasionally.
- Remove from oven and let stand for 10 minutes before carving.
- Warm remaining sauce and serve on the side.

Spiced Lamb Chops with Ginger Crisps

Level: Easy
Serves 4
Preparation Time: 45 minutes

8	(1½-inch) thick lamb chops
4	teaspoons ground coriander
2	teaspoons firmly packed dark brown sugar
1	teaspoon ground black pepper
½	teaspoon salt, optional
½	cup peeled, finely julienned fresh ginger
2	tablespoons canola oil
1	tablespoon salted butter

- Pat lamb chops dry with paper towels and prick with a fork.
- Combine coriander, brown sugar, pepper and optional salt in a small bowl.
- Rub mixture on both sides of lamb chops. Allow chops to sit at room temperature for 15 minutes.
- Fry julienned ginger in oil in a medium-size skillet until it turns a pale golden color. Transfer ginger crisps to a paper towel to drain. Set aside for garnish.
- Melt butter in skillet and sauté lamb chops for 4-6 minutes per side, depending on the degree of doneness preferred.
- Transfer to serving platter and top with ginger crisps.

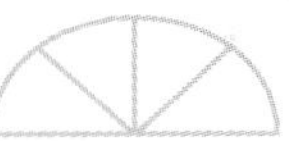

Herb Baked Lamb Chops

Level: Easy
Serves 4
Preparation Time: 2½ hours

4	(2-inch) thick lamb chops
	All-purpose flour, to coat chops
2	tablespoons unsalted butter
¼	cup wine vinegar
2	tablespoons extra-virgin olive oil
¼	cup fresh lemon juice
3	tablespoons Worcestershire sauce
½	cup water
½	teaspoon dried oregano
½	teaspoon dried thyme
2	bay leaves
2	tablespoons unsalted butter, melted
¼	teaspoon garlic salt
¼	teaspoon white pepper
2	medium onions, sliced

- Preheat oven to 325 degrees.
- Flour lamb chops and brown in 2 tablespoons melted butter in a medium-size skillet over high heat. Set aside and keep warm.
- Combine vinegar, oil, lemon juice, Worcestershire sauce, water, oregano, thyme, bay leaves, butter, garlic salt and white pepper in a 11x7x2-inch baking dish. Stir.
- Add lamb chops and sliced onions to vinegar mixture.
- Bake, uncovered, 2 hours.

A Missouri Window

Kansas City has more miles of boulevards than Paris and more fountains than any city except Rome. It also has more miles of freeway per capita than any metro area with more than 1 million residents.

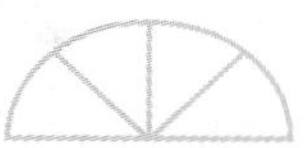

A Missouri Window

In 1945, Japan signed documents of surrender ending World War II in the Pacific on the deck of the USS Missouri.

Lamb Spinach Roulade

Level: Good Cook
Serves 10
Preparation Time: 3 hours

¾	pound white button mushrooms, chopped
3	green onions, minced, white and green parts
6	tablespoons butter
8	slices wheat bread
2	(10-ounce) packages frozen spinach, thawed and squeezed dry
3	ounces feta cheese
¾	teaspoon salt, divided
⅛	teaspoon black pepper
1	(4½-pound) leg of lamb, butterflied and deboned
	Salt and black pepper, to taste
1	cup beef stock, or water
2	tablespoons dry red wine
1	teaspoon instant beef bouillon granules

- Preheat oven to 325 degrees.
- Sauté mushrooms and green onions in butter in a medium-size skillet until tender. Remove from heat.
- Tear bread into pieces and place in mushroom mixture.
- Add spinach, feta cheese, ½ teaspoon salt and ⅛ teaspoon pepper. Toss to mix.
- Sprinkle inside of leg of lamb with salt and pepper to taste. Spread with spinach stuffing.
- Roll up lamb and tie with string. Place lean side down on a rack in a roasting pan. Insert a meat thermometer into the thickest portion.
- Bake at 325 degrees for 2½ hours (30-35 minutes per pound) or until thermometer registers 160 degrees.
- Remove from oven and place on a large warm platter to rest for 15 minutes. Tent with aluminum foil.
- Remove rack from roasting pan. Skim pan juices. Add water, wine, bouillon granules and ¼ teaspoon salt.
- Bring just to a boil over medium-high heat, stirring to deglaze roasting pan. Pour into serving bowl.
- Remove string from lamb, cut into slices and serve with sauce.

Apple and Raisin Stuffed Pork Chops

Level: Good Cook
Serves 6
Preparation Time: 2 hours

- 6 pork chops, 1-inch thick and boneless
- 3 cups bread cubes
- 1 medium Rome Beauty or other cooking apple, unpeeled, cored and chopped
- ½ cup raisins
- ¼ pound sharp Cheddar cheese, shredded
- ¼ teaspoon ground cinnamon
- 3 tablespoons butter or margarine, melted
- ¼ cup orange juice

- Cut pocket in each chop along the fatty side.
- Toss together all other ingredients.
- Preheat oven to 350 degrees. Coat a 13x9x2-inch baking dish with cooking spray.
- Stuff pork chops and arrange in baking dish.
- Add remaining stuffing between chops.
- Bake covered for 1¼ hours.
- Uncover and bake 15 minutes longer to brown chops.

Artichoke and Ham Rolls

Level: Easy
Serves 8-12
Preparation Time: 1 hour

- 16 slices Swiss cheese
- 2-3 (14-ounce) cans artichoke hearts, halved
- 16 cooked ham slices, ¼-inch thick
- 1 (10¾-ounce) can cream of chicken soup
- 1 (8-ounce) carton sour cream
- ½ cup grated Parmesan cheese
- ½ cup Sauterne or Rhine wine, or sweet white wine
- Ground paprika

- Preheat oven to 350 degrees.
- Place 1 slice of cheese and ½ of an artichoke on each ham slice.
- Roll and secure with wooden picks.
- Place ham rolls in a 13x9x2-inch casserole dish.
- Combine soup, sour cream, Parmesan cheese and wine. Pour over ham rolls.
- Sprinkle with paprika.
- Bake for 45 minutes.

A Chef's View

Like pairing food with wine, matching seasonings with foods comes with experience and experimentation. No strict rules prevail, but veteran cooks favor certain combinations. Try these various combinations of seasonings with your next meat dish.

- *Ground Beef: curry, basil, marjoram, savory, chili powder*
- *Beef Roasts, Steaks, and Chops: basil, caraway seed, oregano, red pepper, thyme*
- *Veal: lemon pepper, basil, rosemary, oregano*
- *Pork: sage, ginger, cloves (for ham), curry, rosemary*
- *Lamb: rosemary, mint, oregano*

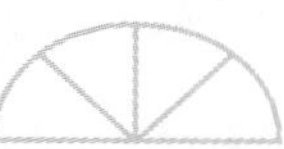

A Culinary Reflection

Coming home from church on Sunday noon, we frequently opened the front door to the aroma of my Mother's pot roast. She would put the roast with bay leaf, a little vinegar, a quartered onion and lots of carrots and potatoes in a slow oven before we left for the service. It was always 'fall off the bone' wonderful when we arrived home. Sometimes we would have a light Sunday supper of popcorn, apples, and oranges while watching Perry Mason or Ben Casey on television. I always knew when I became a mother it would be my job to peel all those oranges, too.

- Judy Corry

Cherry Almond Glazed Pork Roast

Level: Good Cook
Serves 8
Preparation Time: 2½ hours

1 (4-pound) pork loin roast, boned, tied and seasoned
1 (12-ounce) jar cherry preserves
2 tablespoons light-colored corn syrup
¼ cup red wine vinegar
¼ teaspoon salt
¼ teaspoon ground cinnamon
⅛ teaspoon ground cloves
Black pepper, to taste
¼ cup slivered almonds, toasted

- Preheat oven to 325 degrees.
- Place seasoned roast on a cooking rack in a roasting pan and bake for at least 2 hours, or more is necessary.
- Prepare glaze by combining cherry preserves, corn syrup, vinegar, salt, cinnamon, cloves and pepper. Heat to boiling, stirring frequently.
- Reduce heat and simmer 2 minutes. Add almonds. Cover and keep sauce warm.
- Baste roast 2 times during last 30 minutes with sauce using no more than ¼ of mixture.
- Serve remainder of heated sauce with roast.

Pork Orange Tenderloin

Level: Easy
Serves 6
Preparation Time: 2 hours

2 (12-ounce) pork tenderloins
1 cup orange juice
¼ cup olive oil
3 garlic cloves, minced
⅓ cup soy sauce
2 tablespoons fresh rosemary leaves, chopped or 2 teaspoons dried
Black pepper, freshly ground
Fresh rosemary sprigs, optional, for garnish

- Place pork in a glass baking dish.
- Combine orange juice, oil, garlic, soy sauce and rosemary. Mix well. Pour over tenderloins, cover and refrigerate at least one hour or overnight. Rotate meat at least once.
- Preheat oven to 400 degrees.
- Drain marinade and reserve.
- Place tenderloins in a casserole dish and season generously with pepper.
- Roast until cooked through, approximately 20-25 minutes.
- Bring reserved marinade to a boil for 3 minutes, stirring at least twice.
- Slice tenderloins and serve, passing marinade separately.
- Garnish with sprigs of fresh rosemary, if desired.

Raspberry Sauce

Level: Quick and Simple
Yield: 2 cups
Preparation Time: 10 minutes

2 (10-ounce) jars raspberry preserves
¼ cup red wine vinegar
2 tablespoons soy sauce
½ tablespoon prepared horseradish
½ tablespoon catsup
1 tablespoon garlic powder

- Combine all ingredients and whisk until blended.
- Serve warm or at room temperature over medallions of pork tenderloin.

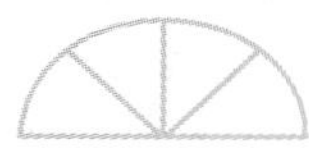

A Show-Me Specialty

Eggplant Creole is a specialty of Glenn's Café in downtown Columbia, Missouri. Glenn's specializes in Cajun and New Orleans style dishes using fresh seafood and vegetables in all of their recipes.

Glenn's Café
29 South Ninth Street
Columbia
573-443-3094

A Chef's View

Andouille (an-DOO-ee; ahn-DWEE) is a spicy, heavily smoked sausage made from pork chitterlings and tripe. French in origin, andouille is a specialty of Cajun cooking. It's traditionally used in specialties like jambalaya and gumbo, and makes a spicy addition to any dish that would use smoked sausage. Andouille is especially good served cold as a hors d'oeuvre.

Glenn's Café Eggplant Creole

Level: Easy
Serves 6
Preparation Time: 45 minutes

2	tablespoons olive oil
4	ounces andouille sausage, diced
1	medium onion, diced
3	celery ribs, diced
1	large green bell pepper, seeded and diced
1	tablespoon dried thyme leaves
1	tablespoon dried oregano leaves
½	teaspoon cracked black pepper
1	tablespoon salt, or to taste
4	garlic cloves
2	large eggplants, peeled and 1-inch dice
	Dash hot pepper sauce, or to taste
½	cup white wine
½	cup red wine
1	(12-ounce) can diced tomatoes
	Cooked rice

- Heat olive oil in large skillet.
- Add sausage and lightly brown. Add onion, celery, bell pepper and brown.
- Combine thyme, oregano, black pepper, salt and garlic. Add to sausage mixture. Stir and cook 1 minute.
- Mix eggplant into sausage. Cook until lightly browned.
- Add hot pepper sauce, white and red wines and tomatoes. Simmer until eggplant is softened and mixture has thickened.
- Serve over hot cooked rice.

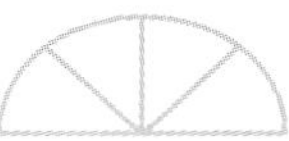

Clove Studded Ham with Orange Rum Glaze

Level: Good Cook
Serves 25-30
Preparation Time: 2½ hours

1	(16-pound) precooked smoked ham with bone-in
	Whole cloves, to cover ham surface
¼	cup Dijon mustard
1	cup dark brown sugar, firmly packed
2	cups canned pineapple chunks, with syrup
1	cup bitter orange marmalade
1	cup dark rum
3	bunches red seedless grapes, cut into small bunches

- Preheat oven to 350 degrees.
- Peel skin from ham and trim fat to leave a ¼-inch layer all around.
- Score fat layer on ham in a diamond pattern with a sharp knife.
- Place ham in a large shallow baking pan lined with foil.
- Insert cloves at points of diamonds in ham fat.
- Spread mustard over ham with flexible rubber spatula.
- Sprinkle brown sugar evenly over the top.
- Bake for 30 minutes.
- Heat pineapple chunks with syrup and marmalade together in a saucepan while ham is baking. Stir constantly.
- Remove from heat, add rum and stir.
- Remove ham from oven, pour sauce over ham, return to oven and bake for an additional 1½ hours, basting frequently. Use a meat thermometer to check for doneness.
- Remove ham from oven and place on serving platter.
- Decorate top of ham with pineapple chunks, held in place by wooden picks.
- Arrange grapes around ham.
- Slice ham very thin and serve on biscuits or bread with a selection of mustards and chutney.
- Cook's Tip: Remove extra pineapple chunks from pan with a slotted spoon. Set aside. Skim fat off pan juices. Add juices to pineapple, heat, and serve alongside ham in a gravy boat.

A Chef's View

To remove some of the salt and add moisture to the ham, soak overnight in water before cooking.

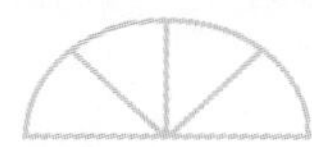

A Missouri Window

'Tis the greatest crossroads the world has ever seen.'

– Senator Thomas Hart Benton, Kansas City

A Chef's View

Grilling Tips:

- *Never salt meat before grilling. Salt will draw moisture from the meat causing it to be dry.*
- *Remove meat from the refrigerator 20-30 minutes before placing on the grill.*
- *Brush cold grill with oil or spray with oil to prevent sticking.*
- *For delicate items such as fish, shrimp or asparagus use an oiled grill basket for easy turning.*
- *At your next marshmallow roast, grease the prongs of the long handled fork to prevent any sticking.*

Marsala Honey Glazed Ham

Level: Easy
Serves 32
Preparation Time: 3 hours

1 (10-pound) smoked ham, low sodium, fully cooked
1 teaspoon ground allspice
24 whole cloves
¼ cup honey
1 cup sweet Marsala wine
Cooking spray

- Preheat oven to 275 degrees.
- Trim rind and excess fat from ham, leaving ¼-inch thick layer of fat.
- Score sides and top of ham in a diamond pattern and sprinkle allspice over ham. Press cloves into cross cuts on ham surface.
- Place ham on a broiler pan coated with cooking spray.
- Drizzle ham with honey and bake for 30 minutes.
- Pour ½ cup wine over ham and bake an additional 30 minutes.
- Baste ham with ½ cup of wine and bake an additional 1 hour and 10 minutes or until ham is heated.
- Place ham on a platter and tent with foil. Let stand for 15 minutes before cutting.

Killer Brats

Level: Easy
Serves 12
Preparation Time: 1 hour

12 bratwurst
2 (12-ounce) cans beer
Water
1 large yellow onion, chopped
12 hot dog buns, split and toasted
Stone ground mustard
Chopped onion
Pickle relish
Sauerkraut, warmed

- Place bratwurst in a large stockpot.
- Pour beer over bratwurst and add enough water to cover sausages.
- Chop onion and add to pot.
- Bring bratwurst to a boil over medium high heat.
- Reduce heat and simmer 30 minutes. Remove bratwurst and drain.
- Grill bratwurst over a charcoal fire until golden brown.
- Serve on toasted buns with stone ground mustard and other condiments such as chopped onion, pickle relish and sauerkraut.

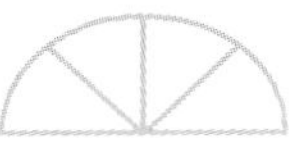

Pork Cutlets with Mushrooms

Level: Good Cook
Serves 4
Preparation Time: 40 minutes

6	tablespoons extra-virgin olive oil, divided
4	boneless loin pork cutlets, ½-inch thick each
½	pound oyster mushrooms, cleaned and roughly sliced
½	pound chanterelle mushrooms, cleaned and cut in half if large
½	cup white wine
	Salt and freshly ground black pepper, to taste

- Heat 3 tablespoons olive oil in a large sauté pan.
- Season pork cutlets with salt and pepper and add to heated pan. Sauté for 1 minute.
- Add mushrooms to pan and continue to sauté until golden brown, about 5-7 minutes.
- Turn cutlets over and stir mushrooms.
- Continue to sauté for 4-5 minutes, then deglaze pan with wine. Cook for 1 more minute and then add remaining 3 tablespoons of olive, swirling pan to emulsify.
- Season with salt and freshly ground black pepper, to taste. Serve.

Pizza Biscuits

Level: Easy
Serves 8
Preparation Time: 40 minutes

2	tubes buttermilk biscuits, 10 per tube
2	cups pizza sauce
	Pepperoni, sliced or chopped
	Sliced ripe olives
	Sliced fresh mushrooms
	Chopped green bell peppers
	Sliced green onion, white and green parts
	Mozzarella cheese, shredded

- Preheat oven to 325 degrees. Coat a 12x9x2-inch baking pan with cooking spray.
- Cut each buttermilk biscuit into four pieces and place in a large mixing bowl.
- Add pizza sauce and any of the desired toppings. Stir.
- Turn into baking pan.
- Bake 20 minutes.
- Take from oven and sprinkle cheese on top and return to oven until cheese is melted.
- Cut and serve.

A Missouri Window

Thomas Hart Benton was a very influential Missouri artist. By the age of seven, people already saw his remarkable drawing abilities. His abilities progressed beyond his imagination, and by the 1930s, he had become the most important muralist in America and was selected to be the first artist featured on the cover of Time magazine. In 1935 he decide to share his artistic knowledge with others. He became a teacher at the Kansas City Art Institute. Throughout his life, he produced many murals including a very famous one in the Missouri State Capitol and another one in the Truman Library. He painted for the remainder of his life. In fact he died with his brush in hand overlooking his final mural that he had just finished.

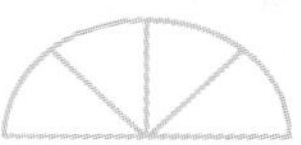

A Chef's View

Everything tastes better when it's cooked on a grill - even low-fat food like fish or skinless chicken.

◆ *Don't throw away dried herbs that have been sitting on your kitchen shelves for years. Moisten a handful, and sprinkle them over hot coals before grilling to add extra flavor.*

◆ *Express your creativity in grilling by marinating food before you cook it. Steeping meat, poultry, seafood or vegetables for anywhere from a few minutes to several hours imparts flavors that complement the natural taste of the foods.*

◆ *Reduce fat by coating the food rack with cooking spray before placing food over the fire instead of brushing oil on it. Food won't stick, and cleanup will be easier.*

◆ *Hinged grill baskets prevent small pieces of food from falling through the food rack and you don't have to turn pieces individually.*

Spicy Indian Barbecue Sauce

Level: Easy
Yield: 1⅔ cups
Preparation Time: 15 minutes

1	medium onion, thinly sliced and separated into rings
2	garlic cloves, minced
½	teaspoon grated fresh ginger
1	tablespoon cooking oil
1	teaspoon curry powder
½	cup barbecue sauce
1	teaspoon ground paprika
½	teaspoon salt
¼	teaspoon hot pepper sauce, or to taste
½	cup unflavored low-fat yogurt

- Cook onion, garlic and ginger in hot oil in a 1-quart saucepan until onion is golden brown.
- Stir in curry powder and cook 1 minute more.
- Add barbecue sauce, paprika, salt and hot pepper sauce; bring to boil.
- Reduce heat and simmer uncovered for 5 minutes; stir occasionally.
- Remove sauce from heat and cool slightly.
- Stir in yogurt and place sauce in a blender. Cover and process until smooth.
- Brush sauce onto chicken or pork the last 20 minutes of grilling.

A Bird's - Eye View

Poultry

A Missouri Window

River Heritage

Tall, wooded bluffs tower above the Mississippi River in the picturesque eastern border of the state. Gently rolling countryside dips into valleys, while creeks wind through fertile farmland. River towns and quaint country villages charm guests with their turn-of-the-century architecture, antique shops, and historical sites. Streams, rivers, and trails wind their way through forested hillsides and scenic bluffs.

The first French settlers came to Saint Genevieve in 1735. Today, this colonial village features roughly 50 historic buildings built in the French Creole style. Indian artifacts and Civil War relics are on display at the Saint Genevieve Museum. Cape Girardeau, the largest of these picturesque river towns, is a city that treasures its historical roots.

At the Trail of Tears State Park in Jackson, the solitude of the dark green forest and the limestone bluffs embrace the majesty of the Mississippi River. This park is a portion of the route that Cherokee Indians took on their forced march to a reservation in Oklahoma. Near Burfordville is Bollinger Mill with a four-story gristmill and covered bridge. The area from Fredericktown north to Bonne Terre was once the world's largest lead-mining district. At Bonne Terre, wide passageways of the world's largest man-made caverns overlook scuba divers in its billion-gallon underground lake.

Photos: The Trail of Tears State Park & Bolinger Mill, Cape Girardeau County

In the early days of what was then called the Medical Auxiliary, the Cape Girardeau County Medical Society Alliance served primarily as a group supporting physicians and spouses. Over the years, the Alliance has contributed to the health of the community and accomplished much in the process.

Cape Girardeau County Area Medical Society Alliance

The Alliance prides itself in knowing that it helps educate nurses through scholarships; in beautifying the community by planting trees in honor and remembrance of doctors; in teaching high school students CPR; and in encouraging elementary students to make good choices through *Project Charlie*. The Medical Alliance was instrumental in working toward the passing of a tax to support a county health unit. Area charitable organizations have been the benefactors of funds raised by Alliance members who spend countless hours working together for this purpose. Special interest groups, such as book clubs, are springing up and ideas are being shared.

Cape Girardeau County Alliance has had three members serve as MSMA Alliance presidents: Gladys Drace, 1941-42, Carol Sparkman, 1990-91, and Nona Nan Chapman, 1995-96. Mrs. Sparkman also served as president of the Southern Medical Association Auxiliary in 2001-2002.

Chicken Breasts Lombardy

Level: Good Cook
Serves 6-8
Preparation Time: 1¼ hours

2	cups sliced fresh mushrooms
¼	pound (1 stick) butter or margarine, divided
12	chicken breast halves, skinned and boned
½	cup all-purpose flour
¾	cup Marsala wine
½	cup chicken stock
½	teaspoon salt
⅛	teaspoon black pepper
½	cup (2-ounces) shredded fontina or mozzarella cheese
½	cup grated Parmesan cheese
¼	cup chopped green onion, white and green parts

- Sauté mushrooms in 2 tablespoons butter or margarine until tender. Set aside.
- Cut each chicken breast half in half lengthwise. Place between 2 sheets of wax paper, flatten to ⅛-inch thickness, using a meat mallet or rolling pin.
- Dredge chicken pieces in flour.
- Melt 2 tablespoons butter in a large skillet. Fry 5-6 pieces chicken at a time until golden in color. Fry remaining chicken, adding butter or margarine as needed. Drain on paper towels.
- Reserve pan drippings in skillet.
- Place browned chicken breasts in a lightly greased 13x9x2-inch baking dish, overlapping edges.
- Sprinkle reserved mushrooms over chicken.
- Add wine and stock to reserved pan drippings in skillet. Bring to a boil, reduce heat and simmer uncovered for 10 minutes, stirring occasionally.
- Stir in salt and black pepper. Pour sauce evenly over chicken.
- Combine cheeses and green onion; sprinkle over chicken.
- Bake, uncovered, at 450 degrees for 12-14 minutes.
- Broil 6 inches from heat 1-2 minutes or until top is lightly browned.

A Chef's View

Fried or baked chicken is especially delicious when it has first been marinated in the refrigerator overnight in buttermilk, milk or sour cream.

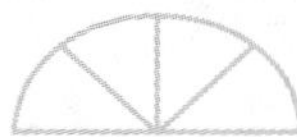

A Missouri Window

Get Your Kicks on Missouri's Route 66

It's more than just a road. It's a ribbon that winds around the soul of a country. America's 'Mother Road' was the primary east-west travel route for decades. Step back to a time when hamburgers were a nickel, optimism was everywhere, and a real adventure meant a driving trip, but not just anywhere. It meant a trip down the Mother Road, the Main Street of America, a place to get your kicks. It meant Route 66.

Apricot Chicken with Garden Rice

Level: Good Cook
Serves 12
Preparation Time: 10 hours

6	(whole) chicken breasts, skinned, boned and halved
1	(12-ounce) can apricot nectar
1	teaspoon ground allspice
½	teaspoon salt
¼	teaspoon ground ginger
¼	teaspoon black pepper
¾	cup apricot preserves
¼	cup apricot brandy, optional
½	cup chopped pecans, toasted
	Windows' Garden Rice

- Place chicken breasts in a 13x9x2-inch glass baking dish.
- Combine nectar, allspice, salt, ginger and black pepper. Pour nectar mixture over chicken. Cover and marinate 8 hours in refrigerator.
- Remove chicken from refrigerator and allow to rest 30 minutes at room temperature.
- Cover with aluminum foil and bake in a 350 degree preheated oven for 30 minutes.
- Uncover, drain and discard liquid.
- Heat preserves in a saucepan over low heat until melted. Brush over chicken.
- Drizzle with apricot brandy, if desired.
- Bake uncovered at 350 degrees for an additional 25 minutes. Baste occasionally with preserves.
- Sprinkle with toasted pecans before serving.
- Serve with or over *Windows'* Garden Rice.

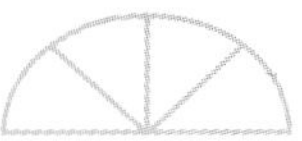

Garden Rice

Level: Easy
Serves 12
Preparation Time: 45 minutes

3 cups white rice, cooked in chicken stock, seasoned with salt and ground white pepper
3 cups wild rice, cooked in chicken stock, seasoned with salt and ground white pepper
1 cup finely chopped onion
1 cup finely chopped celery
2 garlic cloves, minced
1 cup shredded carrots
4 tablespoons butter

- Keep prepared rice warm.
- Cook and stir onion, celery, garlic and carrots in butter in a medium-size skillet.
- Add to prepared rice and toss.
- Cook's Tip: Use a commercial long grain and wild rice combination without the seasoning packet.

Asparagus Artichoke Chicken

Level: Good Cook
Serves 10-12
Preparation Time: 1½ hours

2½ cups chicken stock, divided
4 tablespoons all-purpose flour
1½ cups shredded Cheddar, Swiss or Monterey Jack cheese, divided
5 cups diced cooked chicken
2 (15-ounce) cans asparagus pieces, drained
2 (14-ounce) cans marinated artichoke hearts, drained and quartered

- Preheat oven to 350 degrees. Coat a 13x9x2-inch glass baking dish with cooking spray.
- Whisk constantly ½ cup chicken stock with 4 tablespoons flour in a saucepan over medium heat until smooth.
- Add the remaining chicken stock and 1 cup cheese. Cook and stir until cheese melts and sauce thickens.
- Pour cheese mixture over diced chicken and mix well.
- Layer half the chicken mixture, all the asparagus and artichoke hearts, then the remaining chicken mixture in baking dish.
- Sprinkle with ½ cup cheese.
- Bake for 30-45 minutes or until bubbly.
- Cook's Tip: Can be served alone or over cooked rice.

A Chef's View

For most purposes, broth, bouillon, and stock can be used interchangeably. Broth is simply the liquid left after poaching meat and/or vegetables. Since the cooking time is not very long, the liquid isn't very flavorful, but is suitable for soup or even some sauces. The term bouillon originated in the mid 1800s and came from the French verb bouilliv, meaning 'to boil.' It probably was used to make broth sound more appealing. Simmering meat, bones, vegetables, and herbs in water for a long period of time makes a flavorful stock. This extended cooking time extracts the flavor from the meat and the gelatin from the bones, creating a rich, flavorful liquid.

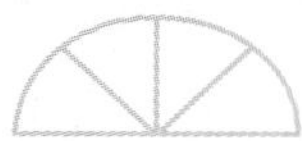

A Missouri Window

'Where there is no vision, there is no hope.'

– George Washington Carver

Carver, born a slave in Diamond, Missouri, received the Theodore Roosevelt Medal in 1939 for his valuable contributions to science.

He experimented with many things in his lifetime. One of these was the peanut. Carver showed that if he planted peanuts in the soil, the growing peanuts would improve the soil and farmers could grow bigger and better crops. Instead of wasting the peanuts he grew, Carver invented other uses, such as cereals, oils, dyes, soaps, and food substitutes.

Cheese Soufflé with Chicken Mushroom Sauce

Level: Expert Cook
Serves 8
Preparation Time: 3 hours

6	tablespoons butter
⅓	cup all-purpose flour
2	cups milk, heated until warmed
3	cups shredded mild Cheddar cheese
6	eggs, separated
½	teaspoon cream of tartar
1	teaspoon dried dill weed, optional
	Windows' Chicken Mushroom Sauce

- Melt butter in a saucepan over medium heat. Stir in flour.
- Add heated milk mixture and stir until thick and bubbly. Stir in cheese until melted.
- Beat egg yolks until thick and lemon-colored.
- Add cheese mixture slowly to egg yolks, stirring constantly. Cool slightly.
- Beat egg whites and cream of tartar until stiff peaks form.
- Slowly fold egg yolk and cheese mixture into the beaten egg whites.
- Pour into 8 ungreased 1-cup soufflé cups. At this time soufflés may be covered tightly with freezer wrap or aluminum foil and frozen until needed.
- Bake soufflés by setting cups into a shallow water bath of boiling water that reaches ½ the height of the soufflé cups.
- Bake for 20 minutes in a preheated 300 degree oven.
- Soufflés are baked when a knife is inserted in the center and comes out clean.
- Serve immediately with *Windows'* Chicken Mushroom Sauce.
- Cook's Tip: Bake frozen soufflés for 1 hour and 15 minutes in a preheated 300 degree oven.

Chicken Mushroom Sauce

Level: Easy
Yield: 3 cups
Preparation Time: 10 minutes

10 fresh mushrooms, chopped
3 tablespoons butter
2 tablespoons all-purpose flour
Salt and black pepper, to taste
½ cup light cream
1 cup sour cream
¼ cup sherry
1 cup cooked chicken breast, chopped

- Cook mushrooms in butter. Add flour and mix well.
- Season with salt and black pepper to taste.
- Add cream and cook, stirring constantly, until the sauce is thickened.
- Add sour cream, sherry and chicken until thoroughly heated.
- Spoon over soufflés.

Chicken and Rice Casserole with Cashews

Level: Easy
Serves 6
Preparation Time: 1½ hours

3 chicken breasts, poached, skinned, boned and cubed
1 medium onion, chopped
1 small green bell pepper, diced
½ teaspoon minced garlic
1 (4-ounce) can sliced mushrooms, drained
2 cups chicken consommé
1¼ cups raw rice, cleaned and rinsed
½ teaspoon cayenne pepper
½ cup cashew nuts

- Preheat oven to 350 degrees. Coat a 11x7x2-inch glass casserole dish with cooking spray.
- Cook and stir chicken, onion, green pepper and garlic in a skillet until onion is tender.
- Add mushrooms, consommé, rice and cayenne pepper. Stir and heat until warm.
- Pour mixture into casserole dish. Cover with aluminum foil.
- Bake for 1 hour.
- Sprinkle cashews on top of casserole before serving.

A Chef's View

Freshen poultry, after washing, by rubbing it with a cut lemon or orange.

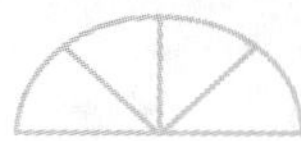

A Show-Me Specialty

Hot Chicken Salad is a specialty of the Jefferson City Country Club.

Jefferson City Country Club
516 Country Club Drive
Jefferson City

Hot Chicken Salad Topping

Level: Easy

Yield: 1½ cups

Preparation Time: 10 minutes

½ cup shredded Swiss cheese

½ cup shredded provolone cheese

½ cup crushed potato chips

- Combine Swiss cheese, provolone cheese and potato chips. Toss.

Chef Ron's Hot Chicken Salad

Level: Good Cook
Serves 8-10
Preparation Time: 1 hour

10	chicken breasts, boneless, skinless, in bite-size pieces
½	pound (2 sticks) butter, divided
½	cup chopped red bell pepper
½	cup chopped yellow bell pepper
½	cup sliced leeks, white part only
½	cup fresh coarsely chopped parsley
½	cup chopped celery
½	cup grated carrots
2	cups sliced fresh mushrooms
1	teaspoon dried rosemary leaves
1	teaspoon ground white pepper
½	teaspoon granulated garlic powder
	Salt, to taste
2	cups chicken stock
1	cup cream sherry
½	cup all-purpose flour
1	cup heavy cream
½	cup sour cream
	Windows' Hot Chicken Salad Topping
1	pound angel hair pasta, cooked al dente

- Sauté chicken, in batches, in 3 tablespoons butter. Add additional butter as needed. Drain. Reserve chicken in a large mixing bowl.
- Add bell peppers, leeks, parsley, celery, carrots, mushrooms, rosemary, ground white pepper and garlic powder to mixing bowl with chicken. Salt to taste. Toss.
- Bring chicken stock and cream sherry to boil in a saucepan.
- Prepare a roux by melting 8 tablespoons butter and gradually adding 8 tablespoons flour to a skillet. Whisk after each addition. Cook until the flour taste is eliminated and mixture is thick, approximately 4 minutes. Do not brown.
- Add roux to chicken stock mixture. Simmer until stock thickens.
- Remove from heat and add heavy cream and sour cream. Mix well.
- Combine sauce and chicken-vegetable mixture. Mix well.
- Preheat oven to 350 degrees.
- Pour mixture into a large greased baking dish or 2 smaller baking dishes.
- Prepare topping. Sprinkle mixture evenly over top of casserole(s).
- Bake for 25-30 minutes or until cheese topping is golden brown and sides just begin to bubble.
- Serve over angle hair pasta.
- Cook's Tip: Garnish, as desired. Serve with fresh fruit.

Chicken Chalupas

Level: Easy
Serves 5-6
Preparation Time: 1½ hours

- 1 (2-3 pound) chicken, poached, skinned, boned and diced into bite-size pieces
- 4 (10¾-ounce) cans cream of chicken soup
- 1 (12-ounce) carton sour cream
- 1 large onion, chopped
- 1 (6-ounce) can crushed tomatoes and mild green chiles
- 1 (12-piece) package soft tortillas, 10-inch rounds
- 1 (16-ounce) package shredded Cheddar cheese

- ◆ Preheat oven to 350 degrees. Coat a 12x10x2-inch baking dish with cooking spray.
- ◆ Combine soup, sour cream, onion, and crushed tomatoes and chiles in a saucepan.
- ◆ Cook soup mixture over medium heat for 5 minutes.
- ◆ Assemble chalupas one at a time by filling a tortilla with 3 tablespoons chicken, 4 tablespoons sauce and 3 tablespoons cheese.
- ◆ Roll and place seam side down in a baking dish. Assemble remaining chalupas.
- ◆ Cover chalupas with remaining chicken, sauce and cheese.
- ◆ Bake until cheese is melted and bubbly, approximately 30 minutes.
- ◆ Cook's Tip: Garnish with additional cheese before serving, if desired.

A Chef's View

Use leftover flour tortillas to make easy, sweet snacks. Lightly spray each flour tortilla with nonstick butter-flavored spray coating; then sprinkle evenly with sugar and ground cinnamon. Using a pizza cutter, cut each tortilla into strips or triangles. Place the pieces on a baking sheet and bake in a 350 degree oven for 8-10 minutes or until crisp. Eat the sweet snacks alone or serve with vanilla ice cream.

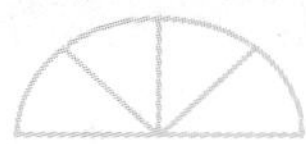

A Missouri Window

The drive along the bluffs over the Big Piney River at Devil's Elbow is perhaps the prettiest spot along Missouri's Route 66. In Lebanon, stop by the 1940s Munger-Moss Motel, a real Route 66 landmark. Springfield's Shrine Mosque's eye-popping Arabian Nights architecture may seem out of place in the heart of the Missouri Ozarks, but entertainers have played here since the 1950s. Today, performers still ring the rafters with concerts for every style and taste. You might think you've gone back in time as you drive through the Town Square in Carthage, with its splendid Victorian houses. A stop at the meticulously restored 1940s Route 66 Drive-In Theatre is also a must.

Chicken Divan

Level: Good Cook
Serves 8
Preparation Time: 8 hours

8	chicken breasts, skinned and boned
2	cups sour cream
2	tablespoons lemon juice, freshly squeezed
2	teaspoons Worcestershire sauce
¼	teaspoon crushed celery seed
1	teaspoon ground paprika
1	garlic clove, minced
½	teaspoon salt
⅛	teaspoon ground white pepper
1	(12-ounce) bag herbed stuffing mix
1	cup seasoned bread crumbs
¼	pound (1 stick) butter, melted
1	(10¾-ounce) can golden mushroom soup
¼	cup fresh parsley, finely chopped
2	tablespoons sherry or sweet white wine
½	teaspoon minced garlic
½	teaspoon onion powder

- Place chicken breasts in a glass baking dish.
- Mix sour cream, lemon juice, Worcestershire sauce, celery seed, paprika, garlic, salt and white pepper together.
- Pour sour cream mixture over chicken, being sure to coat all breasts. Cover with plastic wrap and refrigerate 6-8 hours.
- Combine stuffing mix and bread crumbs. Roll chicken in stuffing mixture and pat into chicken to coat completely.
- Place chicken breasts in greased baking dish 1 inch apart. Refrigerate until ready to bake.
- Pour melted butter over chicken and bake at 350 degrees for 1 hour.
- Prepare sauce by combing mushroom soup, parsley, sherry, garlic and onion powder. Heat to just boiling.
- Serve sauce over chicken.

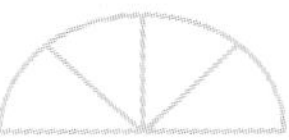

Chicken in Three Cheese Sauce

Level: Easy
Serves 4-6
Preparation Time: 45 minutes

- 3 whole chicken breasts, skinned, boned and halved
- 3 tablespoons olive oil, for sautéing
- Salt and black pepper, to taste
- 1 (10¾-ounce) can cream of mushroom soup
- ½ cup milk
- 1 cup (4-ounces) shredded Cheddar cheese
- ¼ cup freshly grated Parmesan cheese
- 2 tablespoons crumbled Gorgonzola cheese
- 1 teaspoon lemon juice
- ¼ teaspoon parsley flakes
- 1 tablespoon dry sherry

- Preheat oven to 350 degrees. Coat a 15x10x2-inch glass baking dish with cooking spray.
- Pan-fry chicken in olive oil, removing just before chicken browns.
- Season chicken with salt and pepper. Place in a baking dish.
- Combine soup, milk, cheeses, lemon juice, parsley and sherry in a saucepan. Cook over medium heat until blended.
- Pour sauce over chicken and bake uncovered for 30 minutes.
- Cook's Tip: To prepare in a slow cooker, pan-fry and season chicken as directed. Add to slow cooker with remaining ingredients. Cook on low for at least 2 hours.

A Chef's View

Freezing chicken is easy. Cook 1 pound of boneless chicken breast or thighs to get 2 cups chopped; or cook whole chicken to get 3 cups chopped. Freeze chopped cooked chicken up to one month. To freeze uncooked chicken, place chicken pieces in individual zip-top plastic bags; then place individual packages in a large heavy-duty zip-top freezer bag, and label. Freeze chicken pieces up to six months and whole chickens up to one year.

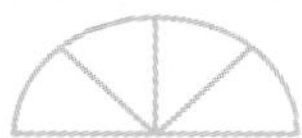

Enchilada Sauce

Level: Easy

Yield: 2 cups

Preparation Time:
30 minutes

2½ cups tomato sauce

2 tablespoons oil

1 tablespoon ground cumin seeds

½ teaspoon chili powder

¼ teaspoon black pepper

◆ Combine all ingredients in a medium-size saucepan and simmer for 30 minutes.

◆ Cool.

Enchilada Topping

Level: Easy

Yield: 3 cups

Preparation Time:
5 minutes

1½ cups Enchilada Sauce

1¼ cups stewed tomatoes

¼ cup chopped green chiles, drained

◆ Combine all ingredients and mix well.

Chicken Enchiladas

Level: Good Cook
Serves 6-8
Preparation Time: 1 hour

Windows' Enchilada Sauce
Windows' Enchilada Topping
3 cups shredded cooked chicken
1 medium onion, chopped
1½ (15-ounce) cans stewed tomatoes, drained
½ cup chopped green chiles
¾ cup sliced ripe olives
½ teaspoon chili powder
1 teaspoon ground cumin seeds
½ teaspoon black pepper
1 pound Monterey Jack cheese, shredded
1 pound Cheddar cheese, shredded
10 (8-inch) round flour tortillas
Fresh parsley, for garnish
Sour cream, for garnish
Guacamole, for garnish

- Prepare Enchilada Sauce according to recipe directions.
- Prepare Enchilada Topping according to recipe directions.
- Combine chicken, onion, tomatoes, chiles, olives, chili powder, cumin and black pepper in a large saucepan. Simmer for 15 minutes.
- Preheat oven to 350 degrees. Coat a 13x9x2-inch baking dish with cooking spray.
- Combine shredded cheeses.
- Brush each tortilla with 2 tablespoons Enchilada Sauce. Top each with 3-4 tablespoons of the chicken mixture and 2-3 tablespoons cheese.
- Roll and place seam side down in baking dish.
- Combine remaining Enchilada Sauce and Enchilada Topping and pour over enchiladas.
- Top with remaining cheese.
- Bake for 20-25 minutes.
- Garnish with parsley and serve with sour cream and guacamole toppings.

Rosemary Walnut Chicken

Level: Good Cook
Serves 6
Preparation Time: 45 minutes

4	tablespoons olive oil, divided
¾	cup coarsely chopped walnuts, toasted, divided
1	tablespoon plus ½ teaspoon rosemary, divided
2½	garlic cloves, minced, divided
¾	teaspoon salt, divided
¼	cup all-purpose flour
¼	teaspoon black pepper
6	boneless, skinless chicken breast halves
1	tablespoon thyme
2	cups dry white wine
2	cups chicken stock
¼	cup balsamic vinegar
½	cup crumbled feta cheese
¼	cup thinly sliced green onions

- Heat 1 tablespoon olive oil in a small skillet.
- Add ½ cup walnuts, ½ teaspoon rosemary, ½ teaspoon minced garlic and ¼ teaspoon salt. Sauté for 3-4 minutes or until walnuts are toasted.
- Mix flour, ½ teaspoon salt and pepper in a shallow dish. Dredge chicken in flour mixture.
- Heat 3 tablespoons olive oil in a large skillet over medium-high heat. Add chicken and cook for 3 minutes on each side or until light brown. Remove chicken to a warm platter and keep warm.
- Reduce heat to medium. Add remaining garlic, 1 tablespoon rosemary and thyme to skillet. Stir and cook for 2 minutes.
- Stir in wine, chicken stock and vinegar. Simmer for 10-12 minutes or until thickened, stirring occasionally.
- Return chicken to skillet. Simmer for an additional 10-12 minutes or until chicken is cooked through.
- Sprinkle feta cheese over chicken.
- Place chicken on individual heated serving plates.
- Spoon sauce over chicken. Sprinkle with green onions and remaining ¼ cup toasted walnuts.
- Serve immediately.

A Missouri Window

The first train of the Atlantic-Pacific Railway, which became the St. Louis-San Francisco Railway, or 'Frisco,' arrived in 1870.

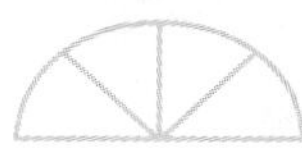

A Missouri Window

Situated within a day's drive of 50% of the U.S. population, Branson and the Tri-Lakes area serves up to 65,000 visitors daily. Branson has been a 'rubber tire' destination with the vast majority of tourists arriving by vehicles, RVs and tour buses. Branson has also become one of America's top motor coach vacation destinations with an estimated 4,000 buses arriving each year.

Chicken Stir-Fry

Level: Good Cook
Serves 2-4
Preparation Time: 2½ hours

2	tablespoons stir-fry oil, divided
2	tablespoons sherry
1	tablespoon soy sauce
3	tablespoons stir-fry seasoning, divided
10	ounces chicken breast, skinned, boned and cut in ½-inch cubes
2	cups snow peas, fresh, if available
1	red bell pepper, sliced in thin strips
1	yellow bell pepper, sliced in thin strips
4	green onions, chopped, white and green parts
1	cup sliced mushrooms
¾	cup chicken stock
2	teaspoons cornstarch
¼	cup slivered almonds, for garnish
	Cooked rice

- Combine 1 tablespoon oil, sherry, soy sauce and 1 tablespoon stir-fry seasoning.
- Add cubed chicken breast. Marinate for 2 hours or overnight.
- Preheat stir-fry pan on medium heat. Add ½ tablespoon oil.
- Stir-fry, adding one at a time, in order: snow peas, sliced peppers, green onions and mushrooms.
- Season with remaining 2 tablespoons stir-fry seasoning. Remove vegetables from pan.
- Add ½ tablespoon oil to fry pan. Add chicken cubes and stir-fry until cooked through.
- Mix chicken stock with cornstarch.
- Return vegetables to stir-fry pan with chicken. Add cornstarch mixture and stir, allowing sauce to thicken.
- Garnish with almonds.
- Serve with or over cooked rice.

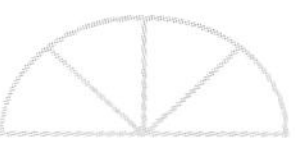

Clary's Chicken Piccata

Level: Good Cook
Serves 2
Preparation Time: 1 hour

2	(4-ounce) boneless chicken breasts
2	eggs, beaten
¼	cup plus 1 tablespoon heavy cream, divided
1	cup freshly grated Parmesan cheese
1	tablespoon chopped fresh parsley
1	tablespoon all-purpose flour, plus additional for dusting
2	teaspoons minced garlic
	Salt and black pepper, to taste
2	tablespoons butter
¼	cup dry white wine
¼	cup lemon juice
1	tablespoon minced shallots
2	tablespoons capers, drained
4-8	tablespoons cold butter
	Cooked pasta

- Pound chicken breasts extremely thin.
- Whisk eggs, ¼ cup heavy cream, freshly grated Parmesan cheese, parsley, flour, garlic, salt and black pepper until smooth.
- Heat a nonstick skillet and melt 2 tablespoons butter.
- Dredge chicken in flour then dip in egg batter.
- Pan-fry chicken in melted butter until both sides are golden. Set aside and keep warm.
- Combine wine, lemon juice, shallots, capers and 1 tablespoon heavy cream in a small saucepan. Reduce until almost dry.
- Remove from heat. Swirl in individual butter chunks by the tablespoon until sauce is thickened.
- Adjust salt and black pepper.
- Top chicken with wine sauce and serve with pasta.

A Show-Me Specialty

Chicken Picatta is one of the most popular main course selections according to James Clary, chef/owner of Clary's Restaurant in Springfield, Missouri.

Clary's Restaurant
3014 East Sunshine Street
Springfield

A Chef's View

Capers are pungent little flower buds found on bushes native to the Mediterranean and part of Asia. The buds are hand-picked and sun-dried then packed in vinegar or brine. If possible, select capers packed in brine and rinse before using to remove excess salt. Most capers are imported from Italy, Morocco, and Greece; however, the petite nonpareil variety from the south of France is considered to be the finest.

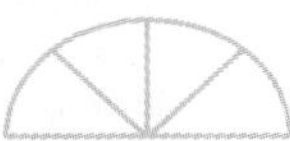

A Missouri Window

In Eminence in southern Missouri, the Alley Spring Grist Mill Historic Site was built in 1894 and is part of the Ozarks National Scenic Riverways.

Cranberry Chicken

Level: Easy
Serves 8
Preparation Time: 1½ hours

1	(6-ounce) package wild and long grain rice
1	(16-ounce) can whole-berry cranberry sauce
1	tablespoon margarine
1	tablespoon lemon juice, freshly squeezed
1	tablespoon Worcestershire sauce
1	tablespoon soy sauce
8	chicken breasts halves, skinned and boned

- Prepare rice mix according to package directions.
- Preheat oven to 350 degrees.
- Combine cranberry sauce, margarine, lemon juice, Worcestershire sauce and soy sauce in a saucepan. Stir.
- Bring cranberry mixture to boiling over medium heat.
- Place cooked rice in bottom of a greased 2½-quart baking dish.
- Arrange chicken pieces over rice and pour sauce over chicken.
- Bake for 1 hour.

Lemon Pecan Chicken

Level: Easy
Serves 4
Preparation Time: 1 hour

1	cup parsley sprigs, chopped
½	cup pecan pieces
½	cup grated Parmesan cheese
⅓	cup peanut oil
2	garlic cloves, minced
3	tablespoons dried basil leaves
3	tablespoons lemon juice, freshly squeezed
1½	pounds chicken breasts, skinned and boned

- Preheat oven to 350 degrees. Spray a 12x8x2-inch baking dish with cooking spray.
- Combine parsley, pecans and Parmesan cheese reserving ⅔ of the mixture.
- Blend remaining parsley mixture with oil, garlic, basil and lemon juice.
- Place chicken in baking dish and cover with oil mixture.
- Sprinkle remaining parsley cheese mixture over chicken.
- Bake for 50-60 minutes.

Crunchy Chicken Cauliflower

Level: Easy
Serves 8
Preparation Time: 40 minutes

1	large head cauliflower, cut into florets
1	(10¾-ounce) can cream of chicken soup
1	(8-ounce) carton sour cream
¼	teaspoon black pepper
2	celery ribs, diced
½	small onion, diced
1	cup (4-ounces) shredded sharp Cheddar cheese
1	(5-ounce) can water-packed chunk chicken, drained and rinsed
1	red bell pepper, cut into ½-inch pieces
2	cups crushed Cheddar and sour cream potato chips

- Preheat oven to 350 degrees. Coat a 13x9x2-inch baking dish with cooking spray.
- Cook cauliflower in boiling water until crisp-tender. Drain.
- Stir together soup, sour cream and black pepper in a medium-size bowl.
- Fold in drained cauliflower, celery, onion, cheese, chicken and red bell pepper.
- Pour into baking dish.
- Sprinkle top with potato chips.
- Bake for 25 minutes.

A Missouri Window

In Mark Twain's words, "cauliflower is nothing but cabbage with a college education." The name comes from the Latin caulis, meaning stalk, and floris, meaning flower. Cauliflower comes in three colors: white, green, and purple.

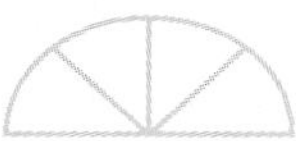

A Missouri Window

Often referred to as Missouri's "Little Grand Canyon," Grand Gulf State Park offers a chance to view a variety of natural wonders. The 322-acre park presents the most spectacular collapsed cave system in the Ozarks. Part of the cave's roof forms one of the largest natural bridges in the state, spanning 200 feet with an opening 75 feet high and 50 feet wide. The "Grand Gulf" stretches for nearly a mile with walls almost 130 feet high, making the chasm deeper than it is wide.

Indian Chicken Kebabs

Level: Good Cook
Serves 4-6
Preparation Time: 8 hours

2	pounds chicken breasts, skinned and boned
1	lemon, juiced
½	teaspoon ground ginger
½	teaspoon garlic paste
2	teaspoons finely chopped fresh cilantro
½	teaspoon hot pepper sauce
½	teaspoon salt
½	cup unflavored low-fat yogurt
½	teaspoon tandoori paste, or a few drops of red food coloring mixed with 1 tablespoon tomato paste
2	tablespoons canola oil
½	cup egg yolk, (2-3 eggs)
	Cooked rice

- Cut chicken into 1-inch cubes. Mix with lemon juice and set aside for 30 minutes.
- Blend remainder of ingredients, except egg yolks, in a food processor until smooth.
- Add mixture to chicken and marinate for 6-8 hours or overnight in refrigerator.
- Heat oil in a skillet. Carefully add chicken and marinade. Simmer on low heat in a covered saucepan for 10 minutes or until chicken is cooked.
- Remove chicken from sauce and with the help of tongs, thread chicken onto skewers, leaving ½ inch gap between pieces. If using wooden skewers, soak skewers in water for ½ hour before using.
- Preheat oven to 300 degrees.
- Place skewers over a broiler pan. Cover skewers with aluminum foil and cook for 5-6 minutes.
- Remove broiler pan from oven, rotate skewers and brush chicken with egg yolk.
- Return to oven and broil for an additional 3 minutes, rotating once.
- Remove skewers and serve kebabs over rice.

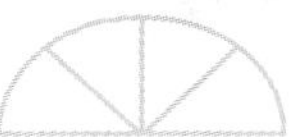

Lemon Apricot Chicken

Level: Easy
Serves 6
Preparation Time: 40 minutes

4	tablespoons butter or margarine, melted and divided
1	egg
2	tablespoons water
1	cup buttermilk biscuit baking mix
1	tablespoon grated lemon peel
¼	teaspoon garlic powder
6	chicken breast halves, skinned and boned
⅔	cup apricot preserves
2	tablespoons lemon juice
½	teaspoon soy sauce
¼	teaspoon ground ginger
6	lemon slices, for garnish

- Preheat oven to 425 degrees.
- Spread 1 tablespoon melted margarine in a 15x10x1-inch jelly-roll pan.
- Whisk egg with 2 tablespoons water in a medium-size bowl.
- Combine baking mix, lemon peel and garlic powder in a shallow bowl. Mix.
- Flatten chicken breasts to ½-inch thickness.
- Dip chicken into egg mixture, then coat with baking mix.
- Place coated chicken in jelly-roll pan.
- Drizzle with remaining 3 tablespoons melted margarine.
- Bake uncovered for 20 minutes. Turn and bake an additional 10 minutes.
- Prepare lemon-apricot sauce by combining preserves, lemon juice, soy sauce and ginger. Heat through.
- Cut chicken crosswise into ½-inch slices. Pour lemon-apricot sauce over chicken.
- Garnish chicken with lemon slices.

A Chef's View

Create a lemon twist garnish by cutting a ⅛-inch thick slices from a lemon. Cut halfway across each slice, stopping at the center, and twist the ends of the slice in opposite directions.

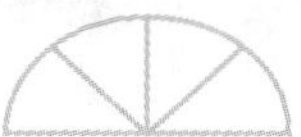

A Missouri Window

'I'm beginning to learn that it is the sweet, simple things in life which are the real ones after all.'

~ Laura Ingalls Wilder, Mansfield, Missouri

Scalloped Chicken

Level: Easy
Serves 10-12
Preparation Time: 1½ hours

1	(8-ounce) package (3½ cups) herb-seasoned stuffing
3	cups cubed cooked chicken
¼	pound (1 stick) butter or margarine
½	cup all-purpose flour
¼	teaspoon salt
	Black pepper, to taste
4	cups chicken stock
6	eggs, slightly beaten
	Windows' Pimiento Mushroom Sauce

- Preheat oven to 325 degrees. Coat a 13x9x2-inch baking dish with cooking spray.
- Prepare stuffing according to directions for dry stuffing.
- Spread stuffing in bottom of baking dish and top with cooked chicken.
- Melt butter in a skillet. Blend in flour, salt and black pepper. Add stock, stirring for 3 minutes or until mixture thickens. Cool slightly.
- Stir a small amount of hot flour mixture into eggs, to temper. Pour into remaining flour mixture and mix.
- Pour sauce over chicken and bake for 40-45 minutes or until a knife inserted halfway to center comes out clean.
- Remove from oven and let stand 5 minutes to set.
- Serve by cutting into squares, placing on individual plates and spooning *Windows'* Pimiento Mushroom Sauce over each square.

Pimiento Mushroom Sauce

Level: Quick and Simple
Yield: 2 cups
Preparation Time: 15 minutes

1	(10¾-ounce) can cream of mushroom soup
1	cup sour cream
¼	cup milk
¼	cup pimiento, chopped
½	teaspoon onion powder
¼	teaspoon garlic powder

- Heat and stir all ingredients until hot.

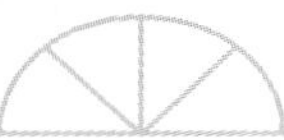

Springfield Cashew Chicken

Level: Easy
Serves 4
Preparation Time: 1 hour

4	large chicken breast halves, skinned, boned and diced into bite-size pieces
½	cup milk
2	tablespoons water
2	eggs, well beaten
	Salt, to taste
2	tablespoons cornstarch
1½	cups chicken stock
2	tablespoons oyster sauce
1	teaspoon granulated sugar
	Black pepper, to taste
1	cup all-purpose flour
	Vegetable oil, for frying
1	cup cashew nuts
½	cup chopped green onion, white and green parts
	Soy sauce
4	servings cooked rice

- Marinate chicken in milk, water, eggs and seasoned with salt for 20 minutes.
- Dissolve cornstarch in a small amount of stock in a saucepan. Whisk in remaining stock.
- Blend in oyster sauce, sugar and black pepper.
- Whisk sauce over medium-high heat until it boils and begins to thicken. Set aside.
- Coat chicken with flour.
- Heat oil in a heavy skillet. Drop chicken into hot oil piece by piece to prevent clumping. Fry chicken until crisp and drain on paper towels.
- Arrange chicken on serving dish, sprinkle with cashews and green onion.
- Reheat sauce and pour over chicken.
- Serve immediately with soy sauce and hot rice.

A Chef's View

Created in China a thousand years ago, the wok is the perfect vessel for health-conscious cooks. Foods prepared with rapid-fire cooking retain their nutrition, taste, color, and crispness. It is not essential to use a wok to stir-fry - a good heavy skillet will do. Stir-frying is the primary method of cooking in a wok, but a wok is also perfect for boiling, steaming, deep-fat frying, or braising food. Vegetable oil and peanut oil are the oils of choice for stir-frying. Both can be heated to a high temperature without smoking. Never substitute butter of margarine. If foods are too wet they will not stir-fry well. Pat dry on paper towels before cooking.

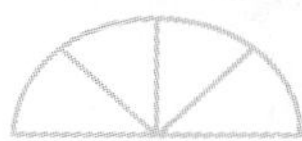

A Chef's View

A croquette is usually a mixture of minced meat or vegetables, a thick white sauce and seasonings that is formed into small cylinders, ovals or rounds, dipped in beaten egg and then bread crumbs, and deep-fried until crisp and brown. It is a way to use uneaten meat or vegetables.

A Missouri Window

The 74th General Assembly adopted Mozarkite as the official state rock on July 21, 1967.

Turkey Croquettes

Level: Easy
Serves 4
Preparation Time: 45 minutes

½	cup mayonnaise
½	teaspoon salt
2	tablespoons minced onion
1	garlic clove, minced
⅛	teaspoon black pepper
1	teaspoon Worcestershire sauce
1	tablespoon chopped parsley
2	tablespoons cold water
2	cups chopped cooked turkey
1	cup fresh bread crumbs
2	cups finely crushed saltine crackers

- Preheat oven to 450 degrees.
- Stir together mayonnaise, salt, onion, garlic, pepper, Worcestershire sauce and parsley.
- Add water, turkey and bread crumbs. Mix well.
- Let stand for 5 minutes.
- Shape into 8 croquettes and roll in cracker crumbs.
- Bake for 15-20 minutes.
- Cook's Tip: Serve with a creamed gravy, if desired.

Turkey Jo's

Level: Quick and Simple
Serves 6
Preparation Time: 30 minutes

1	pound 90% lean ground turkey or beef
½	cup chopped onion
1	(8-ounce) can tomato sauce
½	cup chunky tomato salsa
1	tablespoon brown sugar substitute
6	calorie-reduced hamburger buns, split and toasted

- Coat a medium-size skillet with cooking spray.
- Brown meat and onion in skillet.
- Add tomato sauce, salsa and sugar substitute.
- Lower heat and simmer 15-20 minutes.
- Serve on toasted buns.

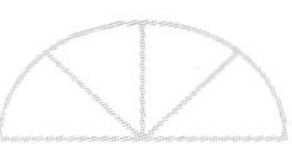

Turkey Hash

Level: Good Cook
Serves 6
Preparation Time: 40 minutes

⅓	cup all-purpose flour
1	(8-ounce) package sliced fresh mushrooms
½	green pepper, chopped
1	medium onion, chopped
4	tablespoons butter, melted
2	cups chicken stock
1	cup half-and-half
2½	cups chopped cooked turkey
1	teaspoon salt
½	teaspoon ground black pepper
3	tablespoons dry white wine
⅓	cup chopped roasted red pepper, drained
½	cup toasted sliced almonds
2	teaspoons chopped fresh sage
	Cornbread or *Windows'* Polenta

- Brown flour in a skillet over medium heat, stirring often.
- Sauté, in separate skillet, mushrooms, green pepper and onion in butter until tender.
- Add flour to mushroom mixture, stirring until smooth. Gradually stir in stock and half-and-half; cook until thickened, stirring constantly.
- Stir in turkey, salt and black pepper. Simmer 5-7 minutes.
- Add wine, red pepper, almonds and sage; cook until thoroughly heated.
- Serve turkey hash over cornbread or *Windows'* Polenta.

A Chef's View

Polenta is a staple of northern Italy, and is a mush made from cornmeal. It can be eaten hot with a little butter or cooled until firm, cut into squares and fried. Polenta is sometimes mixed with cheese such as Parmesan or Gorgonzola. It can be served as first course or side dish and makes hearty breakfast fare. See Windows' Polenta.

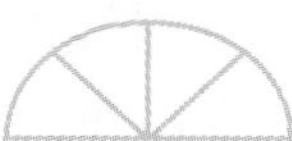

A Chef's View

Turkey is one of the leanest meats. Skinless, boneless turkey tenderloins cook quickly and are low in calories.

Grilled Turkey with Fresh Peach Salsa

Level: Good Cook
Serves 2
Preparation Time: 4 hours

⅓	cup red wine vinegar
4	tablespoons fresh lime juice, divided
½	cup canola oil, divided
2	tablespoon honey
2	jalapeño peppers, seeded and minced, divided
1	(8-ounce) turkey breast tenderloin
½	teaspoon salt
1	large ripe peach, peeled, stoned and diced
1	tomatillo, husked and diced
⅓	cup diced red bell pepper
1	tablespoon diced red onion
2	tablespoons minced fresh cilantro

- Prepare barbecue grill.
- Whisk vinegar, 2 tablespoons lime juice, ¼ cup oil, honey and ½ of minced jalapeño pepper until well blended. Add to zip-top plastic freezer bag.
- Add turkey to marinade in zip-top bag. Refrigerate for at least 2 hours, turning several times.
- Prepare salsa by whisking 2 tablespoons lime juice, ¼ cup oil and salt until well blended. Stir in peach, tomatillo, bell pepper, onion, remaining minced jalapeño and cilantro.
- Cover and chill for 2 hours.
- Heat barbecue grill to medium.
- Grill turkey tenderloin over medium coals until cooked, approximately 15-20 minutes.
- Slice tenderloin and serve with salsa.

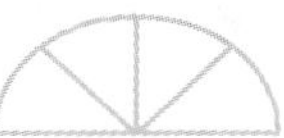

Turkey Breast Medallions with Pecan Honey Glaze

Level: Easy
Serves 4
Preparation Time: 40 minutes

1	(1½-pound) boneless turkey breast, skinned
	Salt, to taste
	Pepper, as desired
2	cups all-purpose flour
6	eggs
⅔	cup milk
	canola oil, as needed
1¼	cups honey
1¼	cups roasted pecans, finely chopped

- Slice turkey breast into 12, 2-ounce medallions.
- Combine salt, pepper and flour.
- Beat eggs and milk together.
- Heat ½-inch oil in a heavy medium-size skillet.
- Dredge turkey in flour mixture, dip into egg mixture and again in flour.
- Fry turkey on one side until golden. Turn, and brown other side until completely cooked. Drain on paper towels.
- Heat honey and stir in pecans.
- Place turkey on a heated platter and top with honey-pecan mixture. Serve immediately.

A Missouri Window

Travel the famous Route 66 but detour to Spencer - a ghost town created when the highway was rerouted. Here, a rare stretch of the original Route 66 concrete road still exists. Continuing your drive, you finally arrive in Joplin - the western end of Route 66 in Missouri. Though the road continues west for another thousand miles or so, you can relax here, knowing you've seen the finest of Route 66.

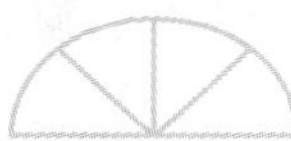

A Chef's View

After the Thanksgiving or Christmas holidays freeze left-over turkey and use later in recipes like meat loaf, soups, salads and hash. Turkey meatballs can be served in a light brown mushroom sauce over rice or as an appetizer.

Spinach and Turkey Meat Loaf

Level: Easy
Serves 4-6
Preparation Time: 1¼ hours

1 pound ground turkey
1 (10-ounce) package frozen chopped spinach, thawed and pressed to remove excess water
1 egg, beaten
¾ cup dry bread crumbs
½ cup chopped onion
1 tablespoon chopped fresh parsley
3 tablespoons ketchup
2 teaspoons fresh lemon juice
½ teaspoon soy sauce
¼ teaspoon ground black pepper
2 tablespoons milk

- Preheat oven to 350 degrees.
- Mix turkey, spinach, egg, bread crumbs, onion, parsley, ketchup, lemon juice, soy sauce and black pepper.
- Moisten with skim milk.
- Shape into a loaf and place in a 9x5x3-inch pan and cover with aluminum foil.
- Bake for 30 minutes. Remove foil and bake for an additional 30 minutes.
- Remove meat loaf from oven and cool 5-10 minutes in pan before slicing.
- Cook's Tip: Serve with a mushroom sauce like the *Windows'* Pimiento Mushroom Sauce.

A Kaleidoscope of Confections

Desserts & Sweets

A Missouri Window

Gateway

The first glimpse of the 630-foot Gateway Arch of St. Louis is a reminder of the historic role the city played in the westward expansion of America. The nearby Old Cathedral, the oldest church in St. Louis, sits across the street from the Old Courthouse, the site of the Dred Scott trial. The riverfront offers many entertaining possibilities, and not far away, the shopping is spectacular at St. Louis Centre or the completely restored Union Station.

Forest Park features the Saint Louis Art Museum, the Zoo, the Muny Opera and the Science Center, with life-size animated dinosaurs. Nearby is the historic Cathedral Basilica of Saint Louis, which houses one of the world's largest collections of mosaic art. Stroll through St. Louis' historic neighborhoods of Laclede's Landing, Soulard, the Hill, and Central West End, all of which provide great places for good shopping and fine food.

Just northwest of St. Louis is the French village of St. Charles with its Lewis and Clark Center, the first Missouri state Capitol building, and a quaint restored riverfront historic district. Southwest of St. Charles is the Daniel Boone Home, where the Boone family settled in the late 1790s.

Photos: The Arch &
Missouri Botanical Garden, St. Louis

St. Louis Metropolitan Medical Society Alliance

From the time St. Louis was settled, medicine was a pioneer art in the area. A group of physicians meeting on Christmas Day in 1835 formed the first medical society in Missouri and the physician spouses also gathered to support the profession of medicine.

In 1925, following the newly formed American Medical Association Auxiliary, which had commenced in 1922, the St. Louis spouses started their own Auxiliary, which just recently celebrated its 75th anniversary.

Long before it was fashionable to fight violence, the St. Louis Medical Alliance has been advocating for strong health programs in the community. Through volunteerism and funding, the Alliance has supported family care at St. Martha's Hall, a St. Louis shelter. Recent health endeavors include a program stressing reduction in teen pregnancies and dating abuse through a media blitz and education in area schools. The *Baby, Think It Over* project, *Shaken Baby* programs, and water intoxication programs are also ongoing and successful.

Currently, the St. Louis Alliance is working in coalition with the Girl Scouts in *Project PAVE - Project Anti-Violence*, which is a pilot program directed at kindergarten through fifth grades for five St. Louis area counties. This project includes the *Hands Are Not For Hitting* program, the anti-bullying campaign, and conflict resolution techniques.

Today, the St. Louis Metropolitan Medical Society Alliance is dedicated to the continued improvement of health, promotion of health education, encouraging participation of volunteers in activities that meet health needs and support health-related charitable endeavors.

The following St. Louis members have served as MSMA Alliance presidents: Mrs. Willard Bartlett, 1928-29; Mrs. Hudson Talbot, 1933-34; Mrs. Walter Kirschner, 1936-37; Mrs. Frank Davis, 1942-43; Mrs. August Werner, 1948-49; Mrs. John O'Connell, 1949-50; Betty Sutter, 1952-53; Sue Shepard, 1956-57; Mrs. Armand Fries, 1957-58; Venus Schattyn, 1962-63; Mrs. Delevan Calkins, 1964-65; Annabel Valach, 1971-72; Delores Ruhling, 1979-80; Chris Bohigian, 1985-86; Marge Perkins, 1992-93; and Elizabeth Huffaker, 1993-94. Mrs. Sutter also served as an American Medical Association Alliance president.

Caramel Brownies

Level: Easy
Yield: 24 bars
Preparation Time: 40 minutes

1	(14-ounce) package vanilla caramels, unwrapped
⅔	cup evaporated milk, divided
1	stick plus 4 tablespoons butter, melted
1	(18.25-ounce) box German chocolate cake mix, without pudding added
1	cup pecans, chopped
2	cups milk chocolate morsels

- Preheat oven to 325 degrees. Butter a 13x9x2-inch rectangular baking pan.
- Melt caramels and ⅓ cup evaporated milk substitute in a double boiler over medium heat, stirring until smooth.
- Melt butter in a saucepan over low heat, add ⅓ cup evaporated milk substitute, boxed cake mix and pecans. Mix well.
- Pat half of cake mixture into baking pan. Bake for 6 minutes.
- Remove from oven, spread caramel mixture over top while both cake and mixture are hot.
- Sprinkle chocolate morsels over caramel sauce. Crumble remaining half of cake mixture over top of chocolate morsels.
- Return to the oven and bake for an additional 15-20 minutes. Do not overbake.
- Cool in pan. Cut into squares.

A Missouri Window

Jefferson National Expansion Memorial consists of the Gateway Arch, the Museum of Westward Expansion, and St. Louis' Old Courthouse. During a nationwide competition in 1947-48, architect Eero Saarinen's inspired design for a 630-foot stainless steel arch was chosen as a perfect monument to the spirit of the western pioneers. Construction of the Arch began in 1963 and was completed on October 28, 1965. The Arch has foundations sunken 60 feet into the ground, and is built to withstand earthquakes and high winds. It sways up to 1-inch in a 20-mph wind, and is built to sway up to 18 inches.

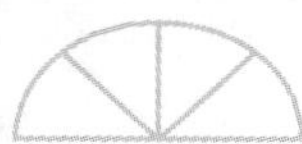

A Chef's View

A slice of soft bread placed in the package of hardened brown sugar will soften it again in a couple of hours. A sack of lumpy sugar won't be if you place it in the refrigerator for 24 hours.

Chocolate Pecan Squares

Level: Easy
Serves 9
Preparation Time: 6 hours

1	cup pecans, finely chopped
1	cup all-purpose flour
¼	pound (1 stick) butter or margarine, softened
1	(8-ounce) package cream cheese, softened
1	cup confectioners' sugar
1	(5-ounce) package instant chocolate pudding mix
1	(8-ounce) carton frozen whipped topping, thawed
1	milk chocolate bar, grated

- Preheat oven to 350 degrees. Butter an 8x8x2-inch square baking pan.
- Mix pecans, flour and butter. Press into pan and bake for 8-12 minutes. Watch carefully. Cool.
- Beat softened cream cheese and sugar together. Pour over cooled crust.
- Prepare chocolate pudding according to package directions. Pour over cream cheese mixture.
- Cover chocolate pudding with whipped topping mix and grated chocolate bar.
- Refrigerate at least 4 hours.
- Serve chilled.

Pecan Pie Bars

Level: Easy
Yield: 16 bars
Preparation Time: 1 hour

- 2 cups all-purpose flour
- ½ cup granulated sugar
- ⅛ teaspoon salt
- ½ pound (2 sticks) plus 4 tablespoons butter, divided
- 1 cup brown sugar, firmly packed
- 1 cup light corn syrup
- 4 large eggs, lightly beaten
- 2¾ cups finely chopped pecans
- 1 teaspoon vanilla extract

- ◆ Preheat oven to 350 degrees. Grease a 13x9x2-inch rectangular baking pan.
- ◆ Combine flour, granulated sugar and salt in a large bowl. Cut in ¾ cup butter thoroughly with a pastry blender until mixture resembles very fine crumbs.
- ◆ Press mixture evenly into greased pan.
- ◆ Bake for 17-20 minutes or until lightly browned.
- ◆ Combine brown sugar, corn syrup, and ½ cup butter in a saucepan; bring to boil over medium heat, stirring gently. Remove from heat.
- ◆ Stir one-fourth of hot mixture into beaten eggs. Add to remaining hot mixture. Mix well.
- ◆ Fold in pecans and vanilla extract.
- ◆ Pour pecan mixture over baked crust.
- ◆ Bake an additional 35 minutes or until set.
- ◆ Cool completely in pan on a wire rack. Cut into bars.

A Missouri Window

The mighty Mississippi River forms Missouri's eastern border. The wide Missouri River winds across the state from west to east.

A Chef's View

When you buy chocolate, you are paying for the quality of the beans from which it was made and the texture of the finished product. Look for chocolate that is shiny on the outside, of uniform color and texture, and should melt like butter on the tongue.

White chocolate is not true chocolate. It is usually a mixture of sugar, cocoa butter, milk solids, lecithin, and vanilla. If cocoa butter is not on the label, the product is confectionery coating, not white chocolate.

Triple Chocolate Fudge Brownies

Level: Easy
Yield: 16 bars
Preparation Time: 40 minutes

3	ounces quality bittersweet chocolate, chopped
1	ounce unsweetened chocolate, chopped
6	tablespoons unsalted butter, cut into pieces
¾	cup granulated sugar
1	teaspoon vanilla extract
2	large eggs
½	teaspoon salt
½	cup all-purpose flour
½	cup semisweet chocolate morsels

- Preheat oven to 350 degrees. Butter and flour an 8-inch square baking pan, shake out excess flour.
- Melt bittersweet and unsweetened chocolates and butter over low heat in a heavy 1½-quart saucepan. Stir until smooth.
- Remove from heat. Cool to lukewarm and whisk in sugar and vanilla extract.
- Add eggs, 1 at a time, whisking well until mixture is glossy and smooth.
- Stir in salt and flour just until combined.
- Fold in chocolate morsels.
- Spread batter evenly in pan and bake in middle of oven 25-30 minutes, or until tester comes out with crumbs adhering to it.
- Cool brownies completely in pan on a rack before cutting into 16 squares.
- To store, layer brownies between sheets of wax paper in an airtight container at room temperature for up to 5 days.

Almond Crunch Cookies

Level: Good Cook
Yield: 4 dozen
Preparation Time: 2 hours

1	cup plus 3 tablespoons granulated sugar, divided
1	cup confectioners' sugar
½	pound (2 sticks) butter or margarine, softened
1	cup canola oil
1	teaspoon almond extract
2	eggs
3½	cups all-purpose flour
1	cup whole wheat flour
1	teaspoon baking soda
1	teaspoon salt
1	teaspoon cream of tartar
2	cups almonds, coarsely chopped
1	(7.5-ounce) package almond brickle baking morsels

- Preheat oven to 350 degrees.
- Combine 1 cup granulated sugar, confectioners' sugar, butter and oil. Beat until well blended using an electric mixer.
- Add almond extract and eggs, one at a time, mixing well after each egg.
- Combine flours, baking soda, salt and cream of tartar in a separate bowl.
- Add flour mixture gradually into creamed sugar mixture, using low speed of mixer, until well blended.
- Stir in chopped almonds and brickle baking morsels.
- Refrigerate 30 minutes.
- Shape dough into 1¾-inch balls. Roll balls in remaining granulated sugar and place 4 inches apart on an ungreased cookie sheet.
- Dip tines of a fork in sugar and then make a crisscross pattern on top of each cookie.
- Bake 12-18 minutes, until edges are golden brown.
- Cool 1 minute on cookie sheet and then remove to wire rack to complete cooling.

A Chef's View

Cookie Tips

- *Baked cookies freeze well and can be stored for several months. Pack as airtight as possible. When ready to use, thaw in refrigerator and warm in oven for a few minutes. They will taste fresh-baked.*
- *When sprinkling sugar on cookies, put sugar in shaker first. Dry flavored gelatin may be added to sugar for variation.*
- *Cut bar cookies or rolled cookies with a pizza cutter.*
- *To keep cookies tender when rolling them out, use confectioners' sugar instead of flour. Out of confectioners' sugar? Blend 1 cup granulated sugar and 1 tablespoon cornstarch in blender at medium speed for 2 minutes.*
- *Add 2 eggs and ½ cup of cooking oil to any flavor of cake mix and you have a quick batch of cookies. Raisins, nuts or coconut can be added. Drop by the teaspoonful onto slightly greased cookie sheets. Bake at 350 degrees for 8 to 10 minutes.*

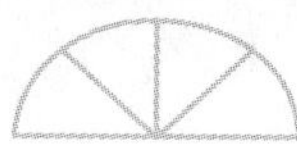

A Chef's View

Cookies that are too crisp may have too much sugar in the dough while cookies that are too soft usually have too much liquid in proportion to the flour.

Amish Sour Cream Sugar Cookies

Level: Easy
Yield: 3 dozen
Preparation Time: 8-12 hours

½	pound (2 sticks) butter, softened
1½	cups granulated sugar
2	eggs
1½	teaspoons vanilla extract
4½	cups all-purpose flour, sifted
1	teaspoon salt
1	teaspoon baking soda
1	teaspoon baking powder
½	teaspoon ground nutmeg
1	cup sour cream
	Granulated sugar for sprinkling

- Cream butter and sugar until light and fluffy.
- Add eggs and vanilla extract; mix well.
- Combine flour, salt, baking soda, baking powder and nutmeg.
- Add flour mixture and sour cream alternately to butter mixture.
- Cover dough with plastic wrap and chill 8-10 hours.
- Preheat oven to 375 degrees.
- Roll a small amount of dough on a lightly floured board to a ⅛-inch thickness.
- Cut with cookie cutter, place on parchment paper and sprinkle with sugar.
- Bake for 8-10 minutes.
- Cook's Tip: To keep cookies tender, use confectioners' sugar instead of flour to dust rolling pin and board.

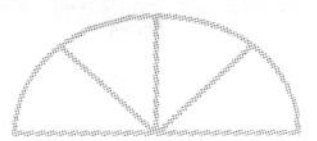

Double Chocolate Chip Cookies

Level: Easy
Yield: 3-4 dozen
Preparation Time: 1 hour

1	cup solid vegetable shortening
1	cup brown sugar, firmly packed
1	cup granulated sugar
3	eggs
3½	cups all-purpose flour
2	teaspoons baking soda
2	teaspoons cream of tartar
	Dash salt
1	teaspoon vanilla extract
12	ounces semisweet chocolate morsels
1	cup nutmeats, chopped, optional

- Preheat oven to 350 degrees.
- Cream shortening and gradually add sugars and beat until fluffy.
- Add eggs, one at a time. Beat well after each addition.
- Combine flour, baking soda, cream of tartar and salt. Gradually add to butter mixture. Mix.
- Add vanilla extract, chocolate morsels and optional nutmeats. Mix.
- Drop by well-rounded teaspoonful onto an ungreased cookie sheet. Bake for approximately 7 minutes.
- Cool on cookie sheet for one minute. Remove to wire rack to complete cooling.

A Culinary Reflection

Summers during college I worked in the Sierras, living in a tent-top cabin, using kerosene lamps for light, and eating less than gourmet food. My sister sent a huge jar of homemade cookies up the mountain. These were squirreled away by my roommate and myself so we wouldn't have to share. Periodically my roommate would say as we enjoyed a late night treat, 'These cookies have a most unusual flavor.' I would agree as we both munched on another cookie. One day I walked outside the cabin in daylight with a cookie and was horrified to see it coated with a greenish-blue matter. Gagging, I carried the jar to the trash. My roommate screamed, 'Don't throw them away! They haven't made us sick.' We later learned that my sister had read in a cookbook that placing slices of fresh raw apple in the cookie jar would keep cookies from getting hard. The dark, moist, closed environment had been the perfect growing condition for mold.

- Nancy Thompson

A Missouri Window

'The Missouri and the Mississippi River have made a deeper impression on me than any other part of the world.'

- T.S. Eliot

A Culinary Reflection

When I was a child and my grandmother would make pies and cobblers, usually gooseberry, and there was always just enough dough left over to let me roll it out. Using a glass or a cookie cutter, I made little 'cookies' that we covered with sugar and cinnamon and baked together. So, now, of course, I do this with my children.

- Donna Corrado

Giant Peanutty Pizza Cookies

Level: Easy
Yield: 2 pizzas
Preparation Time: 1 hour

½ pound (2 sticks) margarine, softened
1 cup peanut butter
1 cup granulated sugar
1 cup brown sugar, firmly packed
2 eggs
1¼ cups all-purpose flour
1 teaspoon baking soda
½ teaspoon salt
2¼ cups quick-cooking rolled oats
1 cup candy-coated chocolate pieces, divided

- Preheat oven to 325 degrees. Line pizza pans with foil. Coat with butter-flavored cooking spray.
- Cream margarine, peanut butter and sugars until light and fluffy.
- Add one egg at a time. Beat well after each addition.
- Combine flour, baking soda and salt in a bowl.
- Add flour mixture gradually to creamed butter mixture. Mix well.
- Stir in oats and ⅓ cup candies.
- Place half of dough on each pizza pan.
- Spread dough to within 1 inch of edge of each pan.
- Sprinkle each cookie with ⅓ cup of remaining candy.
- Bake for 30-35 minutes or until light brown.
- Cool 10 minutes in pan; remove to wire rack and complete cooling.

Peanut Butter Cup Cookies

Level: Quick and Simple
Yield: 3 dozen
Preparation Time: 30 minutes

1 roll refrigerator peanut butter cookie dough
36 miniature peanut butter cups

- Preheat oven to 375 degrees.
- Slice cookie dough into 1-inch thick slices.
- Cut each slice into 4 equal pieces. Place each piece into a miniature muffin cup.
- Bake for 10 minutes; remove cookies from oven.
- Press peanut butter cup into each cookie. Cool completely before removing from pan.

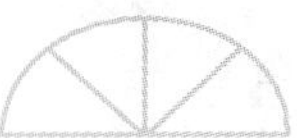

Gingersnaps

Level: Easy
Yield: 3 dozen
Preparation Time: 1½ hours

1 stick plus 4 tablespoons butter, use no substitute
1 cup granulated sugar
1 egg, beaten
4 tablespoons molasses
1 teaspoon ground cinnamon
1 teaspoon ground allspice or cloves
1 teaspoon ground ginger
2 teaspoons baking soda
⅛ teaspoon salt
2 cups sifted all-purpose flour
Granulated sugar

- Preheat oven to 350 degrees.
- Cream butter and sugar in a large mixing bowl.
- Add egg and beat until well-blended.
- Stir in molasses, spices, baking soda and salt.
- Mix in sifted flour. Dough should be rather stiff.
- Form dough into walnut-size balls. Roll each in granulated sugar and place approximately 2 inches apart on an ungreased baking sheet.
- Bake for 12 minutes.
- Cool on wire racks.
- Cook's Tip: Store in an airtight cookie tin with waxed paper or plastic wrap between cookie layers.

Luscious Lemon Fondue

Level: Quick and Simple
Yield: 2 cups
Preparation Time: 5 minutes

1 (11.25-ounce) jar lemon curd
⅓ cup sweetened condensed milk
¼ cup half-and-half
Freshly grated lemon peel, optional

- Combine lemon curd, condensed milk and half-and-half.
- Spoon fondue into a footed compote dish. Garnish with lemon peel.
- Serve surrounded with pears, gingersnaps and pound cake.

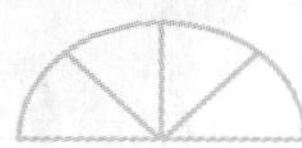

A Culinary Reflection

Easter was a favorite holiday of mine as a child. It was before Holy Week when my mother, grandmother, aunts, and cousins would gather to bake Easter cookies. They were made with dates, nuts, almonds, walnuts, and pistachios. As a young girl, I was allowed to decorate the cookies with designs using special tweezers. The best part was when the first batch came out of the oven and at once, they would be all gone!

- Sana Saleh

Lemon Oat Shortbread

Level: Easy
Yield: 5 dozen
Preparation Time: 2 hours

1	pound (4 sticks) butter, softened
1⅓	cups confectioners' sugar
4	teaspoons finely grated lemon peel, firmly packed
2½	cups all-purpose flour
2	cups quick oats, uncooked
½	teaspoon baking powder
½	teaspoon salt, optional

- Beat butter, sugar, and lemon peel until creamy.
- Combine flour, oats, baking powder and salt.
- Add flour and oat mixture gradually to creamed butter mixture. Mix well.
- Divide dough in half. Wrap each half in plastic wrap. Chill 1 hour or until dough is firm.
- Preheat oven to 325 degrees.
- Remove one portion of dough from the refrigerator.
- Sprinkle confectioners' sugar on a pastry cloth. Roll dough into a 10-inch square. Using a sharp knife or rotary cutter, cut into 30 rectangles, 3x1-inch.
- Transfer rectangles to ungreased cookie sheet 2 inches apart. Pierce each cookie three times with a fork.
- Repeat with remaining dough.
- Bake 18-20 minutes or until lightly browned.
- Cool 1 minute on cookie sheet. Remove shortbread to wire rack and cool completely.
- Store shortbread in an airtight container between sheets of waxed paper.

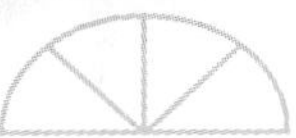

Maple Praliné Biscotti

Level: Good Cook
Yield: 3 dozen
Preparation Time: 1½ hours

2	cups all-purpose flour
1	teaspoon baking powder
¼	teaspoon salt
5	tablespoons butter, softened and divided
½	cup brown sugar, firmly packed
½	cup granulated sugar
4	teaspoons maple extract, divided
2	eggs
¾	cup chopped pecans or walnuts, toasted
1	cup confectioners' sugar
4-5	tablespoons milk

- Preheat oven to 350 degrees.
- Stir flour, baking powder and salt in a small bowl. Set aside.
- Cream 4 tablespoons butter in a large bowl. Gradually add brown sugar and granulated sugar. Beat until fluffy and well mixed.
- Beat in 1 teaspoon maple extract. Add eggs one at a time and beat until smooth.
- Fold in nuts.
- Gently stir in flour mixture, until just blended.
- Divide dough in half. Roll each half into a 12x1½-inch log.
- Place logs on a lightly greased cookie sheet and bake for 25 minutes or until logs begin to crack. Remove from oven.
- Reduce heat to 300 degrees.
- Remove logs to a cutting board and slice each log diagonally into ½-inch slices.
- Lay slices on cookie sheet and bake an additional 10 minutes.
- Cool on racks.
- Mix confectioners' sugar, 1 tablespoon softened butter, 3 teaspoons maple extract and milk until smooth.
- Dip top edge of each biscotti in glaze. Place on waxed paper.
- Cook's Tip: Change flavoring in both cookie dough and glaze to almond, lemon, apricot or pistachio extract. Biscotti can also be dipped in finely chopped nutmeats after dipping in glaze.

A Chef's View

Biscotti (bee-SKAW-toh; bee-SKAWT-tee) is a twice-baked Italian biscuit that is made first by baking it in a loaf, then slicing the loaf and baking the slices. The result is an intensely crunchy cookie that is perfect for dipping into dessert wine or coffee. Biscotti can be variously flavored with hazelnuts or almonds.

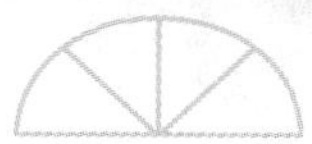

A Chef's View

Granulated sugar is the most used sugar in baking. Brown sugar is less processed sugar than white sugar. It is lighter in weight and also contains more moisture than white; therefore it should be packed when measuring.

A Chef's View

Cake Problem Chart I

- *If Cake Falls:*
  - *Oven not hot enough*
  - *Undermixing*
  - *Insufficient baking*
  - *Opening oven door during baking*
  - *Too much leavening, liquid or sugar*
- *If Cake Peaks in Center:*
  - *Oven too hot at start of baking*
  - *Too much flour*
  - *Not enough liquid*
- *If Cake Sticks to Pan:*
  - *Cake cooled in pan too long*
  - *Pan not greased and floured properly*
- *If Cake Cracks and Falls Apart:*
  - *Removed from pan too soon*
  - *Too much shortening, leavening or sugar*

Stress Reliever Cookies

Level: Easy
Yield: 15 dozen
Preparation Time: 2 hours

3 cups brown sugar, firmly packed
1½ pounds (6 sticks) butter or margarine, or half of each
6 cups oatmeal
1 tablespoon baking soda
3 cups all-purpose flour
½ cup granulated sugar
Butter and sugar, for glazing

- Preheat oven to 350 degrees.
- Mix all ingredients except granulated sugar in a large bowl. Mash, knead and squeeze.
- Form dough into nickel-size balls.
- Place on an ungreased cookie sheet approximately 2 inches apart.
- Butter bottom of a small glass, dip glass in granulated sugar and mash balls flat. Butter glass only once or twice but re-dip glass in sugar for each cookie.
- Bake for 10-12 minutes.
- Cool on cookie sheet before removing cookies to a wire rack.
- Cook's Tip: Recipe can be cut in half.

Ice Cream Cone Cupcakes

Level: Easy
Yield: 1 dozen
Preparation Time: 45 minutes

1 large box ice cream cone cups, flat-bottomed
1 (18.25-ounce) box cake mix, any flavor

- Preheat oven as specified in cake mix directions.
- Prepare cake mix as directed.
- Fill cones ½ full with cake mix. Set upright, next to each other, in a cake pan with sides, so as not to allow tipping.
- Bake for 10-12 minutes or until a cake tester inserted into the center comes out clean.
- Cool at room temperature.
- Top cake with a favorite icing and decorate for special occasions.

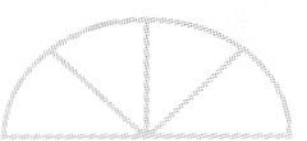

Brown Sugar Pumpkin Crumb Cake

Level: Easy
Serves 12-15
Preparation Time: 1 hour

1 (40-ounce) can solid pack pumpkin
1 (12-ounce) can evaporated milk
3 eggs, beaten
1 cup brown sugar, firmly packed
½ teaspoon ground ginger
¼ teaspoon ground cloves
1 teaspoon ground cinnamon
1 teaspoon salt
1 (18.25-ounce) box yellow cake mix
¼ pound (1 stick) butter, slightly softened
1 cup pecans, chopped
1 cup heavy cream, whipped

- Preheat oven to 350 degrees. Butter a 13x9x2-inch rectangular baking pan.
- Combine pumpkin, milk, eggs, brown sugar, ginger, cloves, cinnamon and salt. Mix well with an electric mixer.
- Pour into baking pan.
- Blend cake mix and butter until crumbly. Stir in chopped nuts.
- Sprinkle over pumpkin mixture.
- Bake for 50 minutes or until a cake tester inserted into the center comes out clean.
- Serve with whipped cream.

A Culinary Reflection

Talk about getting lost in the translation! We were living in Germany and had attended a beautiful buffet. The host asked if I would like another piece of cake to which I replied with the American expression, 'only if you twist my arm.' Days later, I was still sore and bruised!

~ Mary Shumann

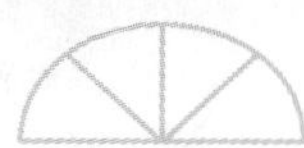

A Chef's View

It is important to use the correct form of flour for baking. If you substitute one flour for another, you could significantly change the texture of a dessert. Flour should be stored in an airtight container in a cool dry place.

- *All-purpose flour is a blend of high-gluten hard wheat and low-gluten soft wheat milled from the inner part of the wheat. It contains no germ or bran and is enriched, by law, with niacin, riboflavin, thiamin, and iron.*
- *Bleached and unbleached are two types of all-purpose flour that can be used interchangeably.*
- *Bread flour is a high-gluten blend ideal for yeast breads.*
- *Cake or pastry flour is a fine-textured, soft wheat flour with a high starch content that makes particularly tender cakes and pastries.*

Buttery Pound Cake

Level: Easy
Yield: 2 loaves
Preparation Time: 1½ hours

½ pound (2 sticks) butter, softened
3 cups granulated sugar
6 eggs, separated
¼ teaspoon baking soda
3 cups cake flour
1 cup sour cream
½ teaspoon vanilla extract
½ teaspoon almond extract
Confectioners' sugar, for garnish
Whipped cream, for garnish

- Preheat oven to 325 degrees. Butter two 9x5x3-inch loaf pans.
- Cream butter and sugar in a large bowl.
- Beat in egg yolks, one at a time.
- Combine baking soda with cake flour in a medium bowl.
- Mix sour cream and extracts in another small bowl.
- Add cake flour mix and sour cream mixture alternately to creamed butter and sugar.
- Beat egg whites until stiff. Fold into cake mixture.
- Pour into loaf pans and bake 1 hour or until a cake tester inserted into the center comes out clean.
- Cool cakes in pan for 10 minutes. Remove from pans and complete cooling on a wire rack.
- Serve.
- Cook's Tip: Sprinkle cakes with confectioners' sugar or top each slice with a dollop of fresh whipped cream.

Mandarin Orange Coconut Cake

Level: Easy
Serves 6-8
Preparation Time: 45 minutes

- 1 (18.25-ounce) box yellow butter cake mix
- 4 eggs
- ½ cup canola oil
- 1 (11-ounce) can Mandarin orange slices, with juices
- 1 (16-ounce) carton frozen whipped topping, thawed
- 1 (4-ounce) carton sour cream
- 1½ cups granulated sugar
- 3 cups shredded coconut, divided
- Freshly grated orange peel

- Preheat oven to 350 degrees. Grease and flour three 8-inch or 9-inch round cake pans. Line bottoms with parchment paper.
- Prepare cake mix with eggs, oil and oranges. Mix on medium speed of electric mixer for 4 minutes.
- Divide batter between prepared pans. Bake for 20 minutes or until done.
- Cool in pans for 5 minutes and then invert on cooling rack. Cool completely before icing.
- Mix whipped topping, sour cream, sugar and 1 cup coconut to make frosting.
- Frost cake. Use remaining coconut on the sides and top of cake.
- Sprinkle fresh orange peel on top of cake.
- Refrigerate cake.
- Cook's Tip: An alternate frosting recipe mixes a 20-ounce can of crushed pineapple with juices, a 3.25-ounce box of vanilla instant pudding and an 8-ounce carton of thawed frozen whipped topping mix. Frost cake. Refrigerate cake after frosting.

A Missouri Window

St. Louis is often called, 'The Gateway to the West' and 'Home of the Blues.' Auguste Chouteau founded Saint Louis in 1764.

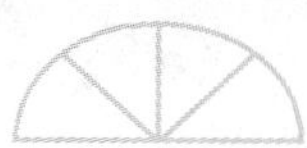

A Chef's View

Rarely, in this day and age do we keep buttermilk in our refrigerators. If you are out, simply add 2 tablespoons white vinegar to 1 cup milk and stir to thicken.

Milk Chocolate Cake

Level: Easy
Serves 12
Preparation Time: 1 hour

¼	pound (1 stick) butter, softened
1½	cups granulated sugar
2	eggs, unbeaten
2	cups cake flour, sifted
½	teaspoon salt
1	cup buttermilk
1	teaspoon vanilla extract
2	bitter chocolate squares
1	teaspoon baking soda
1	tablespoon apple cider vinegar
	Prepared chocolate frosting
	Whipped topping mix with chocolate, optional

- Preheat oven to 350 degrees. Grease a 13x9x2-inch rectangular baking pan.
- Cream butter with electric mixer and gradually add sugar. Beat well.
- Add eggs one at a time beating well after each addition.
- Sift flour and salt together on waxed paper. Set aside.
- Mix buttermilk and vanilla extract. Set aside.
- Melt chocolate in a double boiler over hot water or in the microwave.
- Alternately add flour mixture and buttermilk mixture to creamed butter and sugar. Blend well.
- Stir in melted chocolate.
- Dissolve baking soda in the vinegar and add to batter. Mix well.
- Pour batter into baking pan and bake for 35-40 minutes or until done. Cool.
- Ice with chocolate frosting.
- Cook's Tip: Instead of frosting cake, sprinkle with confectioners' sugar topped with a dollop of whipped cream and milk chocolate shavings.

Mississippi Mud Cake

Level: Easy
Serves 8-10
Preparation Time: 1 hour

2	cups granulated sugar
1	pound (4 sticks) butter, divided
4	eggs, slightly beaten
4	teaspoons vanilla extract, divided
1½	cups all-purpose flour
⅔	cup unsweetened cocoa powder, divided
¼	teaspoon salt
½	(10-ounce) package miniature marshmallows
1	(16-ounce) box confectioners' sugar
½	cup evaporated milk
1½	cups chopped nuts, divided

- Preheat oven to 300 degrees.
- Cream 2 cups granulated sugar and 2 sticks butter until smooth.
- Add eggs and 3 teaspoons vanilla extract. Mix well.
- Sift flour, ⅓ cup cocoa powder and salt. Add to creamed butter mixture. Beat.
- Fold 1 cup chopped nuts into batter.
- Pour into a greased 13x9x2-inch baking pan.
- Bake 35 minutes.
- Remove cake from oven. Sprinkle top with miniature marshmallows.
- Return cake to a 350 degree oven for 10 minutes.
- Cool cake on wire rack for 1 hour.
- Prepare icing by combining confectioners' sugar and cocoa powder in a medium bowl.
- Add evaporated milk, 2 sticks melted butter, 1 teaspoon vanilla extract. Beat until smooth. Add ½ cup chopped nuts.
- Spread over cooled cake.

A Chef's View

Good cooks know that the batter is the key to a good cake. Always let butter, cream cheese and eggs reach room temperature before using. Shortening should be soft so that it resembles whipped cream when beaten with sugar. Instead of adding flavorings last, try adding to the creamed butter and sugar. The batter absorbs the flavoring more readily this way.

A Culinary Reflection

One of our family's Christmas traditions was to have a birthday cake for Baby Jesus. The cake was prepared ahead of time, decorated in red and green, of course. It was baked in a fluted tube pan and centered with a large Christmas candle. The candle was lit on Christmas day and the cake was served with Christmas dinner.

~ Margaret (Peggy) Hausheer

Oatmeal Cake with Brown Sugar Glaze

Level: Good Cook
Serves 12
Preparation Time: 1 hour

1¼	cups boiling water
1	cup quick or old-fashioned oats, uncooked
½	pound (2 sticks) butter, softened and divided
1	cup granulated sugar
1½	cups brown sugar, firmly packed and divided
1	teaspoon vanilla extract
2	eggs
1½	cups all-purpose flour
1	teaspoon baking soda
½	teaspoon salt
1	teaspoon cinnamon
¼	teaspoon ground nutmeg
½	cup half-and-half
1	cup shredded coconut
½	cup nuts, chopped

- Pour boiling water over oats in a large bowl. Cover and let stand 20 minutes.
- Preheat oven to 350 degrees. Grease and flour a 13x9x2-inch rectangular baking pan.
- Beat 1 stick butter until creamy. Gradually add white sugar and 1 cup brown sugar. Beat until fluffy.
- Stir in vanilla extract and eggs.
- Add oats mixture. Mix well.
- Sift together flour, baking soda, salt, cinnamon and nutmeg.
- Stir into creamed mixture.
- Pour batter into pan and bake for 50-55 minutes. Do not remove cake from pan when baked.
- Prepare glaze by combining 1 stick butter, ½ cup brown sugar, half-and-half, coconut and nutmeats. Mix well.
- Spread evenly over cake.
- Broil until frosting becomes bubbly.
- Cake may be served warm or cold.
- Cook's Tip: Serve with a dollop of whipped cream and sprinkle with additional toasted nutmeats.

Missouri Peanut Butter Mud Cake with Fudge Frosting

Level: Easy
Serves 24
Preparation Time: 1 hour

- 2 cups all-purpose flour
- 2 cups granulated sugar
- 1 teaspoon baking soda
- ½ teaspoon salt
- 2 large eggs, lightly beaten
- ½ cup buttermilk
- 1½ cups creamy peanut butter
- ½ pound (2 sticks) butter
- ¼ cup unsweetened cocoa powder
- 1 cup water
- *Windows'* Fudge Frosting

- ◆ Preheat oven to 325 degrees. Lightly coat a 15x10x1-inch rectangular pan with cooking spray.
- ◆ Sift flour, sugar, baking soda and salt together into a large bowl.
- ◆ Stir in beaten eggs and buttermilk.
- ◆ Add peanut butter and mix well. Batter will be stiff.
- ◆ Melt butter in a heavy saucepan over medium heat.
- ◆ Whisk water into the cocoa powder until smooth.
- ◆ Add cocoa mixture to butter and whisk until combined. Bring to a boil, whisking constantly. Remove from heat.
- ◆ Combine cocoa and butter mixture with dry ingredients. Stir until smooth.
- ◆ Pour batter into pan and bake for 20-25 minutes or until a cake tester inserted into the center comes out clean.
- ◆ Prepare *Windows'* Fudge Frosting and spread over warm cake.

Fudge Frosting

Level: Easy
Yield: 3 cups
Preparation Time: 20 minutes

¼ pound (1 stick) butter
¼ cup unsweetened cocoa powder
⅓ cup milk
1 (1-pound) box confectioners' sugar, sifted
1 teaspoon vanilla extract

- ◆ Melt butter in a saucepan over medium heat.
- ◆ Whisk milk into cocoa powder until smooth.
- ◆ Add cocoa mixture to melted butter, whisk and bring to a boil.
- ◆ Remove cocoa mixture from heat and gradually add confectioners' sugar. Stir until smooth.
- ◆ Stir in vanilla extract.
- ◆ Spread icing over warm cake.

A Culinary Reflection

In planning a meal for our young couples group at church, I was assigned to the dessert committee. We were all to make the same dessert using the same recipe. The chair of the committee called and said to make a white sheet cake, cover it with a tub of whipped topping, and put a can of blueberries on top. I did step one and two, opened the can of blueberries and thought 'this won't work.' I even called the chair back and she reassured me not to worry, but to just throw them on top. So I did and all the topping curdled and dissolved into the cake. It looked horrible and though I did what she had instructed, I was sure that this was not right. We got to the meeting and all the other desserts looked beautiful, not the purple soggy mess like mine! She had neglected to tell me to use blueberry pie filling, not blueberries in liquid. She had said she used a recipe that would not fail, but it did for me!

~ Mary Eleanor Farrell

Blueberry Citrus Cake

Level: Good Cook
Yield: 1 cake
Preparation Time: 1 hour

1 (2-layer) package lemon cake mix
½ cup plus 2 tablespoons orange juice, divided
½ cup water
⅓ cup canola oil
3 eggs
1½ cups fresh blueberries
3½ tablespoons finely shredded orange peel
2½ tablespoons finely shredded lemon peel
4 ounces cream cheese, softened
¼ cup butter, softened
3 cups sifted confectioners' sugar
1 cup heavy cream, whipped
Orange peel curls

- Preheat oven to 350 degrees. Grease and flour two 8- or 9-inch round cake pans.
- Combine cake mix, ½ cup orange juice, water, canola oil and eggs in a large mixer bowl. Beat at low speed for 30 seconds. Beat at medium speed for 2 minutes.
- Fold in blueberries, 1½ tablespoons orange peel and 1½ tablespoons lemon peel.
- Spoon batter into cake pans.
- Bake for 35-40 minutes or until a cake tester inserted near the center comes out clean.
- Cool in pans on wire racks for 10 minutes. Invert layers onto wire racks to cool completely.
- Prepare frosting by creaming cream cheese and butter in a medium mixer bowl until light and fluffy.
- Add confectioners' sugar and 2 tablespoons orange juice and beat until smooth.
- Add the whipped cream, 2 tablespoons orange peel and 1 tablespoon lemon peel. Beat at low speed until blended.
- Spread frosting between layers and over the top and side of cake.
- Sprinkle with orange peel curls.
- Store, covered, in the refrigerator.

Ozark Mountain Fresh Apple Cake

Level: Easy
Serves 12-16
Preparation Time: 1 hour

- 3 cups granulated sugar, divided
- 3 cups plus 2 tablespoons all-purpose flour, divided
- 1 teaspoon baking soda
- 1 teaspoon salt
- 1 teaspoon ground cinnamon
- 3 cups peeled, chopped McIntosh or other cooking apples
- 2 eggs, slightly beaten
- 1 cup canola oil
- 5 teaspoons vanilla extract, divided
- ¾ cup chopped pecans or walnuts
- ½ cup coconut, flaked or shredded
- ½ cup brown sugar, firmly packed
- 4 tablespoons melted butter
- 1 cup water

- ◆ Preheat oven to 350 degrees.
- ◆ Sift together 2 cups sugar, 3 cups flour, baking soda, salt and cinnamon.
- ◆ Add chopped apples and toss, coating apples.
- ◆ Blend in eggs, oil and 2 teaspoons vanilla extract. Mixture will be very thick.
- ◆ Fold in nuts and coconut.
- ◆ Spread into a 12x9x2-inch ungreased baking pan.
- ◆ Bake for 40-50 minutes. Do not overbake.
- ◆ Prepare topping for cake by combining 1 cup granulated sugar, ½ cup brown sugar, 2 tablespoons flour and melted butter in a saucepan.
- ◆ Add water slowly into sugar mixture and stir well. Mix in 1 tablespoon vanilla extract.
- ◆ Cook topping over medium heat, stirring often until thickened and clear.
- ◆ Pierce top of cake with fork or a cake tester.
- ◆ Pour sauce over hot cake.
- ◆ Serve warm or cooled.

A Chef's View

If your cake recipe calls for nuts, heat them first in the oven, then dust with flour before adding to the batter to keep them from settling to the bottom of the pan.

To make substitute for cake flour: measure 1 tablespoon cornstarch in bottom of ½-cup measure and then fill cup with all-purpose flour. The general rule is 2 tablespoons cornstarch in the bottom of a 1-cup measuring cup and then filled with all-purpose flour.

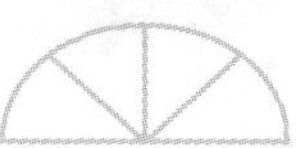

A Chef's View

A good alternative to regular pastry crust is Sugar Cookie Crust. Mix ¾ cup flour with 2½ tablespoons sugar in a bowl. Add 1 lightly beaten egg, ¼ cup softened butter, and ½ teaspoon vanilla extract, and mix well to form a dough. Press evenly into the bottom of a greased 9-inch springform pan. Bake at 350 degrees for 12-15 minutes or until light brown. Cool on wire rack.

Pumpkin Cheesecake with Gingersnap Crust

Level: Easy
Serves 10-12
Preparation Time: 6 hours

1	cup gingersnap crumbs
3	tablespoons butter, melted
1	teaspoon ground cinnamon
2	tablespoons brown sugar
4	(8-ounce) packages cream cheese, softened
1½	cups granulated sugar
5	eggs
¼	cup all-purpose flour
2	teaspoons pumpkin pie spice
1	(14-ounce) can solid pack pumpkin
2	tablespoons light rum
1	pint heavy cream, whipped
	Ground cinnamon

- Preheat oven to 325 degrees. Coat a 10-inch springform pan with cooking spray.
- Combine gingersnap crumbs, melted butter, cinnamon and brown sugar.
- Line bottom of springform pan with gingersnap mixture. Pat firm and chill.
- Beat softened cream cheese until fluffy.
- Add sugar gradually and mix well.
- Add eggs, one at a time, beating well after each addition.
- Mix in flour, pumpkin pie spice, pumpkin and rum.
- Pour batter over crust.
- Bake for 1½ to 1¾ hours or until filling is set.
- Cool, then refrigerate for several hours.
- Garnish with whipped cream and a sprinkle of cinnamon.

White Chocolate Cake Supreme

Level: Good Cook
Serves 6-8
Preparation Time: 1½ hours

8	ounces white chocolate, divided
1	stick plus 2 tablespoons butter, divided
2	cups granulated sugar
5	eggs, separated and divided
2	teaspoons vanilla extract, divided
2½	cups cake flour
	Salt, divided
1	teaspoon baking soda
1	cup buttermilk
1	cup confectioners' sugar
3	tablespoons hot water

- Preheat oven to 350 degrees. Line three 8-inch round cake pans with parchment paper.
- Melt 4 ounces chocolate in top of double boiler over hot water. Cool.
- Cream 1 stick butter with granulated sugar until fluffy.
- Add 4 egg yolks, one at a time and beat well after each addition.
- Blend in melted chocolate and 1 teaspoon vanilla extract and mix well.
- Sift flour, ½ teaspoon salt and baking soda together. Add alternately with buttermilk. Beat well.
- Beat 4 egg whites until stiff. Fold egg whites into cake batter.
- Pour batter into the three 8-inch round cake pans and bake for 30-40 minutes.
- Cool cakes for 5 minutes in pan and then invert on cooling racks.
- Prepare frosting by melting 4 ounces of white chocolate in top of double boiler over hot water.
- Blend in confectioners' sugar, pinch of salt and hot water. Add 1 egg yolk and beat well.
- Add 2 tablespoons butter, one at a time, beating well after each addition.
- Stir in 1 teaspoon vanilla extract and pinch of salt.
- Makes enough frosting to ice the tops of each of the three layers when assembling the cake.
- Cook's Tip: Individuals with certain health problems should be aware that the frosting contains a raw egg yolk.

Italian Cream Cake

Level: Good Cook

Serves 15

Preparation Time: 1 hour

1¼ cups butter, softened, divided

2 cups granulated sugar

5 egg yolks

2 cups all-purpose flour, sifted

1 teaspoon baking soda

1 cup buttermilk

2 teaspoons vanilla extract, divided

1 (3-ounce) can flaked coconut

6 egg whites, stiffly beaten

1 (8-ounce) package cream cheese

1 pound confectioners' sugar, sifted

- Preheat oven to 350 degrees. Grease and flour a 13x9x2-inch cake pan.
- Combine 1 cup butter, granulated sugar, egg yolks, flour, baking soda and buttermilk in a large bowl and mix well.
- Stir in 1 teaspoon vanilla and coconut. Fold in egg whites.
- Pour into cake pan and bake for 40 minutes. Cool in pan.
- Prepare icing by beating cream cheese, confectioners' sugar, ¼ cup butter and 1 teaspoon vanilla until of spreading consistency. Spread over cooled cake.

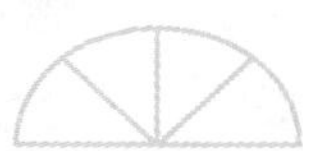

Raspberry Sauce

Level: Expert Cook

Yield: 2½ cups

Preparation Time: 10 minutes

2 (6-ounce) packages frozen raspberries

1⅓ cups granulated sugar

4 tablespoons cornstarch

4 tablespoons lemon juice

- Puree raspberries to produce approximately 2½ cups raspberry puree.
- Combine raspberry puree, sugar and cornstarch in a saucepan. Bring raspberry mixture to a boil. Boil for 2 minutes, stirring constantly.
- Remove from heat and stir in lemon juice.

Raspberry Topping

Level: Expert Cook

Yield: 4 cups

Preparation Time: 10 minutes

1 cup reserved Raspberry Sauce

1-2 tablespoons cherry-flavored liqueur

1½ cups fresh raspberries, or frozen, thawed

- Combine reserved Raspberry Sauce, cherry liqueur and raspberries.
- Drizzle over cheesecake before serving.

Raspberry Ribbon Cheesecake

Level: Expert Cook
Serves 8
Preparation Time: 8-12 hours

Windows' Raspberry Chocolate Wafer Crust
Windows' Raspberry Sauce
Windows' Raspberry Topping
3 (8-ounce) packages cream cheese, softened
½ cup granulated sugar
2 tablespoons all-purpose flour
1 teaspoon vanilla extract
2 egg whites
1 cup heavy cream

- Preheat oven to 350 degrees.
- Prepare Raspberry Chocolate Wafer Crust, Raspberry Sauce and Raspberry Topping. Set aside.
- Beat cream cheese, sugar, flour and vanilla extract until fluffy.
- Add egg whites. Beat on low speed until just blended.
- Stir in heavy cream.
- Pour half of filling into prepared Raspberry Chocolate Wafer Crust. Top with 1½ cups Raspberry Sauce.
- Spoon remaining filling over sauce.
- Bake at 375 degrees for 35-40 minutes or until center is nearly set.
- Remove from oven and immediately run knife around pan to loosen crust.
- Cool on wire rack. Refrigerate 8-12 hours before serving.
- Spoon Raspberry Topping over cheesecake as served.

Raspberry Chocolate Wafer Crust

Level: Expert Cook
Yield: 1 crust
Preparation Time: 15 minutes

2 cups chocolate wafer crumbs, approximately 20 wafers
5 tablespoons plus 1 teaspoon butter, melted
3 tablespoons granulated sugar

- Combine wafer crumbs, melted butter and sugar. Press into the bottom and 1½-inches up the sides of a greased 9-inch springform pan. Chill until firm.

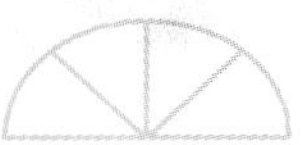

Hardware Café Hot Fudge Peanut Cheesecake

Level: Easy
Serves 8
Preparation Time: 4 hours

1½	cups graham cracker crumbs, approximately 12 whole crackers
5	tablespoons plus 1 teaspoon butter, melted
¼	cup granulated sugar
1	(8-ounce) package cream cheese, softened
1	cup confectioners' sugar
⅓	cup peanut butter
3	cups frozen nondairy whipped topping, thawed
¼	cup peanuts, chopped
¼	cup *Windows'* Hot Fudge Sauce, heated

- Preheat oven to 350 degrees.
- Mix graham cracker crumbs, butter and granulated sugar together. Press into a 9-inch springform pan.
- Bake at 350 degrees for 10 minutes. Cool.
- Beat cream cheese, confectioners' sugar and peanut butter until creamy.
- Stir whipped topping and peanuts into cream cheese mixture.
- Pour into crust in springform pan. Smooth top and chill in refrigerator until set.
- To serve, cut into slices and drizzle with *Windows'* Hot Fudge Sauce.

Hot Fudge Sauce

Level: Easy
Yield: 1½ cups
Preparation Time: 5 minutes

1	cup granulated sugar
2	tablespoons unsweetened cocoa powder
2	tablespoons butter, use no substitute
⅞	cup evaporated milk
1	teaspoon vanilla extract

- Mix sugar and cocoa powder over low heat for 2 minutes, stirring constantly.
- Add butter and milk. Bring to a boil.
- Boil for 2 minutes, stirring constantly.
- Remove from heat and add vanilla extract.
- Serve over ice cream.

A Show-Me Specialty

Hot Fudge Peanut Cheesecake is a specialty of the Hardware Café on the town square in Liberty, Missouri.

Hardware Café
5 East Kansas
Liberty
816-792-3500

A Chef's View

Cake Problem Chart II

- *If Cake Crust is Sticky:*
  - *Insufficient baking*
  - *Oven not hot enough*
  - *Too much sugar*
- *If Cake Texture is Heavy:*
  - *Overmixing when flour and liquid added*
  - *Oven temperature too low*
  - *Too much shortening, sugar or liquid*
- *If Cake Texture is Coarse:*
  - *Inadequate mixing or creaming*
  - *Oven temperature too low*
  - *Too much leavening*
- *If Cake Texture is Dry Overbaking:*
  - *Overbeaten egg whites*
  - *Too much flour or leavening*
  - *Not enough shortening or sugar*

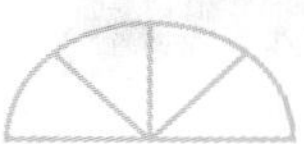

A Chef's View

To freeze pie pastry, shape pie dough into a disk and wrap in plastic wrap and foil. It can also be rolled and fitted into a pie pan or tart pan and wrapped in plastic wrap. To thaw, leave wrapped and let stand at room temperature for 2 hours or longer.

A Chef's View

There are over 30 species of mint, the two most popular and widely available being peppermint and spearmint. Mint is available fresh, dried, as an extract, and as an oil. Most popular of the mints are peppermint, which is more pungent and has a peppery flavor, while spearmint has a milder flavor and fragrance.

Candy Apple Walnut Pie

Level: Easy
Serves 6-8
Preparation Time: 1 hour

6 cups thinly sliced Granny Smith or Rome apples, with or without peel
⅔ cup walnuts, chopped
½ cup cinnamon red hot candies
⅓ cup plus 2 tablespoons granulated sugar, divided
⅓ cup all-purpose flour
2 (9-inch) frozen deep-dish pastry crusts

- Preheat oven to 375 degrees.
- Toss together in a large bowl apples, walnuts, cinnamon candies, ⅓ cup sugar and flour.
- Pour into one frozen pie crust.
- Break or crumble second frozen pie crust into very small pieces and toss with remaining 2 tablespoons sugar. Sprinkle over apples.
- Bake for 55-60 minutes or until candies melt and bubble up through the crumbled crust.
- Cool completely on wire rack before serving.

Frozen Juice Pie

Level: Easy
Serves 6-8
Preparation Time: 4 hours

1 (6-ounce) can frozen juice concentrate, orange, lime or pink lemonade
1 (8-ounce) carton frozen fat-free whipped topping
1 (14-ounce) can fat-free condensed skim milk
1 ready-made graham cracker or chocolate pie crust
Sprigs of mint, for garnish
Fresh fruit slices, for garnish

- Mix frozen juice and whipped topping together.
- Add condensed milk and mix well.
- Pour into pie crust.
- Freeze. When ready to serve garnish top of pie with a sprig of fresh mint or a slice of fresh fruit.
- Cook's Tip: Use *Windows'* Chocolate Wafer Pie Crust instead of ready-made. Experiment with different juices. Pour into individual serving cups without pie crust or freeze in scooped out oranges.

Chocolate Bourbon Pecan Pie

Level: Good Cook
Serves 10
Preparation Time: 1½ hours

1	(9-inch) pastry crust, unbaked
3	eggs, slightly beaten
¾	cup light-colored corn syrup
3	tablespoons granulated sugar
3	tablespoons brown sugar, firmly packed
3	tablespoons butter, softened
1	teaspoon vanilla extract
⅛	teaspoon salt
½	cup pecans, finely chopped
⅓	cup bourbon
1	(6-ounce) package semisweet chocolate morsels
1½	cups pecan halves
	Whipped cream

- Preheat oven to 350 degrees.
- Combine eggs, corn syrup, granulated sugar, brown sugar, butter, vanilla extract and salt in a large mixing bowl. Mix well.
- Stir in chopped pecans and bourbon.
- Pat chocolate morsels lightly onto the bottom of unbaked pastry shell.
- Pour filling gradually on top of chocolate morsels.
- Arrange pecan halves on top of filling.
- Bake for 1 hour or until knife inserted near the center comes out clean.
- Cover edges of pie loosely with foil the last 30 minutes to prevent overbrowning.
- Cool on wire rack.
- Serve pie with a dollop of freshly whipped cream.

A Chef's View

Pastry Problem Chart

- *Tough Pastry:*
  - *Too little fat*
  - *Too much water*
  - *Overmixing*
  - *Too much flour*
  - *Kneading the dough*
- *Crumbly Crust:*
  - *Too little water*
  - *Too much fat*
  - *Self-rising flour used*
  - *Insufficient mixing*
- *Soggy Lower Crust:*
  - *Filling too moist*
  - *Oven temperature too low*
  - *Too much liquid in pastry*
- *Crust Shrinks:*
  - *Too much handling*
  - *Pastry stretched in pan*
  - *Dough uneven in thickness*
  - *Rolling dough back and forth with rolling pin*

A Chef's View

Key Lime Pie is not green. Florida purists insist that a Key lime pie be made from true Key limes, thereby giving the pie its traditional yellow color. The trick is to squeeze the Key limes while they are in season. Freeze the juice in ice cube trays and store cubes in freezer bags. This way you will have the makings of Key Lime Pie all year round.

Key Lime Pie

Level: Easy
Serves 6-8
Preparation Time: 20 minutes

1	(9-inch) prepared deep-dish graham cracker crust
6	egg yolks
3½	cups sweetened condensed milk
1	teaspoon cornstarch
¾	cup Key lime juice
	Whipped cream, for garnish
	Lime slices, for garnish

- Preheat oven to 275 degrees.
- Beat egg yolks at high speed using a mixer for 5-10 minutes or until stiff but still fluffy.
- Add condensed milk. Beat at medium speed for 2 minutes. Scrape side of bowl.
- Stir cornstarch into lime juice and mix well.
- Add cornstarch mixture to egg mixture. Beat at low speed for 2 minutes.
- Spoon into prepared pie shell.
- Bake for 30 minutes or until pie is set but not brown.
- Remove to a wire rack to cool.
- Garnish with whipped cream and lime slices.
- Store in refrigerator.

Coconut Pie

Level: Easy
Serves 8
Preparation Time: 1 hour

1	cup granulated sugar
4	tablespoons melted butter
2	tablespoons all-purpose flour
3	eggs, beaten
1	teaspoon vanilla extract
1	cup buttermilk
1	cup grated coconut
1	(9-inch) pie crust, fluted and unbaked

- Preheat oven to 300 degrees.
- Mix all ingredients together.
- Pour into pie crust and bake for 1 hour.
- Cool before serving.

Lemon Custard Ice Cream Pie

Level: Expert Cook
Serves 8
Preparation Time: 1½ hours

- 1 cup all-purpose flour
- 6 tablespoons butter, softened, use no substitute
- ¼ cup confectioners' sugar
- 2 eggs, beaten
- ¾ cup granulated sugar
- 2 tablespoons all-purpose flour
- 3 tablespoons lemon juice, freshly squeezed
- 1 teaspoon grated lemon peel
- 1 quart lemon custard ice cream
- 1 cup heavy cream
- 2 tablespoons granulated sugar
- 1 teaspoon vanilla extract
- 1 lemon, cut into 8 thin slices, for garnish
- Toasted almonds, for garnish

- ◆ Preheat oven to 350 degrees.
- ◆ Make a shortbread crust by blending 1 cup flour, butter and confectioners' sugar.
- ◆ Press into bottom and sides of a 9-inch pie pan.
- ◆ Bake for 15 minutes.
- ◆ Mix together eggs, ¾ cup granulated sugar, 2 tablespoons flour, lemon juice and peel.
- ◆ Pour over hot crust and bake an additional 20 minutes.
- ◆ Remove from oven and let cool completely.
- ◆ Fill cooled crust with slightly softened lemon custard ice cream.
- ◆ Freeze.
- ◆ Whip heavy cream, add 2 tablespoons sugar and vanilla extract. Beat until stiff.
- ◆ Swirl whipped cream over top of pie. Garnish with lemon slices or toasted almonds.
- ◆ Freeze pie 3 hours before serving.
- ◆ Remove from freezer 10 minutes prior to serving and cut with a knife warmed under hot water.

Chocolate Wafer Pie Crust

Level: Quick and Simple

Yield: 1 crust

Preparation Time: 20 minutes

1½ (8.5-ounce) packages chocolate wafers

1½ teaspoons freshly grated Key lime peel

3 tablespoons cold butter

3 tablespoons granulated sugar

- ◆ Preheat oven to 350 degrees.
- ◆ Grease lightly the bottom and side of a 9-inch springform pan or regular 9-inch pie plate.
- ◆ Process wafers in a food processor with a metal blade to form coarse crumbs.
- ◆ Add the lime peel, butter and sugar to wafer crumbs. Process until mixed.
- ◆ Press into prepared pan.
- ◆ Bake for 12 minutes. Let stand until cool.

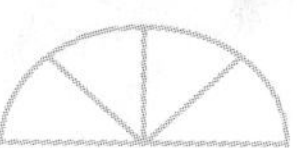

A Culinary Reflection

One of my first memories of my Grandmother was the early morning pie pick-up. She would start making the pies very early because the cars came up the lane by 3-4:00 a.m. The beautiful pies were all packed in wooden pie racks and carried off to the local restaurants. She made them at home until health rules required them to be made at the restaurants. She didn't drive so my mother started driving and helping her with the pies at the restaurants. As long as I can remember they could do 20-30 of the prettiest and best-tasting pies in an hour.

- Millie Bever

No Crust German Chocolate Pie

Level: Easy
Serves 6-8
Preparation Time: 4 hours

3	eggs
1	cup granulated sugar
¼	cup all-purpose flour
¼	pound (1 stick) butter or margarine
4	(1-ounce) squares German chocolate
1	teaspoon vanilla extract
1	cup pecans, chopped

- Preheat oven to 350 degrees. Coat a 9-inch pie plate with cooking spray.
- Beat eggs in a large bowl.
- Combine sugar and flour in a medium-size bowl.
- Add sugar mixture to eggs and beat for 3 minutes.
- Melt butter with chocolate over low heat, or in microwave. Stir in vanilla extract.
- Pour chocolate mixture into egg mixture. Beat.
- Fold in chopped pecans.
- Pour into pie plate.
- Bake for 25 minutes.
- Cool completely. Wrap in foil and freeze.
- Remove from freezer 2 hours before serving.

Pecan Pie

Level: Easy
Yield: 2 pies
Preparation Time: 1 hour

2	(9-inch) pastry crusts, deep-dish and unbaked
3	eggs, beaten
1	cup granulated sugar
3	tablespoons all-purpose flour
1	cup white corn syrup
3	tablespoons butter, softened
1	tablespoon vanilla extract
1	cup pecans

- Beat eggs thoroughly with electric mixer.
- Add sugar, flour and syrup to eggs and mix. Combine with softened butter and vanilla extract. Mix well.
- Stir in pecans.
- Pour into the pastry crusts.
- Bake for approximately 45 minutes. Test for doneness.
- Cool on a wire rack.

No Crust Pumpkin Pie

Level: Easy
Serves 6
Preparation Time: 2 hours

⅔	cup granulated sugar
⅓	cup low-fat biscuit baking mix
2	tablespoons butter
1	(13-ounce) can evaporated skim milk
2	eggs
2½	teaspoons ground pumpkin pie spice
1	(15-ounce) can solid pack pumpkin
2	teaspoons vanilla extract

- Preheat oven to 325 degrees.
- Coat a 9-inch pie plate lightly with cooking spray.
- Place all ingredients in a bowl and beat until smooth.
- Pour into pie plate. Bake 50-60 minutes or until knife comes out clean. Cool. Refrigerate unused pie.
- Cook's Tip: If desired, top individual pieces with low-fat whipped topping.

Mango Pie

Level: Easy
Serves 8
Preparation Time: 1¼ hours

	Windows' Never Fail Pie Crust, unbaked
4	cups (4 or 5 large) mangoes, peeled and cut into ½-inch slices
½	cup granulated sugar
1	tablespoon almond extract
2	teaspoons cinnamon powder
2	tablespoons all-purpose flour, or more as needed
1	teaspoon shredded lemon peel
2	teaspoons lemon or lime juice
1	egg, beaten with 2 tablespoons water
	Whipped cream or ice cream, for garnish

- Bake bottom crust as directed by recipe in a 9-inch deep pie plate.
- Mix together mango slices, sugar, almond extract, cinnamon, flour, peel and juice. Mixture should be moist but not wet.
- Pour into baked crust.
- Reduce oven temperature to 350 degrees.
- Roll out other half of pie dough and fit over pie. Crimp edges and brush with an egg and water wash. Cut vents in top and bake 45-50 minutes.
- Serve warm with fresh whipped cream or a scoop of ice cream.

A Culinary Reflection

My mother always shone when making her annual pumpkin pie for Thanksgiving. I remember one year when I was young my father took his much anticipated first bite, then immediately asked, 'What is wrong with this pie?' Everyone then proceeded to taste the pie and the reaction was the same. Mom figured out that she had used salt in place of the sugar while preparing the pie! This is something we reminisce over every Thanksgiving. Another Thanksgiving while eating the famous pumpkin pie, Dad was getting ready to dress the pie with whipped cream and while shaking the whipped cream can, it exploded up onto the ceiling instead of the pie.

- Kathy Weigand

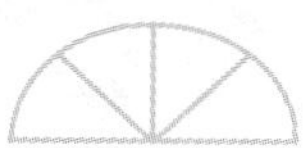

A Chef's View

It's always hard to get that first piece of pie out of the pie pan without breaking it. To make it easier, cut two pieces before you remove the first one. That extra cut makes the pie a little more flexible and less likely to break.

A Culinary Reflection

I remember sitting in my grandmother's kitchen and watching her make 'perfect' pie crust. There was never a recipe that she followed. It was all done by sight and feel. She tried to teach me this talent but I believe like so many talents, it is something you are born with. In her memory, I do keep trying to make a pie crust from scratch.

- Maria Gates

Peach Cream Pie

Level: Easy
Yield: 1 pie
Preparation Time: 1 hour

¼	pound (1 stick) butter
1½	cups all-purpose flour
½	teaspoon salt
4	cups sliced fresh peaches, approximately 8 medium peaches
¾	cup plus ⅓ cup granulated sugar, divided
⅓	cup plus 2 tablespoons all-purpose flour, divided
1	egg, slightly beaten
1	teaspoon vanilla extract
¼	teaspoon salt
1	cup sour cream
4	tablespoons butter
1	teaspoon ground cinnamon

- Preheat oven to 350 degrees.
- Mix together 1 stick butter, 1½ cups flour and ½ teaspoon salt until crumbly. Press into a 10-inch pie plate.
- Combine peaches, ¾ cup sugar, 2 tablespoons flour, egg, vanilla extract and ¼ teaspoon salt.
- Fold in sour cream.
- Pour fruit mixture into pie crust and bake for 45 minutes.
- Prepare topping by mixing together ⅓ cup sugar, ⅓ cup flour, 4 tablespoons butter and cinnamon until crumbly.
- Remove pie from oven. Sprinkle topping on hot pie. Return pie to oven and bake an additional 30-40 minutes or until brown. Watch carefully.

Pumpkin Pecan Pie

Level: Easy
Serves 6-8
Preparation Time: 1¼ hours

1	(9-inch) pastry crust, deep-dish and unbaked
3	eggs, slightly beaten
1	(15-ounce) can solid pack pumpkin
¾	cup granulated sugar
½	cup dark corn syrup
1	teaspoon vanilla extract
¾	teaspoon ground cinnamon
1	cup pecans, chopped
	Cinnamon flavored whipped cream, optional, for garnish
	Cinnamon, optional, for garnish

- Preheat oven to 350 degrees.
- Combine eggs, pumpkin, sugar, corn syrup, vanilla extract and cinnamon with an electric mixer at low speed.
- Pour filling into prepared pie crust.
- Sprinkle with pecans.
- Bake for 50-55 minutes or until knife inserted near center of pie comes out clean.
- Cool on wire rack.
- Serve with whipped cream sprinkled with ground cinnamon, if desired.

A Culinary Reflection

When I lived in Switzerland for a few years, I decided we should prepare a Thanksgiving meal for our hosts, who were French and Swiss. A turkey was an almost impossible find, and there were NO cranberries and NO canned pumpkin. So, I laboriously boiled a gourd /squash, and tried to scrape the insides to make a stringy, bitter, flat pumpkin pie. Our foreign friends never knew the difference. The regional wine flowed and it was truly a treasured memory.

~ Angela Zylka

A Chef's View

Curious about rhubarb? From April to June, tangy tart rhubarb is at its peak. Botanically a vegetable, it is usually enjoyed as a fruit. The leggy stalks, resembling celery, are most often sweetened for use in pies, preserves, and sauces. A favorite flavor combination in England is rhubarb and ginger, whereas Americans and Missourians have traditionally combined rhubarb with strawberries. Be sure to remove and discard any leaves that may be left on the stalks. The leaves can be toxic if consumed. Look for stalks that are crisp and of medium thickness. If juice runs out when you puncture the stalk, you know the rhubarb is fresh.

Rhubarb Pie

Level: Good Cook
Serves 6
Preparation Time: 1 hour

- 2 (9-inch) pastry crusts, deep-dish and unbaked
- 1½ cups plus 1 tablespoon granulated sugar, divided
- ½ teaspoon ground nutmeg
- 1 tablespoon butter, softened
- 3 eggs, divided
- 3 tablespoons all-purpose flour
- 3 cups rhubarb, cleaned and cut into bite-size pieces

- ◆ Preheat oven to 350 degrees.
- ◆ Blend sugar, nutmeg and butter.
- ◆ Add 2 beaten eggs and flour. Beat until smooth.
- ◆ Arrange rhubarb in a 9-inch crust. Pour egg mixture over. Top with second pastry crust cut in shapes or in strips to crisscross top of pie.
- ◆ Brush with egg wash and sprinkle lightly with 1 tablespoon granulated sugar.
- ◆ Bake for 30 minutes or until crust is lightly browned.
- ◆ Cool and serve.

Never Fail Pie Crust

Level: Easy
Yield: 2 crusts
Preparation Time: 20 minutes

- 2 cups sifted all-purpose flour
- 1 teaspoon salt
- ¼ cup cold water
- ¾ cup solid vegetable shortening

- ◆ Sift flour and salt together.
- ◆ Measure out ⅓ cup of the dry mixture and combine with water to form a paste.
- ◆ Cut shortening into remaining flour mixture until pieces the size of small peas are formed.
- ◆ Add paste and stir with fork until mixture forms a ball.
- ◆ Divide dough into two parts and roll each out to desired size.
- ◆ To bake pie crust only, bake for 10 minutes in a 450 degree oven.

Strawberry Meringue Crust Pie

Level: Expert Cook
Serves 8
Preparation Time: 5 hours

4	egg whites, at room temperature
½	teaspoon cream of tartar
¼	teaspoon salt
1	teaspoon vanilla extract
1	cup granulated sugar
2	cups plus 2 tablespoons sifted confectioners' sugar, divided
¼	pound (1 stick) butter
3	egg yolks
1	tablespoon lemon juice
1	teaspoon grated lemon peel
1	pint fresh strawberries or other berries, rinsed, drained and hulled, reserving some berries for garnish
½	cup heavy cream, whipped

- Preheat oven to 275 degrees. Butter a 9-inch pie plate.
- Combine egg whites, cream of tartar, salt and ½ teaspoon of vanilla extract in a large mixer bowl. Beat until partially stiff.
- Add granulated sugar gradually, beating egg whites until stiff.
- Spread meringue approximately 1-inch thick over the buttered pie plate, building up a high fluffy border.
- Bake for 1 hour or until meringue is cream colored and feels dry and firm. Meringue shell will crack while baking.
- Let cool in pan.
- Cream 2 cups confectioners' sugar, butter and egg yolks until light and fluffy. Fold in lemon juice and peel.
- Spread over cooled meringue shell.
- Arrange cleaned and dry berries over creamy layer, pressing down lightly.
- Whip heavy cream, remaining 2 tablespoons confectioners' sugar and ½ teaspoon vanilla extract until stiff.
- Spread over berries.
- Refrigerate for several hours or overnight.
- To serve, garnish with reserved berries.

A Chef's View

When topping a pie with meringue, be sure to coat the entire top surface with at least a ¾-inch thickness of meringue, bringing it right down to the outside lip of the dish and making sure all the edges are completely sealed. To decorate, pull a knife upward through the meringue to make tall peaks or place some of the meringue in a pastry bag (or zip-top bag with the corner cut away) and pipe or squeeze on fluted edges or patterns.

To brown meringue, preheat the broiler to 500 degrees and place the dish under the broiler for about 3 minutes, allowing the edges and peaks of the meringue to turn light brown. Watch closely, as the meringue can burn quickly.

A Show-Me Specialty

Apple Maple Dessert with Custard Sauce is a specialty of the American Bounty Restaurant in Washington, Missouri.

American Bounty Restaurant
430 West Front Street
Washington
636-390-2150

American Bounty Apple Maple Dessert with Custard Sauce

Level: Expert Cook
Serves 6
Preparation Time: 2 hours

1	teaspoon butter
¾	teaspoon granulated sugar
1	cup all-purpose flour
1	cup granulated sugar
1½	teaspoons baking powder
½	cup milk
2	eggs, lightly beaten
2	tablespoons maple syrup or maple-flavored syrup
2	medium Granny Smith apples, peeled, cored and thinly sliced
1	cup heavy cream
⅔	cup granulated sugar
1	egg, beaten
2	egg yolks, beaten
1	cup semi-dry white wine

- Preheat oven to 350 degrees.
- Butter 6 (6-ounce) custard cups or 3 (½-inch) jumbo muffin cups, using 1 teaspoon butter. Sprinkle lightly with the ¾ teaspoon sugar.
- Combine flour, 1 cup sugar and baking powder in a medium mixing bowl.
- Add milk, 2 eggs and maple syrup. Beat until smooth.
- Arrange apples in bottom of custard or muffin cups.
- Pour batter on top of apples until ¾ full.
- Bake for 30-35 minutes or until golden and a cake tester inserted into the center comes out clean. Make custard sauce while dessert is baking.
- Cool 10 minutes. Loosen sides and remove dessert from cups to individual serving plates.
- Serve warm with custard sauce.
- Make the custard sauce by combining heavy cream, ⅔ cup sugar, 1 beaten egg and 2 beaten egg yolks in a saucepan.
- Cook and stir with metal spoon until slightly thickened.
- Remove saucepan from heat and immediately place in a bowl of ice water to prevent overcooking. Stir 1-2 minutes until cool. Strain if necessary. Set aside.
- Bring 1 cup wine to just boiling in a saucepan. Reduce heat and boil gently until reduced to ¼ cup, approximately 15 minutes.
- Remove wine from heat and cool. Stir wine into the custard mixture.
- Store sauce, covered, in refrigerator.
- Makes approximately 1⅔ cups sauce.

Sweet Potato Pie with Poppy Seed Cheddar Crust

Level: Good Cook
Serves 8
Preparation Time: 2½ hours

	Windows' Poppy Seed Cheddar Pie Crust
2	pounds sweet potatoes
3	tablespoons butter, divided
½	teaspoon ground cinnamon
3	seedless oranges, peeled, pith removed and sectioned
¾	cup chopped pecans or cashews, toasted
¾	teaspoon salt
1	tablespoon honey
⅓	cup wheat germ
½	cup grated Cheddar cheese

- ◆ Prepare pastry crust according to recipe directions.
- ◆ Peel potatoes, cut into chunks and boil until soft.
- ◆ Drain potatoes, add butter and cinnamon; then mash.
- ◆ Fold in oranges, toasted nuts, salt and honey.
- ◆ Pour into pastry crust, level and bake for 45-50 minutes or until a knife inserted near the center of the pie comes clean. Cool.
- ◆ Ten minutes before serving prepare topping by mixing together wheat germ, grated cheese and 1 tablespoon butter.
- ◆ Sprinkle over pie. Place pie under a broiler on a middle rack until topping begins to melt and brown lightly.
- ◆ Serve warm.

Poppy Seed Cheddar Crust

Level: Good Cook

Yield: 9-inch crust

Preparation Time: 15 minutes

4 tablespoons butter, cold

1 cup all-purpose flour

Dash salt

½ cup Cheddar cheese

3 tablespoons poppy, caraway or sesame seeds

2-3 tablespoons cold water

◆ Add all ingredients except water to mixing bowl. Cut in butter.

◆ Sprinkle water over mixture, 1 tablespoon at a time; toss with a fork.

◆ Mix lightly until all flour is moistened and dough pulls away from side of bowl. Add additional water as necessary but no more than 1-2 tablespoons.

◆ Gather into ball. Roll out dough on floured board to ⅛-inch thickness and 2 inches larger than pie pan. Ease dough into pan, trim and flute edges.

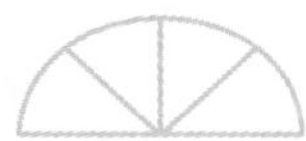

A Culinary Reflection

Food and friends go together. Each Thanksgiving weekend for the last 26 years, my husband and I have hosted an Italian cookie bake for friends. We bake all the traditional Italian cookies, about 250+ dozen and then share them among the 6 families who come to participate in the fun and work of baking cookies. The tradition started the first year we were married when my husband's father, cousin, aunt, and uncle came to 'show this Croatian girl' how to make the 'special Italian cookies.' This event is so popular that even the high school- and college-aged kids give their friends our telephone number for the weekend. Everyone is welcome! We bake, sing, play musical instruments, visit, and eat the entire weekend. Everybody participates and does their share. What a wonderful time to spend with friends, and their families, we hope to have for a lifetime.

~ Carol Jean Stipetich DeFeo

Bananas Foster

Level: Good Cook
Serves 4-6
Preparation Time: 30 minutes

4 tablespoons unsalted butter
⅔ cup dark brown sugar, firmly packed
4 large ripe bananas, peeled and sliced ½-inch thick
8 tablespoons dark rum
4 tablespoons banana liqueur
4 tablespoons white rum
Dash ground cinnamon
French-vanilla ice cream
Whipped cream
Toasted pecans or almonds

- Melt butter and brown sugar in a heavy-duty skillet over low heat, stirring, until sugar dissolves and sauce is bubbly.
- Add sliced bananas and cook in syrup for approximately 3 minutes until bananas are well coated with syrup. Turn bananas several times.
- Add rums, banana liqueur and cinnamon. Baste bananas with syrup.
- Using a fireplace match, carefully ignite liqueur. Shake skillet and spoon flaming sauce over bananas until liqueur burns off.
- Serve bananas and sauce over French vanilla ice cream.
- Top with whipped cream and sprinkle with toasted pecans or almonds.

Brinkman's Baklava

Level: Expert Cook
Yield: 36 bars
Preparation Time: 1 hour

1½	cups granulated sugar, divided
¾	cup water
1½	cups honey
1	(2-inch) cinnamon stick
4	orange slices, cut ¼-inch thick
4	lemon slices, cut ¼-inch thick
1	(16-ounce) package phyllo leaves
2	cups walnuts, chopped
1	cup almonds, chopped
½	teaspoon ground cinnamon
¼	teaspoon nutmeg
¾	pound (3 sticks) unsalted butter, melted

- Combine ¾ cup sugar and ¾ cup water for syrup. Bring to boil stirring constantly to dissolve sugar.
- Add honey, cinnamon stick, orange slices and lemon slices. Simmer 10 minutes. Strain, cool and set aside.
- Preheat oven to 325 degrees.
- Mix walnuts, almonds, ¾ cup sugar, cinnamon and nutmeg together.
- Place two phyllo sheets on a buttered jelly-roll pan. Brush top sheet with melted butter and continue stacking 10 sheets, buttering every other one.
- Sprinkle ⅓ dry nut mixture on last phyllo sheet.
- Add 6 more phyllo sheets, brushing every other one with butter.
- Sprinkle ⅓ dry nut mixture on last phyllo sheet.
- Add 6 more phyllo sheets, brushing every other one with butter.
- Sprinkle with last ⅓ dry nut mixture on last phyllo sheet.
- Stack all remaining sheets on top, brushing every other one with butter and brushing the top leaf with butter. Trim edges so that all sheets fit into the jelly-roll pan.
- With a sharp knife, cutting from a long side, make 8 diagonal cuts at 1½-inch intervals, cutting through only the top layer of phyllo.
- Then at one corner, make 9 cuts at 1½-inch intervals to make diamonds, cutting through only the top layer of phyllo.
- Bake for 60 minutes. Turn oven off and leave pan in oven for 60 minutes.
- Remove pan from oven. Pour cooled syrup on top of baklava.
- Cut all the way through baklava, following the diamond cuts. Cool.

A Culinary Reflection

As a young girl, I volunteered through Girl Scouts at our local hospital as a "pink lady." This experience led me to a health care profession starting as an operating room scrub nurse in high school. After the birth of our first son, his first outing was a picnic at the farm of a local surgeon. Our prestigious cardio-vascular surgeon from Chicago, Dr. Brinkman, showed up a little late. Late, because he was taking his baklava to the picnic warm. I had never tasted anything quite like this in South Dakota before. I met his wife, who also had a baby recently, and was invited to their home to first-hand learn the baklava technique and get a copy of the recipe. Dr. Brinkman and his wife, who have since moved back to Chicago, would be honored to know their recipe and friendship helped lead me to my new medical family, and also that I have continued to make their baklava for 25 years now as one of my family's favorite recipes.

~ Lori Jones

A Chef's View

Evaporated milk is whole, unsweetened milk that has been cooked to reduce the water content by 60 percent; evaporated skim milk contains .5 percent butterfat. Do not substitute sweetened condensed milk for evaporated milk or vice versa.

Sweetened condensed milk is milk that has been cooked to reduce the water content by about 60 percent and has 40-45 percent added sugar. Do not substitute evaporated milk for this product or vise versa.

Cheese Flan with Caramel Sauce

Level: Good Cook
Serves 8-10
Preparation Time: 3 hours

1	(12-ounce) can sweetened condensed milk
1	(12-ounce) can evaporated milk
1	teaspoon vanilla extract
1	(8-ounce) package cream cheese, softened, cut into one-inch squares
6	eggs, beaten
1	cup granulated sugar
2	tablespoons freshly grated lime peel

- Preheat oven to 350 degrees. Prepare a roasting pan containing approximately 1 inch of hot water.
- Combine condensed milk, evaporated milk, vanilla extract and cream cheese in a blender. Process until smooth.
- Add beaten eggs and blend well. Set flan liquid aside.
- Make caramel sauce by melting sugar over high heat in a heat-resistant 8x3-inch round glass baking dish. Swirl dish so as to distribute sugar as it melts. Do not let sugar burn.
- Pour flan liquid carefully into caramel sauce in baking dish. The crackling noise is sugar breaking not glass.
- Set flan baking dish in roasting pan containing hot water.
- Bake for 1 hour. Remove flan from oven.
- Cool and chill.
- Unmold onto a platter with a lip to catch caramel sauce from flan.
- Top with grated lime.

Chocolate Nut Torte

Level: Expert Cook
Serves 6-8
Preparation Time: 1 hour

1	(6-ounce) package semisweet chocolate morsels
¼	pound (1 stick) butter
⅔	cup granulated sugar
3	eggs
½	cup cake flour
½	cup walnuts
1	cup heavy cream
½	cup instant pre-sweetened cocoa powder mix
½	cup raspberry jam
	Chocolate shavings, optional

- Preheat oven to 350 degrees. Generously butter a 9-inch round cake pan. Line pan with parchment paper and butter paper.
- Add chocolate morsels to food processor bowl fitted with a metal blade. Pulse several times to chop.
- Melt butter. While hot, pour through the small feed tube into chocolate with machine running.
- Add sugar to chocolate mixture and continue mixing.
- Keep machine running while adding eggs, one at a time. Mix 1 minute.
- Remove lid. Pour flour over chocolate surface and then add nuts. Replace lid. Pulse 1 second on, one second off, one second on, one second off, one second on. Do not do any additional mixing.
- Pour chocolate batter into prepared pan.
- Bake for 20-25 minutes. Torte will rise slightly and then sink in center.
- Cool torte in pan. Chill.
- Combine cream and cocoa powder. Stir and refrigerate to chill.
- Whip cream and cocoa until stiff enough to spread.
- Remove torte from pan to a serving plate, do not leave inverted.
- Spread raspberry jam over top leaving a ½-inch edge around the outside of the layer.
- Frost top and sides with the whipped cream mixture.
- Refrigerate until ready to serve.
- Garnish with chocolate shaving, if desired.

A Chef's View

A torte is a rich cake, often made with little or no flour. Pair it with chocolate and flavored fruit preserves and you have "heaven on earth." Decorate with chocolate curls by allowing a bar of milk chocolate, or semisweet chocolate to come to room temperature. Carefully draw a vegetable peeler across the bar of chocolate to make long, thin strips. They will curl as you cut them. For narrow curls use the narrow side of the chocolate bar and for wide curls use the broad surface.

A Chef's View

A mousse is a rich airy dish that can be either sweet or savory and hot or cold. Chocolate mousse is a standard dessert on the menu in many restaurants. It can be the perfect light dessert after a filling meal. The fluffiness of a dessert mousse is usually due to the addition of whipped cream or beaten egg whites.

Chocolate Peanut Butter Mousse Cake

Level: Good Cook
Yield: 1 cake
Preparation Time: 2 hours

1	(18.25-ounce) box devil's food cake mix, without pudding
2½	cups heavy cream, divided
1	(10-ounce) package peanut butter morsels
2	teaspoons vanilla extract
1	tablespoon butter
⅔	cup semisweet chocolate morsels

- Prepare and bake cake according to package directions using two 8-inch round baking pans.
- Cool cake in pans on wire racks for 10 minutes. Remove cakes from pans to wire racks and cool completely.
- Combine ⅔ cup heavy cream and peanut butter morsels in a small saucepan. Cook over low heat, stirring constantly, until morsels melt and mixture is smooth.
- Remove peanut butter mixture from heat, stir in vanilla extract and cool 25 minutes.
- Beat 1⅓ cups heavy cream until soft peaks form. Stir one-third of whipped cream into peanut butter mixture. Fold in remaining whipped cream.
- Spread peanut butter mixture between cake layers. Cover and chill.
- Bring remaining ½ cup heavy cream and butter to a boil in a small saucepan. Add chocolate morsels, remove from heat and let stand 5 minutes. Stir until morsels melt and mixture is smooth.
- Pour glaze over cake.
- Serve warm, or chill and then serve at room temperature.

Coffee Crème Brûlée

Level: Good Cook
Serves 8
Preparation Time: 6 hours

1	egg
6	egg yolks
⅔	cup granulated sugar
1¾	cups heavy cream
1¾	cups milk
2	tablespoons coffee-flavored liqueur
1½	tablespoons instant espresso powder
¼	cup brown sugar, firmly packed
2	quarts hot water

- Preheat oven to 325 degrees.
- Whisk together egg, egg yolks and sugar. Set aside.
- Combine cream and milk in a heavy saucepan. Stirring constantly, cook over medium-high heat until mixture just comes to a boil.
- Add liqueur and espresso powder. Stir until espresso powder dissolves.
- Pour milk mixture in a steady stream into egg mixture. Whisk and skim off any froth.
- Pour into 8 ungreased ½-cup ramekins. Set ramekins in a shallow baking pan. Place in oven and add enough hot water to pan to reach halfway up sides of ramekins.
- Bake for 45-60 minutes or until custards are just set but still tremble slightly.
- Remove ramekins from pan and cool completely.
- Cover custards loosely with plastic wrap and chill for at least 4 hours.
- Set broiler rack so that custards will be 2-3 inches from heat and preheat broiler.
- Place ramekins on baking sheet. Sift brown sugar evenly over custards.
- Broil for 2 minutes or until sugar is melted and caramelized. Rotate baking sheet for even broiling and watch closely to avoid burning.
- Chill for 20 minutes.
- Serve.

A Chef's View

To caramelize is to heat sugar until it liquefies and becomes a clear syrup ranging in color from golden to dark brown. Granulated or brown sugar can also be sprinkled on top of food and placed under a heat source, such as a broiler until the sugar melts and caramelizes.

A Culinary Reflection

Every Christmas for as long as I can remember, my mother made all sorts of candy and cookies. My favorite was (and still is) her divinity. It was never too hard or too soft. She always put food coloring in it so that some of it was red and some of it was green. It absolutely melted in your mouth. When I asked her for the recipe, she gave me all the ingredients. But then she told me that the real key was choosing the right, humidity-free day, and the unique way she stirred it only once with her special wooden spoon, and then placed the spoon on the handle of the pan while it boiled so that anything left on the spoon dripped into the boiling mixture. I have never been able to duplicate her process, nor has my divinity ever been successful.

~ Kathy Riscoe

Indian Pudding

Level: Easy
Serves 6
Preparation Time: 35 minutes

2	tablespoons butter
½	cup molasses
2	cups whole or 2% milk
¼	cup granulated sugar
¼	cup cornmeal
¼	teaspoon ground nutmeg
¼	teaspoon ground ginger
3	large eggs, beaten
½	teaspoon vanilla extract
	Vanilla ice cream or frozen custard

- Melt butter in microwave, in a microwave-safe baking dish, on high for 35 seconds or until melted. Set aside.
- Mix molasses, milk, sugar, cornmeal, nutmeg and ginger in a 3-quart microwave-safe baking dish.
- Cover and cook on high in microwave for 5 minutes. Stir.
- Cook, covered and on high, for an additional 5-10 minutes, or until thickened. Stir once or twice.
- Beat eggs into melted butter.
- Add the molasses mixture slowly to eggs and butter, stirring constantly. Blend in vanilla extract.
- Cover and refrigerate until ready to bake and serve.
- Pour into six, 5-ounce microwave-safe, custard cups.
- Place cups in microwave in a circle with a 1-inch space between them.
- Cook uncovered on medium for 10-12 minutes, or until a knife inserted ½-inch from the center comes out clean. Reposition the custards once, halfway through the cooking.
- Let stand for 10 minutes.
- Serve warm, topped with ice cream or frozen custard.

Creamy Caramel Dip

Level: Easy
Yield: 3 cups
Preparation Time: 1 hour

¾ cup brown sugar, firmly packed

1 (8-ounce) package cream cheese, softened

1 (8-ounce) carton sour cream

1 teaspoon vanilla extract

2 teaspoons lemon juice, freshly squeezed

1 cup cold milk

1 (3.4-ounce) package instant vanilla pudding mix

Assorted fresh fruit

- Beat brown sugar and cream cheese until smooth and fluffy.
- Add sour cream, vanilla extract, lemon juice, milk and pudding mix, beating well after each addition.
- Cover and chill for at least 1 hour.
- Serve as a dip for fruit.
- Cook's Tip: Slice fruit, place in individual serving dishes, top with two or three tablespoons of the dip and garnish with a fresh strawberry or sprig of mint.

Old-Fashioned Bread Pudding with Whiskey Sauce

Level: Good Cook
Serves 9
Preparation Time: 1 hour

4	cups French bread, torn into pieces
2	cups milk
½	cup chopped dates or raisins
3	eggs, slightly beaten
1½	cups granulated sugar, divided
¼	pound (1 stick) butter, melted and divided
1	tablespoon vanilla extract
2	teaspoons ground cinnamon
1	egg yolk
2	tablespoons water
2	tablespoons bourbon

- Preheat oven to 350 degrees.
- Combine bread pieces, milk, chopped dates or raisins in a large bowl. Let mixture stand for 5 minutes or until bread is softened, stirring often.
- Grease an 8-inch square baking pan.
- Beat together 3 eggs, 1 cup of sugar, 4 tablespoons of melted butter, vanilla extract and cinnamon.
- Stir egg mixture into bread mixture until blended. Pour into prepared pan.
- Bake for 40-45 minutes or until a knife inserted in the center comes out clean.
- Combine 4 tablespoons melted butter in a small saucepan. Stir in ½ cup sugar, egg yolk and water.
- Cook over medium heat, stirring often, for 5-6 minutes or until sugar dissolves and mixture thickens.
- Remove from heat and stir in bourbon.
- Serve bread pudding with bourbon sauce.

A Chef's View

'Waste not, want not,' has to be a phrase applied to bread pudding. It is a simple, delicious baked dessert made with at least day-old dry bread, milk, eggs, sugar, chopped fruit and nuts. Buttering bread slices before adding the liquid mixture was the traditional way to begin making bread pudding. All bread puddings may be served hot or cold with cream or a spiced sauce.

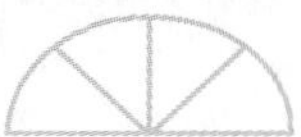

Hot Fudge Sauce to Die For

Level: Easy

Yield: 5 cups

Preparation Time: 45 minutes

½ pound (2 sticks) butter, use no substitute

4½ cups confectioners' sugar

1⅓ cups evaporated milk

4 ounces unsweetened chocolate

- Melt butter in the top of a double boiler.
- Add sugar and milk. Stir until sugar is dissolved.
- Add chocolate, stirring until chocolate is melted and mixture is smooth.
- Continue to cook over hot water for 30 minutes without stirring.
- Remove from heat and stir until creamy smooth.
- Keep refrigerated and reheat over boiling water.

Coffee and Peaches Cream Puffs

Level: Good Cook
Serves 12
Preparation Time: 20 minutes

12	*Windows'* Cream Puff Shells
2	cups heavy cream
4	tablespoons granulated sugar
2	teaspoons freeze-dried coffee
6-8	fresh ripe freestone peaches

- Pour cold heavy cream into a mixing bowl.
- Slowly stir in sugar and coffee. Dissolve both completely.
- Return cream mixture to refrigerator until chilled.
- Whip cold heavy cream until peaks stand on their own.
- Slice peaches.
- Split the puff pastry. Remove any damp dough.
- Mound whipped filling and 4-5 peach slices in bottom half of pastry. Replace top of puff and sprinkle with confectioners' sugar.
- Cook's Tip: Fill remaining puffs, as desired. Add sweetened cocoa powder to whipped cream for a mocha filling. Use a prepared flavored pudding as filling and drizzle a chocolate glaze over puffs with a sprinkling of toasted pecans.

Cream Puff Shells

Level: Good Cook
Yield: 2 dozen
Preparation Time: 1 hour

1	cup milk
¼	pound (1 stick) unsalted butter, cut into small cubes
¼	teaspoon salt
1	tablespoon granulated sugar
1	cup high-gluten or all-purpose flour
4-5	eggs, at room temperature
	Windows' Coffee and Peaches Cream Filling

- Preheat oven to 400 degrees. Prepare a lightly buttered baking sheet.
- Bring milk and butter to boil in a heavy saucepan. Add salt and sugar.
- Add flour and stir until smooth, over high heat, with a wooden spoon.
- Continue stirring until the paste becomes dry and does not cling to the sides of the pan or the spoon.
- Remove pan from heat for approximately 2 minutes.

continued on next page

Cream Puff Shells continued

- Add eggs one at a time, beating vigorously after each addition until batter is very smooth. Dough has reached proper consistency when a small amount will stand erect if scooped up on the end of the spoon.
- Fill pastry bag with puff mixture. To form a puff, hold pastry bag tube close to greased baking sheet and allow pastry to bubble up around tube until desired size is reached. Space 3 inches apart.
- Puffs may also be formed with a spoon.
- Bake puff shells for 10 minutes in a 400 degree oven or until lightly browned.
- Reduce oven temperature to 350 degrees and bake for approximately 25 minutes longer.
- Do not remove from oven until puffs are firm to the touch.
- Cool puffs away from any draft before filling.
- Cut puffs horizontally with a sharp knife. Remove any inside damp dough filaments.
- Fill with *Windows'* Coffee and Peaches Cream Filling.

Peaches Flambé

Level: Good Cook
Serves 2-3
Preparation Time: 5 minutes

3 tablespoons unsalted butter
¼ cup granulated sugar
⅓ cup dark brown sugar, firmly packed
1 ounce peach schnapps
½ ounce orange-flavored liqueur
3 fresh peaches, peeled and pitted, or 2 cups sliced canned peaches
¼ cup white rum
Vanilla or peach ice cream
Fresh peach slices, for garnish
Mint sprigs, for garnish

- Melt butter in a sauté pan.
- Add sugars and caramelize.
- Pour peach schnapps and orange-flavored liqueur carefully into a sauté pan; heat sauce until bubbly.
- Combine peaches and sauce mixture. Spoon sauce over peaches to coat.
- Add rum and bring mixture back to boil.
- To flambé, light a long fireplace match and ignite sauce by placing match to edge of skillet. Let sauce come to boil and burn down.
- Serve over vanilla or peach ice cream.
- Garnish with a fresh peach slice and a sprig of mint.

A Chef's View

Ripen peaches at room temperature. When ripe, store in the refrigerator. Peaches are a great source of potassium, vitamin A and fiber.

A Show-Me Specialty

Peaches Flambé is a specialty of the Country Club Hotel and Spa in Lake Ozarks. Try this dessert while enjoying the jazz combos that entertain weekend dinner guests.

Country Club Hotel and Spa
HH & Carol Road
Lake Ozark
573-964-6438

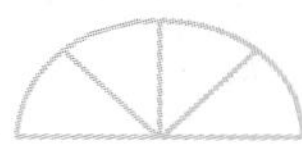

A Chef's View

For a crisp, cool sorbet to prepare the palate, combine 1 cup sugar and the strained juice of 1 lemon with 1 cup water in a saucepan and bring to a boil over low heat, stirring to dissolve the sugar. Boil for 1½ to 2 minutes. Cool to room temperature and whisk in ¾ cup water and 2 cups Riesling wine. Freeze covered, for 4 hours or until firm, whisking several times until smooth. Spoon into 6 chilled serving glasses and garnish with sprigs of mint and lemon twists.

Orange Chocolate Mousse

Level: Good Cook
Serves 8-10
Preparation Time: 1 day

2	cups milk chocolate morsels
2	(8-ounce) packages cream cheese, softened
¼	teaspoon salt
1½	cups brown sugar, firmly packed and divided
4	eggs, separated
2	cups heavy cream
1	teaspoon vanilla extract
2	tablespoons orange-flavored liqueur
1	cup chocolate shavings

- Melt chocolate morsels over hot water in a double boiler. Cool 10 minutes.
- Blend cream cheese, salt and 1 cup brown sugar with an electric mixer.
- Beat egg yolks into cream cheese mixture. Stir into melted chocolate.
- Beat egg whites until stiff in a separate bowl. Gradually add remaining ½ cup brown sugar while beating.
- Fold egg white mixture into chocolate-cream cheese mixture.
- Whip heavy cream until stiff. Fold into chocolate-cream cheese mixture with vanilla extract and orange-flavored liqueur.
- Divide mousse evenly between stemmed wide-mouth red-wine glasses. Cover with plastic wrap.
- Serve with additional whipped cream and chocolate shavings on top.
- Cook's Tip: Some individuals with certain health problems will not be able to eat a dish containing raw eggs.

Praliné Pecan Popcorn

Level: Easy
Yield: 11 cups
Preparation Time: 1 hour

- ¾ cup brown sugar, firmly packed
- ¾ cup maple syrup
- ¼ pound (1 stick) butter
- 2 teaspoons vanilla extract
- 2 cups pecan halves
- 10 cups buttered popcorn, with no unpopped kernels

- Preheat oven to 250 degrees. Butter a 15x10x1-inch jelly-roll pan
- Combine brown sugar, maple syrup and butter in a small heavy saucepan.
- Bring to boil over medium-high heat, stirring often. Reduce heat to medium, cook 2 minutes, stirring often.
- Remove from heat and stir in vanilla extract.
- Place pecans in a large enough bowl to hold popped corn.
- Drizzle sugar mixture over pecans, tossing to coat. Add popped corn, 2 cups at a time, stirring until well coated.
- Spoon popcorn mixture on jelly-roll pan.
- Bake for 1 hour, stirring mixture every 15 minutes with a large spoon.
- Cool completely. Store in an airtight container.

Buttery Toffee Squares

Level: Easy
Yield: 48 bars
Preparation Time: 2 hours

- 1 pound (4 sticks) butter, use no substitute
- 1 pound brown sugar
- 2 cups pecans, chopped
- 1 pound milk chocolate morsels

- Melt butter and add brown sugar in a saucepan. Cook over medium heat until the mixture crackles in cold tap water (270-290 degrees). Stir constantly.
- Add nuts and stir.
- Spread mixture into a buttered jelly-roll pan with a metal spatula.
- Sprinkle chocolate morsels on top and spread with a metal spatula until melted.
- Refrigerate until cold.
- Cut into squares.
- Store between pieces of waxed paper or parchment in a tightly sealed container.

Chocolate Praliné Ice Cream Topping

Level: Easy
Yield: 3 cups
Preparation Time: 10 minutes

⅔ cup brown sugar, firmly packed

1 stick plus 2 tablespoons butter or margarine

1 cup heavy cream

1 (6-ounce) package semisweet chocolate morsels

1 cup pecans, chopped

- Combine sugar, butter and heavy cream in a saucepan. Bring to a boil over medium heat, stirring constantly.
- Reduce heat and simmer 2 minutes, stirring constantly.
- Add chocolate morsels. Stir until melted and smooth.
- Stir in pecans and serve warm over ice cream or a dessert.
- Store in refrigerator and reheat in microwave or over boiling water.

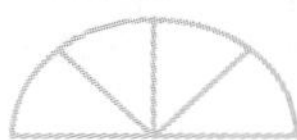

A Chef's View

Originally from the Limousin region, this country-French dessert can be made with any fresh fruit though cherries are traditional. Plums, peaches or pears can also be used.

Raspberry Clafouti

Level: Easy
Serves 6
Preparation Time: 40 minutes

¾	cup all-purpose flour
¾	cup confectioners' sugar
¼	teaspoon salt
4	large eggs, lightly beaten
1	cup milk, warmed
2	tablespoons butter, melted
1½	teaspoons vanilla extract
1½	cups raspberries, washed
	Whipped cream or light cream

- Preheat oven to 375 degrees. Generously butter a 9-inch glass pie dish.
- Sift together flour, sugar and salt.
- Make a well in middle and add eggs. Whisk mixture until it is smooth and blended.
- Stir in warmed milk, butter and vanilla extract.
- Pour ½ cup batter into glass pie dish and bake approximately 6 minutes, just until set.
- Remove from oven and arrange raspberries in pan. Carefully pour remaining batter over raspberries.
- Bake an additional 30 minutes.
- Remove from oven and cut into wedges. Serve with whipped cream or light cream.

Quick n' Yummy Ice Cream

Level: Easy
Serves 1
Preparation Time: 5 minutes

	Crushed ice
6	tablespoons salt
½	cup whole milk
1	tablespoon granulated sugar
¼	teaspoon vanilla extract

- Fill a gallon-size zip-top bag half-full with ice and salt.
- Add milk, sugar and vanilla extract to a quart-size zip-top bag. Seal bag.
- Put quart bag inside of gallon bag of ice and seal.
- Shake for approximately 5 minutes.
- Cook's Tip: Add chocolate shavings, candy-coated chocolate pieces or cookie crumbs to ice cream.

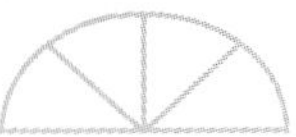

Rhubarb Crisp

Level: Easy
Serves 6
Preparation Time: 1 hour

6	cups fresh or frozen rhubarb, cut into 1-inch slices
1½	cups granulated sugar, divided
2	tablespoons water
1	cup all-purpose flour
½	teaspoon ground cinnamon
⅛	teaspoon salt
¼	pound (1 stick) margarine
2	tablespoons water
	Whipped cream or light cream

- Preheat oven to 350 degrees.
- Mix rhubarb with 1 cup sugar and 2 tablespoons water.
- Pour fruit mixture into a 13x9x2-inch baking dish.
- Mix flour, ½ cup sugar, cinnamon and salt in a medium-size bowl.
- Cut in margarine.
- Sprinkle mixture evenly over rhubarb.
- Bake for 50 minutes or until rhubarb is tender.
- Serve warm with a dollop of whipped cream or light cream.

Banana Ice Cream

Level: Easy
Yield: 1 gallon
Preparation Time: Varies

2	cups whole milk
1¾	cups granulated sugar
½	teaspoon salt
2	cups half-and-half
1	tablespoon vanilla extract
4	cups heavy cream
6	medium bananas, mashed

- Scald milk until bubbles form around edge of pan. Remove from heat.
- Add sugar and salt; stir until dissolved.
- Stir in half-and-half, vanilla extract and heavy cream.
- Cover and refrigerate thirty minutes.
- Add mashed bananas to chilled mixture before freezing. Stir.
- Freeze as directed by ice cream freezer directions.
- Keep in refrigerator freezer until ready to serve.

A Chef's View

If you have a food processor and want to make pastry, combine 3 cups of flour, ½ teaspoon salt, and 1 cup plus 2 tablespoons shortening in a food processor container and pulse until the mixture resembles coarse crumbs. Add about 6 tablespoons ice water 1 tablespoon at a time, mixing until the mixture holds together. Shape into 2 balls. The recipe will make 2 pastry crusts. Use in your favorite recipes. For filled crusts, fit the pastry into a pie plate and prick bottom and side with a fork. Bake at 475 degrees for 8 to 10 minutes or until light brown.

A Culinary Reflection

I remember sitting on the rug, neatly folded and placed atop the crank ice cream maker, while each of us kids would take our 'turn.' Dad would bring fresh farm cream and eggs home from his route, and before it spoiled, Mom would always mix up a batch of homemade ice cream. Dad always got the last 'turn' and we would have to weigh it down to keep it from tipping. He was really strong!

~ Lori Jones

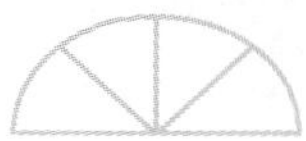

A Chef's View

Add confectioners' sugar to whipping cream before beating. The whipped cream stands up well even if it is not used immediately. Whipping cream retains its shape if, when whipping, you add ½ to 1 teaspoon of light corn syrup per half pint of cream.

White Chocolate Bread Pudding with White Chocolate Sauce

Level: Expert Cook
Serves 6
Preparation Time: 1½ hours

1	(8-ounce) loaf French bread, cut into 1-inch cubes
3½	cups heavy cream, divided
1	cup whole milk
½	cup granulated sugar
18	ounces quality white chocolate, coarsely chopped
7	large egg yolks
2	large eggs
	Golden raisins, optional
	Toasted slivered almonds, optional

- Preheat oven to 275 degrees.
- Arrange bread cubes on baking sheet. Bake until light golden and dry, approximately 10 minutes. Cool completely.
- Increase oven temperature to 350 degrees.
- Combine 3 cups heavy cream, milk and sugar in a heavy 3-quart saucepan. Bring to simmer over medium heat, stirring until sugar dissolves.
- Remove from heat and add 10 ounces, approximately 1¾ cups, white chocolate. Stir until melted and smooth.
- Whisk 7 egg yolks and 2 eggs together in a large bowl.
- Add warm chocolate mixture to eggs and whisk.
- Place bread cubes in a 12x7x2-inch glass baking dish.
- Pour half of chocolate mixture over cubes. Press bread cubes into the chocolate. Let stand 15 minutes.
- Fold in remaining chocolate mixture.
- Cover dish with foil and bake for 45 minutes.
- Uncover and bake until top is golden brown, approximately 15 minutes.
- Remove baking dish from oven and cool slightly on a wire rack.
- Bring remaining ½ cup cream to simmer in a heavy saucepan. Remove saucepan from heat and add remaining 8 ounces white chocolate. Stir until melted and smooth.
- Serve warm white bread pudding with warm white chocolate sauce.
- Pudding may be refrigerated after cooking and warmed at 350 degrees for 35 minutes before the addition of the warm chocolate sauce.
- Cook's Tip: Golden raisins and toasted slivered almonds may be added for another flavor treat.

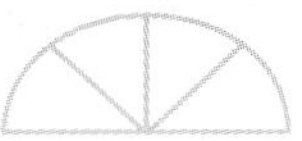

Cranberry Ice Sorbet

Level: Easy
Serves 10-12
Preparation Time: 30+ minutes

4	cups cranberries, rinsed
3	cups water, divided
2	cups granulated sugar
1	tablespoon gelatin, dissolved in ½ cup cold water
2	lemons, freshly squeezed

- Wash and drain cranberries.
- Cook cranberries in 2½ cups water until berries stop popping.
- Drain and reserve juice. Remove and discard skins from berries.
- Add sugar to cranberry pulp and cook until sugar is dissolved. Stir constantly.
- Dissolve gelatin in ½ cup cold water. Add gelatin to cranberry mixture. Stir and cool.
- Stir in lemon juice.
- Pour into a 9x5x3-inch loaf pan and freeze.
- Stir occasionally as sorbet freezes.

A Chef's View

Sorbet, the French word for 'sherbet' which the Italians call 'sorbetto.' Ices or granitas are also names used for the savory or lightly sweetened sorbets that are customarily served either as a palet refresher between courses of a meal or as a dessert. Ices or granitas have become popular in replacing ice cream sherbets. Traditional sorbet, however, contains no milk and has a softer consistency than sherbet.

Farmington's Ice Cream Sherbet

Level: Easy
Yield: 1 gallon
Preparation Time: Varies

2	(16-ounce) cans apricots, chopped
3½	cups granulated sugar
4	oranges, juiced
2	lemons, freshly squeezed
2	cups heavy cream
	Pineapple juice or water, to fill gallon ice cream freezer
10	maraschino cherries, for color

- Combine apricots and sugar in a saucepan. Boil for 3 minutes, stirring constantly. Cool mixture.
- Add orange juice, lemon juice and heavy cream. Mix well.
- Pour into ice cream freezer container.
- Add pineapple juice or water to fill gallon ice cream freezer container.
- Stir in maraschino cherries for color appeal.
- Freeze according to directions given with ice cream freezer.

A Missouri Window

At the St. Louis World's Fair in 1904, the ice cream cone was invented. An ice cream vendor ran out of cups and asked a waffle vendor to help by rolling up waffles to hold ice cream.

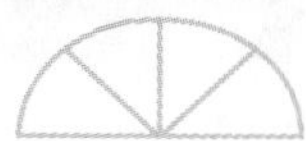

A Chef's View

Make chocolate-covered spoons by placing 12 ounces of semisweet chocolate chip morsels and 1 teaspoon of shortening in a microwave-safe bowl. Microwave on high for 1 minute. Whisk the mixture (the shortening will keep it smooth) until melted. If not warm enough to melt, heat again until mixture is melted. Immediately dip the bowls of the spoon's tip down into the chocolate and place on a waxed paper-lined tray. Let stand at room temperature until firm. Cover spoons in colored plastic wrap and tie with ribbons to use for guests or as gifts.

A Chef's View

Although most store-bought peanut butter is homogenized, some of the oil may still rise to the top of the jar if it stands undisturbed on a shelf for a long time. To prevent this, store the jar upside down. For a real treat, try peanut butter made from nothing but peanuts ground to order. It contains no added fats, stabilizers, or sweeteners.

Chocolate Chip Cookie Truffles

Level: Easy
Yield: 4 dozen
Preparation Time: 1 hour

½ pound (2 sticks) butter, softened
½ cup brown sugar, firmly packed
¼ cup granulated sugar
¼ cup thawed egg substitute
1 teaspoon vanilla extract
1¼ cups all-purpose flour
1 cup mini-semisweet chocolate morsels
¾ cup chopped pecans
1 (12-ounce) package semisweet chocolate morsels
1½ tablespoons solid vegetable shortening

- Cream butter, gradually adding sugars; beat well.
- Add egg substitute and vanilla extract; beat well.
- Combine flour and butter mixture. Mix well.
- Stir in mini-chocolate morsels and chopped pecans.
- Cover and chill 30 minutes.
- Shape tablespoonfuls of mixture into 1-inch balls. Cover and freeze balls, on jelly-roll pan, until firm.
- Melt the 12-ounce package of chocolate morsels with shortening in a double boiler or microwave.
- Using two forks or a dipping tine, quickly dip frozen truffles into melted chocolate, coating completely.
- Place on waxed paper to harden. If desired, decorate with white chocolate drizzle using a pastry tip.
- Store truffles in refrigerator 2-3 days in an airtight container.
- Cook's Tip: Place truffles in decorative seasonal miniature muffin cups if giving for a gift.

Butterscotch Crunch

Level: Quick and Simple
Yield: 3 dozen
Preparation Time: 20 minutes

1 (8-ounce) package butterscotch morsels
½ cup peanut butter
3 cups high-protein rice-and-wheat cereal

- Heat butterscotch and peanut butter in a pan until bits are melted. Stir to keep from burning.
- Pour over cereal. Mix to coat cereal.
- Drop by teaspoonful onto waxed paper. Let cool.
- Store between waxed paper in a tightly covered container.

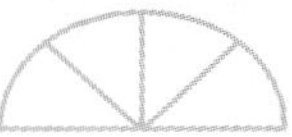

Chocolate Nut Neapolitans

Level: Easy
Yield: 64 pieces
Preparation Time: 2 hours

6 (1-ounce) squares semisweet chocolate, coarsely chopped
3 tablespoons creamy peanut butter, divided
8 (1-ounce) squares premium white chocolate, coarsely chopped
1 (7-ounce) bar milk chocolate, coarsely chopped
¼ cup unsalted roasted peanuts, chopped

- Line an 8-inch square pan with aluminum foil; extend at least 3 inches over sides. Coat with cooking spray.
- Combine semisweet chocolate and 1 tablespoon peanut butter in a microwave-safe bowl.
- Microwave on HIGH for 1 minute. Stir and microwave an additional 15 seconds to 1 minute, or until chocolate melts.
- Spread chocolate into prepared pan. Chill 15 minutes or just until firm.
- Combine white chocolate and 2 tablespoons peanut butter in previously used microwave-safe bowl. Microwave on HIGH 1 minute. Stir and microwave 30 seconds, if necessary. Stir until smooth.
- Spread white chocolate mixture over semisweet layer in pan. Chill pan 15 minutes.
- Place milk chocolate in same baking dish. Microwave on HIGH 1 to 1½ minutes. Stir well.
- Spread milk chocolate evenly over white chocolate layer.
- Sprinkle with peanuts. Cover and chill candy 1½ hours or until set.
- Score candy into 2-inch squares with a thin-bladed knife. Remove from pan by lifting candy by foil handles.
- Cut candy into 2-inch squares with knife. Place each 2-inch square on a cutting board and cut into 4 pieces.
- Store between pieces of waxed paper in an airtight container.

A Chef's View

Try to make candy on dry days. The candy does not set as well on humid or rainy days. Use the best quality sugar. Is there a difference between beet sugar and cane sugar? Not really, after processing, the two sugars are chemically the same.

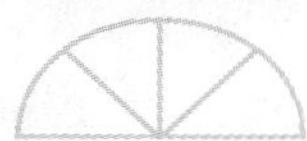

A Chef's View

Today marshmallows are commercially made from corn syrup, gelatin, gum arabic and flavorings. However, once they were created from the sweetened extract of the roots of the marshmallow plant. Marshmallows come in two sizes, regular and miniature and can be white or pastel colors.

A Chef's View

Cut marshmallows by using scissors dipped in water. When roasting marshmallows spray skewers or tree sticks lightly with a butter-flavored cooking spray or margarine.

Marshmallow Happy Pops

Level: Quick and Simple
Yield: 12 pops
Preparation Time: 30 minutes

- 1 bag large marshmallows
- 1 package chocolate candy coating
- Candy sprinkles
- 12 flat wooden sticks

- Spread waxed paper on a cookie sheet.
- Thread 2 marshmallows onto each flat wooden stick.
- Melt candy coating in microwave, stirring until smooth.
- Dip marshmallow sticks into melted coating.
- Sprinkle candy bits on marshmallows.
- Set on waxed paper until dry.
- Cook's Tip: Wrap pops in cellophane and tie with ribbon, appropriate for the holiday.

Tutti-Frutti Candy

Level: Easy
Yield: 4-6 dozen
Preparation Time: 40 minutes

- 20 ounces confectioners' coating, milk or white chocolate
- 2 cups miniature marshmallows, colored and fruit-flavored
- 2 cups crispy rice cereal
- 2 cups salted peanut halves
- 2 cups fruited cereal

- Melt confectioners' coating in the microwave.
- Stir in marshmallows, cereals and peanuts, being careful not to break up cereal.
- Drop by a well-rounded tablespoonful onto a greased cookie sheet.
- Chill.
- Store in an airtight container between sheets of parchment or waxed paper.

Acknowledgments, Sources & Index

WINDOWS *across* MISSOURI

a culinary view

Acknowledgments & Sources

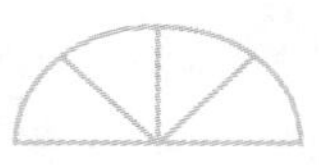

Windows Across Missouri Core Committee

Co-Chairs: Joan M. H'Doubler and Lizabeth Starnes Fleenor

Treasurer: Lori Jones

Co-Editors: Carol Jean DeFeo and Jana Wolfe

Marketing: Eileen Chalk

Windows Across Missouri Sponsors

Donors

Eileen and David E. Chalk, MD, Washington
Carol Jean and Fred G. DeFeo, MD, Kansas City
Lori and Jeffrey T. Jones, MD, Joplin
Missouri State Medical Association

Contributors

Mary Kay McPhee, Kansas City
Becky and Thomas Moore, MD, Joplin
Rhonda and Scott Wade, MD, Savannah

Friends

Diane Acuff, St. Joseph
Yvonne Backstrom, Joplin
Joanne Bamshad, Highland Park, IL
Pattye Barbee, Columbia
Judy Corry, Springfield
Barbara Domann, Springfield
Eileen and Gary A. Dyer, MD, St. Joseph
Ina May Fakhoury, Kansas City
Lizabeth Starnes Fleenor, Jefferson City
Joan M. and Charles E. H'Doubler, MD, Springfield
Richard A. Heimburger, MD, Jefferson City
Susan E. Hollinger, Prairie Village, KS
Elizabeth and William Huffaker, MD, St. Louis
Mary Hunkeler, Shawnee Mission. KS
Jasper-Newton Metropolitan Medical Society
Joan W. Jones, Columbia
Jeri Lynn Joseph, Joplin
Sandy and Harold Kanagawa, MD, Jefferson City
Rosalie and Rolf Krojanker, MD, St. Louis
Jean and Carl Kruse, MD, Palmyra
Lafayette-Ray County Medical Society, Carrollton
Marilyn Lee, Kansas City
Jan Long, Marthasville
Barbara Majzoub, Joplin
Marge and David Perkins, MD, Chesterfield
Valine and Peter D. Perll, MD, Mexico
Marjorie R. Peterson, Springfield
Nancy Rankin, Joplin
Kathy Riscoe, Joplin
Sana and George Saleh, MD, Kansas City
Debbie Sanfelippo, Jefferson City
Debbie Schaaf, St. Joseph
Jewell Schweitzer, Springfield
Diana F. Shaplin, Ballwin
Mary Shuman, St. Joseph
Deborah Smith, St. Joseph
St. Louis Metropolitan Medical Society Alliance
Charlotte Stradford, Columbia
Elizabeth H. Sutter, St. Louis
Anne Turnbaugh, Jefferson City
Vicki and Richard Voszler, MD, Cape Girardeau
Allene and Michael Wright, MD, St. Joseph

For Your Information

Along with original and cherished Missouri recipes, *Windows Across Missouri* includes favorites served in Missouri restaurants. These restaurant recipes are marked as a "Show-Me Specialty" and lists the restaurant information with the recipe. They are also found in the index under "Show-Me Specialty."

Game hunting and fishing are popular sports in Missouri. We hope that the recipes under *Sporting Views - Fish, Seafood & Game* offer new ways to prepare your bounty. For the young chefs, kid-friendly recipes are marked in the index under "Kid-Friendly," and may require adult supervision.

Windows Across Missouri followed style and editing guidelines set forth in:

- *The Recipe Writer's Handbook;* 1997 - Barbara Gibbs Ostmann & Jane L. Baker
- *The New Food Lover's Companion;* 2001 - Third Edition; Sharon Tyler Herbst

Missouri facts and history were contributed by:

- Missouri Mansion Preservation, Inc.
- The Missouri Division of Tourism
- The Missouri Department of Natural Resources
- The Missouri Department of Conservation

Additional photographs by:

- Wendy Poepsel, Photographics, Washington
- Vivian Brill, Silk Purse Graphics, St. Louis

Alliance Presidents whose vision created *Windows Across Missouri - A Culinary View*

Becky Moore	Jasper-Newton Counties	1997-1998
Judy Corry	Greene County	1998-1999
Beverly Murrell, MD	Boone County	1999-2000
Eileen Chalk	Tri-County	2000-2001
Rhonda Wade	Buchanan County	2001-2002
Carol Jean DeFeo	Kansas City	2002-2003

DeNovo Committee - Original Concept for *Windows Across Missouri - A Culinary View*

Gayle Vilmer	Chair of DeNovo Committee	1996-2000
Maura Taylor	Chair of DeNovo Committee	2001-

A special thank-you to our computer consultant,
Fred G. DeFeo, MD,
for his invaluable assistance.

Alliance History Authors

Stacey Ayers
Jean Alvillar
Millie Bever
Lora Blair
Susie Blatt
Nona Nan Chapman
Sherri Ciliberti
Joan M. H'Doubler
Iris Hunt
Betsy Jelley
Barbie Lyons
Mary Kay McPhee
Sandy Mitchell
Majorie Peterson
Mary Shuman
Anne Turnbaugh
Gill Waltman

Proofreaders

Millie Bever
Ranae Butler
Eileen Chalk
Donna Corrado
Judy Corry
Carol Jean DeFeo
Eileen Dyer
Lizabeth Starnes Fleenor
Joan M. H'Doubler
Lori Jones
Becky Jungermann
Liz Kagan
Michele Kennett
Symie Menitove
Jackie Remis
Kathy Riscoe
Mary Shuman
Anne Turnbaugh
Kathy Weigand
Allene Wright
Angela Zylka

Testing Coordinators

Vegetables - Boone
*Lori Gigantelli
Ann Cohen

Breads - Boone
*Patty Kenter
Cindy Beale

Healthy/Lite - Quad
*Carla Bosley

Casseroles - Clay-Platte
*Lea Morrison

Soups and Salads - Cole
*Debbie Sanfelippo
Anne Turnbaugh

Main Dishes - Greene
*Joe Meystrik
Joan M. H'Doubler
Jana Wolfe

Desserts - Jasper-Newton
*Lori Jones
Cynthia Black
Becky Moore

Appetizers - St. Louis
*Millie Bever
Angela Zylka

Miscellaneous - Tri-County
*Susie Blatt

Beverages - Kansas City
*Carol Jean DeFeo

**denotes Chair*

Recipe Contributors

Loretta Allebach
Marjory Allen
American Bounty Restaurant
Andrea's Restaurant
Genevieve Atcheson
Lois Baird
June Barelli
Ester Bauman
Bevo Mill Restaurant
Audrey Bermine
Millie Bever
Lora Blair
Joy Blake-Krug
Susie Blatt
Sarah McBride Blick
George M. Bohigian, MD
Ann Herzog Bondurant
Darlene Bonsanti
Carla Bosley
Polly Bowles
Joan Brown
Rochelle Buckner
Simon Bullen
Ranae Butler
Glenn's Café
Elizabeth E. Campbell, MD
Janet Campbell
Susan Carr
Eileen Chalk
Nona Nan Chapman
Julie Cheche
Chef Patrick Chow-Yuen
Shirley Christensen
Sherri Ciliberti
Chef James Clary
Jill Cohen
Virginia Coppinger
Donna F. Corrado
Judy Corry
Country Club Hotel
Elizabeth Couper
Barbara Crader
Canden Crie
Jack L. Croughan, MD
Carol Jean DeFeo
Fred G. DeFeo, MD
Barbara Domann
Mary Ann Duff
Ruth Ann Dunn
Beulah Dysart
Denniese Dysart, LPC
EBT Restaurant
Johanna B. Echols
Anneliese Engelmann
Ina May Fakhoury
Ardyce Fee
Mary Feldmeier
Lizabeth Starnes Fleenor
Felecia Fleishman
Jan K. Frank
G. Ronald Garrett
Peggy Garrett
Bette Geiger
Chef Leo Geismar
Taney German
Mareen Gill
Roberta Goldman
Marie Gomez
Andrea Greer
Edna Gutzmer
Marge Hahn
Hardware Café
Jay Harms
Sylvia Hartwig
Kathie Hazuka
Joan M. H'Doubler
Mary Catherine Heimburger
Marge Heyer
Geraldine Hill
Sheryl Hoehner
Gail Holand
Susan Hollinger
Betty Huffaker
Mary Hunkeler
Iris Bage Hunt
Jefferson City Country Club
Lori Jones
Harold Kanagawa, MD
Sandy Kanagawa
Melinda Kimlinger
Sharan Klingner
Jackie Krafft
Mollie O. Krafka
Nora Kyger
Shari Layle
Joann Leib

Recipe Contributors, continued

Julie Lentz
Janet Lillis
John Lillis
Mary Lovern
Kathryn Lucas
Martha Jane Lurie
Judy Madden
S.D. Madduri, MD
Carmen Mallouk
Marge Mangum
Chef Brian Manhardt
Leanna McLaughlin
Mary Kay McPhee
Symie D. Menitove
Sandy Meridy
Jan Meyer-Simon
Joe Meystrik
Virginia Miller
Pat Mills
Colleen Miner
Missouri Governor's Mansion
Sandra Mitchell
Kay Moellenhoff
Becky Moore
Thomas Moore, MD
Lea Morrison
Virginia G. Muench
Sarah Muegge
Jeanne M. Murphy
Beverly Murrell, MD
Amy Nichols
Paradise Grill
Martina M. Parker
Marge Perkins
Marjorie Peterson
Catherine L. Platt
Michelle Poire
Mary Pope
Jaya Reddy
Pat Reid
Anne Richardson, RN
Jean Richardson
Rick's Café
John Rollo, MD
Chef Ron
Jackie Sanders
Debbie Sanfelippo
Vicki Saviano
Venus E. Schattyn
Elaine Schmidt
Kathryn Schmidt
Bonnie Shacktner
Susan Shepherd
Mary Shuman
Maxine Sklenar
Charles Small
Deborah Smith
Michelle Cody Smith
Patsy Smith
Wilda Stacey
Cathy Starnes
Cara Stauffer
Stephenson's Apple Farm Restaurant
Deborah Stinnett
Kathryn Stipetich
Shawna Stout
Dee Dee Strauss
Shirley Stroud
C.C. 'Cork' Swarens
Nancy Thompson
Marcella Throne
Robin Till
Twin Oaks Country Club
Gayle Vilmer
Rhonda Wade
Jean Wankum
Kathy Weigand
Donna Weiss
James Weiss, MD
Karen Wempe
Milly K. Wicks
Melanie Brown Wilkens
Virginia Willoughby
Ruthanne Jones Wise
James B. Wolfe, MD
Jana Wolfe
Shelia Wright
Andy Wright, MD
Chef Patrick Chow Yuen
Chef Stephan Zeppenfeldt
Angela Zylka

The MSMA Alliance would like to thank all of those who contributed to *Windows Across Missouri.*

Testers

Lynne Barr
Cindy Beale
Millie Bever
Cynthia Black
Susie Blatt
Carla Bosley
Rochelle Buckner
Eileen Chalk
Sherri Ciliberti
Ann Cohen
Judy Corry
Pam Detten
Mary Ann Duff
Ina May Fakhoury
Mary Eleanor Farrell
Alicia Fernandez
Gina Fuller
Lori Gigantelli
Mary Ann Granger
Cindy Gregston
Lori Jones
Sandy Kanagawa
Patty Kenter
Ann Koppers
Ellen Landsbaum
Julie Lentz
Karen Lieurance
Missy Little
Luanne Loggan
Joe Meystrik
Chris Mittman
Becky Moore
Lea Morrison
Nancy Rankin
Joanne Reardon
Sana Saleh
Debbie Sanfelippo
Kay Schaumann
Kathy Steinberg
Melanie Talbot
Anne Turnbaugh
Jana Wolfe
Cindy Wyrsch
Angela Zylka

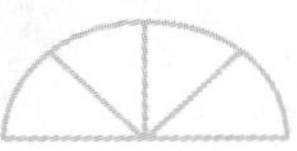

A

A Chef's View

Antipasto Platter ... 16
Banana Wafer Sandwich ... 19
Bouquet Garni ... 120
Café au Lait ... 40
Café Cubano ... 40
Cake Flour ... 275
Cakemix Cookies ... 259
Cake Problem Charts ... 266, 279
Cappuccino ... 40
Children's Cooking Hints ... 159
Chili-Cheese Croutons ... 110
Chive Butter ... 59
Chocolate-Covered Spoons ... 308
Cinnamon Butter ... 46
Citrus Butter ... 46
Confectioners' Sugar ... 259
Cookie Tips ... 259
Cool Lemon Sorbet ... 302
Demi-Glace ... 203
Egg Substitutes ... 64
Egg Wash ... 184
Espresso ... 40
Food Processor Pastry Crust ... 305
Garlic Spread ... 56
Green Onion Butter ... 204
Grilled Corn ... 160
Grilling Tips ... 224, 226
Herb Butter ... 59
Herbed Cheese Spread ... 56
Honey-Pecan Butter ... 46
Last Minute Appetizers ... 34
Latte ... 40
Lemon Butter ... 59
Macciato ... 40
Make Buttermilk ... 270
Maple Butter ... 46
Marinated Tomatoes ... 169
Meringue ... 289
Mocha ... 40
Pastry Problem Chart ... 281
Peach-Mint Vinegar ... 146
Pecan Butter ... 59
Quick Cheese Appetizer ... 22
Red Seafood Sauce ... 181
Removing Tomato Skins and Seeds ... 141
Rice Tips ... 135
Special Spuds ... 164
Spice Use Tips ... 219
Strawberry Butter ... 46
Stuffed Tomatoes ... 17
Sugar Cookie Crust ... 276
Sweet Cinnamon Croutons ... 107
Sweet Tortilla Snacks ... 235
'Tator Tricks ... 163
Trout Handling Tips ... 176
White Roux ... 108

A Show-Me Specialty

American Bounty Apple Maple Dessert with Custard Sauce ... 290
Andrea's Southwestern Guacamole ... 14
Bevo Mill Famous Cheddar Cheese and Chive Biscuits ... 53
Chef Ron's Hot Chicken Salad ... 234
Clary's Chicken Piccata ... 241
Dried Cherry and Almond Chicken Salad in Wonton Cups ... 21
EBT Gazpacho ... 105
Glenn's Café Blackened Red Drum Fish ... 178
Glenn's Café Eggplant Creole ... 222
Hardware Café Hot Fudge Peanut Cheesecake ... 279
Missouri Governor's Mansion Basil Vinaigrette ... 99
Paradise Grill Sirloin Peppered Steak with Armagnac ... 205
Rick's Lampe Scampi and Angel Hair Pasta ... 130
Rick's Salmon Napoleon ... 179
Savory Palmiers ... 26
Stephenson's Apple Farm Frozen Fruit Salad ... 77
Twin Oaks Country Club Linguine with Feta Cheese and Shrimp ... 125

Appetizers (also see Dips and Spreads)

Asian Vegetable and Beef Turnovers ... 19
Baja Shrimp Nachos ... 22
Bleu Cheese Fingers ... 21
Chinese Chicken Wings ... 20
Dried Cherry and Almond Chicken Salad in Wonton Cups ... 21
Gingered Shrimp ... 23
Hallelujah Ham Loaves ... 22
Lobster Deviled Eggs ... 26
Mushroom Pinwheel Fingers ... 25
Orange Pecans ... 32
Pecan Stuffed Dates ... 20
Petite Crab Cakes ... 23
Phyllo Lobster Triangles ... 24
Savory Palmiers ... 26
Tangy Ranch Snack Mix ... 33

Apples

American Bounty Apple Maple Dessert with Custard Sauce ... 290
Apple and Raisin Stuffed Pork Chops ... 219
Apple Cider Spritzer ... 34
Apple Gruyère Tart ... 61
Apple Horseradish Sauce ... 175
Apple Soup ... 106
Apple Volcanoes ... 145

Apple Yams 166
Apples N' Almond Toffee Brickle Dip 14
Bacon Apple Toast 62
Candy Apple Walnut Pie 280
Chicken Fruit Toss 81
Chilled Apple Soup 104
Chunky Apple Pancakes with Cinnamon Butter 71
Cinnamon Apple Bars 68
Fresh Apple Fruit Salad with Pecans 75
Ozark Mountain Fresh Apple Cake 275
Quail with Wild Rice, Sage and Apples 194
Red Cabbage and Apples 154
Wild Rice with Apples and Sun-Dried Cherries 141

Apricots and Apricot Gelatin

Apricot Chicken with Garden Rice 230
Apricot Soup 103
Apricot Stuffed Goose 190
Baked Apricots with Gingersnap Crumbles 145
Coconut Pecan Apricot Salad 95
Farmington's Ice Cream Sherbet 307
Fruity Wild Rice 137
Lemon Apricot Chicken 245

Artichokes

Artichoke and Ham Rolls 219
Artichoke Rice Salad 83
Asparagus Artichoke Chicken 231
Baked Italian Artichoke Spread 27
Christmas Angel Pasta 124
Green Chile Artichoke Spread 28
Tortellini and Vegetable Medley 86

Asparagus

Asparagus Artichoke Chicken 231
Asparagus Aspic with Horseradish 93
Buttery Lemon Asparagus 150
Penne with Asparagus and Shaved Ham 135
Roasted Asparagus and Mushrooms with Rosemary 150

Avocados

Andrea's Southwestern Guacamole 14
Avocado Dressing 96
Avocado Feta Salsa 33
Tortellini and Vegetable Medley 86

B

Bananas

Banana Ice Cream 305
Bananas Foster 292
Chocolate Chip Banana Muffins 50
Honey Nectar Shake 35
South Seas Fruit Salad 76

Beans and Peas

Adzuki Bean Burgers 152
Carrot Ring 155
Chicken Stir-Fry 240
Corn and Black Bean Salsa 30
Fiesta Dip 16
Green Bean and Feta Salad with Walnuts 91
Green Bean and Onion Salad with Bleu Cheese 92
Green Beans, Potatoes and Ham in Redeye Gravy 108
Hobo Beans 151
Hummus 17
Mexican Stack Buffet Salad 82
Not Just for New Year's Day Black-Eyed Peas 31
Penne Spinach Casserole 126
Spicy Black-Eyed Peas and Sausage 110
Taco Soup 110
Tagliatelle with Wild Mushrooms, Peas and Prosciutto 128
Tangy Green Bean and Pea Salad 94
White Chili 111

Beef

Asian Vegetable and Beef Turnovers 19
Baked Stroganoff 209
Beef Stock 119
Beef Rouladen 206
Cabbage Rolls in Tomato Sauce 210
Curried Beef Pita 211
Dad's Taverns 212
Grilled Teriyaki Marinated Filet Mignon 204
Hobo Beans 151
Medallions of Beef Tenderloin in Brandy Tomato Sauce 203
Mexican Stack Buffet Salad 82
Noodles with Beefy Three Cheese Sauce 134
Okra and Ground Beef Casserole 208
Paradise Grill Sirloin Peppered Steak with Armagnac 205
Porcupines 212
Reuben Sandwich Casserole 209
Snuggly Dogs 213
Taco Soup 110
Tailgate Brisket 207

Beets, Orange 153

Beverages

Apple Cider Spritzer 34
Café Con Leche 40
Children's Fruit Juicy Punch 35
Cranapple Frostee 36
Cranberry Tea 39
Edible Flowered Ice Ring 38
English Custard Float 37
Holiday Wassail 41
Honey Nectar Shake 35
Iced Almond Tea 36
Pineapple Octopus Bubbles 38
Raspberry Punch 38
Russian Tea 42
Spicy Mocha Mix 42
Summer Orange Smoothie 39
White Hot Chocolate 40

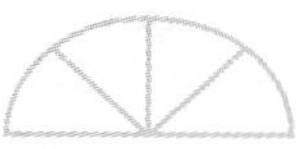

Blueberries
Blueberry Citrus Cake ... 274
Marinated Fruits of Summer ... 146
Sherried Fruit Compote ... 148
Breads
Bevo Mill Famous Cheddar Cheese and Chive Biscuits ... 53
Chili-Cheese Croutons ... 110
Chocolate Chip Banana Muffins ... 50
Date Nut Loaf ... 46
Dill Bread ... 55
Flaky Tomato Basil Biscuits ... 54
Glazed Citrus Loaf ... 45
M M M M M Muffins ... 51
Missouri State Fair Blue Ribbon Zucchini Bread ... 47
Onion Shortcake ... 52
Orange Glazed Poppy Seed Bread ... 48
Puffed Cheese Twists ... 60
Pumpkin Bread ... 49
Quick Focaccia ... 56
Refrigerator Dinner Rolls ... 57
Sally Lunn Bread ... 58
Seasoned Pita Crisps ... 60
Sour Cream Corn Muffins ... 51
Sweet Cinnamon Croutons ... 107
Tuscan Bread ... 59
Yorkshire Popovers ... 54
Breakfast
Apple Gruyère Tart ... 61
Bacon Apple Toast ... 62
Caramel Soaked French Toast ... 66
Chunky Apple Pancakes with Cinnamon Butter ... 71
Cinnamon Apple Bars ... 68
Cinnamon Pecan Coffee Cake ... 69
Decadent Cinnamon Rolls ... 70
Gourmet Waffles ... 72
Italian Brunch Casserole ... 62
Kentucky Hot Browns ... 63
Nutty Granola ... 72
Orange Pecan French Toast ... 67
Peppered Shrimp and Eggs ... 64
Sausage and Egg Strata ... 65
Sausage, Egg and Potato Casserole ... 65
Sweet and Gooey Bubble Bread ... 67
Venison Breakfast Sausage ... 199
Broccoli Salad, Mango ... 91
Butter
Chive Butter ... 59
Cinnamon butter ... 46
Citrus Butter ... 46
Green Onion Butter ... 204
Herb Butter ... 59
Honey-Pecan Butter ... 46
Lemon Butter ... 59
Maple Butter ... 46
Pecan Butter ... 59
Strawberry Butter ... 46

C

Cabbage
Cabbage Rolls in Tomato Sauce ... 210
Red Cabbage and Apples ... 154
Cakes (see Desserts)
Candies (see Desserts)
Cantaloupe Soup ... 103
Carrots
Carrot Ring ... 155
Copper Pennies ... 156
Garden Rice ... 231
Mushroom Veggie Burgers ... 161
Casseroles
Apple Yams ... 166
Armenian Rice ... 136
Asparagus Artichoke Chicken ... 231
Baked Cauliflower and Swiss Cheese ... 157
Baked Stroganoff ... 209
Baked Vermicelli with Spinach and Mushrooms ... 123
Caramel Soaked French Toast ... 66
Chicken and Noodle Casserole ... 132
Chicken and Rice Casserole with Cashews ... 233
Christmas Angel Pasta ... 124
Crunchy Chicken Cauliflower ... 243
Green Chile Corn Squares ... 160
Hobo Beans ... 151
Holiday Party Potatoes ... 164
Italian Brunch Casserole ... 62
Jalapeño Corn ... 161
Mexicorn Corn Soufflé ... 159
Noodles with Beefy Three Cheese Sauce ... 134
Okra and Ground Beef Casserole ... 208
Penne Spinach Casserole ... 126
Potato Cheese Puff ... 165
Reuben Sandwich Casserole ... 209
Sausage and Egg Strata ... 65
Sausage, Egg and Potato Casserole ... 65
Scalloped Chicken ... 246
Scalloped Corn and Oysters ... 185
Seafood Medley ... 182
Shrimp and Rice Supreme ... 187
Spinach Soufflé ... 169
Springfield Cashew Chicken ... 247
Summer Squash Casserole ... 168
Sweet Potato Casserole with Praliné Topping ... 167
Tomato Pie ... 153
Tuna Jackstraws ... 177
White Cheddar Cheese Grits ... 142
Cauliflower
Baked Cauliflower and Swiss Cheese ... 157
Crunchy Chicken Cauliflower ... 243

Italian Oven Fried Cauliflower ... 158

Caviar Cream Cheese Spread ... 10

Cereals and Grains (also see Rice)

Apple Volcanoes ... 145
Butterscotch Crunch ... 308
Crockery Cooker Polenta ... 139
Giant Peanutty Pizza Cookies ... 262
Lemon Oat Shortbread ... 264
M M M M M Muffins ... 51
Nutty Couscous ... 138
Nutty Granola ... 72
Oatmeal Cake with Brown Sugar Glaze ... 272
Polenta ... 139
Stress Reliever Cookies ... 266
Tutti-Frutti Candy ... 310
White Cheddar Cheese Grits ... 142

Cheese

Apple Gruyère Tart ... 61
Baked Cauliflower and Swiss Cheese ... 157
Bevo Mill Famous Cheddar Cheese and Chive Biscuits ... 53
Bleu Cheese Fingers ... 21
Camembert Sauté ... 9
Cheese Soufflé with Chicken Mushroom Sauce ... 232
Chicken Enchiladas ... 238
Chicken in Three Cheese Sauce ... 237
Chunky Gorgonzola Dip ... 9
Clam and Cheese Dip ... 30
Grecian Cheese Round ... 10
Green Bean and Feta Salad with Walnuts ... 91
Green Bean and Onion Salad with Bleu Cheese ... 92
Hallelujah Ham Loaves ... 22
Herbed Goat Cheese ... 11
Maytag White Cheddar Cheese Soup ... 109
Mexican Stack Buffet Salad ... 82
Mozzarella Baked Eggplant ... 158
Parmesan Wine Rice ... 136
Party Cheese Pâté ... 12
Poppy Seed Cheddar Crust ... 291
Puffed Cheese Twists ... 60
Roquefort Sauce ... 215
Strawberry Cheddar Cheese Carousel ... 13
Sweet Potato Pie with Poppy Seed Cheddar Crust ... 291
Tomato and Mozzarella Stuffed Peppers ... 166
White Cheddar and Bleu Cheese Fondue ... 32
White Cheddar Cheese Grits ... 142
White Chili ... 111

Cheesecakes (see Desserts)

Cherries and Cherry Preserves

Blushing Cherry Mold ... 94
Cherry Almond Glazed Pork Roast ... 220
Dried Cherry and Almond Chicken Salad in Wonton Cups ... 21
Roasted Duck Breast with Cherry Sauce ... 189
Wild Rice with Apples and Sun-Dried Cherries ... 141

Chicken (see Poultry)

Chocolate (see Desserts)

Clams

Clam and Cheese Dip ... 30
New England Clam Chowder ... 114

Coconut

Coconut Ginger Rice ... 135
Coconut Pecan Apricot Salad ... 95
Coconut Pie ... 282
Italian Cream Cake ... 277
Mandarin Orange Coconut Cake ... 269
Marinated Fruits of Summer ... 146
Mexican Stack Buffet Salad ... 82
Ozark Mountain Fresh Apple Cake ... 275
Sweet Potato Casserole with Praliné Topping ... 167

Cookies (see Desserts)

Corn

Corn and Black Bean Salsa ... 30
Corn Relish ... 89
Crockery Cooker Polenta ... 139
Green Chile Corn Squares ... 160
Jalapeño Corn ... 161
Mexicorn Corn Soufflé ... 159
Onion Shortcake ... 52
Polenta ... 139
Scalloped Corn and Oysters ... 185
Taco Soup ... 110
Tangy Ranch Snack Mix ... 33
White Cheddar Cheese Grits ... 142

Crab (see Seafood)

Cranberries, Cranberry Juice and Cranberry Sauce

Cranberry Chicken ... 242
Cranapple Frostee ... 36
Cranberry Fruit Salad ... 95
Cranberry Ice Sorbet ... 307
Cranberry Tea ... 39

Cucumbers

Cool Cucumber Sauce ... 34
Cucumber Yogurt Dip ... 16
EBT Gazpacho ... 105

D

Dates

Date Nut Loaf ... 46
Pecan Stuffed Dates ... 20

Desserts

Cakes

Blueberry Citrus Cake ... 274
Brown Sugar Pumpkin Crumb Cake ... 267
Buttery Pound Cake ... 268
Cake Flour ... 275
Cake Problem Charts ... 266, 279
Chocolate Nut Torte ... 295
Chocolate Peanut Butter Mousse Cake ... 296

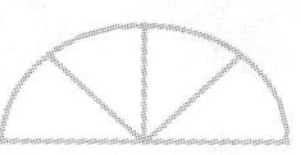

Italian Cream Cake ... 277
Mandarin Orange Coconut Cake ... 269
Milk Chocolate Cake ... 270
Mississippi Mud Cake ... 271
Missouri Peanut Butter Mud Cake with Fudge Frosting ... 273
Oatmeal Cake with Brown Sugar Glaze ... 272
Ozark Mountain Fresh Apple Cake ... 275
White Chocolate Cake Supreme ... 277

Candies

Butterscotch Crunch ... 308
Chocolate Chip Cookie Truffles ... 308
Chocolate Nut Neapolitans ... 309
Marshmallow Happy Pops ... 310
Tutti-Frutti Candy ... 310

Cheesecakes

Hardware Café Hot Fudge Peanut Cheesecake ... 279
Pumpkin Cheesecake with Gingersnap Crust ... 276
Raspberry Ribbon Cheesecake ... 278

Cookies and Bars

Almond Crunch Cookies ... 259
Amish Sour Cream Sugar Cookies ... 260
Buttery Toffee Squares ... 303
Cakemix Cookies ... 259
Caramel Brownies ... 255
Chocolate Pecan Squares ... 256
Cookie Tips ... 259
Double Chocolate Chip Cookies ... 261
Giant Peanutty Pizza Cookies ... 262
Gingersnaps ... 263
Lemon Oat Shortbread ... 264
Maple Praliné Biscotti ... 265
Peanut Butter Cup Cookies ... 262
Pecan Pie Bars ... 257
Stress Reliever Cookies ... 266
Sweet Tortilla Snacks ... 235
Triple Chocolate Fudge Brownies ... 258

Crusts

Chocolate Wafer Pie Crust ... 283
Food Processor Pastry Crust ... 305
Never Fail Pie Crust ... 288
Pastry Problem Chart ... 281
Poppy Seed Cheddar Crust ... 291
Raspberry Chocolate Wafer Crust ... 278
Sugar Cookie Crust ... 276

Cupcakes

Ice Cream Cone Cupcakes ... 266

Frostings and Toppings

Chocolate Praliné Ice Cream Topping ... 303
Confectioners' Sugar ... 259
Fudge Frosting ... 273
Hot Fudge Sauce ... 279
Hot Fudge Sauce to Die For ... 300
Raspberry Sauce ... 278
Raspberry Topping ... 278

Pies

Candy Apple Walnut Pie ... 280
Chocolate Bourbon Pecan Pie ... 281
Coconut Pie ... 282
Frozen Juice Pie ... 280
Key Lime Pie ... 282
Lemon Custard Ice Cream Pie ... 283
Mango Pie ... 285
Meringue ... 289
No Crust German Chocolate Pie ... 284
No Crust Pumpkin Pie ... 285
Pastry Problem Chart ... 281
Peach Cream Pie ... 286
Pecan Pie ... 284
Pumpkin Pecan Pie ... 287
Rhubarb Pie ... 288
Strawberry Meringue Crust Pie ... 289
Sweet Potato Pie with Poppy Seed Cheddar Crust ... 291

Puddings and Desserts

American Bounty Apple Maple Dessert with Custard Sauce ... 290
Banana Ice Cream ... 305
Bananas Foster ... 292
Brinkman's Baklava ... 293
Cheese Flan with Caramel Sauce ... 294
Coffee and Peaches Cream Puffs ... 300
Coffee Crème Brûlée ... 297
Cranberry Ice Sorbet ... 307
Cream Puff Shells ... 300
Creamy Caramel Dip ... 298
Farmington's Ice Cream Sherbet ... 307
Indian Pudding ... 298
Luscious Lemon Fondue ... 263
Old-Fashioned Bread Pudding with Whiskey Sauce ... 299
Orange Chocolate Mousse ... 302
Peaches Flambé ... 301
Praliné Pecan Popcorn ... 303
Quick n' Yummy Ice Cream ... 304
Raspberry Clafouti ... 304
Rhubarb Crisp ... 305
White Chocolate Bread Pudding with White Chocolate ... 306

Dips and Spreads

Andrea's Southwestern Guacamole ... 14
Apples N' Almond Toffee Brickle Dip ... 14
Avocado Feta Salsa ... 33
Baked Italian Artichoke Spread ... 27
Camembert Sauté ... 9
Caviar Cream Cheese Spread ... 10
Chinese Ginger Garlic Dip ... 15
Chunky Gorgonzola Dip ... 9
Clam and Cheese Dip ... 30
Cool Cucumber Sauce ... 34

Corn and Black Bean Salsa ... 30
Cottage Spinach Dip ... 15
Creamy Caramel Dip ... 298
Cucumber Yogurt Dip ... 16
Fiesta Dip ... 16
Garlic Spread ... 56
Grecian Cheese Round ... 10
Green Chile Artichoke Spread ... 28
Herbed Boursin ... 11
Herbed Cheese Spread ... 56
Herbed Goat Cheese ... 11
Hummus ... 17
Jezebel Sauce ... 31
Not Just for New Year's Day Black-Eyed Peas ... 31
Party Cheese Pâté ... 12
Peanut Butter Yogurt Dip ... 19
Pineapple Cheese Ball ... 13
Santa Fe Salsa ... 33
Shiitake Mushroom Spread ... 29
Spinach Tofu Dip ... 17
Strawberry Cheddar Cheese Carousel ... 13
Summer Tomato Relish ... 18
White Cheddar and Bleu Cheese Fondue ... 32

E

Easy

Amish Sour Cream Sugar Cookies ... 260
Andrea's Southwestern Guacamole ... 14
Apple Horseradish Sauce ... 175
Apple Soup ... 106
Apple Yams ... 166
Apples N' Almonds Toffee Brickle Dip ... 14
Apricot Soup ... 103
Artichoke and Ham Rolls ... 219
Artichoke Rice Salad ... 83
Asian Chicken Salad ... 84
Asian Egg Drop Soup ... 108
Asian Vegetable and Beef Turnovers ... 19
Asparagus Aspic with Horseradish ... 93
Autumn Pumpkin Bisque ... 107
Avocado Feta Salsa ... 33
Bacon Apple Toast ... 62
Baja Shrimp Nachos ... 22
Baked Apricots with Gingersnap Crumbles ... 145
Baked Italian Artichoke Spread ... 27
Baked Stroganoff ... 209
Baked Vermicelli with Spinach and Mushrooms ... 123
Banana Ice Cream ... 305
Basil Tomato Soup ... 109
Beef Stock ... 119
Bleu Cheese Fingers ... 21
Blushing Cherry Mold ... 94
Brown Sugar Pumpkin Crumb Cake ... 267
Buttery Lemon Asparagus ... 150
Buttery Pound Cake ... 268
Buttery Toffee Squares ... 303
Camembert Sauté ... 9
Candy Apple Walnut Pie ... 280
Cantaloupe Soup ... 103
Caramel Brownies ... 255
Caramel Soaked French Toast ... 66
Carolina Crab Cakes with Rémoulade Sauce ... 181
Carrot Ring ... 155
Catfish with Yogurt Horseradish Glaze ... 174
Caviar Cream Cheese Spread ... 10
Chicken and Noodle Casserole ... 132
Chicken and Rice Casserole with Cashews ... 233
Chicken Chalupas ... 235
Chicken Fruit Toss ... 81
Chicken in Three Cheese Sauce ... 237
Chicken Mushroom Sauce ... 233
Chicken Stock ... 120
Chilled Apple Soup ... 104
Chocolate Chip Cookie Truffles ... 308
Chocolate Nut Neapolitans ... 309
Chocolate Pecan Squares ... 256
Chocolate Praliné Ice Cream Topping ... 303
Christmas Angel Pasta ... 124
Chunky Apple Pancakes with Cinnamon Butter ... 71
Chunky Gorgonzola Dip ... 9
Cinnamon Apple Bars ... 68
Coconut Pecan Apricot Salad ... 95
Cinnamon Pecan Coffee Cake ... 69
Coconut Ginger Rice ... 135
Coconut Pie ... 282
Cool Cucumber Sauce ... 34
Copper Pennies ... 156
Corn and Black Bean Salsa ... 30
Corn Relish ... 89
Cottage Spinach Dip ... 15
Cranapple Frostee ... 36
Cranberry Chicken ... 242
Cranberry Fruit Salad ... 95
Cranberry Ice Sorbet ... 307
Creamy Caramel Dip ... 298
Crispy Potato Pancakes ... 163
Crockery Cooker Polenta ... 139
Crunchy Chicken Cauliflower ... 243
Cucumber Yogurt Dip ... 16
Curried Beef Pita ... 211
Dad's Taverns ... 212
Deep Fried Catfish and Onion Rings ... 173
Deer Jerky ... 199
Double Chocolate Chip Cookies ... 261
Dried Cherry and Almond Chicken Salad in Wonton Cups ... 21
EBT Gazpacho ... 105
Enchilada Sauce ... 238

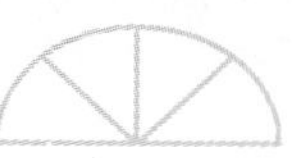

Enchilada Topping ... 238
Farmington's Ice Cream Sherbet ... 307
Fettuccini with Shrimp Sauce ... 129
Flaky Tomato Basil Biscuits ... 54
Fresh Apple Fruit Salad with Pecans ... 75
Fried Green Tomatoes ... 170
Fried Okra ... 162
Frozen Juice Pie ... 280
Fudge Frosting ... 273
Garden Rice ... 231
Garlic and Orange Baked Tomatoes ... 169
German Potato Salad ... 90
Giant Peanutty Pizza Cookies ... 262
Gingered Shrimp ... 23
Gingersnaps ... 263
Glazed Lamb Roast ... 216
Glenn's Café Blackened Red Drum Fish ... 178
Glenn's Café Eggplant Creole ... 222
Grecian Cheese Round ... 10
Greek Pasta Salad ... 85
Green Bean and Feta Salad with Walnuts ... 91
Green Bean and Onion Salad with Bleu Cheese ... 92
Green Beans, Potatoes and Ham in Redeye Gravy ... 108
Green Chile Artichoke Spread ... 28
Green Chile Corn Squares ... 160
Grilled Acorn Squash ... 151
Grilled Salmon Chardonnay ... 178
Grilled Teriyaki Marinated Filet Mignon ... 204
Grilled Trout with Apple Horseradish Sauce ... 175
Hallelujah Ham Loaves ... 22
Hardware Café Hot Fudge Peanut Cheesecake ... 279
Herb Baked Lamb Chops ... 217
Herbed Boursin ... 11
Herbed Goat Cheese ... 11
Hobo Beans ... 151
Holiday Party Potatoes ... 164
Holiday Wassail ... 41
Honey Nectar Shake ... 35
Hoonoono Lau Ai Palani ... 99
Hot Chicken Salad Topping ... 234
Hot Fudge Sauce ... 279
Hot Fudge Sauce to Die For ... 300
Ice Cream Cone Cupcakes ... 266
Iced Almond Tea ... 36
Iced Strawberry Soup ... 104
Indian Pudding ... 298
Italian Baked Trout ... 176
Italian Brunch Casserole ... 62
Italian Oven Fried Cauliflower ... 158
Jalapeño Corn ... 161
Key Lime Pie ... 282
Killer Brats ... 224
Lamb Marinade ... 216
Lemon Apricot Chicken ... 245
Lemon Oat Shortbread ... 264
Lemon Pecan Chicken ... 242
Linguine with Basil Tomato Sauce ... 125
Lobster Deviled Eggs ... 26
Macaroni with Turkey Marinara Sauce ... 133
Mandarin Orange Coconut Cake ... 269
Mandarin Orange Salad ... 78
Mango Broccoli Salad ... 91
Mango Pie ... 285
Mango Sticky Rice ... 140
Marinated Fruits of Summer ... 146
Marsala Honey Glazed Ham ... 224
Mayfair Dressing ... 100
Medallions of Veal with Shiitake Mushrooms ... 214
Mexican Stack Buffet Salad ... 82
Mexicorn Corn Soufflé ... 159
Milk Chocolate Cake ... 270
Mississippi Mud Cake ... 271
Missouri Peanut Butter Mud Cake with Fudge Frosting ... 273
Mozzarella Baked Eggplant ... 158
Mushroom and Onion Stuffed Shrimp ... 185
Mushroom Pinwheel Fingers ... 25
Mushroom Veggie Burgers ... 161
Never Fail Pie Crust ... 288
No Crust German Chocolate Pie ... 284
No Crust Pumpkin Pie ... 285
Noodles with Beefy Three Cheese Sauce ... 134
Nutty Couscous ... 138
Nutty Granola ... 72
Onion Shortcake ... 52
Orange Beets ... 153
Orange Oriental Salad ... 79
Orange Pecan French Toast ... 67
Oranges in Red Wine Sauce ... 147
Ozark Mountain Fresh Apple Cake ... 275
Parmesan Wine Rice ... 136
Party Cheese Pâté ... 12
Pasta with Smoked Salmon ... 131
Peach Cream Pie ... 286
Pecan Pie ... 284
Pecan Pie Bars ... 257
Pecan Stuffed Dates ... 20
Penne Spinach Casserole ... 126
Penne with Asparagus and Shaved Ham ... 135
Peppered Shrimp and Eggs ... 64
Petite Crab Cakes ... 23
Pheasant in Sour Cream ... 192
Pine Nut Wild Rice Salad ... 138
Pineapple Cheese Ball ... 13
Pineapple Surprise Salad ... 96
Pizza Biscuits ... 225
Poached Salmon with Spinach ... 180
Polenta ... 139
Porcupines ... 212

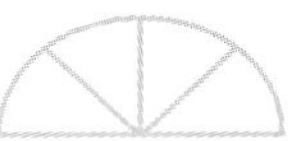

Pork Orange Tenderloin ... 221
Potato Cheese Puff ... 165
Praliné Pecan Popcorn ... 303
Puffed Cheese Twists ... 60
Pumpkin Bread ... 49
Pumpkin Cheesecake with Gingersnap Crust ... 276
Pumpkin Pecan Pie ... 287
Quick Focaccia ... 56
Quick n' Yummy Ice Cream ... 304
Raspberry Clafouti ... 304
Red Cabbage and Apples ... 154
Red Wine Sauce ... 192
Rémoulade Sauce ... 181
Reuben Sandwich Casserole ... 209
Rhubarb Crisp ... 305
Roasted Asparagus and Mushrooms with Rosemary ... 150
Rosemary Hollandaise ... 167
Russian Tea ... 42
Sally Lunn Bread ... 58
Santa Fe Salsa ... 33
Sapsago Dressing ... 100
Sauce for Duck or Goose ... 189
Sausage and Egg Strata ... 65
Sausage, Egg and Potato Casserole ... 65
Savory Palmiers ... 26
Scalloped Chicken ... 246
Scalloped Corn and Oysters ... 185
Seafood in Sunny Lime Butter Sauce ... 183
Seasoned Pita Crisps ... 60
Sherried Fruit Compote ... 148
Shiitake Mushroom Spread ... 29
Shrimp and Rice Supreme ... 187
Shrimp Pasta Salad ... 88
Skillet Rice with Tomatoes ... 141
Snuggly Dogs ... 213
Sour Cream Corn Muffins ... 51
South Seas Fruit Salad ... 76
Spaghetti with Roasted Vegetable Sauce ... 127
Spiced Lamb Chops with Ginger Crisps ... 216
Spicy Black-Eyed Peas and Sausage ... 110
Spicy Indian Barbecue Sauce ... 226
Spinach and Turkey Meat Loaf ... 252
Spinach Soufflé ... 169
Springfield Cashew Chicken ... 247
Stephenson's Apple Farm Frozen Fruit Salad ... 77
Strawberry and Pretzel Salad ... 97
Strawberry Blooms ... 148
Strawberry Cheddar Cheese Carousel ... 13
Strawberry Romaine Salad ... 80
Stress Reliever Cookies ... 266
Summer Squash Casserole ... 168
Sweet and Gooey Bubble Bread ... 67
Taco Soup ... 110
Tailgate Brisket ... 207
Tangy Green Bean and Pea Salad ... 94
Tangy Ranch Snack Mix ... 33
Textured Vegetable Protein Soup ... 118
Tomato Pie ... 153
Tomato Tortellini Soup ... 115
Top Secret Marinade ... 207
Tortellini and Vegetable Medley ... 86
Triple Chocolate Fudge Brownies ... 258
Tuna Jackstraws ... 177
Tuna Lemon Mold ... 98
Turkey Breast Medallions with Pecan Honey Glaze ... 251
Turkey Croquettes ... 248
Tutti-Frutti Candy ... 310
Twin Oaks Country Club Linguine
with Feta Cheese and Shrimp ... 125
Vegetable Stock ... 120
Vegetable Tofu Stir Fry ... 170
Venison Game Stock ... 200
Venison Sauce ... 200
Vichyssoise ... 105
White Cheddar Cheese Grits ... 142
White Chili ... 111
White Hot Chocolate ... 40
Wild Rice with Apples and Sun-Dried Cherries ... 141
Winter Fruit Compote ... 149
Yorkshire Popovers ... 54

Eggplant

Glenn's Café Eggplant Creole ... 222
Mozzarella Baked Eggplant ... 158

Eggs

Asian Egg Drop Soup ... 108
Egg Substitute ... 64
Egg Wash ... 184
Italian Brunch Casserole ... 62
Lobster Deviled Eggs ... 26
Peppered Shrimp and Eggs ... 64
Sausage and Egg Strata ... 65
Sausage, Egg and Potato Casserole ... 65

Expert Cook

American Bounty Apple Maple Dessert
with Custard Sauce ... 290
Brinkman's Baklava ... 293
Cheese Soufflé with Chicken Mushroom Sauce ... 232
Chocolate Nut Torte ... 295
Decadent Cinnamon Rolls ... 70
Kentucky Hot Browns ... 63
Lemon Custard Ice Cream Pie ... 283
Medallions of Beef Tenderloin in Brandy Tomato Sauce ... 203
Paradise Grill Sirloin Peppered Steak with Armagnac ... 205
Phyllo Lobster Triangles ... 24
Raspberry Chocolate Wafer Crust ... 278
Raspberry Ribbon Cheesecake ... 278
Raspberry Sauce ... 278
Raspberry Topping ... 278

Risotto ... 140
Roast Duckling à l'Orange ... 188
Strawberry Meringue Crust Pie ... 289
White Chocolate Bread Pudding with White Chocolate ... 306

F

Fish

Catfish with Yogurt Horseradish Glaze ... 174
Deep Fried Catfish and Onion Rings ... 173
Glenn's Café Blackened Red Drum Fish ... 178
Grilled Fish Steaks ... 176
Grilled Salmon Chardonnay ... 178
Grilled Trout with Apple Horseradish Sauce ... 175
Italian Baked Trout ... 176
Pasta with Smoked Salmon ... 131
Poached Salmon with Spinach ... 180
Rick's Salmon Napoleon ... 179
Seafood in Sunny Lime Butter Sauce ... 183
Tilapia Almondine ... 177
Trout Handling Tips ... 176
Tuna Jackstraws ... 177
Tuna Lemon Mold ... 98

Fruit (see individual fruits)

G

Game

Apricot Stuffed Goose ... 190
Deer Jerky ... 199
Hasenpfeffer ... 195
Pan Roasted Pheasant with Shiitake Mushrooms ... 191
Pheasant in Sour Cream ... 192
Quail in Madeira Wine ... 193
Quail with Wild Rice, Sage and Apples ... 194
Roast Duckling à l'Orange ... 188
Roasted Duck Breast with Cherry Sauce ... 189
Taco Soup ... 110
Tangy Venison Stew ... 197
Venison Breakfast Sausage ... 199
Venison Patties with Mushroom Gravy ... 196
Venison Wellington ... 198

Good Cook

Adzuki Bean Burgers ... 152
Almond Crunch Cookies ... 259
Apple Gruyère Tart ... 61
Apricot Chicken with Garden Rice ... 230
Apricot Stuffed Goose ... 190
Armenian Rice ... 136
Asparagus Artichoke Chicken ... 231
Bananas Foster ... 292
Beef Rouladen ... 206
Blueberry Citrus Cake ... 274
Cabbage Rolls in Tomato Sauce ... 210
Cheese Flan with Caramel Sauce ... 294
Chef Ron's Hot Chicken Salad ... 234
Cherry Almond Glazed Pork Roast ... 220
Chicken Breasts Lombardy ... 229
Chicken Divan ... 236
Chicken Enchiladas ... 238
Chicken in Three Cheese Sauce ... 237
Chicken Stir-Fry ... 240
Chocolate Bourbon Pecan Pie ... 281
Chocolate Chip Banana Muffins ... 50
Chocolate Peanut Butter Mousse Cake ... 296
Clary's Chicken Piccata ... 241
Clove Studded Ham with Orange Rum Glaze ... 223
Coffee and Peaches Cream Puffs ... 300
Coffee Crème Brûlée ... 297
Crab Strudel ... 184
Cream Puff Shells ... 300
Creole Gumbo ... 112
Date Nut Loaf ... 46
Dill Bread ... 55
English Custard Float ... 37
Fruity Wild Rice ... 137
Glazed Citrus Loaf ... 45
Green Peppercorn Sauce ... 214
Grilled Turkey with Fresh Peach Salsa ... 250
Hasenpfeffer ... 195
Indian Chicken Kebabs ... 244
Italian Cream Cake ... 277
Lamb Spinach Roulade ... 218
Lobster Bisque ... 113
Maple Praliné Biscotti ... 265
Maytag White Cheddar Cheese Soup ... 109
Missouri State Fair Blue Ribbon Zucchini Bread ... 47
New England Clam Chowder ... 114
Oatmeal Cake with Brown Sugar Glaze ... 272
Okra and Ground Beef Casserole ... 208
Old-Fashioned Bread Pudding with Whiskey Sauce ... 299
Orange Chocolate Mousse ... 302
Orange Glazed Poppy Seed Bread ... 48
Pan Roasted Pheasant with Shiitake Mushrooms ... 191
Peaches Flambé ... 301
Poppy Seed Cheddar Crust ... 291
Pork Cutlets with Mushrooms ... 225
Quail in Madeira Wine ... 193
Quail with Wild Rice, Sage and Apples ... 194
Refrigerator Dinner Rolls ... 57
Rhubarb Pie ... 288
Rick's Lampe Scampi and Angel Hair Pasta ... 130
Rick's Salmon Napoleon ... 179
Roasted Duck Breast with Cherry Sauce ... 189
Rosemary Walnut Chicken ... 239
Seafood Medley ... 182
Shrimp and Coconut Milk Curry ... 186
Stuffed Veal Tenderloin ... 215
Sweet Potato Casserole with Praliné Topping ... 167
Sweet Potato Pie with Poppy Seed Cheddar Crust ... 291

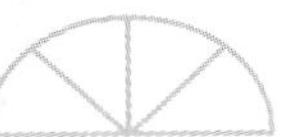

Tagliatelle with Wild Mushrooms, Peas and Prosciutto 128
Tangy Venison Stew 197
Tempura Roasted Peppers 87
Tomato and Mozzarella Stuffed Peppers 166
Turkey Hash 249
Tuscan Bread 59
Venison Breakfast Sausage 199
Venison Patties with Mushroom Gravy 196
Venison Wellington 198
Walterspiel Potato Soup 116
White Chocolate Cake Supreme 277

Grapes

Clove Studded Ham with Orange Rum Glaze 223
Cranberry Fruit Salad 95
Fresh Apple Fruit Salad with Pecans 75
Summer Fruit Kebabs 146

Green Beans (see Beans and Peas)

Grilling Recipes

Grilled Acorn Squash 151
Grilled Fish Steaks 176
Grilled Salmon Chardonnay 178
Grilled Teriyaki Marinated Filet Mignon 204
Grilled Trout with Apple Horseradish Sauce 175
Grilled Turkey with Fresh Peach Salsa 250
Grilling Tips 224, 226
Paradise Grill Sirloin Peppered Steak with Armagnac 205
Rick's Salmon Napoleon 179

K

Kid-Friendly

Ants on a Log 159
Apple Volcanoes 145
Butterscotch Crunch 308
Children Cooking Hints 159
Children's Fruit Juicy Punch 35
Circus Salad 76
Ice Cream Cone Cupcakes 266
Marshmallow Happy Pops 310
Peanut Butter Cup Cookies 262
Peanut Butter Yogurt Dip 19
Pineapple Octopus Bubbles 38
Pizza Biscuits 225
Porcupines 212
Quick n' Yummy Ice Cream 304
Snuggly Dogs 213
Spicy Mocha Mix 42
Tangy Ranch Snack Mix 33
Tuna Jackstraws 177
Tutti-Frutti Candy 310

L

Lamb

Glazed Lamb Roast 216
Herb Baked Lamb Chops 217
Lamb Marinade 216
Lamb Spinach Roulade 218
Spiced Lamb Chops with Ginger Crisps 216

Lemon

Honey Lemon Dressing 98
Lemon Apricot Chicken 245
Lemon Custard Ice Cream Pie 283
Lemon Oat Shortbread 264
Lemon Pecan Chicken 242
Luscious Lemon Fondue 263

Lobster (see Seafood)

M

Mandarin Oranges (see Oranges)

Mangoes

Mango Broccoli Salad 91
Mango Pie 285
Mango Sticky Rice 140
South Seas Fruit Salad 76

Mushrooms

Baked Vermicelli with Spinach and Mushrooms 123
Cheese Soufflé with Chicken Mushroom Sauce 232
Chef Ron's Hot Chicken Salad 234
Chicken Breasts Lombardy 229
Chicken Mushroom Sauce 233
Green Peppercorn Sauce 214
Lamb Spinach Roulade 218
Medallions of Beef Tenderloin in Brandy Tomato Sauce 203
Medallions of Veal with Shiitake Mushrooms 214
Mushroom and Onion Stuffed Shrimp 185
Mushroom Miso Soup 117
Mushroom Pinwheel Fingers 25
Mushroom Veggie Burgers 161
Pan Roasted Pheasant with Shiitake Mushrooms 191
Pimiento Mushroom Sauce 246
Pork Cutlets with Mushrooms 225
Quail in Madeira Wine 193
Rick's Lampe Scampi and Angel Hair Pasta 130
Roasted Asparagus and Mushrooms with Rosemary 150
Seafood Medley 182
Shiitake Mushroom Spread 29
Shrimp and Rice Supreme 187
Tagliatelle with Wild Mushrooms, Peas and Prosciutto 128
Turkey Hash 249
Venison Patties with Mushroom Gravy 196

N

Nuts

Almond Crunch Cookies 259
Bleu Cheese Fingers 21
Brown Sugar Pumpkin Crumb Cake 267
Buttery Toffee Squares 303
Candy Apple Walnut Pie 280
Caramel Brownies 255
Cherry Almond Glazed Pork Roast 220

Chicken and Rice Casserole with Cashews ... 233
Chocolate Bourbon Pecan Pie ... 281
Chocolate Chip Cookie Truffles ... 308
Chocolate Nut Neapolitans ... 309
Chocolate Nut Torte ... 295
Chocolate Pecan Squares ... 256
Chocolate Praliné Ice Cream Topping ... 303
Cinnamon Pecan Coffee Cake ... 69
Coconut Pecan Apricot Salad ... 95
Cranberry Fruit Salad ... 95
Date Nut Loaf ... 46
Dried Cherry and Almond Chicken Salad in Wonton Cups ... 21
Fresh Apple Fruit Salad with Pecans ... 75
Fruity Wild Rice ... 137
Green Bean and Feta Salad with Walnuts ... 91
Green Bean and Onion Salad with Bleu Cheese ... 92
Hardware Café Hot Fudge Peanut Cheesecake ... 279
Lemon Pecan Chicken ... 242
Maple Praliné Biscotti ... 265
Mississippi Mud Cake ... 271
Missouri State Fair Blue Ribbon Zucchini Bread ... 47
No Crust German Chocolate Pie ... 284
Nutty Couscous ... 138
Nutty Granola ... 72
Orange Pecan French Toast ... 67
Party Cheese Pâté ... 12
Pecan Pie ... 284
Pecan Pie Bars ... 257
Pecan Stuffed Dates ... 20
Pineapple Cheese Ball ... 13
Praliné Pecan Popcorn ... 303
Pumpkin Pecan Pie ... 287
Rosemary Walnut Chicken ... 239
Springfield Cashew Chicken ... 247
Strawberry Cheddar Cheese Carousel ... 13
Sweet Potato Casserole with Praliné Topping ... 167
Tilapia Almondine ... 177
Turkey Breast Medallions with Pecan Honey Glaze ... 251
Tutti-Frutti Candy ... 310

O

Okra
Creole Gumbo ... 112
Fried Okra ... 162
Okra and Ground Beef Casserole ... 208

Onions
Deep Fried Catfish and Onion Rings ... 173
Glazed Pearl Onions ... 162
Green Bean and Onion Salad with Bleu Cheese ... 92
Onion Shortcake ... 52

Oranges and Orange Juice
Blushing Cherry Mold ... 94
Chicken Fruit Toss ... 81
Circus Salad ... 76
Holiday Wassail ... 41
Mandarin Orange Coconut Cake ... 269
Mandarin Orange Salad ... 78
Marinated Fruits of Summer ... 146
Orange Beets ... 153
Orange Chocolate Mousse ... 302
Orange Glazed Poppy Seed Bread ... 48
Orange Oriental Salad ... 79
Orange Pecan French Toast ... 67
Orange Pecans ... 32
Oranges in Red Wine Sauce ... 147
Summer Fruit Kebabs ... 146
Sweet Potato Pie with Poppy Seed Cheddar Crust ... 291
Winter Fruit Compote ... 149

P

Pasta
Asian Chicken Salad ... 84
Baked Stroganoff ... 209
Baked Vermicelli with Spinach and Mushrooms ... 123
Beef Rouladen ... 206
Chef Ron's Hot Chicken Salad ... 234
Chicken and Noodle Casserole ... 132
Christmas Angel Pasta ... 124
Clary's Chicken Piccata ... 241
Fettuccini with Shrimp Sauce ... 129
Greek Pasta Salad ... 85
Hasenpfeffer ... 195
Linguine with Basil Tomato Sauce ... 125
Macaroni with Turkey Marinara Sauce ... 133
Noodles with Beefy Three Cheese Sauce ... 134
Pasta with Smoked Salmon ... 131
Penne Spinach Casserole ... 126
Penne with Asparagus and Shaved Ham ... 135
Rick's Lampe Scampi and Angel Hair Pasta ... 130
Shrimp Pasta Salad ... 88
Spaghetti with Roasted Vegetable Sauce ... 127
Tagliatelle with Wild Mushrooms, Peas and Prosciutto ... 128
Tomato Tortellini Soup ... 115
Tortellini and Vegetable Medley ... 86
Twin Oaks Country Club Linguine with Feta Cheese and Shrimp ... 125

Peaches
Coffee and Peaches Cream Puffs ... 300
Grilled Turkey with Fresh Peach Salsa ... 250
Peach Cream Pie ... 286
Peach-Mint Vinegar ... 146
Peaches Flambé ... 301
Sherried Fruit Compote ... 148

Pears
Bleu Cheese Fingers ... 21
Pear Dressing ... 97

Pecans (see Nuts)

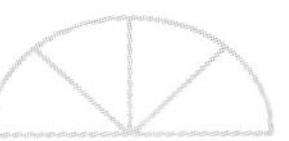

Peppers
EBT Gazpacho ... 105
Green Chile Artichoke Spread ... 28
Green Chile Corn Squares ... 160
Jalapeño Corn ... 161
Santa Fe Salsa ... 33
Summer Tomato Relish ... 18
Tempura Roasted Peppers ... 87
Tomato and Mozzarella Stuffed Peppers ... 166
Pies (see Desserts)
Pineapple
Chicken Fruit Toss ... 81
Clove Studded Ham with Orange Rum Glaze ... 223
Coconut Pecan Apricot Salad ... 95
Marinated Fruits of Summer ... 146
Pineapple Cheese Ball ... 13
Pineapple Octopus Bubbles ... 38
Pineapple Surprise Salad ... 96
Raspberry Punch ... 38
South Seas Fruit Salad ... 76
Winter Fruit Compote ... 149
Pork
Apple and Raisin Stuffed Pork Chops ... 219
Artichoke and Ham Rolls ... 219
Autumn Pumpkin Bisque ... 107
Bacon Apple Toast ... 62
Cabbage Rolls in Tomato Sauce ... 210
Cherry Almond Glazed Pork Roast ... 220
Clove Studded Ham with Orange Rum Glaze ... 223
Green Beans, Potatoes and Ham in Redeye Gravy ... 108
Glenn's Café Eggplant Creole ... 222
Hallelujah Ham Loaves ... 22
Hobo Beans ... 151
Italian Brunch Casserole ... 62
Killer Brats ... 224
Marsala Honey Glazed Ham ... 224
Maytag White Cheddar Cheese Soup ... 109
New England Clam Chowder ... 114
Pecan Stuffed Dates ... 20
Penne with Asparagus and Shaved Ham ... 135
Pizza Biscuits ... 225
Pork Cutlets with Mushrooms ... 225
Pork Orange Tenderloin ... 221
Sausage and Egg Strata ... 65
Sausage, Egg and Potato Casserole ... 65
Savory Palmiers ... 26
Spicy Black-Eyed Peas and Sausage ... 110
Tagliatelle with Wild Mushrooms, Peas and Prosciutto ... 128
Potatoes
Crispy Potato Pancakes ... 163
German Potato Salad ... 90
Green Beans, Potatoes and Ham in Redeye Gravy ... 108
Holiday Party Potatoes ... 164
New England Clam Chowder ... 114
Potato Cheese Puff ... 165
Sausage, Egg and Potato Casserole ... 65
Special Spuds ... 164
'Tator Tricks ... 163
Venison Wellington ... 198
Vichyssoise ... 105
Walterspiel Potato Soup ... 116
Poultry
Chicken
Apricot Chicken with Garden Rice ... 230
Asian Chicken Salad ... 84
Asparagus Artichoke Chicken ... 231
Cheese Soufflé with Chicken Mushroom Sauce ... 232
Chef Ron's Hot Chicken Salad ... 234
Chicken and Noodle Casserole ... 132
Chicken and Rice Casserole with Cashews ... 233
Chicken Breasts Lombardy ... 229
Chicken Chalupas ... 235
Chicken Divan ... 236
Chicken Enchiladas ... 238
Chicken in Three Cheese Sauce ... 237
Chicken Mushroom Sauce ... 233
Chicken Stir-Fry ... 240
Chicken Stock ... 120
Chinese Chicken Wings ... 20
Clary's Chicken Piccata ... 241
Cranberry Chicken ... 242
Crunchy Chicken Cauliflower ... 243
Dried Cherry and Almond Chicken Salad in Wonton Cups ... 21
Indian Chicken Kebabs ... 244
Lemon Apricot Chicken ... 245
Lemon Pecan Chicken ... 242
Rosemary Walnut Chicken ... 239
Scalloped Chicken ... 246
Springfield Cashew Chicken ... 247
White Chili ... 111
Turkey
Grilled Turkey with Fresh Peach Salsa ... 250
Kentucky Hot Browns ... 63
Macaroni with Turkey Marinara Sauce ... 133
Spinach and Turkey Meat Loaf ... 252
Turkey Breast Medallions with Pecan Honey Glaze ... 251
Turkey Croquettes ... 248
Turkey Hash ... 249
Turkey Jo's ... 248
Puddings (see Desserts)
Pumpkin
Autumn Pumpkin Bisque ... 107
Brown Sugar Pumpkin Crumb Cake ... 267
No Crust Pumpkin Pie ... 285
Pumpkin Bread ... 49
Pumpkin Cheesecake with Gingersnap Crust ... 276
Pumpkin Pecan Pie ... 287

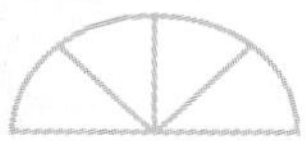

Q

Quail (see Game)

Quick and Simple

Ants on a Log ... 159
Apple Cider Spritzer ... 34
Apple Volcanoes ... 145
Avocado Dressing ... 96
Blender Hollandaise Sauce ... 168
Butterscotch Crunch ... 308
Café Con Leche ... 40
Children's Fruit Juicy Punch ... 35
Chinese Ginger Garlic Dip ... 15
Chocolate Wafer Pie Crust ... 283
Circus Salad ... 76
Crab Louie Salad ... 87
Cranberry Tea ... 39
Elegant Pesto ... 131
Fiesta Dip ... 16
Glazed Pearl Onions ... 162
Gourmet Waffles ... 72
Grilled Fish Steaks ... 176
Honey Lemon Dressing ... 98
Hummus ... 17
Jezebel Sauce ... 31
Luscious Lemon Fondue ... 263
M M M M M Muffins ... 51
Marshmallow Happy Pops ... 310
Missouri Governor's Mansion Basil Vinaigrette ... 99
Mushroom Miso Soup ... 117
Orange Pecans ... 32
Peanut Butter Cup Cookies ... 262
Peanut Butter Yogurt Dip ... 19
Pear Dressing ... 97
Pimiento Mushroom Sauce ... 246
Pineapple Octopus Bubbles ... 38
Raspberry Punch ... 38
Raspberry Sauce ... 221
Raspberry Spinach Salad ... 80
Roquefort Sauce ... 215
Spicy Mocha Mix ... 42
Spinach Tofu Dip ... 17
Strawberries Romanoff ... 149
Summer Fruit Kebabs ... 146
Summer Orange Smoothie ... 39
Summer Tomato Relish ... 18
Tartar Sauce ... 173
Tilapia Almondine ... 177
Turkey Jo's ... 248

R

Raspberries

Marinated Fruits of Summer ... 146
Raspberry Chocolate Wafer Crust ... 278
Raspberry Clafouti ... 304
Raspberry Punch ... 38
Raspberry Ribbon Cheesecake ... 278
Raspberry Sauce ... 278
Raspberry Spinach Salad ... 80
Raspberry Topping ... 278

Rhubarb

Rhubarb Crisp ... 305
Rhubarb Pie ... 288

Rice

Adzuki Bean Burgers ... 152
Apricot Chicken with Garden Rice ... 230
Armenian Rice ... 136
Artichoke Rice Salad ... 83
Baked Stroganoff ... 209
Beef Rouladen ... 206
Cabbage Rolls in Tomato Sauce ... 210
Chicken Stir-Fry ... 240
Coconut Ginger Rice ... 135
Cranberry Chicken ... 242
Creole Gumbo ... 112
Fruity Wild Rice ... 137
Garden Rice ... 231
Glenn's Café Eggplant Creole ... 222
Indian Chicken Kebabs ... 244
Mango Sticky Rice ... 140
Mexican Stack Buffet Salad ... 82
Parmesan Wine Rice ... 136
Pine Nut Wild Rice Salad ... 138
Porcupines ... 212
Quail in Madeira Wine ... 193
Quail with Wild Rice, Sage and Apples ... 194
Rice Tips ... 135
Risotto ... 140
Seafood in Sunny Lime Butter Sauce ... 183
Shrimp and Coconut Milk Curry ... 186
Shrimp and Rice Supreme ... 187
Skillet Rice with Tomatoes ... 141
Springfield Cashew Chicken ... 247
Wild Rice with Apples and Sun-Dried Cherries ... 141

S

Salad Dressings

Avocado Dressing ... 96
Honey Lemon Dressing ... 98
Hoonoono Lau Ai Palani ... 99
Mayfair Dressing ... 100
Missouri Governor's Mansion Basil Vinaigrette ... 99
Pear Dressing ... 97
Sapsago Dressing ... 100

Salads

Artichoke Rice Salad ... 83
Asian Chicken Salad ... 84
Asparagus Aspic with Horseradish ... 93
Blushing Cherry Mold ... 94

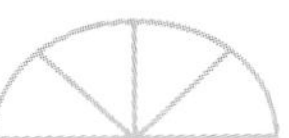

Chicken Fruit Toss ... 81
Circus Salad ... 76
Coconut Pecan Apricot Salad ... 95
Corn Relish ... 89
Crab Louie Salad ... 87
Cranberry Fruit Salad ... 95
Fresh Apple Fruit Salad with Pecans ... 75
German Potato Salad ... 90
Greek Pasta Salad ... 85
Green Bean and Feta Salad with Walnuts ... 91
Green Bean and Onion Salad with Bleu Cheese ... 92
Mandarin Orange Salad ... 78
Mango Broccoli Salad ... 91
Mexican Stack Buffet Salad ... 82
Orange Oriental Salad ... 79
Pine Nut Wild Rice Salad ... 138
Pineapple Surprise Salad ... 96
Raspberry Spinach Salad ... 80
Shrimp Pasta Salad ... 88
South Seas Fruit Salad ... 76
Stephenson's Apple Farm Frozen Fruit Salad ... 77
Strawberry and Pretzel Salad ... 97
Strawberry Romaine Salad ... 80
Tangy Green Bean and Pea Salad ... 94
Tempura Roasted Peppers ... 87
Tortellini and Vegetable Medley ... 86
Tuna Lemon Mold ... 98

Sausage (see Pork)

Sauces and Marinades

Apple Horseradish Sauce ... 175
Blender Hollandaise Sauce ... 168
Chicken Mushroom Sauce ... 233
Cool Cucumber Sauce ... 34
Demi-Glace ... 203
Elegant Pesto ... 131
Enchilada Sauce ... 238
Enchilada Topping ... 238
Green Peppercorn Sauce ... 214
Jezebel Sauce ... 31
Lamb Marinade ... 216
Pimiento Mushroom Sauce ... 246
Raspberry Sauce ... 221
Red Wine Sauce ... 192
Rémoulade Sauce ... 181
Roquefort Sauce ... 215
Rosemary Hollandaise ... 167
Sauce for Duck or Goose ... 189
Spicy Indian Barbecue Sauce ... 226
Tartar Sauce ... 173
Top Secret Marinade ... 207
Venison Sauce ... 200

Seafood

Baja Shrimp Nachos ... 22
Carolina Crab Cakes with Rémoulade Sauce ... 181
Clam and Cheese Dip ... 30
Crab Louie Salad ... 87
Crab Strudel ... 184
Creole Gumbo ... 112
Fettuccini with Shrimp Sauce ... 129
Gingered Shrimp ... 23
Lobster Bisque ... 113
Lobster Deviled Eggs ... 26
Mushroom and Onion Stuffed Shrimp ... 185
New England Clam Chowder ... 114
Peppered Shrimp and Eggs ... 64
Petite Crab Cakes ... 23
Phyllo Lobster Triangles ... 24
Rick's Lampe Scampi and Angel Hair Pasta ... 130
Scalloped Corn and Oysters ... 185
Seafood in Sunny Lime Butter Sauce ... 183
Seafood Medley ... 182
Seafood in Sunny Lime Butter Sauce ... 183
Shrimp and Coconut Milk Curry ... 186
Shrimp and Rice Supreme ... 187
Shrimp Pasta Salad ... 88
Twin Oaks Country Club Linguine with
Feta Cheese and Shrimp ... 125

Soups

Cold

Apple Soup ... 106
Apricot Soup ... 103
Cantaloupe Soup ... 103
Chilled Apple Soup ... 104
EBT Gazpacho ... 105
Iced Strawberry Soup ... 104
Vichyssoise ... 105

Hot

Asian Egg Drop Soup ... 108
Autumn Pumpkin Bisque ... 107
Basil Tomato Soup ... 109
Creole Gumbo ... 112
Green Beans, Potatoes and Ham in Redeye Gravy ... 108
Lobster Bisque ... 113
Maytag White Cheddar Cheese Soup ... 109
Mushroom Miso Soup ... 117
Spicy Black-Eyed Peas and Sausage ... 110
Taco Soup ... 110
Tangy Venison Stew ... 197
Textured Vegetable Protein Soup ... 118
Tomato Tortellini Soup ... 115
Walterspiel Potato Soup ... 116
White Chili ... 111

Stocks

Beef Stock ... 119
Bouquet Garni ... 120
Chicken Stock ... 120
Vegetable Stock ... 120
Venison Game Stock ... 200

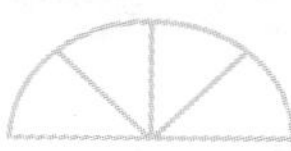

Spinach

Baked Vermicelli with Spinach and Mushrooms 123
Cottage Spinach Dip 15
Lamb Spinach Roulade 218
Penne Spinach Casserole 126
Poached Salmon with Spinach 180
Raspberry Spinach Salad 80
Spinach and Turkey Meat Loaf 252
Spinach Soufflé 169
Spinach Tofu Dip 17
Tomato Tortellini Soup 115

Squash (also see Zucchini)

Grilled Acorn Squash 151
Summer Squash Casserole 168

Strawberries and Strawberry Preserves

Honey Nectar Shake 35
Iced Strawberry Soup 104
Marinated Fruits of Summer 146
Sherried Fruit Compote 148
South Seas Fruit Salad 76
Strawberries Romanoff 149
Strawberry and Pretzel Salad 97
Strawberry Blooms 148
Strawberry Cheddar Cheese Carousel 13
Strawberry Meringue Crust Pie 289
Strawberry Romaine Salad 80
Summer Fruit Kebabs 146

Sweet Potatoes and Yams

Apple Yams 166
Sweet Potato Casserole with Praliné Topping 167
Sweet Potato Pie with Poppy Seed Cheddar Crust 291

T

Tofu

Mushroom Miso Soup 117
Spinach Tofu Dip 17
Textured Vegetable Protein Soup 118
Vegetable Tofu Stir Fry 170

Tomatoes

Basil Tomato Soup 109
Chicken Enchiladas 238
EBT Gazpacho 105
Enchilada Topping 238
Flaky Tomato Basil Biscuits 54
Fried Green Tomatoes 170
Garlic and Orange Baked Tomatoes 169
Linguine with Basil Tomato Sauce 125
Marinated Tomatoes 169
Okra and Ground Beef Casserole 208
Santa Fe Salsa 33
Skillet Rice with Tomatoes 141
Spaghetti with Roasted Vegetable Sauce 127
Spicy Black-Eyed Peas and Sausage 110
Summer Tomato Relish 18
Tomato and Mozzarella Stuffed Peppers 166
Tomato Pie 153
Tomato Tortellini Soup 115

Tuna (see Fish)

Turkey (see Poultry)

V

Veal

Medallions of Veal with Shiitake Mushrooms 214
Stuffed Veal Tenderloin 215

Vegetables (see individual listings)

Venison (see Game)

Z

Zucchini (also see Squash)

Curried Beef Pita 211
Missouri State Fair Blue Ribbon Zucchini Bread 47
Mushroom Veggie Burgers 161

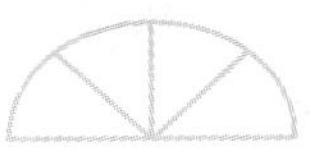

Windows Across Missouri - A Culinary View

Proceeds from Windows Across Missouri
are dedicated to health awareness and education in Missouri communities.

Please complete the form below. Mail, fax or email your order to the addresses and numbers listed below, along with your check or credit card number. Please print legibly so we can ensure your cookbook will reach your shipping destination.

Please send _____ copies of *Windows Across Missouri*	@ $21.50 each	$ ________________
Postage and Handling	@ $ 3.50 each	$ ________________
	Total	$ ________________

Method of Payment:

______Check Enclosed - Make payable to MSMA Alliance

______Visa ______MasterCard

Name as it appears on card ________________________________

Shipping Address ________________________________

City/State/Zip ________________________________

Telephone Number ________________________________

Account Number ____ ____ ____ ____ - ____ ____ ____ ____ - ____ ____ ____ ____ - ____ ____ ____ ____

Expiration Date: Month ____________ Year ____________

Signature ________________________________

How did you learn of *Windows Across Missouri?*

_____	Friend or Family Member	_____	Alliance Member
_____	Bookstore	_____	Newspaper
_____	Catalogue	_____	Other ________________

Missouri State Medical Association Alliance

113 Madison Street ◆ P.O. Box 1028

Jefferson City, Missouri

Tel: 573-636-5151 ◆ Fax: 573-636-8552

Internet: www.msma.org

OFFICE USE ONLY

Number of Cookbooks ____________ Amount ____________ Date Shipped ____________